An Analysis of the Textual Character
of the Bohairic of Deuteronomy

Society of Biblical Literature
Septuagint and Cognate Studies

edited by
Harry M. Orlinsky

Number 9

An Analysis of the Textual Character of the Bohairic of
Deuteronomy
by
Melvin K. H. Peters

Melvin K. H. Peters

AN ANALYSIS OF THE TEXTUAL CHARACTER OF THE BOHAIRIC OF DEUTERONOMY

SCHOLARS
PRESS

Distributed by
Scholars Press
PO Box 5207
Missoula, Montana 59806

An Analysis of the Textual Character of the Bohairic of Deuteronomy
Melvin K. H. Peters

Library of Congress Cataloging in Publication Data

Peters, Melvin K H
    An analysis of the textual character of the
Bohairic of Deuteronomy.

    (Septuagint and cognate studies ; no. ISSN 0145-
2754)
    Bibliography: p.
    1. Bible. O.T. Deuteronomy. Coptic—Versions.
2. Bible.   O.T.   Deuteronomy—Manuscripts,
Coptic. 3. Bible. O.T. Deuteronomy—Criticism,
Textual. I. Society of Biblical Literature. II. Title.
III. Series.
BS1274.C66P47   222'.15'049   78-12958
ISBN 0-89130-264-6

Printed in the United States of America
1   2   3   4   5

Printing Department
University of Montana
Missoula, Montana 59812

7911—UM Printing Services

TABLE OF CONTENTS

FOREWORD

Thanks must be expressed, first of all, to the
Libraries and Museums which supplied microfilms of the
Bohairic manuscripts used in this work. Professor Robert
Hanhart, director of the Septuaginta-Unternehmen in
Göttingen granted permission to use and to copy the col-
lation books of Deuteronomy. The books were made avail-
able through Professor J. W. Wevers, editor of the Göttingen
Genesis and of the forthcoming Deuteronomium. To both these
Professors and to the Septuaginta-Unternehmen the gratitude
of the writer is expressed.

The author is especially grateful to Professor
Wevers for his thorough and instructive supervision of
the research at every stage of its development. He
willingly provided his personal copies of witnesses to
the Greek of Deuteronomy, which would have been difficult
to obtain otherwise. He also made available his introductory
notes and sigla. Professor A. Pietersma gave helpful
suggestions on text critical methods at various stages
of the investigation.

The author's interest in Septuagint research was
aroused by an exposure to Professor Wevers, both in his
publications and in his seminars. Septuagint sub-versions
and Bohairic in particular were considered as a potentially

i

fruitful area for investigation and thus in consultation
with Professor Wevers the present study was undertaken.

The support and confidence of all my friends is
gratefully acknowledged.

Melvin K. H. Peters

Toronto, Canada
May, 1975

Preface to the Scholars Press
IOSCS Monograph Series edition:

I wish to thank Scholars Press for publishing this
dissertation as a monograph. Professor Harry M. Orlinsky,
editor of the SCS monograph series carefully read the
manuscript and recommended its publication. To him I wish
to express my special appreciation. In addition, to the
scholars who encouraged me to publish the work as a whole,
especially Professors Bill Holladay and Walter Harrelson, my
grateful thanks are expressed.

Melvin K. H. Peters
Cleveland, Ohio
JUNE 1978

SIGLA AND ABBREVIATIONS

The system of the Göttingen Septuaginta-Unternehmen, particularly of J. W. Wevers' recent edition of Genesis, is followed throughout this research. Most sources mentioned below are fully referenced in the Wevers edition and those not found there will be described in his forth-coming edition of Deuteronomy. Any abbreviations and sources not used in Wevers' Genesis and those peculiar to the present investigation are explained below.

I. The Greek Textual Witnesses

A. Uncials: A B F M V

B. Papyri: 848 963

C. Textual Families:

<u>O</u> = G-82-376-426

    376' = 376 + 426

<u>oI</u> = 15-64-381-618

    15' = 15 + 64   381' = 381 + 618

<u>oII</u> = 29-58-72-707

    72' = 72 + 707

<u>O</u>" = <u>O</u> + <u>oI</u> + <u>oII</u>   <u>O</u>' = <u>O</u> + <u>oI</u>   <u>O</u>' = <u>O</u> + <u>oII</u>

    <u>oI</u>' = <u>oI</u> + <u>oII</u>

$\underline{C}$ = 16-77-131-500-529-616-739

    16' = 16 + 131   500' = 500 + 739

    529' = 529 + 616

$\underline{cI}$ = 57-73-320-413-528-550-552-761

    57' = 57 + 413 73' = 73 + 320

    550' = 550 + 552 528' = 528 + 761

$\underline{cII}$ = 46-52-313-414-417-422-551-615

    46' = 46 + 313 52' = 52 + 616

    414' = 414 + 551

$\underline{C}$" = $\underline{C}$ + $\underline{cI}$ + $\underline{cII}$ $\underline{C}$' = $\underline{C}$ + $\underline{cI}$ $\underline{C}$' = $\underline{C}$ + $\underline{cII}$

    $\underline{cI}$' = $\underline{cI}$ + $\underline{cII}$

$\underline{b}$ = 19-108-118-314-537

    19' = 19 + 108 118' = 118 + 314

$\underline{d}$ = 44-106-107-125-610

    44' = 44 + 106 107' = 107 + 610

    125' = 125 + 107

$\underline{f}$ = 53-56-129-246-664

    53' = 53 + 664 56' = 56 + 246

$\underline{n}$ = W^I-54-75-127-458-767

    54' = 54 + 127 75' = 75 + 458

$\underline{s}$ = 30-85-130-321-343-344-346-730

    30' = 30 + 730 321' = 321 + 346

    85' = 85 + 130 343' = 343 + 344

$\underline{t}$ = 74-76-134-370-799

    74' = 74 + 134 76' = 76 + 370

$\underline{y}$ = 71-121-318-392-527-619

  71' = 71 + 619   392' = 392 + 527

$\underline{z}$ = 18-68-83-120-122-128-630-669

  18' = 18 + 128   68' = 68 + 122

  630' = 630 + 669

D. Codices Mixti:

  28 55 59 319 407 509 646

  407' = 407 + 509

E. Greek Patristic Witnesses:

Anast	= Anastasius Sinaita (PG 89)
Chr	= Chrysostomus I-XVII (PG 47-64)
Cyr	= Cyrillus Alexandrinus I-X (PG 68-77)
CyrHier	= Cyrillus Hierosolymitanus (PG 33, 331-1180)
Did	= Didymus Alexandrinus (SC 83,84,85; ed. L Doutreleau, 1962)
Epiph	= Epiphanius I-III (GCS 25, 31, 37; ed. K Holl)
Eus	= Eusebius Caesariensis I-II, III 1, IV, VI, VIII 1, 2, (GCS 7, 11, 14; ed. E Klostermann. GCS 23; ed I. A. Heikel. GCS 43, 1.2; ed. K Mras)
Hipp	= Hippolytus
Ant	= περὶ τοῦ ἀντιχρίστου (GCS I, 2; ed. H. Achelis)
Isid	= Isidorus Pelusiota (PG 78)

v

Iust	=	Iustinus Martyr (ed. H. Hemmer and P. Lejay, 1909)
Dial	=	Dialogus cum Tryphone (ed. G. Archambault)
Nil	=	Nilus Ancyranus (PG 79)
Or	=	Origenes I-VI (GCS 2, 3; ed. P. Koetschau GCS 10; ed. E Preuschen. GCS 29; ed W. A. Baerens. GCS 38, 40; ed. E. Klostermann)
Cels	=	Contra Celsum I-IV (SC 132, 136, 147, 150; ed M Borret, 1967-1969)
Phil	=	Philon Iudaeus Alexandrinus (L. Cohn and P. Wendland, Opera, Berlin 1896 ff)
Procop	=	Procopius Gazaeus (PG 87)
PsClem	=	Pseudo-Clementina (GCS 42; ed B. Rehm)
Tht	=	Theodoretus Cyrensis I-V (PG 80-84)
Titus	=	Titus Bostrensis Episcopus (PG 18)

F. The Old Versions:

Lat	=	The Old Latin Version
cod 91	=	Randnoten: Léon, S. Isidoro, Codex Gothicus Legionensis.
cod 92	=	Randnoten: Léon, S. Isidoro 1.3 (Legionensis 2).
cod 94	=	Randnoten: Escorial, Biblioteca de S. Lorenzo 54. V. 35.

```
cod  95 = Randnoten: Madrid, Acad. de la Histo-
          ria 2-3.
cod  96 = Randnoten: Calahorra, Catedral 2.
cod 100 = Lyon, Bibl. de la Ville, Ms 403   1964.
cod 103 = Würzburg. Universitätsbibl. Mp. theol.
          fol 64a. Palimpsest.
cod 104 = München, Bayer. Staatsbibl. Lat. Monac.
          6225.
cod 300 = Verona, Biblioteca Capitolare I (1).
cod 330 = Rom, Bibl. Vat., Regin. lat 11.
cod 410 = Madrid, Bibl. Nacional 10001.
cod 460 = Sinai, St. Katharinenkloster. Slavon. 5
Ambr     = Ambrosius
 Cain    = De Cain et Abel
 Patr    = De patriarchis
 Ps 118  = Expositio de Psalmo CXVIII
 Tob     = De Tobia
Aug      = Augustinus
 C Adim  = Contra Adimantum
 Deut    = Quaestiones de Deuteronomio
 Ios     = Quaestiones de Iesu Nava
 Loc in hept = Locutionum in Heptateuchum
 Perf    = De perfectione iustitiae hominis
 Quaest  = Quaestiones de Genesi
BrevGoth = Breviarium Gothicum
Cassiod = Cassiodorus
 Ps      = Exposito Psalmorum
```

ClemR	=	Clemens Romanus
Cypr	=	Cyprianus
Fortun	=	Ad Fortunatum, de exhortatione martyrii
FirmMat	=	Firmicus Maternus
Fulg	=	Fulgentius
Ep	=	Epistulae
Hes	=	Hesychius of Jerusalem
Hi	=	Hieronymus
C Pel	=	Dialogi contra Pelagianos
Ezech	=	Commentariorum in Hiezechielem libri
Gal	=	Commentarii in epistulam ad Galatus
Is	=	Commentariorum in Esaiam libri
Mal	=	Commentarius in Malachiam
Hil	=	Hilarius
Ps	=	Tractatus super Psalmos
Hiln	=	Quintus Iulius Hilarianus
Pasch	=	De ratione paschae et memsis
Isid	=	Isidor
Fid	=	De fide catholica ex Veteri et Novo Testamento contra Iudaeos ad Florentiam sororem
Lib geneal	=	Liber genealogus
Luc	=	Lucifer of Cagliari
Athan	=	De S. Athanasio
Conven	=	De non conveniendo cum haereticis
Parc	=	De non parcendo in Deum delinquentibus

```
Mart    = Pope Martin I
Opt     = Optatus
 App    = Appendix 10 monumentorum veterum ad
          Donatistarum historiam pertinentium
Or      = Origenes
 Matth  = Commentary on Matthew
Pel     = Pelatius, Brite
 Vita   = De vita christiana
PsAmbr  = Pseudo-Ambrosius
 Lex    = Lex Dei sive Mosaicarum et Romanarum
          legum collatio
PsAug   = Pseudo-Augustinus
 Fulg   = Libellus adversus Fulgentium Donatistam
PsHi    = Pseudo-Hieronymus
 Brev   = Breviarium in Psalmos
Ruf     = Rufinus
 Ex     = Origenis in Ex homiliae
 Num    = Origenis in Nm homiliae
 Reg S Bas = Regula S. Basilii ad monachos
Spec    = Liber de divinis scripturis sive Spec-
          ulum quod fertur S. Augustini
Tert    = Tertullianus
 Ieiunio = De ieiunio adversus psychicos
 Marc   = Adversus Marcionem
 Scorp  = Scorpiace
```

```
Aeth        = Ethiopic Version

Arab        = Arabic Version

Arm         = Armenian Version

Bo          = Original Bohairic

   Bo^A, A  = Paris, Bibl Natl., Coptic 1

   Bo^B, B  = Paris, Bibl. Natl., Coptic 100

   Bo^C, C  = Paris, Bibl Natl., Coptic 56

   Bo^D, D  = London, Brit. Mus. Or., 422

   Bo^E, E  = London, Brit. Mus. Or., 8987

   Bo^F, F  = Oxford, Bodl. Libr. Huntington 33.

   Bo^G, G  = Rome, Bibl. Vat. Copt 1.

   Bo^H, H  = Rome, Bibl. Vat., Coptic 4

   Bo^A', A' = Bo mss A through F

   Bo^B', B' = Bo mss B and E

   Bo^G', G' = Bo mss G and H

   Bo^L     = Lagarde's edition

   Bo^W     = Wilkins' edition

   Bo^LW    = Both printed editions of Bo

Sa          = Sahidic Version

   Sa^1     = A. Ciasca, Sacrorum Bibliorum Fragmenta
              copto-sahidica Musei Borgiani iussu
              et sumptibus S. Congregationis de Pro-
              paganda Fide edita. Tom I Rom 1885.
              Contents: 1:13-38, 3:5-4:22, 4:44-6:14
              8:11-9:24, 11:28-16:7, 16:16-17:1
```

Sa^2 = R. Kasser, Papyrus Bodmer XVIII, Deut I-X, 7 en sahidique. Geneve 1962. Contents: 1:1-10:7 (1:1-18 9:26-10:7 fragmentary)

Sa^3 = E. A. Wallis Budge, Coptic Biblical Texts in the Dialect of Upper Egypt. London 1912. (= Brit. Mus. Or. 7594) Contents: 1:39-2:19 4:48-8:3 9:7-13:17 14:17-18:10 19:1-20:6 22:3-26:10 28:1-6 9-12 14-31:10 31:12-14 31:16-fin libri

Sa^4 = W. C. Till and P. Sanz, Eine griechisch-koptische Odenhandschrift, Monumenta biblica et ecclesiastica 5. Rome 1939 Contents: 32:2-13 14-39 43 fragmentary

Sa^5 = C. Wessely, Griechische und Koptische Texte Theologischen Inhalts II, III and IV, Studien zur Paleographie und Papyruskunde IX, XII, XIV. Contents: 1:3-7 13:12-14:5 32:1-15 39-43 33:18-28 34:7-12

Sa^6 = J. Schleifer, Sahidische Bibel-Fragmente aus dem British Museum zu London. Sitzungsb. d. Kais. A. d. W. in Wien, philos.-hist. Kl. 162, 6. Wien 1909. Brit. Mus. Or 4717 (1). Contents: 32:30-43

Sa^7 = id, 164, 6. Wien 1911. Contents: 1:23-30

Sa^8 = id, Bruchstücke der sahidischen Bibel-übersetzung. id 170, 1. Wien 1912. Brit. Mus. Or. 4916 (2). Contents: 21:8-16

Sa[9] = A. E. Brooke, Sahidic Fragments of the Old
Testament. J Th S 8 (1906) 73-74. Paris,
Bibl. Nat., Copte 129[1] f.93 Contents:
32:14-16 17-19 21 22 24-25

Sa[10] = O. von Lemm, Sahidische Bibelfragmente III.
Bulletin de l'Académie Impériale des
Sciences de St.-Pétersbourg. Ve Série,
XXV, 4. St.-Pétersbourg 1906. Paris, Bibl.
Nat., Copte 130[5], f. 137. Contents: 21:5-12
13-15 fragmentary

Sa[11] = W. Till, Saidische Fragmente des Alten Testamentes. Le Muséon 50 (1937) 175-237. Wien,
Nat. Bibl. K. 9809. Contents: 16:19-22 17:1-6

Sa[12] = L. Th. Lefort, Les Manuscrits Coptes de
l'Université de Louvain. Louvain 1940.
Contents: 7:26-8:1 8:2-3 4-5 7-8 9:24-10:4
fragmentary

Sa[13] = A. Erman, Bruchstücke der oberaegyptischen
Uebersetzung des alten Testamentes. Nachr.
v. d. Kön. G. d. W. u. d. G. A. Universität
zu Göttingen. Nr. 12, Göttingen 1880.
Cod. Bibl. Bodl. Hunt 5. Contents: 8:19-9:24

Sa[14] = W. Pleyte and P. A. A. Boeser, Manuscripts
Coptes du Musée d'Antiquités des Pays-Bas
à Leide. Leiden 1897. Contents: 17:5-14

Sa[15] = Paul E. Kahle, Bala'izah: Coptic texts
from Dein al-Bala'izah in Upper Egypt. Vol.
I, Oxford 1954, 298-301. Contents: 8:1-8

Sa[16] = G. Maspéro, Fragments de la version thébaine
de l'Ancien Testament. Mém. publ. par les
membres de la mission arch. fr. au Caire
VI. 1, Paris 1892. Contents: 1:1-23 5:1
5:3-8 11-15 7:11-13 26:13-19 27:1 28:4-12
59-29:11 32:43-52 33:1-34:8

Sa[17] = New York: J Pierpont Morgan Libr., Copt.
ms 566. (cf Bybliotheca Pierpont Morgan
Codices Coptici photographice expressi.
Roma 1922) Complete (see also p. 359)

Pal   = Palestinian-Syriac Version
Syh   = Syro Hexaplar

G. Printed Greek Editions:
    Ald   = Aldine
    Compl = Complutensian
    Sixt = Sixtine

H. Monographs and Collections:
    Barh = Abū 'l-Farağ--Barhebraeus' Scholia on the
           Old Testament. Edited by M. Sprengling and
           W. C. Graham. Chicago 1931.
    GCS = Die griechischen christlichen Schriftsteller
           der ersten drei Jahrhunderte (Berliner Ausg.)

MSU = Mitteilungen des Septuaginta-Unternehmens, Berlin 1909ff.

PG = Migne, Patrologica, Series Graeca.

SC = Sources Chrétiennes

THGG = J. W. Wevers, Text History of the Greek Genesis MSU XI Göttingen, 1974

I. Other Abbreviations:

* = first hand of a manuscript

c = corrector

c pr m = correction(s) by the first hand

s = suppletor of a manuscript

txt = the text of a manuscript

mg = margin

te = the text of an version

ap = the apparatus of a version

Lat = the following witness is in Latin

+ = add(s)

om,> = omit(s)

⌒ = omission through homoioteleuton

. .]του = in the manuscript concerned του is legible

[ ] = reconstructed reading enclosed

※ = hexaplaric asterisk

÷ = hexaplaric obelus

⟋ = hexaplaric metobelus

Ⓜ = Massoretic Text

```
cf        = confer
cod(d)    = codex (codices)
corr      = corrector
c var     = with variation(s)
fin       = end
fol(l)    = folio(s)
Deut      = the critical text
ex par    = from a parallel passage
hab       = has/have
inc       = uncertain
init      = beginning
LXX       = original Septuagint
mend      = false(ly)
ms(s)     = manuscript(s)
omn       = all manuscripts
pl        = several
pr        = places before
rell      = the remaining evidence
scr       = write(s)/written
sed hab   = but it/they has/have (usually the lemma)
supra lineam = above the line
tr        = transpose(s)
ult       = last (occurrence)
vid       = apparently
```

CHAPTER I

DESCRIPTION OF THE MANUSCRIPTS

There are eight known manuscripts containing the Bohairic of Deuteronomy in European libraries. These[1] are:

A = Paris, Bibl. Natl., Coptic 1, foll. $\overline{o\Gamma}$ (= 73)v - $\overline{\rho\lambda\alpha}$ (= 131)v = foll. 309v - 367v.

B = Paris, Bibl. Natl., Coptic 100, foll. $\overline{c\mu\bar{\jmath}}$ (= 247)r - $\overline{c\bar{q}\theta}$ (= 299)v = foll. 249r - 301v.

C = Paris, Bibl. Natl., Coptic 56, foll. $\overline{\rho\mu\alpha}$ (= 141)r - $\overline{\rho\xi\bar{\jmath}}$ (= 167)v = foll. 140r - 166v.

D = London, Brit. Mus., Or. 422, foll. 305r - 363v.

E = London, Brit. Mus., Or. 8987, foll. $\overline{e}$ (= 5)r - $\overline{\rho\kappa\alpha}$ (= 124)r = foll. 2r - 121r.

F = Oxford, Bodl. Libr., Huntington 33, foll. $\overline{\gamma\kappa\beta}$ (= 422)r - $\overline{\gamma\bar{q}e}$ (= 496)v = foll. 414r - 485v.

G = Rome, Bibl. Vat., Coptic 1, pages $\overline{\gamma N}$ (= 450) - $\overline{\phi N}$ (= 550) = foll. 226v - 276v.

H = Rome, Bibl. Vat., Coptic 4, pages $\overline{\phi\xi e}$ (= 565) - $\overline{\chi\pi\Gamma}$ (= 683) = foll. 1r - 60r.

A (Paris: Bibliothèque Nationale Coptic 1) with Arabic translation.[2]

This is a vellum ms of the entire Pentateuch consisting of 367 folios, each 40 x 28 cm. A colophon to Genesis

1

(fol. 91r) states that the copy of Genesis was finished
on the 19th of Choiak 1073 in the Era of the Martyrs,
i.e., 1356 A.D. A further colophon to Deuteronomy
(fol. 367v) states that the entire volume was completed
three years later. The scribe was a monk named Michael
the son of Abraham.

The folios are numbered consecutively in Arabic numerals on the outside upper corner of the recto of each
folio, and in Coptic numbers on the outside upper corner
of the verso of each folio. Numbers and Deuteronomy are
numbered seriatim (in Coptic) from ⲁ (= 1) to ⲣⲗ̄ⲁ (= 131).
There is an average of 33 lines to the page, and 24
letters to the line. The Arabic translation is to the
right of the Coptic text on each page.

An ornament stands at the beginning of the Book of
Deuteronomy below which is the title "Deuteronomion,"
but divided as ⲆⲉⲨⲦⲉ ⲣⲟⲛⲟ Ⲙⲓⲟⲛ . The words ⲚⲀⲒ Ⲛⲉ
ⲚⲒⲤⲀⲬⲒ ⲚⲦⲉ ⲦⲆⲓⲁⲐⲎⲔⲎ occur twice in 29:1, with the first
instance serving as title. The word Ⲏ̅ⲱⲆⲉ appears as a
title to Chapter 32. The chapters are marked in Roman
numerals in the margins. The manuscript is paragraphed--
each paragraph beginning with a majuscule of the first
letter.

The original scribe has indicated a mistake by a
diagonal line through the error if one letter is involved.
If two or more letters had been incorrectly written, the
scribe drew one or more horizontal lines through them.

The correct letter or letters, if necessary, were written
supra lineam, or in the margin if the correction was long.
Marginal readings are usually written at right angles to
the text. Only one instance of a marginal reading by the
original scribe is written horizontally, that is, parallel
to the text, but it is upside down.

Corrections and additions by a later hand are usually
supra lineam, but the original text is not altered. If
such corrections are made in the margin they appear parallel
to the text.

The text of the ms appears to be damaged at 9:18, 20
and 21. It is difficult to determine whether this was
the result of poor photographic technique, or of a
mutilated original. Since not all the text can be read
in these passages, no e silentio conclusions are valid.
Aside from these passages, the text is clear and easily
readable.

B (Paris: Bibliothèque Nationale Coptic 100) with Arabic
translation.[3]

This is a paper manuscript of the entire Pentateuch
consisting of 302 folios each 28 x 21.5 cm. A colophon
on folio 301v = $\overline{c\overline{q}\theta}$ (= 299)v indicates that it was written
in the year 1521 of the Holy Martyrs = 1805 A.D., by John
the son of Michael.

The manuscript is written in two columns per page.
The folios are numbered consecutively from 1 - 302 on the
outside upper corner of the recto, and from $\overline{\Delta}$ (= 4) to

C̅Y̅Θ (= 299) on the outside upper corner of the verso of
each folio. Folios ⲁ̅ β̅ Γ̅ T̅ (= 1, 2, 3, and 300) are
not numbered in Coptic--the first three bearing the preface
the fourth a subscription. The Coptic scribe made several
mistakes in the numbering of this manuscript. Folios 22v
and 23v both bear the number K̅β (= 22), and folios 29v
and 30v are both numbered K̅H̅ (= 28). This explains the
apparent discrepancy in the numbering. The number of
folio C̅H̅Ϩ (= 247) has been partially erased, so that only
C̅H̅ (= 240) appears. The previous folio number C̅H̅Ε (= 246)
is inadvertently written as C̅λ̅Ϩ (= 237). The numbering
of the folios preceding and following these two is in
order. The Coptic text has an average of 37 lines to
the column and 12 letters to the line. The Arabic translation is to the right of each column of Coptic text.

An ornament appears at the beginning of Deuteronomy
immediately below which is inscribed the title CYN Θεω
ⲠⲒⲘⲁϨ Ε̅ NⲀⲱⲘ NTE ϯⲢⲟⲚⲟⲘⲒⲘⲟⲚ NTE Θεωpⲓⲁ εΘ-
ⲟⲨⲁβ , "With God, The Mighty (one) The fifth Book--
Tetironomimon[4]--of Holy Events." The words NⲀⲒ NЄ NⲒ
which begin the book are written in majuscule. Paragraphs
also begin with a majuscule. Chapter numbers are written
within the loop of the initial majuscule, e.g., ⒻⲣoϨ εⲧⲀⲚ-
ⲔⲟⲦ ; and should this initial letter have no loop the
chapter number is written beside it. The curses beginning
at 27:15 are numbered from β̅ (= 2) to ⲓΓ̅ (= 13). The word
Ϩⲱⲁε occurs as a title to Chapter 32.

Marginal readings are written either in the small space
between the two columns of the page or on the outside margin.
These marginal readings are always written at an angle of
approximately 45° to the main text. If the scribe wrote
more than one letter incorrectly, he drew one horizontal
line through the letters and inserted the correction, if
necessary, supra lineam. If one letter was incorrectly
written, this was indicated by several short diagonal
strokes at its base, and the correct letter, if necessary,
was written supra lineam. The text is on the whole neatly
written, with few corrections or marginal readings.

C (Paris: Bibliothèque Nationale Coptic 56)[5]

This paper manuscript of the Pentateuch consists of
166 folios each 30 x 20 cm. A colophon on fol. 166v =
$\overline{\rho\overline{\varsigma}\varsigma}$ (= 167v) indicates that the ms was completed on
Thursday the 24th of Tobi 1356 E.M. = 1660 A.D.

The manuscript is numbered consecutively with Arabic
numerals on the recto of each folio, and with Coptic
numbers on the verso. There is an average of 34 Coptic
letters to the line, and 44 lines to the page. The text
is not translated.

The Coptic phrase ϹⲨⲚ Ⲑⲉⲱ is preceded by an ornament and followed by the Arabic title at the beginning
of Deuteronomy. The first line of the text is in large
letters. There are no paragraphs, but sometimes the
first letter of a section is a majuscule.

A shortened stroke or elongated dot is frequently

written between words. This stroke functions as a word divider, e.g., βαρνηιοχοϛ but in a number of situations it can be mistaken for an ι or a poorly written ε . The first letters of the recto of a folio are written below the last words of the verso of the preceding folio.

If the scribe wrote one or two letters of a word incorrectly, he indicated his error by two diagonal strokes through the base of the letter(s) thus, ϙοχοϛ Corrections if needed were supra lineam. If more than two letters were incorrectly written, the scribe drew several horizontal lines through these letters. There is one marginal reading in Deuteronomy by the original scribe, and two by later hands. All three readings appear on the outside margin of the page.

The script of this ms is considerably smaller and more cramped than any of the other mss. Reading it is difficult for these reasons.

D (London: British Museum Oriental 422)[6]

This paper manuscript contains the Pentateuch (with lacunae) in Coptic and Arabic. It consists of 364 folios 11 1/2 x 8 in., in quires of 12 folios each. The first preserved quire number is Γ̄ (= 3), and the last is λδ̄ (= 34). The ms is dated (on fol. 63v) in the year 1109 of the Martyrs = 1393 A.D.

The folios are numbered consecutively in Arabic numerals on the outside upper corner of the recto of each

folio. Only the quires are numbered in Coptic, the first
quire number in Deuteronomy being $\overline{\lambda}$ (= 30) and the last
$\overline{\lambda\Delta}$ (= 34). The number of a quire appears on the inside
upper corner of the verso of its final folio. Each page
has an average of 31 lines of approximately 22 letters.
The Arabic translation is to the right of the Coptic text.

The beginning of each book is headed by an ornament.
The title ⲤⲚ ⲐⲈⲰ ⲆⲈⲨⲦⲈⲢⲟⲚⲟⲘⲓⲟⲚ "With God Deuteronomion"
is inscribed immediately below the initial ornament of
Deuteronomy. The manuscript is paragraphed--the first
letter of each paragraph being in majuscule and set out
in the margin. Some chapter numbers are written in Roman
numerals in the margins. The curses of 27:15ff. are
numbered from $\overline{\alpha}$ (= 1) to $\overline{\iota\beta}$ (= 12) in the outside margin.

Mistakes by the first hand are shown by means of
a diagonal line through the incorrect letter, with the
correction supra lineam thus, ⲘⲪ̅ⲁⲃ. Marginal readings
are always written along the outside margin at right
angles to the text.

Worms have eaten into the volume in several places.
This has produced gaps in the outside lower corner of
each folio of Deuteronomy. The gaps are so small in many
places that the text can be easily reconstructed,[7] but the
text is unfortunately lost in several other places. For
a list of the damaged verses see Appendix. No e silentio
conclusions based on these verses are valid.

The following passages are lacking in Deuteronomy,

28:33 - 38, 28:53 - 29:6, 31:26 (the word Ⲇⲓⲁⲑⲏⲕⲏ) to
the end of the book. The script is legible and neat.

E (<u>London: British Museum Oriental 8987</u>)[8]

     This is a paper manuscript of the book of Deutero-
nomy only, in Coptic and Arabic. It consists of 121 folios
each approximately 8 1/2 x 11 in. The date (1796 A.D.) is
given in a subscription to the text, fol. ⲡⲕⲅ̅ (= 123)r.

     The folios are numbered consecutively on the upper
outside corner in Arabic numerals on the recto and Coptic
numbers on the verso of each folio. The first three folios
are numbered in Coptic but not in Arabic numerals. Folio
Ⲇ̅ (= 4)r is therefore the same as fol. 1r. The pages
have approximately 27 lines each with an average of 16
letters. The Arabic translation is to the right of the
Coptic text on all pages.

     The title ⲥⲩⲛ ⲑⲉⲟⲥ ⲡⲓⲙⲁⲅ ⲉ̅ ⲛⲁⲱⲙ ⲛⲧ̅ⲡⲟⲛⲟⲙⲓⲙⲟⲛ ⲛⲧⲉ
ⲑⲉⲱⲣⲓⲁ ⲉⲑⲟⲩⲁⲃ "With God, The Fifth Book--Tetironomimon--
of Holy Events," is inscribed immediately below an initial
ornament. The first words of the text ⲛⲁⲓ ⲛⲉ ⲛⲓⲥⲁϫⲓ
are in majuscule. Each paragraph begins with a majuscule
of its first letter.

     Mistakes by the first hand are indicated by short
diagonal lines through the incorrect letter or letters,
and the correct reading, if necessary, is supra lineam.
The letters of the script are widely spaced and easily
readable.

F (<u>Oxford: Bodleian Library Huntington 33</u>)[9]

    This manuscript of the entire Pentateuch in Coptic and Arabic consists of 495 folios of approximately 7 1/2 x 11 in. A colophon to Deuteronomy states that the manuscript was completed on Tuesday the 19th of Amshir in the year 1390 of the Holy Martyrs, i.e., 1674 A.D., (cf. fol ⲣ̅ⲩ̅ⲋ̅ (= 496)v.

    The folios of Deuteronomy are numbered consecutively from ⲣ̅ⲕ̅ⲃ (= 422) to ⲣ̅ⲩ̅ⲋ̅ (= 496) on the verso, and from 414 to 485 on the recto side of each folio. The Coptic scribe would seem to have numbered three more folios than the librarian who affixed the Arabic numbers, but this is not the case. Coptic consecutive numbers were placed on the verso and recto sides of a single folio in three places, i.e., at ⲩⲡ̅ⲇ (= 484) and ⲩ̅ⲡ̅ⲉ (= 485), ⲣ̅ⲡ̅ⲋ (= 486) and ⲣ̅ⲡ̅ⲍ (= 487), ⲣ̅ⲩ̅ⲁ (= 491) and ⲩ̅ⲩ̅ⲃ (= 492). This explains the apparent discrepancy in the number of folios. There are approximately 27 lines of 20 letters to a page. The Arabic translation is to the right of the Coptic text in all pages.

    The text of Deuteronomy is headed by an ornament, immediately below which appears the title ⲡⲓⲙⲁϩ ⲉ̅ ⲛⲁⲟⲙ ⲛⲧⲉⲧⲡⲟⲛⲟⲙⲓⲙⲟⲛ ⲛⲧⲉ ⲑⲉⲱⲣⲓⲁ ⲉⲑⲟⲩⲁⲃ "The Fifth Book-- Tetironomimon--of Holy Events/Sights." The initial letters of the text ⲛⲁⲓ ⲛⲉ ⲛⲓⲥⲁϫⲓ ⲉⲧⲁⲩ are written in majuscule. The manuscript is paragraphed--each paragraph beginning with a majuscule of the first letter. The title ΠΙΜΑϨ Ē ΝⲀⲞⲘ ΝΤΕ†ⲢⲞⲚⲞⲘΙⲚ appears above the Coptic text of the verso of folios ⲢⲔⲈ (=426) to ⲢⲖⲈ (= 435). The abbreviations ⲒⲤ̅ ⲬⲤ̅ ⲨⲤ̅ ⲐⲤ̅ "Jesus Christ Son of God" appear on folio ⲢⲖ̅ (= 430), and, with variations, at intervals of 10 folios thereafter, i.e., on foll. 440, 450, etc.

The original scribe identified an incorrect letter by drawing several short diagonal strokes through it, and placing the correct letter supra lineam, e.g., ϤⲰⲢⲀⲢ If he wrote more than one incorrect letter, he drew several horizontal lines through them and made the correction, if necessary, supra lineam. An omitted letter is placed supra lineam without change of the text. There are no marginal readings in Deuteronomy. The first letters of the recto of a folio are frequently written at the lower margin of the verso of the preceding folio. The script is neat, and the letters well spaced making the text fully legible.

G (Rome: Vatican Apostolic Library, Coptic 1)[10]

This is a parchment manuscript of the entire Pentateuch, with an Arabic translation. It consists of 276 folios each 335 x 320 mm. The Coptic text has been assigned to the 9th or 10th century, and is by far the oldest of the mss read. A note on folio 276 states that the ms was written by Solomon from Babylon (i.e., old Cairo).

Numbering in Arabic numerals is consecutive for the folios, and appears on the outside upper corner of the recto of each folio. Numbering in Coptic is consecutive for the page, but is written only at the upper outside corner of the verso of each folio. Only the even numbers are written. Each page has 37 lines with an average of 32 letters to the line. The Arabic translation is written on the outside margin of each page; and was added several centuries after the Coptic text was written.[11] A line of Arabic translation is sometimes written between two lines of Coptic as a result. The last two folios of the ms are switched on the microfilm and probably in the ms.

An ornament appears at the beginning of the book of Deuteronomy within which the title ΔΕΥΤΕ ΡΟΝΟ ΜΙΟΝ is inscribed. A decorative border at the end of Chapter 28 seems to indicate a terminus of some kind, for the title ΝΑΙ ΝΕ ΝΙCΑΔΙ ΝΤΕ ϮΔΙΑΘΗΚΗ is written immediately thereafter in a different hand, centred on a line of its own. The title ϨΩΔΗ also appears at the beginning of Chapter 32. The Coptic scribe has indicated the passages where Yahweh converses with Moses and Aaron by a con-tinuous numbering from $\overline{A}$ (= 1) to $\overline{\rho\pi\varepsilon}$ (= 186), running from the beginning of Exodus to the end of Deuteronomy. Those passages in Deuteronomy are numbered $\overline{\rho\pi\beta}$ (= 182) to $\overline{\rho\pi\varepsilon}$ (= 186). The manuscript has paragraphs, marked by a majuscule of the initial letter in the margin.

The scribe used the "round" type[12] of uncials for
the biblical text itself, and the oblong type for titles,
colophons and corrections. The accents are indicated
sometimes by a straight line, sometimes by a dot, sometimes by a dot prolonged by a curved line. Punctuation
is indicated by a dot above the line or by a hyphen between two dots. The ordinary initial letters, which are
written in the margin are slightly larger than the ordinary letters, and are not marked out specially by deco-
rations, etc. The text of Deuteronomy is carefully written
with few corrections and no marginal readings by the
original scribe. If the scribe omitted a letter, he
wrote it above the space in the text to which it logically
belongs, without changing the text itself.

The script is more square than that of any other
manuscript used. It was written apparently with a broad-
nibbed pen so that the letters all tend to have a very
thick profile, e.g., ΜΗѠΟΥ . An unthinking
reader might confuse letters in the square series, e.g.,
Λ Λ and letters in the round series, e.g., ϹЄ Οϴ .
Generally, the hand is attractive and clear.

H (<u>Rome: Vatican Apostolic Library, Coptic 4</u>)[13]

This is a paper manuscript containing the book of
Deuteronomy composed of 59 folios, each 389 x 262 mm. A
subscription to Deuteronomy (folio 60v) dates the com-
pletion of the ms on the 23rd of the month of Megor, the

year 1115 of the Martyrs, i.e., 1399 A.D. A note at the
end of Deuteronomy states that the scribe's name was
Michael.

The folios bear Arabic numbers from 1 - 60 on the
upper outside corner of the recto of each folio, and
Coptic numbers from $\overline{\phi\xi\varsigma}$ (= 566)[14] to $\overline{\chi\pi\Delta}$ (= 684) on
the verso of each folio. The Coptic numbering is con-
secutive for the page, and only the even numbers are
written out. The text of Deuteronomy which begins on
fol. 1r in the Arabic numbering is thus in Coptic $\overline{\phi\xi\epsilon}$
(= 565), but it is not numbered. The scribe apparently
erred when he wrote $\overline{\phi\xi\zeta}$ (= 567) on folio 1v; he should
have written $\overline{\phi\xi\varsigma}$ (= 566).[15] This manuscript also indicates the places where Yahweh speaks to Moses and Aaron
by the numbers Δ (= 1) to $\overline{\rho\pi\varsigma}$ (= 186). In Deuteronomy,
these places are indicated by large decorated letters,
and the numbers $\overline{\rho\pi\beta}$ (= 182) to $\overline{\rho\pi\varepsilon}$ (= 186) are added.
There is an average of 24 letters to a line and 35 lines
to a page. The Arabic translation is to the right of the
Coptic text on all pages.

The title ϭιν Θεω πι ε̄ Ναϣωм ντε мωснс πιπροφнтнс
πιϫωм ντε Δεγτερονομιον πε "With God, The
Fifth Book of Moses the Prophet, (which) is the book of
Deuteronomy" is inscribed below an initial ornament. The
first words of the text Ναι νε νιϭαϫι εταγϭαϫι ммωογ ν
are written in large letters. The manuscript has paragraphs--
each beginning with a majuscule of the first letter set

out in the margin. The first words of Chapter 29 Ναι νε
ΝΙϭΑΧΙ ΝΤΕ†ΔΙΑΘΗΚΗ are written twice, with the first
instance serving as title. The word Ⳬⲱⲗⲏ is written
as a title to Chapter 32. The curses of Chapter 27 are
numbered on the outside margin from ⲁ (= 1) to ⲓⲅ (= 13).
The subscription ⲆⲈⲨⲦⲈⲢⲞⲚⲞⲘⲒⲞⲚ ⲈⲚ ⲎⲢⲏⲚⲏ ⲁⲘⲏⲚ "Deuteronomy
in Peace Amen" is written in large letters on fol. 60r.

The ms is carefully written with few corrections
and only four marginal readings--all by the first hand.
Three of these readings are written at right angles to
the text, the fourth is parallel; all appear in the outside margin. If one or two letters are omitted by the
first hand they are placed supra lineam with no change
to the text, e.g., Ⲇⲟⲧⲉⲥⲑⲉ

The script is neat and "hangs" from lines lightly
impressed in the paper above it. The text of Deuteronomy
is the third part of a three volume work. Evidence for
the view that the three volumes were originally one is
given in the Vatican Catalogue.[16]

References

[1]
Most of these mss carry a double numbering--in
Coptic and in Arabic numerals. Both are given here. The
Coptic is the older of the two numbering systems, and is
therefore given first with its equivalent in Arabic
numerals in brackets. The modern numbering--Arabic
numerals--is given second. Apparent discrepancies in the
number and numbering of the folios of some mss, e.g., A,
B, D, F, are explained in the detailed descriptions.

The information on the descriptions of these mss
was gathered partly from microfilms of their originals
and partly from published catalogues of the libraries in
which the mss are housed. The details found in the catalogues were checked as far as possible against the microfilms, and were verified or corrected as necessary. In
all mss the usual Coptic abbreviations were used, e.g.,
ⲡ̅ⲭ̅ⲥ̅ = ⲡⲉⲭⲟⲓⲥ , ⲡ̅ⲛ̅ⲁ = ⲡ̅ⲛⲉⲩⲙⲁ ⲫ̅ⲧ̅ = ⲫⲛⲟⲩ̅ ⲉⲃ̅ⲩ̅ = ⲉⲃⲟⲗⲁⲃ etc. The ta-
chygraphs ⸗ , or ⌄ , or ⸌ = ⲛ were used in most texts.
Details of scribal idiosyncracies are given only where
they have significance for an understanding of the text.

[2]
See L. Delaporte, "Catalogue Sommaire des Manu-
scrits Coptes de la Bibliothèque Nationale." Revue de
L'Orient Chrétien, 2ème Série Tome IV, pp. 417-418.

[3]
Ibid., Tome V, p. 86.

[4]
This is obviously a corruption of ⲛⲁⲉⲣⲧⲉⲣⲟⲛⲟⲙⲓⲟⲛ
A similar corruption appears at the beginning of Exodus,
where the word in the Coptic title is ⲗⲟⲝⲟⲗⲟⲥ. See also
mss E and F.

[5]
Ibid., pp. 85-86.

[6]
W. E. Crum, Catalogue of the Coptic Manuscripts
in the British Museum. (London: Longmans & Co. 1905),
p. 315.

[7]
In such places, the usual designation [ ] will
be used.

[8]This ms is listed in A. E. Brooke, "The Bohairic Version of the Pentateuch." <u>The Journal of Theological Studies</u>, III (1902), p. 206ff., as British Museum Curzon ms 117, and a brief description is given there. The designation British Museum Or. 8987 is based on the title of the microfilm. The British Museum has advised that Deuteronomy is Curzon 114 and Exodus is 117.

[9]Brooke, <u>op. cit.</u>, lists this ms also and gives a brief description of it. The size of the folios was measured from the microfilm on the basis of the scale of inches and centimeters supplied at the beginning. The figures are therefore only approximate.

[10]A detailed description of this ms is given in <u>Codices Coptici Vaticani; Barberiniani Borgiani Rossiani, Tomus I, Codices Coptici Vaticani</u>, Recensuerunt Adulphus Hebbelynck et Arnoldus Van Lantschoot (Bibliotheca Vaticana 1937), pp. 1-6.

[11]Hebbelynck and Lantschoot, <u>op. cit.</u>, date the translation to the 13th or 14th centuries but suggest that it was not based on the Coptic of this ms. For a good treatment of the Arabic versions of the Penta-teuch, see the dissertation of Joseph F. Rhode, <u>The Arabic Versions of the Pentateuch in the Church of Egypt</u>, (St. Louis: 1921). Folios 97v and 166 of this ms have been published phototypically by Henry Hyvernat, <u>Album de Paléographie copte</u>, (Rome: 1888) tab. XIX, XVIII.

[12]Cf. A. Hebbelynck, "Les κεφάλαια et les τίτλοι des Evangiles." <u>Le Muséon</u> (Louvain 1928) XLI, p. 118

[13]Cf. Hebbelynck and Lantschoot, <u>op. cit.</u>, p. 7. This manuscript was formerly Vatican Coptic 9, according to this catalogue.

[14]I disagree with Hebbelynck and Lantschoot, <u>op. cit.</u>, p. 11, who suggested that on fol. 1v the scribe should have written ⲫ̅ⲝ̅ⲏ̅ (= 568) instead of ⲫ̅ⲝ̅ⲍ̅ (= 567). Such a change would upset the numbering of the remainder of the manuscript. I would suggest rather ⲫ̅ⲝ̅ⲋ̅ (= 566), which would resolve the problem quite simply. In that event, the text of Deuteronomy begins on page ⲫ̅ⲝ̅ⲉ̅ (=565) and the subsequent numbering is in order.

[15]See note 14.

[16]Hebbelynck and Lantschoot, <u>op. cit.</u>, p. 7.

CHAPTER II

CLASSIFICATION OF THE MANUSCRIPTS

The eight mss of the Bohairic of Deuteronomy fall into two groups. The first consists of two mss, G-H, and the second of six mss, A-B-C-D-E-F.

The homogeneity of the first group can easily be shown. In fact, it is virtually certain that H is a copy of G.[1] The passages where Yahweh speaks to Moses and Aaron are numbered in these two mss only. These are also the only two mss numbered by page and not by folio. These external facts suggest similarity, and textual analysis confirms it. The following list is a sampling of the many unique readings[2] of these two mss. The text of G-H is the lemma, the majority reading the variant. The chapter and verse divisions of the editions[3] are conveniently used here.

9:5   ⲉⲑⲃⲉ ⲧ̄ⲙⲉⲧⲁⲥⲉⲃⲏⲥ ⲛⲧⲉ ⲛⲁⲓ ⲉⲑⲛⲟⲥ ⲛⲁ̄ⲉ ⲡ̄⳪ⲥ ⲉⲩⲉⲩⲟⲧⲟⲩ ⲉⲃⲟⲗϩⲁⲧⲍⲏ ⲙⲡⲉⲕϩⲟ] om

9:16   ⲡⲉⲧⲉⲛⲛⲟⲩⲧ̄] om

9:23   ⲡⲉⲧⲉⲛⲛⲟⲩⲧ̄ ⲟⲩⲟϩ] om

9:29   ϧⲉⲛ ⲧⲉⲕⲛⲓϣϯ ⲛϫⲟⲙ ⲛⲉⲙ ϧⲉⲛ ⲧⲉⲕϫⲓϫ ⲉⲧⲁⲙⲁϩⲓ ⲛⲉⲙ ϧⲉⲛ ⲡⲉⲕϫⲫⲟⲓ ⲉⲧϫⲟⲥⲓ] om

10:10 ϧⲉⲛ ⲡⲓⲥⲏⲟⲩ ⲉⲧⲉⲙⲙⲁⲩ ⲟⲩⲟϩ ⲙⲡⲉϥⲟⲩⲱϣ ⲉⲩⲉⲧⲑⲏⲛⲟⲩ] ⲙⲡⲉϥϥⲉⲧⲑⲏⲛⲟⲩ (C var)

11:8   ⲛⲏ ⲁⲛⲟⲕ ⲉⲧϩⲟⲛϩⲉⲛ ⲙⲙⲱⲟⲩ ⲛⲧⲟⲧⲕ ⲙⲫⲟⲟⲩ] om

11:32 ⲧⲏⲣⲟⲩ ⲛⲉⲙ ⲛⲁⲓϩⲁⲡ ⲛⲏ ⲁⲛⲟⲕ ⲉⲧϯ ⲙⲡⲉⲧⲉⲛⲙⲃⲟ ⲙⲫⲟⲟⲩ] om

12:7   ⲡⲉⲕⲛⲟⲩⲧ̄] om

17

12:29   ΟΥΟΖ ΝΤΕΚΕΡΚΛΗΡΟΝΟΜΙΝ ΜΜΟϤ ΟΥΟΖ ΝΤΕΚϢΩΠΙ ΝΖΡΗΙ ϨΕΝ ΠΟΙΚΑϨΙ] om

13:4   ΕΡΕΤΕΝΕϹΩΤΕΜ ΝϹΑ ΤΕϤϹΜΗ ΟΥΟΖ ΕΡΕΤΕΝΕΤΟΥϨΟ ΕΡΟϤ] om

13:18   ΝΗ ΑΝΟΚ ΕΤϨΟΝϨΕΝ ΜΜΩΟΥ ΕΤΟΤΚ ΜⲪΟΟΥ ΕΙΡΙ ΜΠΙΠΕΘΝΑΝΕϤ ΝΕΜ
      ΠΕΘΡΑΝΑϤ ΜΠΕΜΘΟ ΜΠϬΟΙϹ ΠΕΚΝΟΥϮ] om

14:12   ΝΗΕΘΟΥΑΒ ΑΝ ΝΝΕΤΕΝΟΥΟΜΟΥ] ΟΥΟΖ ΝΑΙ ΝΝΕΤΕΝ ΟΥΩΜ ΕΒΟΛ ΝϨΗΤΟΥ

14:24   ΠΕΚΝΟΥϮ ΕΘΡΟΥΜΟΥϮ ΕΠΕϤΡΑΝ ΕΜΑΥ ϪΕ ΕϤΕϹΜΟΥ ΕΡΟΚ ΝϪΕ ΠϬΟΙϹ ΠΕΚΝΟΥϮ] om

15:6   ϪΕ ΠϬΟΙϹ ΠΕΚΝΟΥϮ ΑϤϹΜΟΥ ΕΡΟΚ ΜⲪΡΗϮ ΕΤΑϤϹΑϪΙ ΝΕΜΑΚ ΟΥΟΖ] om

15:18   ΟΥΟΖ ΕϤΕϹΜΟΥ ΕΡΟΚ ΝϪΕ ΠϬΟΙϹ ΠΕΚΝΟΥϮ ϨΕΝ ΟΥΟΝ ΝΙΒΕΝ ΝΗΕΤΕΚΕΑΙΤΟΥ] om

16:2   ΝΕΜ ϨΑΝΕϨΩΟΥ] om

16:2   ΠΕΚΝΟΥϮ] om

16:11   ϨΕΝ ΠΙΜΑ ΕΤΕ ΠϬΟΙϹ ΠΕΚΝΟΥϮ ΝΑϹΟΤΠϤ ΕΜΟΥϮ ΕΠΕϤΡΑΝ ΜΜΑΥ] om

17:1   ΠΕΚΝΟΥϮ] om

17:10   ΟΥΟΖ ΕΚΕΑΡΕΖ ΕΙΡΙ ΝΟΥΟΝ ΝΙΒΕΝ] ΟΥΟΖ ΕΚΕΑΡΕΖ ΚΑΤΑ

17:20   ΕΒΟΛϨΑ ΝΙΕΝΤΟΛΗ] om

18:5   ΕΘΡΕϤΟΖΙ ΕΡΑΤϤ ΜΠΕΜΘΟ ΜΠϬΟΙϹ ΕϤϢΕΜϢΙ ΟΥΟΖ ΕϤϹΜΟΥ ϨΕΝ
      ΠΕϤΡΑΝ ΝΘΟϤ ΝΕΜ ΝΕϤϢΗΡΙ] ΕΘΡΕϤϢΕΜϢΙ ΜΠΕΜΘΟ ΜΠ⳥Ϲ

18:7   ΠΕϤΝΟΥϮ] om

18:15   ΠΕΚΝΟΥϮ] om

18:16   ΠΕΚΝΟΥϮ ι°] om

19:1   ΟΥΟΖ ι°] om

26:19   ΝΤΕΚϢΩΠΙ ϢΑ ΠϢΩΙ] ΝΤΕΚϹΑΠϢΩΙ

34:12   ΤΗΡϤ] om

     The most obvious feature of this list of variants is the
number of omissions that it attests. The reading of the G-H group
is frequently longer than that of the rest of the mss. The task of
determining conclusively whether the longer or shorter reading is

original Coptic is beyond the scope of this chapter, but a workable
hypothesis is possible. Bohairic is a translation from Greek,[4] so
the reading which comes closer to the Greek may normally be considered the original Coptic. A comparison of the Greek with the
list of relevant passages indicates that the longer readings of the
G-H group are original Bohairic.

The list of unique readings of G-H shows not only the affinity
of G to H but simultaneously demonstrates the homogenous nature of
the larger group A-B-C-D-E-F. Further proof of the existence of
two major groups will therefore not be given. The group G-H will
hereafter be referred to as G' and the group A-B-C-D-E-F as A'.

There is, however, one clearly defined sub-group of the larger
group A', namely B-E-F. The Coptic titles[5] of these three mss
suggest a similarity which is confirmed by their texts. They alone
attest the corruption ⲚⲦⲉⲧⲡⲟⲛⲟⲙⲓⲙⲟⲛ of the word "Deuteronomion"
in their titles, and numerous readings unique to them appear in
their texts. The following list is typical of the unique readings
of the B-E-F sub-group. The reading of this sub-group is the lemma,
and the remaining five mss the variant.

1:1   ⲞⲨⲦⲞⲨ] ⲞⲨⲦⲰⲨ

1:1   ⲔⲀⲦⲀⲔⲣⲏⲤⲉⲀ] — ⲔⲣⲏⲤⲉⲀ

1:13   ⲈⲠⲒⲤⲦⲒⲘⲎ] — ⲦⲎⲘⲎ

1:18   ⲚⲦⲉⲦⲉⲚⲀⲒⲦⲞⲨ] ⲈⲦⲉⲦⲉⲚⲚⲀⲀⲒⲦⲞⲨ

1:23   ⲚⲢⲱⲘⲒ] + ⲞⲨⲢⲱⲘⲒ

1:25   ⲪⲎⲉⲦⲀ ⲠϬⲞⲒⲤ] ⲪⲎⲉⲦⲉ .

1:31   ⲈⲦⲀⲨⲚⲀⲨⲀⲚⲞⲨⲱⲕ] ⲈⲦⲀⲨⲨⲀⲚⲞⲨⲱⲕ

1:38   ⲡⲉⲧⲁⲕⲛⲁⲧⲛⲟⲙⲧ] ⲡⲉⲧⲉⲕ·

1:39   ⲫⲏⲉⲧⲁⲩⲥⲱⲟⲣⲛ] ⲫⲏⲉⲧⲉϥ·

1:39   ⲉⲑⲛⲁⲉⲣⲕⲗⲏⲣⲟⲛⲟⲙⲓⲛ] ⲉⲧⲛⲁ·

1:40   ⲁⲣⲉⲧⲉⲛϫⲟⲕ] — ϫⲱⲕ

2:3   ⲕⲱⲧ] ⲉⲣⲉⲧⲉⲛⲕⲱⲧ

2:6   ⲉⲣⲉⲧⲉⲛⲉϣⲱⲡⲓ] — ϣⲱⲡ

2:9   ⲛⲉⲕϩⲃⲏⲟⲩⲓ] ⲛⲓϩⲃ·

2:12 & 22   ⲥⲉⲏⲣ] ⲥⲏⲓⲣ

2:26   ⲛϫⲟϫⲟⲙⲙⲓⲟⲛ] ⲛⲓϫⲟϫⲟⲙⲙⲓⲛ

2:26   ⲕⲏⲁⲑⲱⲙ] ⲕⲉⲁⲙⲱⲑ

2:27   ⲟⲩⲓⲛⲁⲙ ⲛⲉⲙ ⲟⲩⲇⲉ ϫⲁϭⲏ] ⲉⲟⲩⲓⲛⲁⲙ ⲟⲩⲇⲉ ϫⲁϭⲏ

2:32   ⲉⲡⲡⲟⲗⲉⲙⲟⲥ ⲛⲁⲥⲥⲁ] — ⲙⲟⲥ ⲉⲓⲁⲥⲥⲁ (ⲥⲩⲁⲅ)

2:35   ⲁⲛⲩϣⲱⲗⲟⲩ] — ϣⲟⲗ·

2:36   ⲥⲕⲉⲛ] ⲉⲥⲕⲉⲛ (ⲥⲩⲁⲅ)

2:36   ⲉⲛⲉⲇⲟⲧⲟⲩ] ⲛⲉⲛⲥⲇⲟⲧⲟⲩ

2:36   ⲉⲣⲛⲱⲛ] ⲁⲣⲛⲱⲛ

3:4   ⲛⲧⲟⲩⲧⲟⲩ ⲛⲧⲉ ⲁⲣ ⲝ̅ ⲙⲃⲁⲕⲓ] ⲛⲧⲟⲧⲟⲩ ⲝ̅ ⲙⲃⲁⲕⲓ

3:5   ϩⲁⲛⲙⲟⲩⲭⲗⲟⲥ] ϩⲁⲛⲙⲟⲭⲗⲟⲥ (ⲥ ⲩⲁⲣ)

3:11   ⲛⲧⲉⲑⲃⲁⲥⲁⲛ] ⲛⲑⲃⲁⲥⲁⲛ

3:28   ⲫⲏⲉⲧⲉⲕⲛⲁⲩ] ⲫⲏⲉⲧⲁⲕ·

13:7   ⲛⲓⲉⲑⲛⲟⲥ ⲛⲧⲉ ⲛⲓⲛⲟⲩⲧ] ⲛⲓⲛⲟⲩⲧ ⲛⲧⲉ ⲛⲓⲉⲑⲛⲟⲥ

29:1   ⲭⲱⲣⲉⲃ] ⲭⲱⲣⲏⲃ

29:6   ⲡⲉⲛⲛⲟⲩⲧ] ⲡⲉⲧⲉⲛⲛⲟⲩⲧ

29:7   ⲛⲧⲉⲑⲃⲁⲥⲁⲛ] ⲛⲑⲃⲁⲥⲁⲛ

29:10   ⲛⲉⲧⲉⲛⲕⲣⲏⲧⲏⲥ] — ⲕⲣⲓⲧⲏⲥ

29:11   ⲛⲧⲟⲧⲉⲛ] ⲛⲧⲱⲧⲉⲛ

29:14 ΝΑΧω] ΝΑΙΧω

29:15 αλλα] + ΝΕΜ

29:15 ΜΦΟΟΥ ΜΠΑΙΜΑ] ΜΠΑΙΜΑ ΜΦΟΟΥ

29:16 ΜΦΡΗϯ ΓΑΡ ΕΤΑΡΕΤΕΝϭΙΝΙ] ΜΦΡΗϯ ΕΤΑΡΕΤ.

29:17 ΕΡΕΤΕΝΝΑΥ] ΑΡΕΤ.

29:17 ΝΟΥϭωΥ] ΕΝΟΥϭωΥ

29:22 ΕΘΝΑΤΟΥΟΝΟΥ] ΕΤΝΑΤ.

29:27 ΠΚΑϩΙ] ΠΙΚΑϩΙ

29:29 ΝΑΘΟΥΟΝϩ] ΝΕΘΟΥΟΝϩ

     The sub-group B-E-F is not always as unified as this list of
readings would suggest. There are several instances where two
members preserve a unique reading, the third joining the majority
reading. In other cases one manuscript has a slight variant from
the other two in the sub-group, while the majority reading is
different. Six kinds of readings are possible in these circumstances.
(1) BE vs rell, (2) BF vs rell, (3) EF vs rell, (4) BE, F vs rell,
(5) BF, E vs rell, (6) EF, B vs rell. The following list of variants
is presented in the above order. The lemma is the majority reading.

(1)   1:1   ΜΦΑΡΡΑΝ] ΜΦΑΡΑΝ BE

        1:13   ΝϩΑΝΥΓΟΥΜΕΝΟϹ (ϲ var)] ΝϩΑΝΥΓωΜΕΝΟϹ BE

        1:22   ΑΡΕΤΕΝΙ] ΕΡΕΤΕΝΙ BE

        1:28   ΝΑΦωΠ] ΝΑΦωΦ BE

        1:45   ΜΠΕΥϯϩΘΗΥ] ΜΠΕρϯ. BE

        2:9   ΜΠΕΡΕΡϪΑϪΙ 1°] ΜΠΕΡϪΑϪΙ BE

        2:10   ΡΑΦΑΙΜ] ΡΑΦΙΜ BE

        2:11   ΕΥΕΗΠ (ϲ var)] ΕΥΗΠ BE

2:16 ⲁⲣⲍⲉⲓ] ⲍⲉⲓ ΒΕ

2:20 ⲛⲓⲁⲙⲙⲁⲛⲓⲧⲏⲥ] ⲛⲁⲙⲙⲁⲛ ΒΕ

2:22 .ⲉⲙⲁⲩ (ⲋ var)] ⲙⲙⲱⲟⲩ ΒΕ

2:25 ⲛⲛⲓⲉⲑⲛⲟⲥ] ⲛⲛⲏⲉⲑⲛⲟⲥ ΒΕ

3:1 ⲉⲡⲡⲟⲗⲉⲙⲟⲥ] ⲉⲡⲓⲡⲟⲗ· ΒΕ

3:4 ⲁⲣⲕⲱⲃ] ⲁⲣⲕⲱⲃ ΒΕ

3:5 ⲛⲉ] ⲟⲙ ΒΕ

3:9 ⲛⲓⳙⲟⲓⲛⲓⳝ] ⲛⲓⳙⲟⲛ· ΒΕ

3:11 ⲡⲉⳙⳛⲓⲏ] ⲧⲉⳙϭⲓⲏ ΒΕ

3:12 ⲡⲓⲕⲁⲍⲓ] ⲡⲣ ϫⲉⲛ ΒΕ

3:14 ⲓⲁⲓⲣ] ⲁⲓⲉⲣ ΒΕ

3:20 ⲉⲧⲉⳙⲕⲗⲏⲣⲟⲛⲟⲙⲓⲁ] ⲛⲧⲉⳙⲕ· ΒΕ

3:29 ⲡⲉ] ⲟⲙ ΒΕ

13:5 ⳙⲏⲉⲧⲁⲩⲥⲟⲧⲕ] — ⳙⲥⲟⲧⲡⲕ ΒΕ

13:16 ⲛⲛⲟⲩⲕⲟⲧⲥ] ⲛⲟⲩⲕⲟⲧⲥ ΒΕ

29:7 ⲁⲣⲉⲧⲉⲛⲓ] ⲉⲣⲉⲧⲉⲛⲓ ΒΕ

29:18 ⲉⲥⲣⲏⲧ] ⲉⲥⲓⲣⲏⲧ ΒΕ

(2) 1:12 ⲡⲱⲥ] ⲡⲉ̄ⲥ ΒF

1:38 ⲉⲣⲁⲧⳙ] ⲉⲣⲁⲧⲕ ΒF

1:41 ⲛⲛⲉⳙⲥⲕⲉⲩⲟⲥ] ⲛⲣⲉⳙⲥⲕⲉⲩⲟⲥ ΒF

2:10 ⲉⲛⲁⳛⲱⳙ] ⲉⲛⲁⳛⲟⲩ ΒF

3:6 ⲁⲛⲩⲟⲧⲟⲩ] ⲁⲛⲩⲟⲣⲧⲟⲩ ΒF

3:8 ⳙⲁ] ⳙⲉ ΒF

3:9 ϫⲉ ⲥⲁⲛⲓⲱⲣ] ⲛϫⲉ ⲥⲁⲛⲓⲱⲣ ΒF

3:24 ⲛⲧⲁⲙⲉ] ⲛⲧⲁⲙⲁ ΒF

	13:16	NϢHTC] NϢHT BF
(3)	1:11	NKⲰB] NKOB EF
	1:36	ϤⲟⲣⲉⳌ] ⲉϤⲟⲣⲁⳌ E ; ⲁϤⲟⲣⲉⳌ F
	1:46	ⲀⲢⲉⲧⲉNⳌⲉⲙⲤⲒ ι°] ⲉⲢⲉⲧⲉNⳌ.
	3:21	NHⲉⲧⲉKNⲀⲉⲢⳢⲒN⳰ⲞⲢ] NHⲉⲧⲀKNⲀ.
	29:10	ⲈⲢⲀⲧⲉNⲐHNⲞⲨ] ⲉⲢⲉⲧⲉNⲐ.
(4)	1:14	ⲀⲧⲉⲧⲉNⲉⲢⲟⲧⲱ] ⲉⲧⲉⲧⲉNⲉⲢ. BE ; NⲧⲉⲧⲉNⲉⲢ. F
	1:38	Nⲉ ⲉⲧNⲀⲐHⲒⳋ] ⲠⲉⲐNⲀⲦHⲒⳋ BE; Ⲡⲉ ⲉⲐNⲀⲦHⲒⳋ F
	2:16	HⲠⲟⲗⲉⲙⲒⲤⲦHⲤ] ⳢⲉN Ⲡⲟⲗⲉⲙ. BE; ⳢⲉN ⲠⲟⲨⲗⲉⲙ. F
	3:3	NⲐⲂⲀⲤⲀN] NⲧⲉⲐⲂⲀⲤⲀN BE; NⲧⲀⲐⲂ. F
	3:10	ⲉⳆⲢⲀⲒN] ⲀⳆⲢⲀN BE; ⲀⳆⲢⲀⲒN F
	3:13	NNⲒⲢⲀⳤⲀⲒH] NNⲒⲢⲀⳤⲀⲒN BE; NNⲒⲢⲀⳤⲒⲙ F
	29:20	ⲉⳅⲉⲦⲞⲙⲞⳋ] ⲉⲦⲞⳋⲙⲞⳋ BE; ⲉⳅⲉⲦⲞⳋⲙⲞⳋ F
(5)	1:10	ⳌHⲠⲠⲉ ⲦⲉⲦⲉNⲞⲒ] ⳌHⲠⲠⲉ ⲠⲉⲦⲉNⲞⲒ BF; ⳌHⲠⲠⲉ ⲦⲉNⲞⲒ E
	2:28	ⲉⲒⲉⲞⳋⲰⲙ] ⲉⲒⲉⲞⳋⲱⲙK BF; ⲉⲒⲉⲞⳋⲱⲙⳋ E
	13:11	ⲉⲒⲢⲒ] ⲀⲒⲒⲢⲒ BF ; ⲀⲢⲒⲢⲒ E
(6)	1:15	ⲉⲠⲒⲤⲦHⲙH] ⲉⲠⲒⲤⲦⲒⲙH EF; ⲙⲠⲒⲤⲦⲒⲙH B

It is clear that the strongest relationship within the sub-group exists between B and E, and the weakest between E and F. In the light of this evidence, B and E will hereafter be considered as one witness and will be referred to as B'. The remaining mss of the second group A', namely A C Ɗ do not in themselves form a group nor do they follow consistent patterns.

References

[1] Hebbelynck and Lantschoot, op. cit. p. 7, have stated that H is almost surely a copy of G. The many unique readings in these mss, the distribution of paragraphs and the variant readings and omissions common to both suggest that the one was a copy of the other. Brooke, op. cit., p. 259, supports this view. My research confirms it. All of G was collated, then Chapters 1 - 3, 13, and 29 of H. The two mss were together almost always in these chapters. A list of unique readings of G which spanned the entire book was also checked against H, and in every case, the readings were identical. No more of H was collated as a result, and it was assumed that G = H.

[2] A fuller discussion of the unique readings of G-H appears in Chapter III.

[3] See Chapter III.

[4] See Chapter IV. The final word on the Greek Deuteronomy will be given by J. W. Wevers in his edition now in progress.

[5] See Chapter I. ⲡⲓⲙⲁϩ ⲉ̄ ⲛⲁⲩⲙ ⲛⲧⲉϯⲡⲟⲛⲟⲙⲓⲙⲟⲛ ⲛⲧⲉ ⲑⲉⲱⲣⲓⲁ ⲉⲃⲟⲣⲁⲃ is written as the title of these three mss only. Not all of E was collated because it became clear after the first three chapters were collated that the text was copied by the writer of B. (All of B had at that time been collated.) Chapters 13 and 29 of E were also collated to confirm that the apparent dependence remained constant throughout the book. This proved to be accurate.

Chapter III

THE PRINTED EDITIONS

The Bohairic of the Pentateuch is available in printed form in two major editions. The older of these, now out of print was edited in 1731 by David Wilkins in London[1] (hereafter Bo^W), the more recent and more widely accessible, in 1867 by Paul de Lagarde in Leipzig[2] (hereafter Bo^L), this latter being readily available in reprint.[3]

In the introduction to Bo^W, Wilkins claims that it was based on three mss housed at that time in the Vatican, Paris and Bodleian libraries.

> Pentateuchum Copticum ex MS. Vaticano
> Parisiensi & Bodlejano descriptum, ac
> Latina civitate donatum Tibi exhibeo.[4]

He subsequently identifies the mss. The Vatican was vols. 7, 8, and 9 in the series of mss "kept behind a lattice," i.e., Bibl. Vat. 2, 3, and 4, of which Deuteronomy is vol. 4 = H. The Bodleian ms he identifies as Huntington 33 = F. As to the Paris ms he states that it was kept in the Bibliotheca Regia, but was transferred to the Abbey of Saint-Germain-des-Prés for his purposes by his dear friend Montfaucon.

> Aetatem Parisiensis Regii Codicis, quem pro
> singulari erga me affectu celeberrimus Mont-
> fauconius ex Bibliotheca Regia in Abbatiam
> S. Germani a Pratis in meos usus intulit,
> adnotare oblitus eram; forsan quod finito
> hujus codicis examine statim ad alia me con-
> tuli: eam tamen proximis, si quae typis ex-
> scripturus fuero MSS. Copticis inseram.[5]

It has been determined through correspondence with the
Bibliotheque Nationale that the ms most likely used was Bibl.
Natl., Copte 56 = C (1660). The Conservateur en Chef de la
Section Oriental du Département des Manuscrits has informed
me that this ms was acquired in Venice on the 11th of August
1698 by Bernard Montfaucon. She further states, "Ce même
manuscrit provient de l'Abbaye de Saint-Germain-des-prés où
il portait le numéro 20."[6] She also verified that the Bibliothèque Nationale was called Bibliotheca Regiae until 1728.

Initially, it would seem reasonable to assume that
Wilkins' statement is accurate and that he did consult,
whether to copy or to collate, these three mss. And while
it is impossible to determine exactly what he did, one can
fairly accurately reconstruct his most probable modus operandi.

A comparison of the text of Wilkins with the Bodleian ms
F reveals that in matters of orthography, he considered this
ms authoritative. The reason for this seems obvious. The
Bodleian ms was in the same country (England) as Wilkins, and
presumably easily accessible to him. Thus, in all probability,
he used it as a lemma against which he collated his copies/
collations of the Vatican and Paris mss. The following list
of variants is, in the main, unique readings of Bo^W and F.
In some instances B' the congeners of F join them, but if
it is recalled that mss B and E were not in existence at
that time, the agreement is of no textual significance. Bo^L
is used as lemma in this and all subsequent lists of Coptic
readings. This choice is made for convenience only and does
not indicate textual superiority of Lagarde's edition in any way.

1:7 ⲌⲀ ⲚⲎ ⲦⲎⲢⲞⲨ] ⲌⲀⲚ ⲚⲎ ⲦⲎⲢⲞⲨ

1:10 ⲦⲈⲦⲈⲚⲞⲒ] ⲠⲈⲦⲈⲚⲞⲒ = Ⲃ

1:11 ⲚⲈⲦⲈⲚⲒⲞⲦ] ⲚⲈⲦⲈⲚⲒⲞⲨⲦ = Ⲉ

1:11 ⲚⲔⲰⲂ] ⲚⲔⲞⲂ = Ⲉ

1:13 & 15 ⲈⲠⲒⲤⲦⲎⲘⲎ] ⲈⲠⲒⲤⲦⲒⲘⲎ = Ⲃ

1:14 ⲀⲦⲈⲦⲈⲚⲈⲢⲞⲨⲰ] ⲚⲦⲈⲦⲈⲚⲈⲢⲞⲨⲰ

1:15 Ⲛ̄ⲎⲄⲞⲨⲘⲈⲚⲞⲤ] ⲚⲌ̄ⲨⲄⲰⲘ.

1:21 ⲚⲈⲦⲈⲚⲒⲞⲦ] ⲚⲈⲦⲈⲚⲒⲞⲨⲦ

1:25 ⲪⲎⲈⲦⲈ ⲠⲄⲞⲒⲤ] ⲪⲎⲈⲦⲀ ⲠⲦⲞⲤ = Ⲃ

1:28 ⲀⲨⲪⲈⲚⲌ ⲠⲈⲦⲈⲚⲌⲎⲦ] ⲀⲨⲪⲈⲚⲌⲎⲦ

1:31 ⲈⲦⲀⲢⲈⲦⲈⲚⲚⲀⲨ] ⲈⲦⲈⲢⲈⲦⲈⲚⲚⲀⲨ

1:35 ⲚⲚⲞⲨⲒⲞⲦ] ⲚⲚⲞⲨⲚⲞⲨⲦ

1:36 ⲨⲞⲨⲈⲌ] ⲀⲨⲞⲨⲈⲌ

1:38 ⲈⲢⲀⲦⲨ] ⲈⲢⲀⲦⲔ

1:38 ⲠⲈⲦⲈⲔⲚⲀⲦⲚⲞⲘⲦ] ⲠⲈⲦⲀⲔⲚⲀⲦ.

1:39 ⲪⲎⲈⲦⲈⲨⲤⲰⲞⲨⲚ] ⲪⲎⲈⲦⲀⲨ.

1:39 ⲈⲦⲚⲀⲈⲢⲔⲖⲎⲢⲞⲚⲞⲘⲒⲚ] ⲈⲐⲚⲀ.

1:41 Ⲁ ⲠⲒⲞⲨⲀⲒ ⲠⲒⲞⲨⲀⲒ ⲤⲒ] Ⲁ ⲠⲒⲞⲨⲀⲒ ⲤⲒ

2:4 ⲚⲒⲤⲒⲎ] ⲤⲒⲎ

2:4 ⲌⲀⲦⲈⲦⲈⲚⲌⲎ] ⲌⲀⲦⲈⲚⲌⲎ

2:6 ⲈⲢⲈⲦⲈⲚⲈⲨⲰⲠ] ⲈⲢⲈⲦⲈⲚⲈⲨⲰⲠⲒ = Ⲃ'

2:7 ⲚⲌⲂⲎⲞⲨⲒ] ⲚⲈⲔⲌⲂⲎⲞⲨⲒ = Ⲃ'

2:13 ⲚⲐⲰⲦⲈⲚ] ⲐⲰⲦⲈⲚ

2:35 ⲀⲚⲨⲞⲖⲞⲨ] ⲀⲚⲨⲰⲖⲞⲨ = Ⲃ

3:3 ⲚⲐⲂⲀⲤⲀⲚ] ⲚⲦⲈⲐⲂ. Ⲃₒ^Ⲱ Ⲃ'   ⲚⲦⲀⲪⲂ. Ϥ

3:5 ⲌⲀⲚⲘⲞⲬⲖⲞⲤ] ⲌⲀⲚⲘⲞⲨⲬⲖⲞⲤ = Ⲃ'

3:6	ⲉⲧⲁⲛⲁⲓⲥ] ⲛⲧⲁⲛⲁⲓⲥ	
3:12	ⲁⲣⲟⲏⲣ] ⲛⲁⲣⲟⲏⲣ	
3:16	ⲛⲁⲙⲙⲱⲛ] ⲛⲁⲙⲙⲟⲛ	
3:20	ⲕⲟⲧⲩ] ⲕⲟⲧ	
3:21	ϧⲉⲛ ⲡⲓⲥϩⲟⲩ] ⲛⲥϩⲟⲩ	
3:21	ⲛⲏⲉⲧⲉⲕⲛⲁⲉⲣϫⲓⲛⲓⲟϥ] ⲛⲏⲉⲧⲁⲕ.	
3:24	ⲉⲧⲁⲙⲁϩⲓ] ⲧⲁⲙⲁϩⲓ	
3:24	ⲧⲉⲕϫⲟⲙ] ⲡⲉⲕϫⲟⲙ	
3:27	ⲉⲩϥⲟⲧϩ] ⲉⲩϥⲟϩ	
3:28	ⲫⲏⲉⲧⲁⲕⲛⲁⲩ] ⲫⲏⲉⲧⲉⲕ. = B	
4:1	ⲛⲓϩⲁⲡ] ⲛϩⲁⲡ	
4:3	ⲥⲁϥⲁϩⲟⲩ] ⲥⲁϥⲁϩⲱⲟⲩ	
4:6	ⲉⲣⲉⲧⲉⲛⲉⲁⲣⲉϩ] ⲉⲣⲉⲧⲉⲛⲁⲣⲉϩ = B	
4:6	ⲉⲣⲉⲧⲉⲛⲉⲁⲓⲧⲟⲩ] ⲁⲣⲉⲧⲉⲛⲁⲓⲧⲟⲩ	
4:6	ⲛⲏⲉⲧⲛⲁⲥⲱⲧⲉⲙ] ⲛⲏⲉⲑⲛⲁ.	
4:10	ⲉⲛⲁⲥⲁϫⲓ] ⲛⲛⲁⲥⲁϫⲓ	
4:11	ϩⲁⲣⲁⲧⲩ] ϧⲉⲛ ⲣⲁⲧⲩ	
4:12	ⲁⲣⲉⲧⲉⲛⲥⲟⲑⲙⲉⲥ] ⲁⲣⲉⲧⲉⲛⲉⲥⲟⲑⲙⲉⲥ	
4:18	ⲡⲕⲁϩⲓ] ⲡⲓⲕⲁϩⲓ	
4:22	ⲇⲉ] om	
4:23	ⲛⲱⲧⲉⲛ ⲛⲟⲩϥⲱⲧϩ] ⲛⲑⲱⲧⲉⲛ ⲛⲟⲩϥⲟⲧϩ	
4:25	ⲛⲟⲩϥⲱⲧϩ] ⲛⲟⲩϥⲟⲧϩ = B	
4:27	ⲉⲣⲉⲧⲉⲛⲟⲓ ⲛⲕⲟⲩϫⲓ] ⲉⲣⲉⲧⲉⲛ ⲛⲕⲟⲩϫⲓ	
4:27	ⲧⲏⲣⲥ] om = B'	
4:32	ⲇⲉ ⲁⲛ °] ϫⲉ ⲉⲛ	
4:46	ⲙϥⲟⲅⲱⲣ] ϥⲟⲅⲟⲣ	

5:9	ⲛⲛⲏⲉⲧⲙⲟⲥⲧ] ⲛⲛⲓⲉⲑⲙⲟⲥⲧ	Bᵒ^ᵂ F		ⲛⲛⲏⲉⲑ Bʹ
5:11	ⲙⲫⲏⲉⲧⲛⲁϭⲓ] ⲙⲡⲓⲉⲑⲛⲁϭⲓ			
5:11	ⲟⲩⲙⲉⲧⲉⲫⲗⲏⲟⲩ 2°] ⲟⲩⲙⲉⲧⲁⲫⲗⲏⲟⲩ			
5:23	ⲉⲧⲥⲙⲏ] ⲉⲧⲥⲙⲏ = Bʹ			
5:24	ⲧⲉⲩⲥⲙⲏ] ⲉⲧⲉⲩⲥⲙⲏ = Bʹ			
5:26	ⲉⲩⲥⲁϫⲓ] ⲁⲩⲥⲁϫⲓ = Bʹ			
5:28	ⲉⲣⲉⲧⲉⲛⲥⲁϫⲓ] om = Bʹ			
5:28	ⲥⲉⲥⲟⲩⲧⲱⲛ] ⲉⲥⲟⲩⲧⲱⲛ = Bʹ			
5:28	ⲛⲏ ⲧⲏⲣⲟⲩ ⲉⲧⲁⲩⲥⲁϫⲓ] ⲛⲓⲥⲁϫⲓ ⲧⲏⲣⲟⲩ = Bʹ			
5:29	ⲉⲧⲛⲁⲑⲓⲥ] ⲉⲑⲛⲁⲑⲓⲥ			
6:2	ⲉⲧⲍⲟⲛⲍⲉⲛ] ⲉⲧⲍⲱⲛⲍⲉⲛ			
6:7	ⲉⲕⲉⲧⲥⲁⲃⲉ] ⲉⲕⲉⲥⲁⲃⲉ ⲥⲁϫⲓ			
6:7	ⲉⲕⲍⲉⲙⲥⲓ] ⲉⲕⲉⲍⲉⲙⲥⲓ = Bʹ			
6:11	ⲍⲁⲛⲏⲓ] ⲍⲁⲛⲛⲏⲓ			
6:11	ⲍⲁⲛⲓⲁⲍϫⲱⲓⲧ] ⲍⲁⲛⲓⲁⲍⲁϫⲱⲛⲧ			
6:16	ⲉⲛⲓⲉⲛⲧⲟⲗⲏ] ⲛⲛⲓⲉⲛⲧⲟⲗⲏ			
6:21	ⲟⲩϫⲓϫ] ⲛⲟⲩϫⲓϫ			
6:21	ⲉⲥⲁⲙⲁⲍⲓ] ⲉⲥⲉⲙⲁⲍⲓ = Bʹ			
7:1	ⲉⲩⲟⲩϣ] ⲟⲩⲟⲩϣ			
7:1	ⲉⲩϫⲟⲣ 1°] ⲟⲩϫⲟⲣ			
7:1	ⲉⲩϫⲟⲣ 2°] ϫⲟⲣ			
7:2	ⲉⲣⲉⲧⲉⲛϣⲁⲣⲓ] ⲉⲣⲉⲧⲉⲛϣⲁⲣⲉ			
7:4	ⲉⲣⲱⲧⲉⲛ] om = Bʹ			
7:5	ⲛⲟⲩⲯⲩϣⲏⲛ] ⲛⲓⲯⲩϣⲏⲛ = Bʹ			
7:7	ⲟⲩⲕⲟⲧⲓ] ⲟⲩϫⲱⲧⲓ			
7:8	ⲧϫⲓϫ] ⲧⲉⲕϫⲓϫ			

7:9	ⲛ̅ⲛⲏⲉⲧⲉⲣⲅⲁⲧⲁⲡⲁⲛ] ⲛ̅ⲛⲓⲉⲧⲉⲣ·
7:9	ⲍⲁⲛⲩⲟ ⲛ̅ⲱⲟⲩ] ⲛⲁⲛⲱⲟⲩ ⲛ̅ⲩⲟ = ⲃ'
7:15	ⲉⲩⲉⲉⲛⲟⲩ] ⲉⲩⲉⲛⲟⲩ = ⲃ'
7:15	ⲛ̅ⲏⲉⲧⲁⲕⲥⲱⲟⲩⲛⲟⲩ] ⲛⲓⲉⲧⲉⲕⲥⲟⲩⲱⲛⲟⲩ
7:15	ⲉⲧⲙⲟⲥⲧ] ⲉⲑⲛⲁⲙⲟⲥⲧ
7:18	ⲛ̅ⲛⲏⲉⲧⲁⲩⲁⲓⲧⲟⲩ] ⲛ̅ⲛⲓⲉⲧⲁⲩ·
7:20	ⲛ̅ⲁⲉ] ⲉⲭⲉⲛ = ⲃ'
7:22	ⲙⲟⲩⲛⲕ] ⲙⲟⲛⲕ = ⲃ'
7:22	ⲉⲏⲣⲏⲓ] ⲛ̅ϩⲣⲏⲓ
8:7	ⲛⲓⲙⲉⲩⲩⲟⲧ] ⲛⲓⲙⲏⲩⲩⲟⲧ
8:9	ⲛⲟⲩϩⲟⲙⲧ] ⲛⲟⲩϩⲙⲟⲧ
8:13	ⲛⲉⲕⲉϩⲱⲟⲩ] ⲛⲉⲕϩⲱⲟⲩ
8:13	ⲁⲩⲩⲁⲛⲁⲩⲁⲓⲁ⸱] ⲁⲩⲩⲁⲓ
8:15	ⳟϩⲟⲩ ⲉⲩϭⲓⲗⲁⲡⲥⲓ] ⲡⲓϩⲟⲩ ⲉⲩϭⲟⲗⲡⲥⲓⲙ
8:15	ⲛⲉⲙ ⲓ°] ⲟⲙ
8:15	ⲟⲩⲓⲃⲓ] ⲟⲩⲗⲓⲃⲓ
8:16	ⳟⲏⲉⲧⲁⲩⲧⲉⲙⲙⲟⲕ] ＿ⲩⲧⲁⲙⲙⲟⲕ
8:20	ⲛⲏⲉⲧⲉ] ⲛⲏⲉⲧⲁ = ⲃ'
8:20	ⲛⲁⲧⲁⲕⲱⲟⲩ] ⲛⲁⲧⲁⲕⲟⲩ
9:2	ⲁⲕⲥⲱⲧⲉⲙ] ⲉⲕⲥⲱⲧⲉⲙ = ⲃ'
9:10	ⲙ̅ⲡⲓⲧⲏⲃ] ⲙ̅ⲡⲓⲧⲉⲃ = ⲃ'
9:14	ⲉⲩⲁⲟⲣ] ⲉⲩⲁⲱⲣ
9:21	ⲉⲩⲩⲟⲙ] ⲁⲩⲩⲟⲙ = ⲃ'
9:22	ⲡⲓⲡⲓⲣⲁⲥⲙⲟⲥ] ⲡⲓⲣⲁⲥⲙⲟⲥ = ⲃ'
9:22	ⲡⲓⲣⲱⲕϩ] ⲟⲩⲣⲱⲕϩ = ⲃ'
9:23	ⲛⲁ ⲧⲉⲩⲥⲙⲏ] ⲉⲧⲉⲩⲥⲙⲏ = ⲃ'
9:27	ⲉϩⲣⲁⲕ] ⲛ̅ϩⲓ

10:10	ⲉⲣⲁⲧ] ⲟⲙ
10:15	ⲛⲉⲧⲉⲛⲓⲟⲧ] ⲛⲧⲉⲛⲉⲛⲓⲟⲧ
10:17	ⲉⲧⲭⲟⲣ] ⲉⲧⲝⲱⲣ
10:18	ϥⲙⲉⲓ] ϥⲙⲏⲓ
10:21	ⲉⲧⲁⲩⲓⲣⲓ] ⲃⲣ ⲅⲁⲣ = Β'
10:22	ⲡⲟⲩⲁϣⲁⲓ] ⲡⲟⲩϣⲁⲓ
11:4	ⲛⲟⲩⳓⲑⲱⲣ] ⲛⲟⲩⳓⲑⲟⲣ
11:5	ϣⲁⲧⲉⲧⲉⲛⲓ] ⲉϣⲁⲧⲉⲧⲉⲛⲓ
11:10	ⲛⲟⲩⲟⲧ] ⲛⲟⲩⲉⲧ
11:15	ⲛⲧⲉⲕⲥⲓ] ⲛⲧⲉⲕⲥⲉ
11:17	ⲛⲧⲉⲩⲧⲁⳝⲛⲟ] ⲛⲧⲁⲩⲧ·
11:23	ⲉⳓⲭⲟⲣ] ⲉⳓⲭⲱⲣ
11:25	ⲉⳳⲣⲉⲛ] ⲉⳳⲣⲏⲛ
11:28	ⲁⲣⲉⲧⲉⲛ ϣⲧⲉⲙⲥⲱⲧⲉⲙ] ⲉⲣⲉⲧⲉⲛϣ·
11:28	ⲉⲧⲁⲓⳳⲉⲛⳳⲉⲛ] ⲉⲧⲁⲓⳳⲟⲛⳳⲉⲛ = Β'
11:29	ⲁⲣⲉϣⲁⲛ] ⲉⲣⲉϣⲁⲛ
11:30	ⲁⲛ] ⲟⲙ = Β'
11:30	ϥⲣⲏ] ⳝⲣⲉ
12:1	ⲉⲧⲉⲧⲉⲛⲛⲁⲱⲛⳬ] ⲛⲧⲉⲧⲉⲛⲛⲁⲱⲛⳬ = Β'
12:4	ⲡⲉⲧⲉⲛⲛⲟⲩⲧ] ⲡⲉⲛⲛⲟⲩⲧ
12:5	ⲉⲣⲉⲧⲉⲛⲉϣⲉ] ⲉⲩϣⲉ = Β'
12:8	ⲉⲧⲉⲧⲉⲛⲓⲣⲓ] ⲉⲧⲉⲛⲓⲣⲓ
12:17	ⲙⲡⲓⲣⲉⲙⲏⲧ] ⲙⲡⲓⲣⲏⲙⲉⲧ
12:20	ⲁⲥϣⲁⲛⲉⲣⲡⲓⲑⲩⲙⲓⲛ] ⲁⲛϣⲁⲛ· = Β'
13:6	ⲁⲩϣⲁⲛⲧⳳⲟ] ⲁⲩϣⲉⲛⲧⳳⲟ
13:9	ⲛϣⲟⲣⲡ] ⲛϣⲱⲣⲡ
13:14	ⲡⲁⲓⲥⲁⳉⲓ] ⲡⲓⲥⲁⳉⲓ

13:16	ⲚϨⲎⲦⲤ] ⲚϪⲎⲦ
13:17	ⲦⲓⲈⲘⲂⲞⲚ] ⲚⲈⲘⲂⲞⲚ
13:18	ⲀⲢⲈⲦⲈⲚϢⲀⲚⲤⲰⲦⲈⲘ] ⲀⲢⲈⲦⲈⲚⲤⲰⲦⲈⲘ
14:5	ⲞⲢⲎⲄⲀ] ⲞⲨⲢⲎⲄⲀ
14:7	ⲚⲚⲈⲦϤⲰⲢϪ ⲚⲚⲈⲚϬⲞⲠ] ⲚⲒⲈⲦϤⲰⲢϪ ⲈⲚⲈⲚϬⲞⲠ
14:8	ⲈⲂⲞⲖϨⲈⲚ] ϨⲈⲚ = Bʹ
14:9	ⲦⲈⲚϨ] ⲦⲎⲚϨ
14:10	ⲦⲈⲚϨ] ⲦⲎⲚϨ
14:12	ⲠⲒⲚⲞⲨⲢⲒ] ⲠⲒⲘⲞⲢⲒ
14:12	ⲠⲒⲀϪⲰⲘ] ⲠⲒⲀϪⲞⲘ Bₒᵂ Bʹ ; ⲠⲒⲈϪⲞⲘ F
14:13	ⲠⲒⲐⲢⲈ [ⲠⲒⲐⲢⲈⲦⲞⲨⲒ
14:15	ⲠⲒⲈⲖϪⲰⲂ] ⲠⲒⲈⲖϨⲰⲂ
14:16	ⲔⲨⲔⲚⲞⲚ] ⲬⲨⲚⲞⲚ
14:16	ⲌⲒⲠ] ⲌⲒⲠⲚⲈⲚ
14:17	ⲂⲎϪ ⲌⲂⲞⲨⲒ] ϪⲎⲂ ⲌⲂⲞⲨⲒ
14:18	ⲌⲎⲘⲎ] ⲌⲎⲘⲒ
14:21	ⲆⲈ] >
14:22	ⲘϤⲢⲈⲘⲎⲦ] ⲘϤⲢⲎⲘⲎⲦ
14:23	ⲠⲈⲔⲚⲞⲨⲦ] ⲪϮ = Bʹ
14:23	ⲈⲢⲈⲦⲈⲚⲈϬⲒ] ⲈⲐⲢⲈⲦⲈⲚⲈϬⲒ = Bʹ
14:23	ⲚⲚⲒⲈϨⲞⲞⲨ] ⲈⲚⲒⲈϨⲞⲞⲨ
14:24	ⲠⲒⲘⲀⲚϢⲰⲠⲒ] — ϢⲰⲠ
14:25	ⲈⲦⲀⲨⲤⲞⲦⲠⲨ] ⲈⲦⲀⲔⲤ· = Bʹ
14:26	ϨⲀ ⲈⲚⲬⲀⲒ] ϨⲈⲚ ⲬⲀⲒ
14:26	ⲈⲦⲈ 1°] ⲚⲦⲈ
15:6	ⲈⲞⲨⲘⲎϢ 2°] ⲚⲞⲨⲘⲎϢ
15:9	ⲈⲞⲨⲚⲒϢϮ] ⲚⲞⲨⲚⲒϢϮ = Bʹ

15:12 ϩⲉⲛ ϯⲣⲟⲙⲡⲓ] om

15:20 ⲛⲁⲥⲟⲧⲡϥ] ⲛⲥⲟⲧⲡϥ

15:21 ⲟⲩⲃⲉⲗⲗⲉ] ⲃⲉⲗⲗⲉ

15:22 ⲓⲉ] ⲛⲉⲙ

16:4 ⲛϩⲟⲩⲓⲧ] ⲛϩⲟⲩⲏⲧ

16:12 ⲡⲉ] >

16:16 ⲛⲓⲁⲛ ⲍ̅] ⲛⲓⲛⲁⲛ ⲍ̅

16:16 ⲉⲕϣⲟⲩⲓⲧ] ⲉⲧϣⲟⲩⲓⲧ

17:1 ⲙⲡϭⲟⲓⲥ] om = B'

17:2 ⲇⲉ] + ϫⲉ (sic)

17:3 ⲛⲁⲓⲉⲧⲉ] ⲛⲁⲓⲉⲧ

17:4 ⲡⲁⲓⲥⲱϥ] ⲡⲓⲥⲱϥ

17:9 ⲛⲓⲣⲉϥϯϩⲁⲡ] ⲛⲓⲣⲉϥϩⲁⲡ

17:15 ⲉϩⲣⲏⲓ 1°] ⲛϩⲣⲏⲓ

17:20 ⲛⲧⲉϥϣⲧⲉⲙⲣⲓⲕⲓ] ⲉⲧⲉϥϣ.

18:10 ⲉϥⲑⲣⲟ] ⲉϥⲑⲣⲟⲩ

18:11 ⲉϥϫⲟⲩϣⲧ] ⲁϥϣⲓⲛⲓ ⲛⲛⲏⲉⲧϫⲱϣⲧ

18:11 ⲉϩⲁⲛⲙⲏⲓⲛⲓ] ⲛϩⲁⲛ. = B'

18:14 ⲉⲧⲉⲕⲛⲁⲉⲣⲕⲗⲏⲣⲟⲛⲟⲙⲓⲛ] ⲉⲧⲁⲕ.

18:14 ⲛⲁⲕ] ⲛⲁϥ = B'

18:16 ⲛⲛⲉⲛⲛⲁⲩ] ⲛⲛⲉⲛⲉⲛⲁⲩ

18:22 ⲛⲧⲉϥϣⲧⲉⲙϣⲱⲡⲓ] ⲛⲧⲉϥϣⲧⲉⲙϣⲱⲙ

19:4 ⲉⲙⲁⲩ] ⲙⲙⲁⲩ

19:6 ⲫⲏⲉⲧϫⲏϥ] ⲡⲓⲉⲧ.

19:14 ⲉⲛⲓⲑⲟϣ] ⲉⲡⲓⲑⲱϣ

19:14 ⲑⲏⲉⲧⲁⲕⲉⲣⲕⲗⲏⲣⲟⲛⲟⲙⲓⲛ] ⲛⲏⲉⲧⲁⲕ.

19:19 ⲡⲉϥⲥⲟⲛ] ⲡⲉϥⲥⲱⲛ

34

19:21	ⲉⲧⲁⲩⲛⲁⲑⲓⲥ] — ⲛⲁⲑⲏⲓϥ
20:6	ⲙⲙⲟⲩ 2°] om = B'
20:14	ⲛ̄ⲏⲉⲧⲉ] ⲛ̄ⲏⲉⲧⲁ = B'
20:18	ⲛⲟⲩⲥⲱⲩ] ⲡⲟⲩⲥⲱⲩ
20:19	ⲉⲇⲣⲏⲓ] ⲛ̄ⲇⲣⲏⲓ
20:19	ⲉⲡⲓⲥⲟⲃⲧ] ⲉⲡⲉⲕⲥⲟⲃⲧ = B'
21:2	ⲉⲩⲉⲓ] ⲉⲩⲉⲓⲛⲓ = B'
21:6	ⲑⲏⲉⲧⲇⲉⲛⲧ ⲉϥⲏⲉⲧⲁⲩⲙⲁⲩⲩ] ⲛ̄ⲏⲉⲧⲇⲉⲛⲧ ⲉⲧⲁⲩⲙⲁⲩⲩ
21:7	ⲙⲡⲟⲩϥⲱⲛ] ⲙⲡⲟⲩϥⲟⲛ ⲉⲃⲟⲗ = B'
21:7	ⲉⲃⲟⲗ] om = B'
21:8	ⲛ̄ⲧⲉⲩⲧⲉⲙ ⲟⲩⲥⲛⲟⲩ] ⲛ̄ⲧⲉ ⲟⲩⲥⲛⲟⲩ
21:11	ⲛⲓⲩⲱⲗ] ⲡⲓⲩⲱⲗ
21:13	ⲛⲉⲡⲟⲟⲩ] ⲛⲟⲩⲉⲡⲟⲟⲩ = B'
21:15	ϥⲏⲉⲧⲉⲩⲙⲉⲓ] ϥⲏⲉⲧⲁⲩⲙⲉⲓ
21:15	ϥⲏⲉⲧⲉⲩⲙⲟⲥⲧ] ϥⲏⲉⲧⲁⲩ.
21:16	ⲛ̄ⲑⲏⲉⲧⲉⲩⲙⲉⲓ] — ⲙⲏⲓ
21:17	ⲛ̄ⲇⲓⲡⲗⲟⲩⲛ] — ⲗⲟⲛ
21:20	ⲛⲁⲧⲧⲙⲁⲧ] ⲛⲁⲧⲙⲁⲧ = B'
21:20	ⲉⲩⲧⲥⲩⲙⲃⲟⲩⲗⲏ] — ⲃⲱⲗⲏ
21:22	ⲟⲩⲩⲉ] ⲡⲓⲩⲉ
21:23	ⲟⲩⲕⲱⲥ] ⲟⲩⲕⲟⲥ
22:2	ⲁⲛ 1°] om = B'
22:3	ⲙⲡⲉⲩⲡⲃⲟⲥ] — ⲱⲥ
22:5	ⲛ̄ⲥⲡⲓⲙⲓ] ⲛ̄ⲧⲥⲡⲓⲙⲓ = B'
22:6	ⲙ̄ⲡⲉⲕⲡⲟ] ⲛ̄ⲛⲉⲕⲡⲟ
22:12	ⲉⲧⲉⲕⲛⲁⲭⲟⲗⲡ̄ⲕ] — ⲭⲟⲗⲡ̄
22:17	ⲉⲭⲱⲥ] ⲉⲭⲟⲥ = B'

22:26 ⲡⲉϥϣⲫⲏⲣ] ⲙⲡⲉϥϣⲫⲏⲣ

23:1 ϣⲉ] ϣⲁ

23:5 ⲁ ⲡϭⲟⲓⲥ] ⲉⲡ⳯ϭⲥ

23:9 ⲁⲕϣⲁⲛⲓ] ⲁⲕϣⲉⲛⲓ

23:10 ⲉⲟⲩⲟⲛ] ⲟⲩⲟⲛ = Β'

23:11 ⲉⲩⲉⲇⲱⲕⲉⲙ] ⲉⲩⲉⲇⲱⲕ = Β'

23:11 ⲁⲩϣⲁⲛϩⲱⲧⲡ] ⲉⲩ.

23:14 ⲉⲥⲟⲩⲁⲃ] ⲛⲥⲟⲩⲁⲃ

23:16 ⲉⲑⲣⲁⲛⲁⲩ] ⲉⲑⲣⲉⲛⲁⲩ

23:18 ⲛⲟⲩⲡⲟⲣⲛⲏ] ⲛⲛⲟⲩⲡⲟⲣⲛⲏ

23:18 ϩⲁⲛⲃⲟⲧ] ϩⲁⲛϩⲟⲧ

23:19 ⲛⲆⲣⲉ] ⲛⲆⲣⲏ

23:22 ⲁⲕⲩⲧⲉⲙⲟⲩⲱϣ] ⲉⲕϣⲧ.

23:22 ϭⲓ] ⲟⲙ

23:24 ⲉⲏⲟⲕⲓ] ⲙⲙⲟⲕⲓ

24:1 ⲉⲛⲉⲥⲇⲓⲇ] ⲛⲛⲉⲥⲇ.

24:4 ⲉⲧⲉⲩϩⲓⲧⲥ] ⲉⲧⲁⲩϩ.

24:6 ⲉⲧⲉ] ⲛⲧⲉ

24:6 ⲛⲁⲟⲩⲱ] ⲛⲁⲟⲩⲟ

24:8 ⲡⲓⲕⲱⲕ] ⲡⲓⲱⲓⲕ

24:10 ⲉⲛⲭⲁⲓ] ⲛⲭⲁⲓ = Β'

25:1 ⲛⲧⲟⲩⲉⲣⲕⲁⲧⲁⲅⲓⲛⲱⲥⲕⲓⲛ] —ⲟⲥⲕⲓⲛ

25:2 ⲡⲓⲁⲥⲉⲃⲏⲥ] — ⲃⲉⲥ

25:2 ⲧⲉⲩⲙⲉⲧⲁⲥⲉⲃⲏⲥ] — ⲃⲉⲥ

25:3 ⲛⲁϥ] ⲟⲙ = Β'

25:8 ⲁⲩϣⲁⲛⲟϩⲓ] ⲉⲩⲉϣⲁⲛⲟϩⲓ

26:2 ⲛⲓⲁⲡⲁⲣⲭⲏ] ⲡⲓⲁⲡⲁⲣⲭⲏ

26:5	ⲉⲭⲏⲙⲓ] ⲛ̄ⲭⲏⲙⲓ
26:5	ⲁⲩϣⲁⲛⲟⲍⲓ] ⲉⲩⲉϣⲁⲛ·
26:6	ⲉⲩⲛⲁⲩⲧ] ⲁⲣⲛⲁⲩⲧ
26:7	ⲛⲉⲛⲓⲟⲧ̄] ⲛⲓⲓⲟⲧ̄ = ⲃ'
26:8	ⲉⲥⲁⲙⲁⲍⲓ] ⲉⲥⲉ· = ⲃ'
26:10	ⲡⲓⲕⲁⲍⲓ] ⲡⲕ· = ⲃ'
26:11	ⲉⲧϣⲟⲡ] ⲉⲧϣⲱⲡ
26:12	ⲁⲕϣⲁⲛⲇⲱⲕ] ⲁⲕϣⲉⲛ·
26:12	ⲡⲓⲣⲉⲙⲏⲧ] — ⲙⲉⲧ
26:13	ⲙ̄ⲡⲓⲉⲣ] ⲙ̄ⲡⲉⲣ
26:15	ⲇⲟⲣⲩⲧ] ⲇⲱⲩⲧ
26:16	ⲡⲁⲓⲉⲍⲟⲟⲩ] ⲫⲁⲓ·
26:18	ⲉⲧⲁⲩⲭⲟⲥ] ⲉⲧⲁⲕ· = ⲃ'
27:2	ⲛ̄ⲱⲛⲓ] ⲱⲛⲓ
27:7	ⲉⲕⲉϣⲱⲧ] ⲉⲕⲉϣⲟⲧ
27:8	ⲍⲓ ⲛⲓⲱⲛⲓ] ⲍⲓⲱⲛⲓ
27:10	ⲛ̄ⲥⲁ] ⲟⲙ
27:14	ⲉⲩⲉⲉⲣⲟⲩⲱ] ⲉⲩⲉⲣⲟⲩⲱ
27:19	ⲫⲏⲉⲧⲛⲁⲣⲓⲕⲓ] ⲡⲓⲉⲑⲛ·
27:19	ⲛⲉⲙ ͗ⲟ] ⲟⲙ = ⲃ'
27:21	ⲫⲏⲉⲧⲛⲁⲉⲛⲕⲟⲧ ͗ⲟ] ⲡⲓⲉⲑⲛ·
27:23	ⲧⲉⲩϣⲱⲙⲓ] — ϣⲱⲙ
27:26	ⲉⲁⲓⲧⲟⲩ] ⲉⲧⲁⲓⲧⲟⲩ
28:1	ⲧⲏⲣⲟⲩ ͗ⲟ] ⲟⲙ = ⲃ'
28:4	ⲛⲓⲟⲍⲓ] ⲟⲍⲓ
28:5	ⲛ̄ⲏⲉⲧⲛⲁⲥⲱⲇⲡ] ⲛⲓⲉⲑⲛⲁ·
28:7	ⲉⲩⲇⲉⲙⲇⲱⲙ] ⲉⲩⲇⲉⲙⲇⲟⲙ

28:8 ϧⲉⲛ ⲉⲛⲭⲁⲓ] ⲟⲩⲟϩ ϧⲉⲛ ⲛⲉⲛⲭⲁⲓ = Βʹ

28:8 ⲉⲧⲉⲕⲛⲁϩⲓ] ⲛⲧⲉⲕⲛⲁϩⲓ

28:13 ⲛⲟⲩⲥⲁⲧ] ⲛⲛⲟⲩ. = Βʹ

28:14 ⲛⲛⲁⲓⲥⲁⲭⲓ] ⲉⲛⲁⲓ. = Βʹ

28:20 ⲉⲛⲭⲁⲓ] ⲛⲉⲛⲭⲁⲓ

28:20 ϣⲁⲧⲉϥϥⲟⲧⲕ] ϣⲁⲧⲉϥⲉⲧⲕ

28:20 ⲉⲧϩⲱⲟⲩ] ⲉⲧϩⲟⲩⲟ

28:21 ϣⲁⲧⲉϥϥⲟⲧⲕ] ϣⲁⲧⲉϥϥⲱⲧⲕ = Βʹ

28:25 ⲉⲕⲭⲏⲣ] ⲉⲕⲁⲱⲣ

28:29 ⲛⲛⲉⲕⲉϩⲟⲟⲩ] ⲛⲛⲉⲕϩ.

28:29 ⲉⲕⲉⲟⲓ ⲉⲩϭⲓⲛⲭⲟⲛⲥ] ⲉⲕⲉϭⲓⲟⲩ ⲛⲭⲟⲛⲥ

28:33 ⲛⲓⲟⲩⲟⲧ] ⲛⲓⲟⲩⲱⲧ = Βʹ

28:33 ⲉⲕⲉⲉⲣϭⲱⲩⲧ] ⲉⲕⲉϣϭⲟⲧⲩ

28:48 ⲡⲓⲓⲃⲓ] ⲡⲓⲉⲃⲓ = Βʹ

28:49 ⲧϫⲁⲏ] ⲧϫⲁⲉ = Βʹ

28:52 ⲉⲧϭⲟⲥⲓ] ⲧϭⲟⲥⲓ

28:52 ⲉⲧϫⲟⲣ] ⲧϫⲟⲣ

28:52 ⲉⲩⲉϩⲉϫϩⲱⲁⲕ] — ⲟⲁⲕ

28:56 ⲡⲉⲥⲩⲏⲣⲓ] ⲛⲉⲥ.

28:56 ϩⲁⲛⲧⲁⲧⲥⲓ] ϩⲁⲛⲧⲁⲧⲥ

28:57 ⲛⲁϩⲉⲁϩⲱⲁⲕ] — ⲟⲁⲕ

28:58 ⲁⲣⲉⲧⲉⲛϣⲧⲉⲙⲥⲱⲧⲉⲙ] ⲁⲣⲉⲧⲉⲛⲥⲱⲧⲉⲙ = Βʹ

28:64 ⲙⲡⲕⲁϩⲓ 2°] ⲙⲡⲓⲕⲁϩⲓ

28:68 ⲉϫⲣⲏⲓ ⲉⲭⲏⲙⲓ] ⲛϫⲣⲏⲓ ⲛⲭⲏⲙⲓ

29:1 ⲭⲱⲣⲏⲃ] — ⲉⲃ = Βʹ

29:10 ⲉⲣⲁⲧⲉⲛⲑⲏⲛⲟⲩ] ⲉⲣⲉⲧⲉⲛ.

29:11 ⲡⲓϣⲉⲙⲙⲟ] ⲡⲉⲧⲉⲛϣⲉⲙⲙⲟ = Βʹ

29:14 ⲚⲀⲓⲭⲱ] ⲚⲀⲬⲱ = Ⲃ'

29:15 ⲚⲈⲘ ꙇ°] om = Ⲃ'

29:17 ⲉⲚⲟⲩⲥⲱⲩ] Ⲛⲟⲩⲥⲱⲩ = Ⲃ'

29:20 ⲡⲬⲱⲘ] ⲡⲬⲟⲘ

29:22 ⲉⲧⲚⲀⲧⲱⲟⲩⲚⲟⲩ] ⲉⲐⲚⲀ· = Ⲃ'

29:23 ⲉⲐⲟⲩⲉⲧⲟⲩⲱⲧ] ⲉⲐⲟⲩⲟⲧⲟⲩⲱⲧ

29:26 ⲀⲩⲩⲉⲘⲩⲓ] ⲉⲩⲩ· = Ⲃ'

29:27 ⲡⲓⲕⲀⳅⲓ] ⲡⲕ· = Ⲃ'

29:27 ⲡⲬⲱⲘ]—ⲟⲘ

29:29 ⲚⲈⲐⲟⲩⲟⲚⳅ] ⲚⲀⲐ· = Ⲃ'

30:7 ⲚⲎⲉⲧⲘⲟⲥϯ] ⲚⲓⲉⲐⲘ·

30:15 ⳘⲘⲟⲩ] ⲡⲘⲟⲩ

30:19 ⲚⲧⳘⲉ] ⲉⲚⲧⳘⲉ

30:20 ⲚⲈⲘ ⳅ°] om = Ⲃ'

31:1 ⲀⲩⲬⲉⲕⲧⲟⲧⲩ] ⲀⲩⲬⲉⲕⲧⲟⲩ

31:3 ⲚⲧⲉⲕⲉⲣⲕⲗⲏⲣⲟⲚⲟⲘⲓⲚ] ⲚⲧⲉⲕⲕⲗⲎ·

31:5 ⲉⲣⲉⲧⲉⲚⲉⲓⲣⲓ] Ⲁⲣⲉ· = Ⲃ'

31:11 ⲉⲩⲥⲟⲡ] Ⲛⲥⲟⲡ = Ⲃ'

31:16 ⲩⲚⲀⲧⲱⲚⲩ] ⲩⲚⲀⲉⲚⲧⲱⲚⲩ = Ⲃ'

31:16 ⲉⲣⲟⲩ] ⲉⲂⲟⲗ

31:20 ⲉⲓⲉϬⲓⲧⲟⲩ] ⲉⲓϬⲓⲧⲟⲩ

31:20 ⲚⲩⲉⲘⲘⲟ] ⲉⲩⲉⲘⲘⲟ ⲟⲩⲟⳍ

31:24 ⳍⲟⲧⲉ] ⳍⲟⲆⲉ

31:26 ⲘⲡⲀⲓⲬⲱⲘ]—ⲟⲘ

32:1 ⲉⳅⲀⲚⲥⲀⲃⲓ] ⲚⳅⲀⲚⲥⲀⲃⲓ

32:2 Ⲛⲟⲩⲓⲱϯ] Ⲛⲟⲩⲱⲓϯ

32:5 ⲉⲧⲕⲟⲗⲃ] ⲉⲧⲕⲱ· = Ⲃ'

32:6	ⲉⲧⲉⲧⲉⲛ︦ⲧ] ⲛ︦ⲧⲉⲧⲉⲛ︦ⲧ
32:6	ⲁⲩⲑⲁⲙⲓⲟⲕ] —ⲙⲟⲕ
32:8	ⲛⲁ̄ⲉ] ⲇⲉ
32:8	ⲉⲩⲛⲁϫⲱⲣ] —ⲟⲣ = Bʹ
32:9	ⲁⲩϣⲱⲡⲓ] ⲉⲩⲉϣⲱⲡⲓ
32:13	ⲉⲍ︦ⲣⲏⲓ] ⲉ̄ⲣⲏⲓ
32:18	ⲉⲧⲁⲩⲁ̄ϥⲟⲕ] —ⲱⲕ
32:20	ⲉⲩϥⲟⲛⲍ] ⲁⲩϥⲱⲛⲍ
32:21	ϥⲏⲉⲧⲉ 2°] ⲟⲙ
32:27	ⲛⲏⲉⲧ︦ⲧ] ⲛⲓⲉⲧ︦ⲧ
32:27	ⲛⲥⲉⲁ̄ⲟⲥ] ⲛ︦ⲁ̄ⲟⲥ = Bʹ
32:29	ⲉⲛⲁⲓ ⲙⲁⲣⲟⲩϣⲟⲡⲟⲩ] ⲉⲛⲁⲩ ⲙⲁⲣⲟⲩϣⲟⲡⲱⲟⲩ
32:32	ⲧⲟⲩⲃⲱⲛⲁⲗⲟⲗⲓ] ⲧⲟⲩⲃⲟⲛ.
32:33	ⲛⲁ̄ⲣⲁ̄ⲕⲱⲛ] —ⲟⲛ
32:33	ⲛⲁⲧⲧⲁⲗ6ⲟ] ⲛⲁⲧⲁⲧⲁⲗ6ⲟ
32:36	ⲉⲩϣⲏⲗ] ⲉⲩϣⲉⲗ
32:38	ⲛⲟⲩϣⲟⲩϣⲟⲩϣⲓ] ⲛⲓϣ. = Bʹ
32:38	ⲙⲁⲣⲟⲩⲧⲱⲟⲩⲛⲟⲩ] —ⲛⲱⲟⲩ
32:39	ⲡⲉⲑⲛⲁϣⲱⲡ] ⲡⲓⲉⲑⲛ.
32:41	ⲥⲛⲁⲁⲙⲟⲛⲓ] ⲛⲉⲥⲁⲙⲟⲛⲓ
32:41	ⲛⲏⲉⲑⲙⲟⲥ︦ⲧ] ⲉⲑⲙⲟⲥ︦ⲧ = Bʹ
32:42	ⲛⲏⲉⲑⲛⲁϣⲁⲣⲓ] ⲛⲓⲉⲑ.
32:43	ⲛⲏⲉⲑⲙⲟⲥ︦ⲧ] ⲛⲓⲉⲑ.
32:46	ⲛ︦ⲛⲁⲓⲥⲁ̄ⲓ 2°] ⲛ︦ⲛⲁⲥ.
32:46	ⲛ︦ⲧⲉ ⲧ̄ⲁⲓⲛⲟⲙⲟⲥ] ⲛ︦ⲧⲉ ϥⲁⲓⲛⲟⲙⲟⲥ
32:49	ⲁⲙⲟⲩ] ⲟⲩ
32:50	ⲟⲩⲭⲁϥ] ⲁⲩⲭⲁϥ = Bʹ

33:4	ⲫⲏⲉⲧⲁⲩⲍⲉⲛⲍⲱⲛⲧⲉⲛ] ⲫⲏⲉⲧⲁⲩⲍⲉⲛⲍⲱⲛ
33:6	ⲉⲩⲟⲩϭ] ⲉⲩⲱϭ
33:8	ⲛⲓⲟⲣⲱⲛⲍ] ⲛⲓⲟⲣⲍⲓ
33:9	ⲉⲛⲉⲕⲥⲁϫⲓ] ⲉⲡⲉⲕⲥⲁϫⲓ
33:12	ⲍⲟⲣ] ⲍⲱⲣ
33:16	ⲛⲏⲉⲧϣⲏⲡ] ⲛⲓⲉⲧ·
33:16	ⲙⲫⲏⲉⲧⲁⲩⲟⲣⲟⲛⲍϥ] — ⲟⲣⲱⲛⲍϥ
33:17	ⲛⲓⲁⲛⲁⲛϣⲟ] ⲛⲓⲉⲛⲁⲛϣⲟ
33:19	ⲛⲏⲉⲧϣⲟⲡ] ⲛⲓⲉⲧϣⲟⲡ
33:23	ⲛⲏⲉⲧϣⲏⲡ] ⲛⲓⲉⲧϣⲏⲡ
33:24	ⲉϥϣⲏⲡ] ⲉϥϣⲉⲡ
33:24	ⲉϥⲉⲥⲱⲡ] ⲉϥⲉⲥⲟⲡ
33:28	ⲉⲣⲉ] ⲉⲉⲣ ⲋ Ⲃ′
34:9	ⲉⲧⲟⲧϥ] ⲛ̄ⲧⲟⲧϥ
34:11	ⲛⲓϣⲫⲏⲣⲓ] ⲛⲛⲓϣ·
34:11	ⲉⲧⲁⲩⲟⲣⲟⲣⲡϥ] ⲉⲧⲁⲩⲟⲣⲱⲣⲡϥ

Many of these variants are scribal errors in F in turn copied by Wilkins, for example, 1:11, 4:32, 1:28, 23:1, 24:8. This dependence on F has led some scholars[7] to the unnecessary conclusion that Bo[W] was probably based on F alone. But as A. E. Brooke has pointed out, "there is no real reason to doubt the truth of Wilkins' account of his own edition."[8]

In fact, it can also be shown that Bo[W] and the Paris ms C preserve unique readings. The following is a list of variants where Bo[W] and C preserve a reading not found in either F or H. In some instances other mss may join Bo[W] and C; but since we can assume that these were not available to Wilkins, the similarity of readings is of no consequence.

1:22	ϤⲎⲈⲦⲈⲚⲚⲀⲰⲈⲚⲀⲚ] ϤⲎⲈⲦⲈ ⲦⲈⲚⲚⲀⲰⲈⲚⲀⲚ
2:6	ⲈⲢⲈⲦⲈⲚⲈⲞⲨⲰⲘ] ⲈⲢⲈⲦⲈⲚⲞⲨⲞⲘ = AB
4:4	ⲦⲈⲦⲈⲚⲞⲚϢ] ⲦⲈⲦⲈⲚⲞⲨⲰⲚϢ = ABD
4:12	ϢⲈⲚ ⲠⲒⲦⲰⲞⲨ] om
4:20	ⲘϤⲢⲎⲦ = Bo^W AC] ⲚϢⲢⲎⲒ rell
5:29	ⲌⲀⲦⲀⲌⲎ] ⲌⲀⲦⲌⲎ = B
7:15	ⲚⲖⲀⲒⲖⲈⲒ] ⲚⲀⲖⲀⲒⲖⲈⲒ = AB
7:25	ⲚⲞⲨⲚⲞⲨⲦ = Bo^W BC] om rell
8:10	ⲚⲆⲈ ⲠϬⲞⲒⲤ ⲠⲈⲔⲚⲞⲨⲦ] om
11:1	ⲈⲚⲈⲨϤⲀⲢⲈⲌ ⲚⲈⲘ = Bo^W CD] om rell
11:1	ⲚⲈⲨⲈⲚⲦⲞⲖⲎ = Bo^W CD] ⲈⲚⲈⲨⲈⲚⲦⲞⲖⲎ rell
18:11	ⲈⲨⲎⲞⲨⲦ] ⲀⲨⲘⲞⲨⲦ = B
19:4	ⲀⲚ 2°] om ≠ B
20:20	ⲈⲔⲈⲔⲞⲦⳓ] ⲈⲔⲈⲔⲞⲦ = B
22:25	ⲈⲢⲈⲦⲈⲚⲈϢⲰⲦⲈⲂ = Bo^W C] ⲈⲢⲈⲦⲈⲚϢⲰⲦⲈⲂ rell
25:1	ⲘⲠⲒⲀⲤⲈⲂⲎⲤ] ⲘⲠⲒⲀⲤⲈⲂⲈⲤ
25:15	ⲚⲈⲘ ⲚⲐⲎⲘⲒ 1° = Bo^W C] om rell
28:34	ⲚⲎⲈⲦⲈⲔⲚⲀⲚⲀⲨ] ⲚⲎⲈⲦⲈⲔⲚⲀⲨ
28:48	ⲰⲀⲦⲈⳣⳣⲞⲦⲔ] ⲰⲀⲦⲈⳣⲈⲦⲔ Bo^W , ⲰⲀⲦⲈⳣⳣⲈⲦⲔ C
29:3	ⲠⲒⲚⲒⲰⲦ = Bo^W CD] ⲚⲒⲚⲒⲰⲦ rell
30:20	ⲚⲚⲈⲔⲒⲞⲦ] ⲠⲈⲔⲚⲞⲨⲦ
31:16	ⲚⲦⲀⲆⲒⲀⲐⲎⲔⲎ] ⲚⲦⲀ|ⲆⲒⲀⲐⲎⲔⲎ ≠ BD
31:16	ϤⲎⲈⲦⲞⲨⲚⲀⲰⲈⲚⲰⲞⲨ] ϤⲎⲈⲦⲈⲚⲚⲀⲰ = ABD
33:29	ⲦⲤⲎⳓⲒ] ⲈⲦⲤⲎⳓⲒ = B
34:10	ⲠⲢⲞϤⲎⲦⲎⲤ] ⲠⲒⲠⲢⲞϤⲎⲦⲎⲤ = A

This is not a long list. In fact, some of these variants could be accidental; but there are a few clear examples which serve to demonstrate Wilkins' dependence on or at least his acquaintance with ms C, e.g., 4:12, 8:10, 28:34, 29:3, 30:20.

Geographical and paleographical factors may also be
brought to bear on the discussion. Wilkins, by his own ad-
mission, forgot to include the date of ms C because he
turned his attention elsewhere as soon as he finished ex-
amining that ms.[9] This may also indicate a lesser degree
of care taken in collating this ms. As mentioned in Chapter I, the script of C is fairly difficult to read and
quite small by comparison with the other mss. This, together with its location in Paris, whereas Wilkins was in
London, may account in part for the few unique readings.
It is clear that C has influenced Bo^W only slightly but
that it was actually used as Wilkins maintained is now
certain.

It can also be demonstrated that Wilkins used the
Vatican ms H. The following is a list of readings unique
to Bo^W and H. It may be recalled that G' = G-H.

1:7   ⲁⲣⲉⲃⲁ] ⲁⲣⲁⲃⲁ

1:19   Ⲭⲱⲣⲏⲃ] Ⲭⲱⲣⲉⲃ

2:36   ⲟⲩⲟⲍ ⲟⲩⲟⲛ ⲛⲓⲃⲉⲛ] om ⲟⲩⲟⲍ = A

4:3   ⲉⲧⲁ] + ⲡ⳪ⲥ

4:3   ⲙⲃⲉⲣⲫⲉⲣⲱⲫ 1° + 2°] ⲙⲃⲉⲗⲫⲉⲣⲱⲫ = B

9:5   ⲙⲡⲟⲩⲕⲁⲍⲓ = Bo^W DG'] ⲙⲡⲓⲕⲁⲍⲓ rell

9:5   ⲁⲗⲗⲁ] + ⲉⲑⲃⲉ ⲧⲙⲉⲧⲁⲥⲉⲃⲏⲥ ⲛⲧⲉ ⲛⲁⲓⲉⲑⲛⲟⲥ ⲛ⳰ⲭⲉ
         ⲡ⳪ⲥ ⲉⲩⲉⲩⲟⲧⲟⲩ ⲉⲃⲟⲗϩⲁⲧⲍⲏ ⲙⲡⲉⲕⲍⲟ   (c var)

9:6   ⲉⲕⲉⲉⲙⲓ] ⲡⲣ ⲟⲩⲟⲍ

9:8   ⲉⲩⲉⲧⲑⲏⲛⲟⲩ] ⲡⲣ ⲟⲩⲟⲍ

9:9   ⲛⲁⲓⲭⲏ] ⲡⲣ ⲟⲩⲟⲍ

9:10 & 17   ⲃ†] ⲥⲛⲟⲩ†

9:10	ⲚⲀⲢⲤⲒ̈ϨⲎⲞⲨⲦ] þr ⲞⲨⲞϩ
9:13	ⲠⲈϪⲈ] þr ⲞⲨⲞϩ
9:13	ϨⲀⲚⲚⲀⲨⲦⲚⲀϨⲂⲒ] ⲚⲚⲀⲨⲦⲚⲀϨⲂⲒ
9:15	ⲞⲨⲞϩ 2° = Bo^W G'] om rell
9:16	ⲈⲦⲀⲒⲚⲀⲨ] þr ⲞⲨⲞϩ
9:16	ⲠⲈⲦⲈⲚⲚⲞⲨϯ - Bo^W G' (c var)] om rell
9:17	ⲀⲒϬⲒ] fr ⲞⲨⲞϩ
9:17	ⲀⲒϬⲒ ⲚϮⲠⲖⲀϨ ϦⲦ ⲀⲒⲂⲈⲢⲂⲰⲢⲞⲨ = Bo^W G' (c var)] ⲀⲒⲂⲞⲢⲂⲈⲢ ⲚϮⲠⲖⲀϨ ϦϮ rell
9:18	ⲀⲒϮϨⲞ] þr ⲞⲨⲞϩ
9:20	ⲞⲨⲞϩ 1° 2° = Bo^W G'] om rell
9:21	ⲀⲒⲘⲞⲚⲔⲨ] + ⲈⲘⲀϢⲱ
9:22	ⲞⲨⲞϩ 1° 2° 3° = Bo^W G'] om rell
9:22	ⲚⲒⲘϨⲀⲨ] ⲠⲒⲘϨⲀⲨ = D
9:23	ⲠⲈⲦⲈⲚⲚⲞⲨϯ ⲞⲨⲞϩ - Bo^W G'] om rell
9:26	ⲚⲬⲎⲘⲒ] + ϨⲈⲚ ⲦⲈⲔⲚⲒϢϮ ⲚϪⲞⲘ ⲚⲈⲘ ϨⲈⲚ ⲦⲈⲔϪⲒϪ ⲈⲦⲀⲘⲀϨⲒ ⲚⲈⲘ ϨⲈⲚ ⲠⲈⲔϪⲀϤⲞⲒ ⲈⲦϬⲞⲤⲒ (c var)
9:27	ⲚⲞⲨⲘⲈⲦⲀⲤⲈⲂⲎⲤ] + ⲚⲈⲘ ⲈϪⲈⲚ ⲚⲞⲨⲚⲞⲂⲒ (om ⲈϪⲈⲚ G')
9:27	ⲘⲠⲈⲢϪⲞⲨϢⲦ = Bo^W G'] om rell
9:28	ⲈⲐⲂⲈ 2°] þr ⲞⲨⲞϩ
9:29	ⲚⲬⲎⲘⲒ] + ϨⲈⲚ ⲦⲈⲔⲚⲒϢϮ ⲚϪⲞⲘ ⲚⲈⲘ ϨⲈⲚ ⲦⲈⲔϪⲒϪ ⲈⲦⲀⲘⲀϨⲒ
	ⲚⲈⲘ ϨⲈⲚ ⲠⲈⲔϪⲀϤⲞⲒ ⲈⲦϬⲞⲤⲒ (c var)
10:3	ⲞⲨⲞϩ 2° 3° = Bo^W G'] om rell
10:5	ⲈⲦⲀⲒⲒ ⲆⲈ] þr ⲞⲨⲞϩ
10:6	ⲀⲨⲔⲞⲤⲨ] þr ⲞⲨⲞϩ
10:10	ϨⲈⲚ ⲠⲒⲤⲎⲞⲨ ⲈⲦⲈⲘⲘⲀⲨ ⲞⲨⲞϩ ⲘⲠⲈⲨⲞⲨⲰϢ ⲈⲨⲈⲦⲐⲎⲚⲞⲨ = Bo^W G']
	ⲘⲠⲈⲨⲨⲈⲦⲐⲎⲚⲞⲨ rell (c var)
10:11	ⲠⲈϪⲈ Ⲡ̅ϬⲞⲒⲤ] þr ⲞⲨⲞϩ
10:12	ⲞⲨⲞϩ 1° = Bo^W G'] om rell

10:12 ⲚⲈϤⲘⲰⲒⲦ] + ⲦⲎⲢⲞⲨ

10:12 ⲈϢⲈⲘϢⲒ ⲘⲘⲞϤ] ⲈϢⲈⲘϢⲒ ⲘⲠϬ̅Ⲥ̅ ⲠⲈⲔⲚⲞⲨϮ

11:1 ⲞⲨⲞϨ 1° = Bo^{W} G'] om rell

11:3 ⲚⲈⲘ ⲚⲈϤⲘⲎⲒⲚⲒ = Bo^{W} G'] om rell

11:8 ⲚⲎ — ⲘⲪⲞⲞⲨ = Bo^{W} G'] om rell

11:8 ⲚⲦⲈⲦⲈⲚϢⲈⲚⲰⲦⲈⲚ = Bo^{W} G'] om rell

11:13 ⲄⲀⲢ] ⲆⲈ

11:14 ⲞⲨⲞϨ 1° = Bo^{W} G'] om rell

11:15 ⲀⲔϢⲀⲚⲞⲨⲰⲘ] pr ⲞⲨⲞϨ

11:17 ⲞⲨⲞϨ 1° = Bo^{W} G'] om rell

11:20 ⲈⲢⲈⲦⲈⲚⲈⲤϦⲎⲦⲞⲨ] pr ⲞⲨⲞϨ

11:22 ⲈⲘⲞϢⲒ — fin = Bo^{W} G'] om rell

11:23 ⲞⲨⲞϨ 1° = Bo^{W} G'] om rell

11:28 ⲚⲦⲈⲦⲈⲚⲤⲰⲢⲈⲘ] pr ⲞⲨⲞϨ

11:29 ⲈⲤⲈϢⲰⲠⲒ] pr ⲞⲨⲞϨ

11:31 ⲚⲐⲰⲦⲈⲚ] + ⲄⲀⲢ

11:32 ⲈⲢⲈⲦⲈⲚⲈⲀⲢⲈϨ] pr ⲞⲨⲞϨ

11:32 ⲈⲢⲈⲦⲈⲚⲈⲀⲢⲈϨ ⲈⲒⲢⲒ = Bo^{W} G'] ⲈⲢⲈⲦⲈⲚⲈⲒⲢⲒ rell

11:32 ⲦⲎⲢⲞⲨ — fin = Bo^{W} G'] om rell

12:3 ⲈⲢⲈⲦⲈⲚⲈϪⲞⲘϪⲈⲘ] pr ⲞⲨⲞϨ

12:3 ⲚⲞⲨϢϢⲎⲚ] pr ⲞⲨⲞϨ

12:6 ⲈⲢⲈⲦⲈⲚⲈⲒⲚⲒ] pr ⲞⲨⲞϨ

12:7 ⲠⲈⲔⲚⲞⲨϮ = Bo^{W} G'] om rell

12:10 ⲈϤⲈⲐⲢⲈⲦⲈⲦⲈⲚⲘⲦⲞⲚ] pr ⲞⲨⲞϨ

12:11 ⲈⲤⲈϢⲰⲠⲒ] pr ⲞⲨⲞϨ

12:12 ⲈⲢⲈⲦⲈⲚⲈⲞⲨⲚⲞϤ] pr ⲞⲨⲞϨ

12:26 ⲚⲈⲔⲈⲨⲬⲎ = Bo^{W} G'] ⲚⲈⲔϢⲎⲢⲒ rell

12:27 ⲚⲒⲀϤ 2°] pr ⲚⲦⲈ ⲠϬ̅Ⲥ̅ ⲠⲈⲔⲚⲞⲨϮ

12:28 ΝΗ ⲀⲚⲞⲔ = $B_o{}^w$ G' (ⲥ var)] om rell

12:29 ⲞⲨⲞϨ ⲚⲦⲈⲔⲈⲢⲔⲖⲎⲢⲞⲚⲞⲘⲒⲚ — fin = $B_o{}^w$ G' (ⲥ var)] om rell

13:2 ⲚⲦⲈϤⲒ] þr ⲞⲨⲞϨ

13:4 ⲈⲢⲈⲦⲈⲚⲈⲤⲰⲦⲈⲘ — fin = $B_o{}^w$ G'] om rell

13:5 ⲈⲘⲞϢⲒ ϨⲒⲰⲦϤ = $B_o{}^w$ G'] om rell

13:8 ⲚⲚⲈ ⲚⲈⲔⲂⲀⲖ ⲈⲢⲤⲔⲈⲡⲀϫⲒⲚ] ⲞⲨⲆⲈ ⲚⲚⲈⲔⲈⲢⲤⲔⲈⲡⲀϫⲒⲚ

13:10 ⲈⲨⲈⲘⲞⲨ] þr ⲞⲨⲞϨ

13:11 ⲚⲚⲞⲨⲞⲨⲀϨⲦⲞⲦⲞⲨ] þr ⲞⲨⲞϨ

13:16 ⲚⲈⲤϢⲰⲖ Ⲓ°] þr ⲞⲨⲞϨ

13:16 ⲈⲤⲈⲢⲰⲔϨ] þr ⲞⲨⲞϨ

13:16 ⲈⲤⲈϢⲰⲡⲒ] þr ⲞⲨⲞϨ

13:17 ⲞⲨⲞϨ ⲚⲦⲈϤϯ ⲚⲚⲀⲒ ⲚⲀⲔ ⲞⲨⲞϨ = $B_o{}^w$ G' (ⲥ var)] om rell

13:18 ⲚⲎ ⲀⲚⲞⲔ — fin = $B_o{}^w$ G'] om rell

14:12 ⲚⲎⲈⲐⲞⲨⲀⲂ ⲀⲚ ⲚⲚⲈⲦⲈⲚⲞⲨⲞⲘⲞⲨ] ⲞⲨⲞϨ ⲚⲀⲒ ⲚⲚⲈⲦⲈⲚⲞⲨⲰⲘ
ⲈⲂⲞⲖ ⲚϦⲎⲦⲞⲨ

14:21 ⲘⲡⲒϢⲈⲘⲘⲞ = $B_o{}^w$ G'] ⲡⲒϢⲈⲘⲘⲞ rell

14:23 ⲈⲦⲀⲨⲤⲞⲦⲡϤ] + ⲚϪⲈ ⲡ̅Ϭ̅Ⲥ̅ ⲡⲈⲔⲚⲞⲨϯ

14:23 ⲚⲈⲔⲈϨⲰⲞⲨ ⲚⲈⲘ = $B_o{}^w$ G'] om rell

14:24 ⲡⲈⲔⲚⲞⲨϯ Ⲓ° — fin = $B_o{}^w$ G'] om rell

14:25 ⲡⲈⲔⲚⲞⲨϯ ⲈⲢⲞϤ = $B_o{}^w$ G' (ϩⲈⲢⲞϤ G')] om rell

14:26 ϦⲈⲚ ⲚⲒⲈϨⲰⲞⲨ — ⲈⲢⲰⲞⲨ 2° = $B_o{}^w$ G'] om rell

14:26 ⲈⲔⲈⲞⲨⲰⲘ] þr ⲞⲨⲞϨ

14:26 ⲈⲔⲈⲞⲨⲚⲞϤ] þr ⲞⲨⲞϨ

14:29 ⲈϤⲈⲒ] þr ⲞⲨⲞϨ

14:29 ⲈϤⲈⲤⲰ] þr ⲞⲨⲞϨ

14:29 ⲡϬⲞⲒⲤ] + ⲡⲈⲔⲚⲞⲨϯ

14:29 ⲚⲈⲔϨⲂⲎⲞⲨⲒ = $B_o{}^w$ G'] ⲚⲈⲔⲂⲀⲔⲒ rell

46

15:3 ⲘⲠⲈⲕⲤⲞⲚ — fin = Bᴼ ᵂ Gʹ] om rell

15:4 ⲆⲈ ϦⲈⲚ ⲞⲨⲤⲘⲞⲨ = Bᴼ ᵂ] ⲆⲈ ⲞⲨⲎⲒ ⲈⲐⲂⲈ ⲦⲀⲒⲤⲀϪⲒ ϦⲈⲚ ⲞⲨⲤⲘⲞⲨ Gʹ ; om rell

15:4 ⲠⲈⲔⲚⲞⲨϮ = Bᴼ ᵂ Gʹ] om rell

15:4 ϦⲈⲚ ⲠⲒⲔⲀϨⲒ ⲪⲎⲈⲦⲀⲨⲦⲎⲒϤ ⲚⲀⲔ ⲚϪⲈⲠϬⲞⲒⲤ ⲠⲈⲔⲚⲞⲨϮ ϦⲈⲚ ⲞⲨⲤⲔⲖⲎⲢⲞⲤ ⲈⲈⲢⲔⲖⲎ—
ⲢⲞⲚⲞⲘⲒⲚ ⲘⲘⲞⲨ = Bᴼ ᵂ Gʹ] ⲤⲔⲈⲢⲔⲖⲎⲢⲞⲚⲞⲘⲒⲚ ⲘⲠⲒⲔⲀϨⲒ rell

15:5 ⲈϢⲰⲠ ⲆⲈ — ⲚⲒⲂⲈⲚ ⲚⲎ ⲀⲚⲞⲔ = Bᴼ ᵂ Gʹ] ⲀⲔϢⲀⲚ-
ⲀⲢⲈϨ ⲈⲚⲒⲈⲚⲦⲞⲖⲎ rell

15:6 ϪⲈ ⲠϬⲞⲒⲤ ⲠⲈⲔⲚⲞⲨϮ ⲀⲨⲤⲘⲞⲨ ⲈⲢⲞⲔ ⲘⲪⲢⲎϮ ⲈⲦⲀⲨⲤⲀϪⲒ
ⲚⲈⲘⲀⲔ ⲞⲨⲞϨ = Bᴼ ᵂ Gʹ] om rell

15:7 ⲈⲂⲞⲖϦⲈⲚ = Bᴼ ᵂ Gʹ] om rell

15:7 ⲞⲨⲒ ⲚⲦⲈ = Bᴼ ᵂ] ⲞⲨⲒ Ⲛ Gʹ om rell

15:9 ⲚⲦⲈⲨⲈⲢⲠⲞⲚⲎⲢⲞⲤ] þr ⲞⲨⲞϨ

15:9 ⲈⲨⲈϢⲰⲠⲒ] þr ⲞⲨⲞϨ

15:10 ⲠⲈⲔⲚⲞⲨϮ = Bᴼ ᵂ Gʹ] om rell

15:11 ⲈⲒϪⲰⲘⲘⲞⲤ = Bᴼ ᵂ Gʹ] ϮϪⲰⲘⲘⲞⲤ rell

15:14 ⲈⲔⲈϮ ⲚⲀⲨ 2° = Bᴼ ᵂ Gʹ] om rell

15:15 ⲈⲔⲈⲈⲢⲪⲘⲈⲨⲒ] þr ⲞⲨⲞϨ

15:15 ⲀⲨⲤⲞⲦⲔ] þr ⲞⲨⲞϨ

15:17 ⲈⲔⲈⲞⲨⲰⲦⲈⲚ] þr ⲞⲨⲞϨ

15:17 ⲈⲨⲈϢⲰⲠⲒ] þr ⲞⲨⲞϨ

15:18 ⲞⲨⲞϨ ⲈⲨⲈⲤⲘⲞⲨ ⲈⲢⲞⲔ ⲚϪⲈ ⲠϬⲞⲒⲤ ⲠⲈⲔⲚⲞⲨϮ ϦⲈⲚ ⲞⲨⲞⲚ
ⲚⲒⲂⲈⲚ ⲚⲎⲈⲦⲈⲔⲈⲀⲒⲦⲞⲨ = Bᴼ ᵂ Gʹ] om rell

15:19 ⲚⲈⲘ ⲚⲈⲔⲈⲤⲰⲞⲨ = Bᴼ ᵂ Gʹ] om rell

15:19 ⲠⲈⲔⲚⲞⲨϮ = Bᴼ ᵂ Gʹ] om rell

15:19 ⲘⲘⲀⲤⲒ = Bᴼ ᵂ Gʹ] ⲚϢⲀⲘⲒⲤⲒ rell

16:1 ⲈⲔⲈⲒⲢⲒ] þr ⲞⲨⲞϨ

16:2 ⲈⲔⲈϢⲰⲦ] þr ⲞⲨⲞϨ

16:2   ⲡⲉⲕⲛⲟⲩϯ 1° = Bo^W G'] om rell

16:2   ⲛⲉⲙ ϩⲁⲛⲉϩⲱⲟⲩ = Bo^W G' (e var)] om rell

16:2   ⲛϫⲉ ⲡϭⲟⲓⲥ ⲡⲉⲕⲛⲟⲩϯ ⲉⲣⲟⲩ = Bo^W G'] om rell

16:4   ⲛⲛⲉⲁⲩ] pr ⲟⲩⲟϩ

16:7   ⲉⲕⲉⲟⲩⲱⲙ] pr ⲟⲩⲟϩ

16:8   ⲉⲕⲉⲟⲩⲉⲙ = Bo^W G'] ⲟⲩⲱⲙ rell

16:10 ⲉⲕⲉⲓⲣⲓ] pr ⲟⲩⲟϩ

16:10 ⲡⲉⲕⲛⲟⲩϯ 2° = Bo^W G'] om rell

16:11 ϧⲉⲛ ⲡⲓⲙⲁ — fin = Bo^W G'] om rell

16:12 ⲉⲕⲉⲉⲣⲫⲙⲉⲩⲓ] pr ⲟⲩⲟϩ

16:12 ⲟⲩⲟϩ ⲉⲕⲉⲁⲣⲉϩ ⲟⲩⲟϩ ⲉⲕⲉⲓⲣⲓ ⲛⲛⲁⲓⲉⲛⲧⲟⲗⲏ = Bo^W G'] om rell

16:14 ⲛⲉⲙ 3°] om

16:14 ⲉⲧϧⲉⲛ ⲧⲉⲕⲃⲁⲕⲓ 1°] om

16:16 ⲛⲓⲃⲉⲛ = Bo^W G'] om rell

16:16 ⲡⲉⲕⲛⲟⲩϯ ϧⲉⲛ ⲡⲓⲙⲁ ⲉⲧⲉϥⲛⲁⲥⲟⲧⲡϥ ⲛϫⲉ ⲡϭⲟⲓⲥ ϧⲉⲛ = Bo^W G'] om rell

16:17 ϯϫⲟⲙ ⲛⲧⲉ ⲧⲉⲧⲉⲛϫⲓϫ ⲛⲉⲙ = Bo^W G'] om rell

16:18 ⲉⲣⲉⲧϩⲁⲡ] pr ⲟⲩⲟϩ

16:19 ⲛⲛⲉⲛⲃⲁⲗ] ⲛⲛⲓⲃⲁⲗ

16:19 ⲯⲁⲣⲧⲁⲕⲟ] pr ⲟⲩⲟϩ

17:1   ⲡⲉⲕⲛⲟⲩϯ 2° = Bo^W G'] om rell

17:3   ⲁⲣⲓ 1°] pr ⲟⲩⲟϩ

17:4   ⲛⲧⲟⲩⲧⲁⲙⲟⲕ] pr ⲟⲩⲟϩ

17:5   ⲉⲣⲉⲙⲟⲩ] pr ⲟⲩⲟϩ

17:7   ⲉⲕⲉⲱⲗⲓ] pr ⲟⲩⲟϩ

17:8   ϧⲉⲛ ⲡⲓϩⲁⲡ ⲟⲩⲧⲉ ⲟⲩⲥⲛⲟⲩ ⲛⲉⲙ ⲟⲩⲥⲛⲟⲩ ⲛⲉⲙ ⲟⲩⲧⲉ ⲟⲩϩⲁⲡ ⲛⲉⲙ ⲟⲩϩⲁⲡ
        ⲟⲩⲧⲉ ⲡⲓϭⲟϩ ⲛⲉⲙ ⲡⲓϭⲟϩ ⲟⲩⲧⲉ ϯⲁⲛⲧⲓⲗⲟⲅⲓⲁ ⲛⲥⲁⲁⲓ ⲛⲟⲩϩⲁⲡ ϧⲉⲛ
        ⲛⲉⲧⲉⲛⲃⲁⲕⲓ ⲟⲩⲟϩ ⲉⲕⲉⲧⲱⲛⲕ = Bo^W G'] ⲟⲩⲧⲉ ⲟⲩⲥⲟⲛ ⲛⲉⲙ ⲟⲩⲧⲉ ⲟⲩⲥⲟⲛ

ⲚⲈⲘ ⲞⲨⲦⲈ ⲞⲨϨⲀⲠ ⲚⲈⲘ ⲞⲨϨⲀⲠ ⲀⲚⲦⲒⲖⲞⲄⲒⲀ ⲚⲒⲂⲈⲚ ⲤⲀϪⲒ   rell

17:9   ⲈⲔⲈⲒ] ϸⲣ ⲞⲨⲞϨ

17:10   ⲞⲨⲞϨ ⲈⲔⲈⲀⲢⲈϨ ⲈⲒⲢⲒ ⲚⲞⲨⲞⲚ ⲚⲒⲂⲈⲚ = B₀ᵂ G'] ⲞⲨⲞϨ ⲈⲔⲈⲀⲢⲈϨ ⲔⲀⲦⲀ

17:12   ⲈⲔⲈⲰⲖⲒ] ϸⲣ ⲞⲨⲞϨ

17:13   ⲠⲒⲖⲀⲞⲤ ⲓ°] ϸⲣ ⲞⲨⲞϨ

17:14   ⲞⲨⲞϨ ⲓ° = B₀ᵂ G'] om rell

17:14   ⲚⲦⲈⲔϪⲞⲤ] ϸⲣ ⲞⲨⲞϨ

17:16   ϨⲒⲚⲀ ⲚⲚⲈⲨⲐⲢⲈ ϨⲐⲞ ⲀⲨϪⲀⲒ ⲚⲀⲨ = B₀ᵂ G'] om rell

17:17   ⲈⲘⲀⲨⲰ] ϸⲣ ⲚⲀⲨ

17:19   ⲚⲈⲘ ⲚⲀⲒ ⲘⲈⲐⲘⲎⲒ ⲈⲀⲒⲦⲞⲨ ϨⲒⲚⲀ = B₀ᵂ G'] om rell

17:20   ⲈⲂⲞⲖϨⲀ ⲚⲒⲈⲚⲦⲞⲖⲎ = B₀ᵂ G'] om rell

18:3   ⲈⲨⲈϮ] ϸⲣ ⲞⲨⲞϨ

18:3   ⲚⲞⲨⲒⲚⲀⲘ] om

18:4   ⲚⲒⲀⲠⲀⲢⲬⲎ ⲚⲦⲈ 2° = B₀ᵂ G'] om rell

18:5   ⲈⲐⲢⲈⲨⲞϨⲒ ⲈⲢⲀⲦϤ ⲘⲠⲈⲘⲐⲞ ⲘⲠϬⲞⲒⲤ ⲈⲨϪⲈⲚϢⲒ ⲞⲨⲞϨ ⲈⲤⲘⲞⲨ ϦⲈⲚ
      ⲠⲈⲨⲢⲀⲚ ⲚⲐⲞⲨ ⲚⲈⲘ ⲚⲈⲨϢⲎⲢⲒ = B₀ᵂ G'] ⲈⲐⲢⲈⲨϢⲈⲘϢⲒ ⲘⲠⲈⲘⲐⲞ ⲘⲠϬⲤ rell

18:6   ⲠⲒⲘⲀ ⲈⲦⲈϤϢⲞⲠ ϨⲒⲰⲦϤ ⲔⲀⲦⲀ ϮⲈⲦⲈⲢⲈⲠⲒⲐⲨⲘⲒⲚ ⲚϪⲈ ⲦⲈϤⲮⲨⲬⲎ ⲈⲠⲒⲘⲀ
      ϮⲈⲦⲈϤⲤⲞⲦⲠϤ = B₀ᵂ G'] ϪⲈ ⲀⲤⲈⲢⲈⲠⲒⲐⲨⲘⲒⲚ ⲚϪⲈ ⲦⲈϤⲮⲨⲬⲎ rell

18:7   ⲠⲈϤⲚⲞⲨϮ = B₀ᵂ G'] om rell

18:15   ⲠⲈⲔⲚⲞⲨϮ = B₀ᵂ G'] om rell

18:16   ⲠⲈⲔⲚⲞⲨϮ ⲓ° = B₀ᵂ G'] om rell

18:20   ϮⲈⲦⲚⲀⲤⲀϪⲒ] ϸⲣ ⲞⲨⲞϨ

18:22   ⲚⲦⲈϤϢⲦⲈⲘⲒ] ϸⲣ ⲞⲨⲞϨ

19:1   ⲞⲨⲞϨ ⲓ° = B₀ᵂ G'] om rell

21:16   ⲚⲚⲈⲨϨⲨⲠⲀⲢⲬⲞⲚⲦⲀ = B₀ᵂ G'] ⲚⲚⲈⲨϨⲨⲠⲀⲢⲬⲰⲚⲦⲀ rell

26:19   ⲚⲦⲈⲔϢⲰⲠⲒ ⲤⲀⲠϢⲰⲒ = B₀ᵂ G'] ⲚⲦⲈⲔⲤⲀⲠϢⲰⲒ rell

28:15 ⲁⲛ] om

28:57 ⲛⲧⲉ ⲛⲭⲁⲓ = Bo^W G'] ⲛⲧⲉ ⲉⲛⲭⲁⲓ rell

32:5 ⲡⲓϣⲏⲣⲓ] ⲛⲓϣⲏⲣⲓ

33:3 ⲛⲉ⳽ⲭⲓⲝ = Bo^W H] ⲛⲉⲛⲭⲓⲝ rell

34:12 ⲧⲏⲟⲩ = Bo^W G'] om rell

Three major points emerge from an analysis of this list of
unique readings of Bo^W and G'.

(1) Several of the variants involve the addition of the copula
"ⲟⲣⲟ⳽".

(2) The majority of these variants (all but 13) occur between
chapters 9 and 18.

(3) Many readings attested in G are missing in all the other
extant mss.

The fact that Wilkins used mss from the three sources he mentioned should now be established. But he seems to have also used a
manuscript which he does not identify, or to have been an innovative
editor. Brooke seems convinced that he may have composed freely from
Greek into Coptic in places where his mss were deficient, or, in his
opinion, unsatisfactory.[10] The following is a list of readings unique
to Bo^W.

1:1 ⲛ⳽ⲁ⳽] ⲛϣⲁⲣⲓ

1:7 ⲉⲟⲩⲧⲱⲟⲩ] ⳽ⲉⲛ ⲟⲩⲧⲱⲟⲩ

1:7 ⲡⲉⲩϭⲫⲣⲁⲧⲏⲥ] ⲡⲓⲕⲣⲟ ⲉⲩⲫⲣⲁⲧⲏⲥ

1:8 ⲛⲛⲉⲧⲉⲛⲓⲟⲧ] ⲛⲛⲉⲧⲉⲛⲓⲟⲩⲧ

1:10 ⳽ⲏⲡ ⲡⲉ] pr ⲟⲩⲟ⳽

1:13 ⲛ⳽ⲁⲛⲩⲅⲟⲩⲙⲉⲛⲟⲥ] ⲛ⳽ⲁⲛ⳽ⲟⲩⲅⲱⲙⲉⲛⲟⲥ

1:14 ⲁⲧⲉⲧⲉⲛⲉⲣⲟⲩⲱ] pr ⲟⲩⲟ⳽

1:16 ΠΕϤΠΡΟCΙΛΙΤΟC] ΠΕϤΠΡΟCΗΛΙΤΟC

1:17 ΝΝΕΚϨΩΠ] ΝΝΕΚϨΩΤ

1:18 ΕΤΕΤΕΝΝΑΑΙΤΟϤ] ΕΤΕΤΕΝΕΑΙΤΟϤ

1:21 †] ΑϤΤΗΙϤ ΝΩΤΕΝ

1:23 ΟϤϬΙ] ϸⲣ ΟϤΟϨ.

1:23 ΟϤΡΩΜΙ] ΝΟϤΡΩΜΙ ΝΟϤΩΤ

1:25 ΟϤϬΙ] ϸⲣ ΟϤΟϨ

1:25 ΟϤΙΝΙ] ϸⲣ ΟϤΟϨ

1:27 ΕΤΗΙΤΕΝ] ΝΤΕΝΤΕΝ

1:28 ΟΝΝΑϢΕΝΑΝ] ΝΟϢΕΝΑΝ

1:28 ΕϨΡΗΙ] ΕⲐΡΗΙ

1:31 ΜⲪⲢΗⲧⲓ°] ΠΙΜΩΙΤ ΝΤΕ ΠΤΩΟϤ ΜⲠΙΑΜΜΟΡⲢΕΟC ⲆΕ

1:41 ΟΡΕΤΕΝⲐΩΟⲣϤ] ϸⲣ ΟϤΟϨ

1:42 ΕⲆΟΜⲆΕΜ] ΕⲆΕΜⲆΩΜ

1:43 ΜⲠΕΤΕΝCΩΤΕΝ] ϸⲣ ΟϤΟϨ

1:43 ΟΤΕΤΕΝΕΡⲠΟΡΑΒΕΝΙΝ] ϸⲣ ΟϤΟϨ

1:44 ΕⲣΟΜΟ] ΕⲣΜΟ

1:45 ΜⲠϬΟΙC] † ΠΕΝΝΟⲩ†

2:1 ΟΝΚΩΤ] ϸⲣ ΟϤΟϨ

2:4 ϨΟΝϨΕΝ] ϸⲣ ΟϤΟϨ

2:4 ΤΕΤΕΝΝΟCΙΝΙ] ΤΕΝΕΝΝΟCΙΝΙ

2:10 ΟϤΟϨ] ΝΕΜ

2:10 & 11 ΝΝΗΕΤⲆΕΝ ΝΟΚΙΜ] ΝΝΙΕΝΟΚΙΜ

2:12 ΝΙϢΗⲣⲓ ΝΤΕ ΗCΟϤ] ΝΕΝϢΗⲣⲓ ΝΗCΟϤ

2:12 ΟⲩϤΟΤΟⲩ] ΟϤΟϨ ⲟ⳽ⲭⲉⲣ Εⲣⲱⲟⲩ

2:13 CΙΝΙ] ϸⲣ ΟϤΟϨ

2:14 ΜⲠΟΛΕΜΙCΤΗC] † Εⲣⲙⲱⲟⲩⲧ

2:14 †ⲡⲁⲣⲉⲙⲃⲟⲗⲏ] ⲡⲁⲣⲉⲙⲃⲟⲗⲏ

2:16 ⲙⲡⲟⲗⲉⲙⲓⲥⲧⲏⲥ] ⲛⲓ ⲡⲟⲗⲉⲙⲓⲥⲧⲏⲥ

2:16 ⲁⲥϣⲱⲡⲓ] ⲉⲥⲉϣⲱⲡⲓ

2:19 ⲧⲉⲧⲉⲛⲛⲁϩⲱⲛⲧ] ⲫⲣ ⲟⲩⲟϩ

2:20 ⲛⲓϫⲟϫⲟⲙⲙⲓⲛ] ⲛⲓϫⲟⲭⲟⲙⲙⲓⲛ

2:21 ⲉⲁⲣⲟⲛ ϣϫⲟⲙ ⲙⲛⲟⲩ] ⲟⲩⲟϩ ⲉⲩϫⲟⲣ ⲉϩⲟⲧⲉⲣⲟⲛ

2:21 ⲛⲛⲏⲉⲧϣⲟⲡ ϧⲉⲛ ⲛⲁⲕⲓⲙ] ⲕⲉⲛⲓⲉⲛⲁⲕⲓⲙ

2:21 ⲁⲩⲉⲣⲕⲗⲏⲣⲟⲛⲟⲙⲓⲛ] ⲫⲣ ⲟⲩⲟϩ

2:22 ⲁⲩⲉⲣⲕⲗⲏⲣⲟⲛⲟⲙⲓⲛ] + ⲙⲙⲟⲩ ⲟⲩⲟϩ

2:22 ⲙⲡⲟⲩϩⲟ] ⲙⲡⲉⲩϩⲟ

2:23 ⲁⲩϣⲱⲡⲓ] ⲫⲣ ⲟⲩⲟϩ

2:24 ϣⲁⲓ ⲥⲓⲛⲓ] ⲁⲛⲥⲓⲛⲓ

2:25 ϩⲁⲛⲛⲁⲕϩⲓ] ⲫⲣ ⲟⲩⲟϩ

2:26 ⲕⲉⲇⲙⲱⲑ] ⲕⲏⲇⲁⲙⲱⲑ

2:28 ⲉⲓⲉⲥⲱ] ⲫⲣ ⲟⲩⲟϩ

2:28 ⲉⲓⲉⲟⲩⲱⲙ] ⲫⲣ ⲟⲩⲟϩ

2:30 ⲁⲩⲧⲛⲟⲙⲧ] ⲫⲣ ⲟⲩⲟϩ

2:30 ⲛϩⲣⲏⲓ] ⲙⲫⲣⲏⲧ

2:32 ⲛϫⲉ ⲥⲏⲱⲛ] + ⲡⲟⲩⲣⲟ ⲛⲉⲥⲉⲃⲱⲛ

2:32 ⲉⲡⲡⲟⲗⲉⲙⲟⲥ ⲉⲓⲁⲥⲥⲁ] ⲉⲡⲟⲗⲉⲙⲟⲥ ϧⲉⲛ ⲓⲁⲥⲥⲁ

2:34 ⲁⲛⲁⲙⲁϩⲓ] ⲫⲣ ⲟⲩⲟϩ

2:36 ⲙⲡⲉⲃⲁⲕⲓ] ⲙⲡⲉⲡⲃⲁⲕⲓ

2:36 ⲉϩⲣⲏⲓ] ⲉϩⲣⲏⲓ

2:37 ⲡⲕⲁϩⲓ] ⲉⲡⲕⲁϩⲓ

2:37 ⲉⲧⲧⲟⲟⲩϣ] — ⲑⲱϣ

3:1 ⲛⲧⲉ ⲑⲃⲁⲥⲁⲛ] ⲛⲑⲃⲁⲥⲁⲛ

3:1 ⲉⲇⲣⲁⲓⲛ] ⲡⲉⲇⲣⲁⲓⲛ

3:3 ⲛⲉⲙ ⲡⲉⲩⲕⲁϩⲓ ⲧⲏⲣϥ] ⲟⲙ

3:3	ⲈϨⲢⲎⲒ] ⲈϨⲢⲎⲒ
3:3	ⲀⲚϢⲀⲢⲒ] ⲠⲢ ⲞⲨⲞϨ
3:4	ⲝ̄] Ⲛ ⲝ̄
3:4	ⲀⲢⲔⲰⲂ] ⲀⲢⲄⲰⲂ
3:6	ⲀⲚϤⲈⲦ] ⲠⲢ ⲞⲨⲞϨ
3:8	ⲚⲀⲈⲢⲘⲰⲚ] ⲚⲦⲈ ⲀⲢⲚⲰⲚ
3:9	ϪⲈ ⲤⲀⲚⲒⲢ] ⲚϪⲈ ⲤⲀⲚⲒⲢ
3:11	ⲠⲖⲎⲚ ϪⲈ] ϪⲈ ⲠⲖⲎⲚ
3:11	Ⲇ̄ ⲚⲞⲨⲞⲤⲐⲈⲚ] Ⲇ̄ ⲘⲘⲀϨⲒ ⲚⲚⲈⲨⲞⲢⲰϢⲤ
3:13	ⲞⲢⲄⲞⲂ] ⲀⲢⲄⲞ Ⲃ
3:14	ⲠⲒⲘⲞⲄⲀⲐⲒ] ⲠⲒⲘⲀⲄⲀⲐⲒ
3:14	ⲚⲦⲈ ⲀⲨⲂⲰⲆ] ⲚⲦⲀⲨⲰⲐ
3:17	ⲦⲠⲀⲤⲬⲀ] ⲦϤⲀⲤⲄⲀ
3:20	ⲚⲦⲞⲨⲈⲢⲔⲖⲎⲢⲞⲚⲞⲘⲒⲚ] ⲚⲦⲞⲨⲔⲖⲎⲢⲞⲚⲞⲘⲒⲚ
3:21	ⲈⲦⲀ ⲪⲚⲞⲨⲦ ⲀⲒⲦⲞⲨ] ⲈⲦⲀⲨⲀⲒⲦⲞⲨ ⲚϪⲈ Ⲡ︤Ⲟ︦Ⲥ︥ ⲠⲈⲚⲚⲞⲨⲦ
3:24	Ⲡ︦Ⲟ︦Ⲓ︦Ⲥ︦ ϩⲟ] Ⲫ︦Ⲧ︦
3:24	ⲠⲈⲔⲀⲖⲞⲨ] ⲘⲠⲈⲔⲀⲖⲞⲨ
3:26	ⲀⲨϨⲒⲠϨⲞ] ⲀⲠϨⲒⲠϨⲞ
3:27	ⲀⲚⲀⲨ] ⲠⲢ ⲞⲨⲞϨ
3:28	ⲘⲀⲚⲞⲨⲦ] ⲘⲀⲦⲚⲞⲨⲦ
3:28	ϨⲀϪⲈⲚ] ϨⲀⲦⲈⲚϨⲎ
3:28	ⲠⲒⲖⲀⲞⲤ] ⲘⲠⲀⲒⲖⲀⲞⲤ ⲞⲨⲞϨ
3:29	ⲚⲀⲠⲎ] ⲦϨⲈⲖⲖⲞⲦ
4:1	ⲈⲦⲦⲤⲂⲞ] ⲈⲦⲤⲂⲞ
4:1	ⲚⲦⲈⲦⲈⲚⲀϢⲀⲒ] ⲠⲢ ⲞⲨⲞϨ
4:2	ⲚⲚⲈⲦⲈⲚⲰⲖⲒ] ⲠⲢ ⲞⲨⲞϨ
4:4	ϨⲀ] ⲞⲘ

4:9 ⲚⲦⲈ ⲚⲈⲔϢⲎⲢⲒ] ⲚⲚⲈⲔϢⲎⲢⲒ

4:11 ⲞⲨⲤⲀⲢⲀⲐⲎⲚⲞⲨ] ⲤⲀⲢⲀⲐⲎⲚⲞⲨ ; ⲚⲈⲘ ⲞⲨⲚⲒϢϮ ⲚⲤⲘⲎ] om

4:12 ⲞⲨⲤⲘⲎ 1°] ⲈⲞⲨⲤⲘⲎ

4:12 ⲞⲨⲤⲘⲞⲦ] pr ⲞⲨⲞϨ

4:14 ⲀⲚⲞⲔ] pr ⲞⲨⲞϨ

4:16 ⲚⲦⲈⲦⲈⲚⲐⲀⲘⲒⲞ] pr ⲞⲨⲞϨ

4:17 ⲚϨⲀⲖⲎⲦ] ⲚϨⲀⲖⲀⲦ

4:17 ⲚⲎⲈⲦϨⲎⲖ] ⲚⲎⲈⲦϨⲀⲖⲀⲒ

4:19 ⲘⲘⲰⲞⲨ 2°] ⲚⲐⲰⲞⲨ

4:20 ⲀϤⲈⲚⲐⲎⲚⲞⲨ] + ⲈⲂⲞⲖϦⲈⲚ ⲠⲒⲔⲀϨⲒ ⲚⲬⲎⲘⲒ

4:21 ⲘⲂⲞⲚ] ⲀϤⲘⲂⲞⲚ

4:21 ⲈⲐⲂⲈ] om

4:21 ϦⲈⲚ] ⲈⲂⲞⲖϦⲈⲚ

4:23 ⲚⲦⲈⲦⲈⲚⲐⲀⲘⲒⲞ] pr ⲞⲨⲞϨ

4:25 ⲒⲈ ϨⲀⲚϢⲎⲢⲒ] ⲚⲈⲘ ϨⲀⲚϢⲎⲢⲒ

4:25 ⲚⲦⲈⲦⲈⲚⲈⲢⲀⲚⲞⲘⲒⲚ] pr ⲞⲨⲞϨ

4:26 ⲚⲚⲈⲦⲈⲚⲀϢⲀⲒ ⲚⲰϪⲔ] ⲚⲚⲈⲦⲈⲚⲈⲰϪⲔ

4:31 ⲘⲘⲞⲤ ⲚⲰⲞⲨ] + ⲚϪⲈ Ⲡ̅ϭ̅ⲥ̅

4:34 ⲞⲨⲠⲒⲢⲀⲤⲘⲞⲤ] ⲞⲨϭⲰⲚⲦ

4:34 ϦⲈⲚ ⲞⲨⲠⲞⲖⲈⲘⲞⲤ] pr ⲚⲈⲘ

4:37 ⲈⲐⲂⲈ ϪⲈ] ⲈⲐⲂⲈ ⲞⲨϪⲈ

4:37 ⲀϤⲤⲰⲦⲠ] pr ⲞⲨⲞϨ

4:38 ⲚϨⲀⲚⲚⲒϢϮ ⲚⲈⲐⲚⲞⲤ ⲈⲂⲞⲖ] ⲚⲚⲒⲈⲐⲚⲞⲤ ⲚⲚⲒϢϮ ⲚⲈⲘ

4:42 ⲪⲎⲈⲦⲚⲀϤⲰⲦ ⲈⲘⲀⲨ ⲈϤⲈⲰⲚϦ] om

4:42 ⲈϤⲈⲪⲰⲦ] pr ⲞⲨⲞϨ

4:42 ⲚⲚⲒⲂⲀⲔⲒ] ⲚⲚⲀⲒⲂⲀⲔⲒ

4:43 ⲚⲄⲀⲖⲆⲒⲚ] ⲄⲀⲆⲆⲒ

4:45   ϨΙ ΠϢΑϤε] om

4:45   ΦΗΕΤΑϒΤΑΚΟϤ] ΝΗΕΤΑϒΤΑΚΟϤ

4:48   ϨΙΧεΝ] ⳰ ΟϒΟϨ

4:48   αεΡΜωΝ] εΡΜωΝ

4:49   ΦΗΕΤϢΗϤ εΒΟλ] ΝΤε ΠϢΑϤε

5:3   Νετα] ΝΝετα

5:3   ΤΑΙΔΙΑΘΗΚΗ] ΝΤΑΙΔΙΑΘΗΚΗ

5:5   ΜΠετεΝϢεΝωτεΝ] ⳰ ΟϒΟϨ

5:6   ΑΝΟΚ Πε ΠϬΟΙϹ] ΠϬΟΙϹ ΑΝΟΚ

5:7   ΝᾹε ϨΑΝΚεΝΟϒϯ] ΝΙΚεΝΟϒϯ

5:8   ΝΝεΚΘΑΜΙΟ ΝΑΚ] ΝΝεΚΑΙΚ

5:9   ΝΤε ΝΙΙΟϯ εᾹεΝ] ΝΤεΝΙΟϯ ε

5:14   ΠεΚΒωΚ ₂°] ΠεΚΑλΟϒ

5:15   ΑϤεΝΚ] ⳰ ΟϒΟϨ

5:15   ετΟϒΒΟϤ] ⳰ ΟϒΟϨ

5:16   ΝΤεΚεΡ] ⳰ ΟϒΟϨ

5:18/17] tr

5:22   ΝΑΙ] om

5:22   ΑϤϨΗΤΟϒ] ⳰ ΟϒΟϨ

5:22   ϹΝΟϒϯ] ΝΟϒ Β̄

5:22   ΝᾹε ΠϬΟΙϹ ₂°] om

5:27   εΝεϹΟΘΜΟϒ] ⳰ ΟϒΟϨ

5:28   ΝεΝϹΑᾹΙ] ΝΙϹΑᾹΙ

5:28   ϢΑΡΟΙ] ϨΑΡΟΙ

5:31   ΜΑΡΟϒΙΡΙ] ⳰ ΟϒΟϨ

6:5   εΒΟλϨεΝ ΠεΚϨΗΤ ΤΗΡϤ ΝεΜ] om

6:5   ΝεΚΜεϒΙ ΤΗΡΟϒ] ΤεΚΜεϒΙ ΤΗΡϹ

6:8 ⲉⲕⲉⲙⲟⲣⲟⲩ] ⲉⲕⲉⲙⲟⲩⲣⲟⲩ

6:10 ⲉⲛⲁⲛⲉⲩ] ⲡⲣ ⲛⲉⲙ

6:11 ⲛⲉⲙ ⲓ°] om

6:11 ⲛⲧⲉⲕⲟⲩⲱⲙ] ⲡⲣ ⲟⲩⲟϩ

6:13 ⲛⲑⲟⲩ ⲓ°] ⲡⲣ ⲟⲩⲟϩ

6:13 ⲉⲕⲉⲱⲣⲕ] ⲉⲧⲉⲕⲉⲱⲣⲕ

6:16 ⲛⲛⲉⲕⲉⲣⲡⲓⲣⲁⲍⲓⲛ] ⲛⲛⲉⲕⲉⲣϭⲱⲛⲧ

6:16 ⲉⲧⲁⲣⲉⲧⲉⲛⲉⲣⲡⲓⲣⲁⲍⲓⲛ ϧⲉⲛ ⲡⲓⲡⲣⲁⲥⲙⲟⲥ] — ⲉⲣϭⲱⲛⲧ ϧⲉⲛ ⲡⲓϭⲱⲛⲧ

6:18 ⲡⲓⲡⲉⲑⲣⲁⲛⲁⲩ] ⲙⲡⲉⲑⲣⲁⲛⲁⲩ

6:21 ⲛⲁⲛⲟⲓ] ⲁⲛⲛⲟⲓ

6:21 ⲡⲓⲕⲁⲍⲓ] ⲡⲓⲕⲁϩⲓ

6:21 ⲁⲩⲉⲛⲧⲉⲛ] ⲡⲣ ⲟⲩⲟϩ

6:22 ⲟⲩⲟϩ ⲉⲣⲟⲓ ⲛϩⲟϯ] om

6:22 ⲛⲓⲉⲧϩⲱⲟⲩ] ⲛⲏⲉⲧϩⲱⲟⲩ

6:23 ⲛⲧⲉⲩϭⲓⲧⲧⲉⲛ ⲉϧⲟⲩⲛ] om

6:23 ⲛϫⲉ ⲡϭⲟⲓⲥ] ⲉⲧ

7:2 ⲛⲛⲉⲧⲉⲛⲛⲁⲓ] ⲛⲛⲉⲧⲉⲛⲉⲛⲁⲓ

7:4 ⲉⲥⲉⲫⲉⲛϩ] ⲉⲩⲉⲣⲓⲕⲓ

7:4 ⲉⲩⲉⲩⲉⲧⲑⲏⲛⲟⲩ] ⲡⲣ ⲟⲩⲟϩ

7:7 ⲫⲛⲟⲩϯ] om

7:7 ⲧⲉⲧⲉⲛⲉⲣⲕⲟⲩϫⲓ] ⲧⲉⲧⲉⲛⲕⲟⲩϫⲓ

7:7 ⲉⲃⲟⲗ ⲟⲩⲧⲉ] ⲟⲩⲧⲉ ⲉⲃⲟⲗ

7:8 ⲁⲗⲗⲁ] + ⲉⲑⲃⲉ

7:8 ⲁⲩⲙⲉⲛⲣⲉⲑⲏⲛⲟⲩ] ⲁⲩⲙⲉⲛⲣⲓⲧⲧⲉⲛ

7:8 ⲁⲩⲥⲟⲧⲕ] ⲡⲣ ⲟⲩⲟϩ

7:10 ⲛⲛⲉⲩⲱⲥⲕ] ⲛⲛⲉⲩⲉⲱⲥⲕ

7:13 ⲉⲩⲉⲑⲣⲉⲕⲁⲩⲁⲓ] ⲡⲣ ⲟⲩⲟϩ

56

7:13	ⲡⲓⲕⲁϩⲓ] ⲡⲕⲁϩⲓ
7:14	ⲟⲩⲧⲉ] + ⲉⲃⲟⲗ
7:15	ⲉϥⲉⲱⲗⲓ] ⲡⲣ ⲟⲩⲟϩ
7:17	ⲡⲁⲓⲱⲗⲟⲗ] ⲫⲁⲓ ⲱⲗⲟⲗ
7:19	ⲙⲡⲓⲣⲁⲥⲙⲟⲥ] ⲛⲛⲓϭⲱⲛⲧ
7:19	ⲡⲉⲕⲛⲟⲩϯ 2°] ⲡⲉⲧⲉⲛⲛⲟⲩϯ
7:19	ϩⲁⲧⲟⲩϩⲏ] ϩⲁⲧⲟⲩϩⲟ
7:21	ⲡⲓⲱⲇⲉⲛⲉϩ ⲟⲩⲟϩ ⲉⲧⲁⲙⲁϩⲓ] ⲡⲓⲛⲓⲱⲧ ⲛⲉⲙ ⲉⲧⲟⲓ ⲛϩⲟϯ
7:22	ⲛⲧⲟⲩⲁⲱⲁⲓ] ⲡⲣ ⲟⲩⲟϩ
7:23	ⲉϥⲉⲧⲏⲓⲧⲟⲩ] ⲡⲣ ⲟⲩⲟϩ
7:25	ⲉϩⲁⲧ] ⲛⲟⲩϩⲁⲧ
7:25	ⲉⲃⲟⲗ ⲛϩⲏⲧⲟⲩ] ⲟⲙ
7:25	ⲉⲑⲃⲏⲧⲟⲩ] ⲉⲑⲃⲉ ⲫⲁⲓ
7:26	ⲛⲧⲉⲕⲉⲣⲁⲛⲁⲑⲉⲙⲁ] ⲡⲣ ⲟⲩⲟϩ
8:1	ⲛⲁⲓ 2°] ⲛⲏ
8:1	ⲛⲧⲉⲧⲉⲛⲱⲉ] ⲡⲣ ⲟⲩⲟϩ
8:1	ⲛⲧⲉⲧⲉⲛⲉⲣⲕⲗⲏⲣⲟⲛⲟⲙⲓⲛ] ⲡⲣ ⲟⲩⲟϩ
8:2	ⲉⲑⲣⲉϥⲉⲙⲓ] ⲡⲣ ⲟⲩⲟϩ
8:3	ⲁⲩⲑⲣⲉⲕϩⲕⲟ] ⲟⲩⲟϩ ⲁⲩⲑⲣⲉϩⲟⲕⲉⲣⲕ
8:5	ⲁⲣⲓⲉⲙⲓ] ⲡⲣ ⲟⲩⲟϩ
8:7	ⲉⲧⲉ ⲟⲩⲟⲛ] ⲉⲧⲉ ⲟⲩⲛ
8:9	ⲛⲛⲉⲕⲉⲣϣⲇⲉ] ⲡⲣ ⲟⲩⲟϩ
8:10	ⲉⲕⲉⲟⲩⲱⲙ] ⲡⲣ ⲟⲩⲟϩ
8:10	ⲉⲕⲉⲥⲙⲟⲩ] ⲡⲣ ⲟⲩⲟϩ
8:12	ⲛⲧⲉⲕⲥⲓ] ⲡⲣ ⲟⲩⲟϩ
8:16	ⲉⲑⲣⲉ] ⲡⲣ ⲟⲩⲟϩ

8:17	ⲧⲁⲛⲟⲙϯ] ⲧⲁⲭⲟⲙ
8:18	ⲙ̄ⲫⲣⲏϯ] ϣⲁ
8:20	ⲡⲥⲁϫⲓ] ⲧⲥⲙⲏ
9:3	ⲉⲕⲉⲉⲙⲓ] ⲡⲣ ⲟⲩⲟϩ
9:3	ⲉⲩⲉⲩⲟⲧⲟⲩ 2°] ⲡⲣ ⲟⲩⲟϩ
9:4	ⲛⲁⲅⲁⲑⲟⲛ] ⲡⲉⲑⲛⲁⲛⲉⲩ
9:4	ⲁⲗⲗⲁ ⲉⲑⲃⲉ ϯⲙⲉⲧⲁⲥⲉⲃⲏⲥ ⲛⲧⲉ ⲛⲁⲓⲉⲑⲛⲟⲥ ⲡϭⲟⲓⲥ ⲛⲁⲩⲟⲧⲟⲩ ⲉⲃⲟⲗϩⲁⲧϩⲏ
9:5	ⲛⲑⲟⲕ] ⲛⲑⲟⲩ ⲙ̄ⲡⲉⲕϩⲟ] om
9:5	ϩⲓⲛⲁ] ⲡⲣ ⲟⲩⲟϩ
9:5	ϯⲇⲓⲁⲑⲏⲕⲏ] ⲉⲧⲇⲓⲁ ⲑⲏⲕⲏ
9:6	ⲡϭⲟⲓⲥ] + ⲡⲉⲕⲛⲟⲩϯ
9:6	ⲛⲁϯ] ⲉⲩϯ
9:8	ⲟⲛ] om
9:9	ⲉϩⲣⲏⲓ] ⲉⲅ̅ⲣⲏⲓ
9:12	ⲁⲣⲑⲁⲙⲓⲟ] ⲡⲣ ⲟⲩⲟϩ
9:14	ⲉⲛⲁϣϣⲩ] ⲛⲛⲁϣϣⲩ
9:15	ⲉⲧⲁⲓⲕⲟⲧⲧ] ⲡⲣ ⲟⲩⲟϩ
9:15	ⲛⲭⲣⲱⲙ] + ϣⲁ ⲧⲫⲉ
9:15	ⲃ̄ϯ ⲛⲱⲛⲓ] ⲃ̄ ⲛⲛⲓⲙⲉⲧⲙⲉⲑⲣⲉⲩ
9:15	ⲃ̄ϯ 2°] ϯⲃ̄
9:16	ⲁⲣⲉⲧⲉⲛⲑⲁⲙⲓⲟ] ⲡⲣ ⲟⲩⲟϩ
9:16	ⲁⲣⲉⲧⲉⲛⲉⲣⲡⲁⲣⲁⲃⲉⲛⲓⲛ] ⲡⲣ ⲟⲩⲟϩ
9:17	ⲁⲓⲃⲉⲣⲃⲱⲣⲟⲩ] ⲁⲓⲃⲟⲣⲃⲉⲣ
9:17	ⲁⲓϩⲉⲙϩⲱⲙⲟⲩ] ⲡⲣ ⲟⲩⲟϩ
9:19	ⲡⲓⲉⲙⲃⲟⲛ] ⲉⲙⲃⲟⲛ
9:21	ⲉⲑⲛⲏⲟⲩ] ⲉⲩⲓ
9:22	ⲡⲉⲧⲉⲛⲛⲟⲩϯ] om

9:23 ϩⲟⲧⲉ] ⲟⲩⲟϩ ⲉϣⲱⲡ
9:26 ⲛⲧⲉ ⲛⲓⲉⲑⲛⲟⲥ] ⲛⲧⲉ ⲛⲓⲛⲟⲩϯ
9:26 ϧⲉⲛ ⲧⲉⲕⲛⲓϣϯ ⲛϫⲟⲙ] om
9:27 ⲛⲟⲩⲙⲉⲧⲁⲥⲉⲃⲏⲥ] + ⲛⲉⲙ ⲉϫⲉⲛ ⲛⲟⲩⲛⲟⲃⲓ
9:28 ⲡⲓⲙⲁ] ⲛⲓⲙ
9:28 ⲉⲡⲕⲁϩⲓ] ⲉⲡⲟⲩⲕⲁϩⲓ
9:28 ϥⲙⲟⲥϯ] ⲁϥⲙⲟⲥϯ
9:28 ϩⲓ ⲡϣⲁϥⲉ 2°] om
10:3 ⲃ̄ϯ 1°, 2°] ϯⲃ
10:4 ⲁϥⲡⲏⲓⲧⲟⲩ] pr ⲟⲩⲟϩ
10:6 ⲛⲁⲕⲓⲙ] ⲓⲁⲕⲓⲙ ϧⲉⲛ
10:8 ⲛϯⲫⲩⲗⲏ] ⲛⲧⲫⲩⲗⲏ
10:12 ⲉⲙⲟϣⲓ] pr ⲟⲩⲟϩ
10:13 ⲛϧⲏⲧⲟⲩ] om
10:15 ⲙⲙⲱⲟⲩ] ⲉⲣⲱⲟⲩ ⲟⲩⲟϩ
10:15 ⲡⲁⲓ ⲉϩⲟⲟⲩ ⲫⲁⲓ] ⲙⲫⲁⲓ ⲡⲓⲉϩⲟⲟⲩ
10:16 ⲧⲉⲛϣⲟⲧ] ⲛϣⲟⲧ
10:16 ⲙⲡⲉⲣⲉⲣⲛⲁϣⲧ] ⲙⲡⲉⲧⲉⲛⲉⲣⲛⲁϣⲧ
10:18 ϥⲙⲉⲓ] pr ⲟⲩⲟϩ
10:21 ⲛⲏⲉⲧϥⲫⲉⲣⲓⲱⲟⲩ] ϥⲫⲉⲣⲓⲱⲟⲩ
10:22 ⲉϧⲣⲏⲓ] ⲉϩⲣⲏⲓ
11:1 ⲉⲕⲉⲙⲉⲛⲣⲉ] pr ⲟⲩⲟϩ
11:1 ⲡϭⲟⲓⲥ] ⲙⲡϭ̄ⲥ
11:1 ⲛⲉϥⲉⲛⲧⲟⲗⲏ ⲛⲉⲙ ⲛⲉϥ ⲙⲉⲑⲙⲏⲓ] ⲛⲉϥⲙⲉⲑⲙⲏⲓ ⲛⲉⲙ ⲛⲉϥⲉⲛⲧⲟⲗⲏ
11:3 ⲡⲉϥⲕⲁϩⲓ ⲧⲏⲣϥ] ⲙⲡⲉϥⲕⲁϩⲓ ⲛⲓⲃⲉⲛ
11:4 ⲛⲟⲩϩⲁⲣⲙⲁ] pr ⲛⲉⲙ

11:4 ⲛⲉⲙ ⲛⲏ ⲧⲏⲣⲟⲩ ⲉⲧⲁϥⲁⲓⲧⲟⲩ] ⲟⲩⲟϩ ⲛⲏⲉⲧⲁϥⲓⲣⲓ
11:7 ⲛⲉⲧⲉⲛⲃⲁⲗ] pr ϫⲉ
11:8 ⲛⲧⲉⲧⲉⲛϣⲉⲛⲱⲧⲉⲛ] pr ⲟⲩⲟϩ
11:8 ⲛⲧⲉⲧⲉⲛⲉⲣⲕⲗⲏⲣⲟⲛⲟⲙⲓⲛ] ⲉⲉⲣⲕⲗⲏⲣⲟⲛⲟⲙⲓⲛ
11:10 ϣⲁⲩⲧⲥⲱⲟⲩ] pr ⲟⲩⲟϩ
11:16 ⲛⲧⲉⲧⲉⲛⲟⲩⲱϣⲧ] pr ⲟⲩⲟϩ
11:17 ⲉⲣⲉⲧⲉⲛⲉⲧⲁⲕⲟ] pr ⲟⲩⲟϩ
11:18 ⲉⲩⲉϣⲱⲡⲓ] pr ⲟⲩⲟϩ
11:18 ⲉⲣⲉⲧⲉⲛⲉⲙⲟⲣⲟⲩ] ⲉⲑⲣⲉⲧⲉⲛⲙⲟⲩⲣⲟⲩ
11:19 ⲉⲣⲉⲧⲉⲛⲉϯⲥⲃⲱ] pr ⲟⲩⲟϩ
11:20 ϩⲓ ⲛⲓⲟⲩⲉϫⲣⲱⲟⲩ] ϩⲓϫⲉⲛ ⲛⲉϫⲣⲱⲟⲩ
11:21 ⲛⲧⲉ ⲛⲉⲧⲉⲛϣⲏⲣⲓ] ⲛⲧⲉ ⲛⲉⲛϣⲏⲣⲓ
11:22 ⲉⲧⲱⲙⲓ] ⲉⲧⲟⲙⲓ
11:24 ⲉⲧⲉⲧⲉⲛⲛⲁϩⲱⲙⲓ] ⲛⲧⲉⲧⲉⲛⲛⲁϩⲱⲙⲓ
11:30 ⲫⲏⲉⲧϣⲟⲡ] ⲫⲏⲉⲧϣⲱⲡ
11:31 ⲉⲣⲉⲧⲉⲛⲉⲉⲣⲕⲗⲏⲣⲟⲛⲟⲙⲓⲛ ⲙⲙⲟϥ] om
11:32 ⲉϯ] ϯ
12:3 ⲉⲣⲉⲧⲉⲛⲉⲕⲟⲣϫⲟⲩ] ⲉⲣⲉⲧⲉⲛⲉϫⲉⲣⲟⲩ ⲟⲩⲟϩ
12:3 ⲛⲧⲉ] ⲛ
12:3 ⲉⲣⲉⲧⲉⲛⲉⲧⲁⲕⲉ] pr ⲟⲩⲟϩ
12:3 ⲡⲟⲩⲣⲁⲛ ⲉⲃⲟⲗϧⲉⲛ] ⲙⲡⲟⲩⲣⲁⲛⲉⲃⲟⲗ
12:6 ⲛⲏ ⲉⲧⲉⲛⲛⲁⲧⲏⲓⲧⲟⲩ ϧⲉⲛ] om
12:6 ⲡⲉⲧⲉⲛⲟⲩⲱϣ] ⲛⲉⲧⲉⲛⲟⲩⲱϣ
12:7 ⲉⲣⲱⲟⲩ ⲛⲉⲙ ⲛⲉⲧⲉⲛⲏⲓ] ⲛⲉⲙ ⲛⲉⲧⲉⲛⲏⲓ ⲉⲣⲱⲟⲩ
12:9 ⲙⲡⲁⲧⲉⲧⲉⲛⲓ] ⲙⲡⲁⲧⲉⲛⲓ
12:10 ⲉⲣⲉⲧⲉⲛⲉϣⲱⲡⲓ] pr ⲟⲩⲟϩ
12:11 ⲛⲉⲧⲉⲛⲣⲉⲙⲁϯ] ⲛⲉⲧⲉⲛⲣⲉⲙⲏϯ

12:12	ⲉⲧϩⲉⲛ] ⲉⲧϧⲉⲛ	
12:13	ⲉⲧⲉⲕⲛⲁⲛⲁⲩ] ⲉⲧⲉⲕⲛⲁϥⲛⲁⲩ	
12:14	ⲛⲛⲉⲕⲃⲁⲕⲓ] ⲛⲛⲉⲕⲫⲩⲗⲏ	
12:14	ⲛⲉⲙ ⲛⲉⲕⲯⲟⲩⲯⲟⲩⲯⲓ] om	
12:17	ⲛⲁⲛⲉⲕⲉⲥⲱⲟⲩ] ⲛⲉⲕⲉⲥⲱⲟⲩ	
12:20	ⲟⲩⲟⲥⲑⲉⲛ] ⲟⲩⲱⲯⲥⲑⲉⲛ	
12:20	ⲧⲛⲁⲟⲩⲉⲙ] ⲧⲛⲁⲟⲩⲱⲙ	
12:20	ⲉⲟⲩⲉⲙ 1°, 2°] ⲉⲟⲩⲱⲙ	
12:21	ⲡⲓⲧⲟⲡⲟⲥ] ⲡⲓⲙⲁ	
12:21	ⲉⲕⲉⲯⲱⲧ] ϧⲣ ⲟⲩⲟϩ	
12:23	ⲥⲛⲟⲩ] ⲙⲡⲓⲥⲛⲟⲩ	
12:23	ⲛⲛⲟⲩⲟⲩⲱⲙ ⲛⲛⲓⲯⲩⲭⲏ] ⲛⲛⲉⲩⲟⲩⲱⲙⲩ ⲛϫⲉ ⲟⲓⲯⲩⲭⲏ	
12:24	ⲛⲛⲉⲧⲉⲛⲟⲩⲟⲙⲩ] ⲛⲛⲉⲧⲉⲛⲟⲩⲱⲙ	
12:26	ⲟⲩⲟϩ] om	
12:27	ⲉⲕⲉⲓⲣⲓ] ϧⲣ ⲟⲩⲟϩ	
12:28	ⲉϣⲱⲡ] om	
12:28	ⲙⲡⲓⲡⲉⲑⲛⲁⲛⲉⲩ] ⲙⲡⲉⲑⲣⲁⲛⲁⲩ ⲛⲉⲙ ⲡⲉⲑⲛⲁⲛⲉⲩ	
12:30	ⲛⲟⲩⲛⲟⲩϯ] ⲛⲛⲟⲩⲛⲟⲩϯ	
12:31	ⲛⲛⲟⲩⲛⲟⲩϯ 1°] + ϫⲉ	
13:3	ⲛⲥⲁ] ϧⲣ ⲁⲛ	
13:3	ⲡⲓⲣⲉⲩϥⲉⲣⲣⲁⲥⲟⲩⲓ] ϧⲣ ⲛⲧⲉ	
13:3	ⲉⲛⲁⲩ] ⲉⲉⲙⲓ	
13:4	ⲧⲉⲩⲥⲙⲏ] ⲧⲉⲩⲙⲏ	
13:4	ⲉⲣⲉⲧⲉⲛⲉⲧⲟⲩϩⲟ] ⲉⲣⲉⲧⲉⲛⲉⲧⲟⲩϩⲱⲟⲩ	
13:5	ⲉⲥⲱⲣⲙⲉⲕ] ⲉⲥⲱⲣⲙⲉⲕ	
13:5	ⲧⲙⲉⲧⲃⲱⲕ] ⲡⲏⲓ ⲛⲧⲉ ⲧⲙⲉⲧⲃⲱⲕ	
13:7	ⲁⲩⲣⲏⲭⲩ 1°, 2°] ⲁⲩⲣⲏⲭ	
13:10	ⲉⲩⲉϩⲓⲱⲛⲓ] ϧⲣ ⲟⲩⲟϩ	

13:11 ⲡⲓⲗⲁⲟⲥ] ⲡⲓⲥⲗ̄

13:13 ⲟⲩⲟⲛ] ⲛⲟⲩⲟⲛ

13:14 ϩⲏⲡⲡⲉ] ϥⲣ ⲟⲩⲟϩ

13:17 ⲛⲧⲉ ⲡϬⲟⲓⲥ ⲧⲁⲥⲑⲟ] ⲛⲧⲉⲩⲧⲁⲥⲑⲟ ⲛⲭⲉ ⲡϬ̄ⲥ

13:17 ⲛⲧⲉⲕⲑⲣⲉⲕⲁⲩⲁⲓ] ⲟⲩⲟϩ ⲛⲧⲉϥⲉⲣⲁⲩⲁⲓ ⲛⲧⲁⲕ

14:2 ⲛⲁⲩ ⲛⲟⲩⲗⲁⲟⲥ] ⲛⲁⲕ ⲟⲩⲗⲁⲟⲥ

14:2 ⲉϥⲱⲛϧ] ⲉⲩⲥⲉⲃⲧⲟⲧ

14:2 ⲛⲏⲉⲧⲭⲏ ⲙⲡⲉⲛ̄ⲑⲟ] ⲉⲧϫⲓⲝⲉⲛ ⲡϩⲟ

14:5 ⲡⲓⲅⲁⲣⲅⲟⲥ] ⲡⲓⲅⲁⲣⲅⲁⲥ

14:5 ⲅⲁⲙⲏⲗⲟⲡⲁⲣⲇⲁⲗⲓⲥ] ⲕⲁⲙ.

14:6 ⲛⲉⲙ] ⲟⲩⲟϩ ⲉⲧⲱⲗⲓ

14:6 ⲛⲟⲩⲓⲉⲃ] + ⲙⲃ̄

14:6 ⲉⲧⲥⲁⲑⲙⲓ] ⲉⲧⲓⲛⲓ ⲛⲟⲩⲥⲁⲑⲙⲓ

14:6 ⲉⲣⲉⲧⲉⲛⲉⲟⲩⲟⲙⲟⲩ] — ⲟⲩⲱⲙⲟⲩ

14:7 ⲛⲏⲉⲧⲥⲁⲑⲙⲓ] ⲛⲏⲉⲧⲓⲛⲓ ⲛⲟⲩⲥⲁⲑⲙⲓ

14:7 ⲛⲟⲩⲓⲉⲃ] ϥⲣ ⲛⲏⲉⲧⲱⲗⲓ

14:7 ⲥⲉⲥⲁⲑⲙⲓ] ⲥⲉⲓⲛⲓ ⲛⲟⲩⲥⲁⲑⲙⲓ

14:7 ⲛⲭⲉ ⲛⲁⲓ ⲥⲉⲫⲱⲣϫ ⲇⲉ ⲁⲛ] ⲛⲛⲟⲩϥⲫⲟⲣϫ ⲇⲉ

14:7 ϩⲁⲛⲁⲕⲁⲑⲁⲣⲧⲟⲛ] ⲉⲧϬⲁϧⲉⲙ

14:8 ⲩϥⲟⲣϫ ϧⲉⲛ ⲛⲉϥⲓⲉⲃ] ⲉϥⲱⲗⲓ ⲛⲉϥⲓⲉⲃ

14:8 ⲟⲩⲟϩ] + ⲉⲩⲫⲱϫ ⲛⲉϥϬⲟⲡ ⲟⲩⲟϩ ⲛⲛⲉϥⲓⲛⲓ

14:8 ⲩⲥⲁⲑⲙⲓ] ⲛⲉⲩⲥⲁⲑⲙⲓ

14:9 ⲉⲣⲉⲧⲉⲛⲉⲟⲩⲟⲙⲟⲩ] — ⲟⲩⲱⲙⲟⲩ

14:10 ⲛⲏⲉⲧⲉ ⲙⲙⲟⲛ] ⲛⲏⲧⲏⲣⲟⲩ ⲉⲧⲉⲙⲙⲟⲛ

14:13 ⲡⲓⲑⲟⲉ] + ⲡⲓⲉⲃⲱⲕ

14:14 ⲡⲓⲁⲃⲱⲕ] ⲟⲙ

14:16 ϧⲣⲟⲇⲓⲟⲛ] ⲉⲣⲟⲇⲓⲟⲛ ⲛⲉⲙ

14:21 ⲉⲑⲙⲱⲟⲩⲧ] + ⲧⲏⲣⲟⲩ

14:21 ⲛⲛⲉⲕⲫⲉⲥ]—ⲫⲁⲥ

14:23 ⲛⲛⲓⲣⲉⲙⲁⲧ] ⲛⲟⲩⲣⲉⲙⲏⲧ

14:24 ⲛⲧⲉⲕⲩⲧⲉⲙϫⲉⲙϫⲟⲙ] ϥⲣ ⲟⲩⲟⲍ

14:24 ⲡⲓⲧⲟⲡⲟⲥ] ⲡⲓⲙⲁ

14:25 ⲉⲕⲉⲧⲏⲓⲧⲟⲩ] ϥⲣ ⲟⲩⲟⲍ

14:25 ⲉⲕⲉϣⲉⲛⲁⲕ] ϥⲣ ⲟⲩⲟⲍ

14:26 ⲥⲓⲕⲉⲣⲁ] ⲥⲓⲕⲣⲣⲁ

15:3 ⲙⲡⲉⲧⲉⲛⲧⲁⲕ] ⲉⲧⲉⲛⲧⲁⲕ

15:4 ⲛⲛⲉ ⲟⲩⲟⲛ ϣⲱⲡⲓ] ⲛⲛⲉϥⲉϣⲱⲡⲓ

15:4 ⲉⲩⲉⲣϩⲁⲉ] ⲟⲩϩⲏⲕⲓ

15:6 ⲉⲧⲁⲩⲥⲁϫⲓ] ⲁⲩⲥⲁϫⲓ

15:6 ⲉⲕⲉⲉⲣⲇⲁⲛⲓⲥⲧⲏⲥ] ⲉⲕⲉϯϣⲁⲡ

15:6 ⲛⲛⲟⲩⲉⲣⲇⲁⲛⲓⲥⲧⲏⲥ] ⲛⲛⲉⲕⲉⲉⲣⲇ.

15:7 ⲫⲏⲉⲧⲉⲩϯ] ⲫⲏⲉⲧⲉⲩⲧⲏⲓϥ

15:7 ⲛⲛⲉⲕⲛⲁⲩⲧ] ⲛⲛⲉⲕⲉⲛⲁⲩⲧ

15:7 ⲙⲡⲉⲕϩⲏⲧ] ⲡⲉⲕϩⲏⲧ

15:7 ⲛⲛⲉⲕϣⲑⲁⲙ] ⲛⲛⲉⲕⲉϣⲑⲁⲙ

15:8 ⲟⲩⲟⲩⲱⲙ] ⲟⲩⲱⲙ

15:8 ⲙⲙⲟⲩ] ⲛⲑⲟⲩ

15:10 ⲉⲕϯ] ⲉⲕⲉϯ

15:10 ⲉⲧⲉⲕⲉϩⲓ] ⲉⲧⲉⲕⲉϩⲓⲧ

15:11 ⲡⲓⲕⲁϩⲓ] ⲡⲉⲕⲕⲁϩⲓ

15:11 ⲟⲩⲟⲩⲱⲙ] ⲟⲩⲱⲙ

15:12 ⲙⲡⲉⲕⲥⲟⲛ] ⲡⲉⲕⲥⲟⲛ

15:13 ⲁⲕϣⲁⲛⲟⲩⲟⲣⲡϥ] ⲉⲕⲟⲩⲟⲣⲡϥ

15:13 ⲉⲃⲟⲗ 1°] ⲟⲙ

15:13 ⲚⲢⲈⲘϨⲈ] ⲦⲈⲂⲟⲗ Ϩⲁⲣⲟⲕ

15:13 ⲚⲚⲈⲕⲟⲩⲟⲣⲡϥ] ⲚⲚⲈⲕⲉⲟⲩⲟⲣⲡϥ

15:13 ⲈⲂⲟⲗ ϩ·] Ⲉⲣⲟϥ

15:13 ⲈϥϣⲟⲩⲓⲦ] ⲈⲦϣⲟⲩⲓⲦ

15:17 ⲘⲠⲈϥⲘⲁϣϫ] ⲘⲠⲈⲕⲘⲁϣϫ

15:19 ⲚⲚⲈⲕϨⲱⲕ] ϧⲣ ⲞⲨⲆⲈ

16:2 ϨⲀⲚⲈϨⲰⲟⲩ] ⲈϨⲰⲟⲩ

16:5 ⲠⲓⲠⲀⲤⲬⲁ] ⲘⲠⲓⲠⲀⲤⲬⲁ

16:5 ⲚⲚⲒⲂⲀⲔⲒ] ⲚⲦⲈ ⲚⲈⲕⲂⲀⲔⲒ

16:7 ⲈⲔⲈϣⲈⲚⲀⲔ] ϧⲣ ⲟⲩⲟϨ

16:9 ⲈⲀⲔⲈⲣϨⲎⲦⲤ] ⲈⲦⲀⲕⲈⲣϨⲎⲦⲤ

16:11 ⲈⲔⲈⲞⲒⲚⲞⲨ] ϧⲣ ⲟⲩⲟϨ

16:11 ⲚⲀⲤⲞⲦⲠϥ] ⲚⲤⲞⲦⲠϥ

16:12 ⲚⲀⲔⲞⲒ] ⲞⲒ

16:13 ⲚⲀⲔ] ⲚⲦⲀⲔ

16:14 ⲈⲔⲈⲞⲨⲚⲞⲨ] ϧⲣ ⲟⲩⲟϨ

16:14 ⲈⲦϦⲈⲚ ⲦⲈⲔ ⲂⲀⲔⲒ ⁚] ⲈⲦϦⲈⲚ ⲚⲈⲕⲂⲀⲔⲒ

16:15 ⲈⲔⲈⲀⲒⲦⲞⲨ] ⲈⲔⲈⲀⲒⲦϥ

16:15 ⲚϣⲀⲒ] ⲘⲠϣⲀⲒ

16:16 ⲦⲤⲔⲎⲚⲞⲠⲎⲔⲒⲁ] — ⲠⲎⲄⲒⲁ

16:17 ⲚⲦⲈ ⲦⲈⲦⲈⲚϫⲒϫ] ⲚⲦⲈⲦⲈⲚϫⲒϫ

16:20 ⲠⲀⲒⲆⲒⲔⲈⲞⲚ] ⲚⲐⲘⲎⲒ

16:20 ⲚⲦⲈⲔⲈⲣⲔⲗⲎⲣⲞⲚⲞⲘⲒⲚ] ⲚⲦⲈⲔ ⲔⲗⲎⲣ.

17:3 ⲀⲣⲒ] ⲈϩⲒ

17:3 ⲚⲦⲞⲨⲞⲩⲱϣⲦ] ⲟⲩⲟϨ ⲚⲦⲞⲩⲟⲩⲱϣⲦ

17:4 ⲈⲔⲈⲔⲱⲦ] ϧⲣ ⲟⲩⲟϨ

17:5 ⲈⲔⲈⲒⲚⲒ] ϧⲣ ⲟⲩⲟϨ

17:5	ⲉⲣⲉⲧⲉⲛⲉⲍⲓⲱⲛⲓ]	ⲃ̄ ⲟⲩⲟⲍ
17:6	ⲛⲁⲭⲉ]	om
17:8	ⲉⲕⲉⲧⲱⲛⲕ]	ⲉⲕⲧⲱⲛⲕ
17:9	ⲛⲓⲟⲩⲏⲃ]	ⲛⲛⲓⲟⲩⲏⲃ
17:9	ⲛⲛⲓⲉⲍⲟⲟⲩ]	ϧⲉⲛ ⲛⲓⲉⲍⲟⲟⲩ
17:12	ⲉⲧⲛⲁⲓⲣⲓ]	+ ϧⲉⲛ
17:12	ⲛⲟⲩⲙⲉⲧⲣⲉⲩⲍⲓⲡⲍⲟ]	ⲟⲩⲙⲉⲧⲣⲉⲩⲍⲓⲡⲍⲟ
17:12	ⲙⲫⲣⲁⲛ]	ⲟⲩⲣⲁⲛ
17:12	ⲉⲩⲉⲙⲟⲩ]	ⲃ̄ ⲟⲩⲟⲍ
17:14	ⲛⲧⲉⲕϣⲱⲡⲓ]	ⲃ̄ ⲟⲩⲟⲍ
17:15	ⲟⲩⲭⲱ]	ⲉⲭⲱ
17:18	ⲁⲩϣⲁⲛⲍⲉⲙⲥⲓ]	ⲁⲩⲍⲉⲙⲥⲓ
17:18	ⲉⲩⲉⲥϭⲁⲓ]	ⲃ̄ ⲟⲩⲟⲍ
17:18	ⲛⲛⲓⲟⲩⲏⲃ]	ⲛⲓⲟⲩⲏⲃ
17:19	ⲉⲩⲉϣⲱⲡⲓ]	ⲃ̄ ⲟⲩⲟⲍ
17:19	ⲛⲧⲉⲩⲁⲣⲉⲍ]	ⲟⲩⲟⲍ ⲉⲁⲣⲉⲍ
17:20	ⲛⲧⲉⲩϣⲧⲉⲙ]	ⲛⲛⲉⲩϣⲧⲉⲙ
17:20	ⲛⲓⲉⲛⲧⲟⲗⲏ]	ⲛⲛⲓⲉⲛⲧⲟⲗⲏ
18:1	ⲛⲛⲉ ⲧⲟⲓ ϣⲱⲡⲓ]	ⲛⲛⲉⲩⲉϣⲱⲡⲓ
18:1	ⲛⲓⲗⲉⲩⲓⲧⲏⲥ]	ⲛⲗⲉⲩⲓⲧⲏⲥ
18:1	ⲧⲫⲩⲗⲏ]	ⲙ̄ⲧⲫⲩⲗⲏ
18:1	ⲛⲗⲉⲩⲓ]	+ ⲟⲩⲧⲟⲓ
18:2	ⲛⲛⲉⲕⲗⲏⲣⲟⲥ]	ⲛⲛⲉⲩⲕⲗⲏⲣⲟⲥ
18:3	ⲛⲓⲉⲃⲟⲗϩⲓⲧⲟⲧⲩ]	ⲉⲃⲟⲗϩ.
18:3	ⲉⲃⲟⲗϩⲓⲧⲉⲛ]	ⲉⲃⲟⲗϩⲉⲛ
18:3	ⲛⲏⲉⲧϣⲱⲧ]	— ϣⲟⲧ
18:3	ⲛⲓⲟⲩⲟⲭⲓ]	ⲛⲓⲟⲭⲓ

18:5	ϧⲉⲛ ⲛⲉⲛϣⲏⲣⲓ ⲙ̅ⲡⲓⲥⲣⲁⲏⲗ]	om
18:6	ⲉⲧⲉϥϣⲟⲡ]	ⲉϥϣⲱⲡⲓ
18:6	ⲫⲏⲉⲧⲉⲣⲉⲡⲓⲑⲩⲙⲓⲛ]	ⲫⲏⲉⲣⲉⲡⲓⲑ.
18:6	ⲫⲏⲉⲧⲉϥⲥⲟⲧⲡϥ]	ⲫⲏⲉⲧⲉⲥ.
18:7	ⲉⲑⲣⲉϥϣⲉⲙϣⲓ]	ⲉϥⲉϣⲉⲙϣⲓ
18:7	ⲧⲏⲣⲟⲩ]	ⲛⲓⲃⲉⲛ
18:10	ⲉϥⲉⲣⲕⲗⲏⲇⲟⲛⲓⲍⲉⲥⲑⲉ]	ⲉϥⲉⲣⲭⲗⲏ.
18:12	ⲛⲁⲓ]	ⲛ̅ϫⲉ
18:16	ⲡⲉⲛⲛⲟⲩϯ]	ⲡⲉⲕⲛⲟⲩϯ
18:18	ⲉϥⲉⲥⲁϫⲓ]	ϥⲣ ⲟⲩⲟϩ
18:21	ⲉⲧⲁⲓⲥⲁϫⲓ ⲉⲧⲉ ⲙ̅ⲡⲉ ⲡϭⲟⲓⲥ ⲥⲁϫⲓ]	ⲙ̅ⲡⲓⲥⲁϫⲓ ⲫⲏⲉⲧⲁⲩⲥⲁϫⲓ ⲁⲛ ⲛ̅ϫⲉ ⲡ̅ⲟ̅ⲥ̅
18:22	ⲛ̅ⲧⲉϥϣⲧⲉⲙⲓ]	ⲛ̅ⲧⲉϥϣⲧⲉⲙϣⲱⲡⲓ
19:2	ⲙ̅ⲡⲓⲕⲁϩⲓ]	ⲙ̅ⲡⲉⲕⲕⲁϩⲓ
19:3	ⲡⲕⲁϩⲓ]	ⲡⲉⲕⲕⲁϩⲓ
19:4	ⲡⲉ]	ⲇⲉ
19:4	ⲡⲓⲟⲩⲁϩⲥⲁϩⲛⲓ ⲉⲧⲉ ⲉϥϣⲱⲡⲓ]	ⲉϥⲉϣⲱⲡⲓ ⲡⲓⲍⲟⲛϩⲉⲛ
19:4	ⲙ̅ⲡⲓⲣⲉϥϧⲱⲧⲉⲃ]	ⲛ̅ⲣⲉϥϧⲱⲧⲉⲃ
19:4	ⲫⲏⲉⲧⲛⲁϥⲱⲧ]	ⲛ̅ⲧⲉ ⲫⲏⲉⲑⲛⲁϥⲱⲧ
19:4	ⲉϥⲉⲱⲛϧ]	ϥⲣ ⲟⲩⲟϩ
19:5	ⲉⲟⲩⲁϩⲯⲩⲭⲏⲛ]	ⲉⲟⲩ̅ϣⲥ ⲉⲟⲩⲁϩⲯⲩⲭⲏⲛ ⲟⲩⲟϩ
19:5	ⲉⲥⲉⲕⲣⲟⲕϩ]	om
19:5	ⲛ̅ⲧⲉ ⲡⲓⲕⲉⲗⲉⲃⲓⲛ]	ⲛ̅ϫⲉ ⲡⲓⲕⲉⲗⲓⲃⲓ
19:5	ⲛⲟⲩϩ]	ⲛ̅ⲧⲉϥϩⲉⲓ
19:5	ⲙ̅ⲡⲓϣⲉ]	+ ⲟⲩⲟϩ ⲫⲏⲉⲑϩⲓⲧϥ
19:5	ⲛ̅ⲧⲉ ⲩ̅ⲟ]	ⲛ̅ϫⲉ
19:5	ϩⲉⲓ]	om
19:5	ⲉⲃⲟⲗϧⲉⲛ]	ⲉⲃⲟⲗ

19:5	ⲛⲧⲉϥⲙⲁϯ]	ⲛⲧⲉϥϩⲉⲓ
19:6	ⲛⲧⲉϥⲙⲟⲩ]	om
19:6	ⲛϫⲉ ⲫⲁⲓ ⲙⲙⲟⲛ]	ⲟⲩⲟϩ ⲛⲧⲉ ⲫⲁⲓ ⲙⲙⲟⲛ
19:8	ⲛϫⲉ ⲡϭⲟⲓⲥ ⲫⲛⲟⲩϯ]	om
19:8	ⲛⲧⲉϥϯ]	ⲡⲣ ⲟⲩⲟϩ
19:8	ⲫⲏⲉⲧⲁⲩϫⲟⲩ ⲉⲧⲏⲓϥ]	ⲫⲏⲉⲧⲁⲩϫⲱⲩ ⲉⲧ
19:9	ⲟⲩⲟϩ]	om
19:10	ⲡⲉⲕⲕⲁϩⲓ]	ⲡⲓⲕⲁϩⲓ
19:11	ⲛⲧⲉϥϭⲓⲭⲣⲟⲩ]	ⲡⲣ ⲟⲩⲟϩ
19:12	ⲉⲩⲉⲟⲩⲱⲣⲡ]	ⲡⲣ ⲟⲩⲟϩ
19:12	ⲉⲩⲉⲉⲛⲩ]	ⲡⲣ ⲟⲩⲟϩ
19:12	ⲉⲩⲉⲧⲏⲓⲩ]	ⲡⲣ ⲟⲩⲟϩ
19:13	ⲧⲁⲥⲟ]	ⲧⲁⲱ
19:13	ⲛⲁⲑⲛⲟⲃⲓ]	ⲛⲁⲧⲛⲟⲃⲓ
19:15	ⲛⲛⲉⲩϣⲱⲡⲓ]	ⲛⲛⲉϥⲟϩⲓ
19:17	ⲛⲛⲓⲕⲣⲓⲧⲏⲥ]	ⲛⲛⲉⲩϯϩⲁⲡ
19:18	ⲉⲩⲉϣⲓⲛⲓ]	ⲡⲣ ⲟⲩⲟϩ
19:19	ⲉⲣⲉⲧⲉⲛⲉⲱⲗⲓ]	ⲡⲣ ⲟⲩⲟϩ
20:2	ⲉϣⲁⲛ ⲉⲡⲓⲡⲟⲗⲉⲙⲟⲥ]	ⲉⲧⲃⲱⲧⲥ ⲟⲩⲟϩ
20:2	ⲉⲩⲉϧⲱⲛⲧ]	ⲉⲩϧⲱⲛⲧ
20:3	ⲉⲡⲡⲟⲗⲉⲙⲟⲥ]	ⲉⲡⲓ ⲡⲟⲗⲉⲙⲟⲥ
20:5	ⲛⲧⲉ ⲕⲉⲣⲱⲙⲓ]	ⲛⲧⲉϥⲕⲉⲣⲱⲙⲓ
20:5	ⲛⲧⲉϥⲕⲟⲧϥ]	ⲙⲁⲣⲉϥⲕⲟⲧϥ
20:8	ⲉⲣⲉⲡⲉϥϩⲏⲧ]	ⲡⲣ ⲟⲩⲟϩ .
20:8	ⲛⲧⲉϥⲕⲟⲧϥ]	ⲡⲣ ⲟⲩⲟϩ
20:11	ⲛⲧⲟⲩⲁⲟⲩⲱⲛ]	ⲡⲣ ⲟⲩⲟϩ
20:12	ⲛⲧⲟⲩⲓⲣⲓ]	ⲡⲣ ⲟⲩⲟϩ
20:14	ⲉⲕⲉⲟⲩⲱⲙ]	ⲡⲣ ⲟⲩⲟϩ

20:16 ⲚⲚⲈⲦⲈⲚⲦⲁⲚ Ⲇⲉ] ⲚⲎⲈⲦⲁⲚⲈⲢⲰⲚⲒ ⲁⲚ

20:17 ⲠⲒⲄⲈⲢⲄⲈⲤⲈⲞⲤ ⲚⲈⲘ ⲠⲒⲈⲂⲞⲨⲤⲈⲞⲤ] ⲠⲒⲒⲈⲂⲞⲨⲤⲈⲞⲤ ⲚⲈⲘ ⲠⲒⲄⲈⲢⲄⲈⲤⲈⲞⲤ

20:19 ⲂⲈⲚⲒⲠⲒ] ⲂⲈⲚⲒⲠⲒⲒ

20:20 ⲈⲪⲢⲎⲒ ⲈⲬⲈⲚ] ⲈⲪⲢⲎⲒ ⲈⲬⲈⲚ

21:4 ⲈⲤⲚⲀⲨⲦ] ⲦⲈⲤⲚⲀⲨⲦ

21:4 ⲈⲢⲈⲬⲰⲬⲒ] ⲡⲣ ⲟⲩⲟⲍ

21:4 ⲚⲚⲈⲚⲔⲞⲂⲌ] ⲚⲚⲞⲨⲔⲞⲂⲌ

21:5 Ⲭⲱ ⲈⲂⲞⲗ ⲚⲒⲂⲈⲚ ⲚⲈⲘ] om

21:5 ⲀⲚⲦⲒⲗⲞⲄⲒⲀ] ⲦⲀⲚⲦⲒⲗⲞⲠⲀ

21:6 ⲚⲒⲪⲈⲗⲗⲞⲒ] + ⲦⲎⲢⲞⲨ

21:6 ⲪⲎⲈⲦⲀⲨⲬⲈⲬ] ⲪⲎⲈⲦⲀⲨⲬⲰⲔⲒ

21:7 ⲈⲨⲬⲰⲘⲘⲞⲤ] ⲈⲢⲈⲬⲰⲘⲘⲞⲤ

21:8 ⲚⲎⲈⲦⲀⲔⲤⲞⲦⲞⲨ] ⲚⲎⲈⲦⲀⲔⲤⲰⲦⲞⲨ

21:8 ⲰⲠⲒ] + ⲀⲚ

21:10 ⲚⲦⲈⲨⲦⲎⲒ ⲦⲞⲨ] ⲡⲣ ⲟⲩⲟⲍ

21:11 ⲚⲦⲈⲔⲈⲢⲠⲒⲐⲨⲘⲒⲚ] ⲡⲣ ⲟⲩⲟⲍ

21:13 ⲈⲤⲈⲢⲒⲘⲒ] ⲡⲣ ⲟⲩⲟⲍ

21:13 ⲌⲀⲢⲞⲤ] ⲐⲀⲢⲞⲤ

21:14 ⲚⲚⲈⲔⲦⲎⲒⲤ] ⲡⲣ ⲟⲩⲟⲍ

21:15 ⲚⲦⲞⲨⲘⲒⲤⲒ] ⲡⲣ ⲟⲩⲟⲍ

21:16 Ⲛⲧ] ⲉⲧ

21:17 ⲠⲒⲰⲞⲢⲠ ⲘⲘⲒⲤⲒ] ⲎⲠⲒⲰⲀⲘⲒⲤⲒ ⲰⲎⲢⲒ

21:18 ⲚⲦⲞⲨⲦⲤⲂⲰ] ⲡⲣ ⲟⲩⲟⲍ

21:19 ⲈⲢⲈⲈⲚⲨ] ⲡⲣ ⲟⲩⲟⲍ

21:19 ⲚⲈⲘ ⲌⲀ ⲦⲠⲨⲗⲎ ⲚⲦⲈ ⲠⲒⲦⲞⲠⲞⲤ] ⲞⲨⲟⲍ ⲌⲀ ⲚⲒⲢⲰⲞⲨ ⲚⲦⲈ ⲠⲒⲘⲀ

21:20 ⲞⲨⲟⲍ ⲈⲢⲈⲬⲞⲤ] ⲈⲨⲬⲰⲘⲘⲞⲤ

21:20 ⲈⲨⲬⲰⲘⲚⲞⲤ] om

21:22	ⲟⲩⲛⲟⲃⲓ] ⲛⲟⲃⲓ
21:22	ⲛⲧⲉⲧⲉⲛⲁϣⲩ] ϥⲣ ⲟⲩⲟϩ
21:23	ⲛⲛⲉⲡⲉⲩⲥⲱⲙⲁ ⲉⲛⲕⲟⲧ] ⲛⲛⲉⲩⲉⲛⲕⲟⲧ ⲛϫⲉ ⲡⲉⲩⲥⲱⲙⲁ
21:23	ⲛⲛⲉⲧⲉⲛⲥⲱⲩ] ϥⲣ ⲟⲩⲟϩ
22:1	ⲉⲩⲥⲱⲣⲉⲙ] ⲉⲩⲥⲱⲣⲉⲙ
22:2	ⲉⲩⲉϣⲱⲡⲓ] ⲟⲩⲟϩ ⲉⲩⲉϣⲱⲡ ⲓ
22:2	ⲡⲉⲕⲥⲟⲛ 2°] ⲡⲉⲕϣⲛ
22:2	ⲉⲩϩⲉⲛⲧ] ⲙⲡⲉⲩϩⲉⲛⲧ
22:3	ⲛⲧⲁⲕⲟ] ϥⲣ ⲕⲁⲧⲁ
22:5	ⲟⲩⲥϩⲓⲙⲓ] ⲧⲥϩⲓⲙⲓ
22:5	ⲛⲛⲉϩⲱⲟⲩⲧ] ⲛⲛⲉⲩϩⲱⲟⲩⲧ
22:6	ⲓⲉ ϩⲁⲛⲙⲁⲥ ⲓⲉ ϩⲁⲛⲥⲱⲟⲩϩⲓ] ⲟⲩⲙⲁⲥ ⲓⲉ ⲟⲩⲉⲥⲱⲟⲩϩⲓ ⲟⲩⲟϩ
22:6	ⲡⲓⲙⲟϩ] ⲡⲓⲙⲁⲥ
22:7	ⲟⲩⲟⲩⲱⲣⲡ] ⲟⲩⲱⲣⲡ
22:7	ⲛϫⲉ] ⲟⲙ
22:7	ⲛⲁⲕ 2°] ⲉⲣⲟⲕ ⲟⲩⲟϩ
22:8	ⲉⲕⲉⲑⲁⲙⲓⲟ] ϥⲣ ⲟⲩⲟϩ
22:13	ⲛⲧⲉⲩⲙⲉⲥⲧⲱⲥ] ϥⲣ ⲟⲩⲟϩ
22:14	ⲛⲧⲉⲩϩⲓ] ϥⲣ ⲟⲩⲟϩ
22:14	ⲛⲧⲉⲩϫⲉ] ϥⲣ ⲟⲩⲟϩ
22:16	ⲧⲛⲟⲩ] ⲟⲙ
22:17	ⲛⲑⲟⲩ ⲧⲛⲟⲩ] ⲧⲛⲟⲩ ⲛⲑⲟⲩ
22:19	ⲉⲩⲉⲑⲣⲉⲩⲧⲟⲥⲓ] ϥⲣ ⲟⲩⲟϩ
22:20	ϣⲱⲡⲓ] ⲛϣⲱⲡⲓ
22:20	ⲛⲧⲟⲩϣⲧⲉⲙϫⲉⲙ] ϥⲣ ⲟⲩⲟϩ
22:20	ⲙⲉⲧⲡⲁⲣⲑⲉⲛⲟⲥ] ⲛⲟⲩⲙⲉⲧ.
22:21	ⲉⲥⲉⲙⲟⲩ] ϥⲣ ⲟⲩⲟϩ

22:23	ⲟⲩⲁⲗⲟⲩ] ⲁⲗⲟⲩ
22:26	ⲧⲆⲉⲗϣⲁⲓⲣⲓ] ⲛ̄ⲧⲆⲉⲗϣⲁⲓⲣⲓ
22:26	ϭⲓ ⲉⲧⲆⲉⲗϣⲁⲓⲣⲓ] om
22:28	ⲙⲡⲁⲧⲟⲩⲱⲡ] ⲙⲡⲁⲧⲱⲡ
22:28	ⲛ̄ⲧⲉⲩϭⲓⲧⲥ] ϧⲣ ⲟⲩⲟϩ
22:30	ⲛ̄ⲛⲉⲩϭⲱⲣⲡ] ϧⲣ ⲟⲩⲟϩ
23:1	ⲉⲩⲗⲁⲥ] ⲉⲩⲗⲁⲥ
23:6	ⲛ̄ⲛⲉⲕⲧⲁⲓⲉ ⲙⲟⲩⲧ̄] ⲛ̄ⲛⲉⲕⲉⲕⲱⲧ̄
23:7	ⲛ̄ⲣⲉⲙⲛ̄Ⲭⲱⲓⲗⲓ] ⲟⲩⲣⲉⲙⲛ̄Ⲭⲱⲓⲗⲓ
23:8	ⲙⲙⲁϩ Ⲅ̄] ⲙⲙⲁⲩ Ⲅ̄
23:10	ⲉⲩⲉϣⲉⲛⲁⲩ] ϧⲣ ⲟⲩⲟϩ
23:11	ⳓⲣⲏ] ⳓⲣⲉ
23:12	ⲉⲕⲉϣⲉⲛⲁⲕ] ϧⲣ ⲟⲩⲟϩ
23:13	ⲙⲙⲟⲥ] ⲛⲆⲏⲧⲥ
23:13	ⲛⲆⲏⲧⲥ] om
23:14	ⲉⲥⲉϣⲱⲡⲓ] ϧⲣ ⲟⲩⲟϩ
23:16	ⲛⲆⲣⲏⲓ] ⲛ̄ϩⲣⲏⲓ
23:16	ⲛ̄ⲛⲉⲕϩⲉⲆϩⲱⲕⲩ] ⲛ̄ⲛⲉⲕϩⲉⲆϩⲟⲕⲩ
23:20	ⲡⲉⲕⲥⲟⲛ] ⲙⲡⲉⲕⲥⲟⲛ
23:20	ⲛ̄ⲛⲉⲕϣⲁⲡⲩ] ⲉⲕⲉϣⲁⲡⲩ
23:21	ⲉⲩⲉϣⲱⲡⲓ] ϧⲣ ⲟⲩⲟϩ
23:24	ⲉⲕⲉⲟⲩⲉⲙ] ⲉⲕⲉⲟⲩⲱⲙ
23:25	ⲉⲕⲉⲑⲟⲩⲉⲧ] ϧⲣ ⲟⲩⲟϩ
24:1	ⲛ̄ⲧⲉⲩϣⲱⲡⲓ] ϧⲣ ⲟⲩⲟϩ
24:1	ⲁⲥϣⲁⲛϣ̄ⲧⲉⲙϩⲉⲙ] ⲁⲥϣⲁⲛϣ̄ⲧⲉⲙ
24:1	ⲉⲩϣⲏⲩ] ⲉⲩⲙⲏⲩ
24:1	ⲉⲩⲧⲏⲓⲩ] ϧⲣ ⲟⲩⲟϩ
24:3	ⲛ̄ⲧⲉⲩⲙⲉⲥⲧⲱⲥ] ϧⲣ ⲟⲩⲟϩ

24:5	ⲛⲛⲉϥϣⲉ]	ⲛⲛⲉϥⲉϣⲉ
24:5	ⲉⲡⲡⲟⲗⲉⲙⲟⲥ]	ⲉⲡⲓⲡⲟⲗⲉⲙⲟⲥ
24:6	ⲟⲩⲙⲁⲭⲁⲛⲏ]	ⲟⲩⲉⲣⲛⲓ
24:8	ⲉⲧⲟⲩⲛⲁⲍⲉⲛⲍⲉⲛ]	ⲉⲧⲉⲟⲩⲛⲁⲍⲟⲛⲍⲉⲛ
24:9	ⲉⲣⲉⲧⲉⲛⲛⲏⲟⲩ]	ⲉⲣⲉⲧⲉⲛⲉⲑⲛⲏⲟⲩ
24:12	ⲡⲉⲩϩⲍⲃⲟⲥ]	ⲡⲉⲩⳓⲁⲟⲩⲱ
24:13	ⲙⲡⲉⲩϩⲍⲃⲟⲥ 1°, 2°]	— ⲃⲱⲥ
24:13	ⲉⲩⲉⲥⲙⲟⲩ]	ϧⲣ ⲟⲩⲟϩ
24:15	ⲛⲛⲉⲩϣⲟⲩ]	ϧⲣ ⲟⲩⲟϩ
24:15	ⲛⲧⲉⲩϣⲱⲡⲓ]	ϧⲣ ⲟⲩⲟϩ
24:16	ϣⲏⲣⲓ 1°]	ⲛⲓϣⲏⲣⲓ
24:16	ⲓⲱⲧ 2°]	ⲛⲓⲱⲧ
24:17	ⲛⲛⲉⲕⲕⲉⲗⳉ ⲍⲓ]	ⲛⲛⲉⲕⲣⲓⲕⲓ
24:17	ⲛⲛⲉⲕⲉⲗ]	ⲛⲛⲉⲕⲉⲁⲟⲩⲱ
24:17	ⲡϩⲍⲃⲟⲥ]	ⲙⲡⲓϩⲍⲃⲱⲥ
24:17	ⲛⲟⲩⲭⲏⲣⲁ]	ⲛⲧⲉ ⲟⲩⲭⲏⲣⲁ
24:17	ⲛⲁⲟⲩⲱ]	ⲟⲙ
24:18	ⲁⲩⲥⲟⲧⲕ]	ⲁⲩⲥⲱⲧⲕ
24:19	ⲛⲛⲉⲕⲕⲟⲧⲕ]	ϧⲣ ⲟⲩⲟϩ
24:21	ⳓⲱⲗ]	ϣⲱⲗ
25:2	ⲉⲩⲉⲉⲣⲙⲁⲥⲧⲓⲅⲅⲟⲓⲛ]	ϧⲣ ⲟⲩⲟϩ
25:3	ⲉⲣⲱⲟⲩ ⲉϣⲱⲡ ⲇⲉ ⲁϥϣⲁⲛⲧⲟⲩϩⲟ]	ⲟⲙ
25:3	ⲛⲁⲓϣⲁϣ] ⲛⲁⲓ ⲉϣⲱⲡ ⲇⲉ ⲁⲕϣⲁⲛ ⲟⲩⲁϣⲉ ϣⲁϣ
25:5	ⲉⲩⲉⳓⲓⲥ]	ⲉⲩⲉⳓⲓⲧⲥ
25:5	ⲉⲩⲉϣⲱⲡⲓ]	ϧⲣ ⲟⲩⲟϩ
25:9	ⲉⲥⲉⲓ]	ⲉⲥϣⲉⲛⲁⲥ
25:9	ⲉⲥⲉⲉⲣⲟⲩⲱ]	ϧⲣ ⲟⲩⲟϩ

25:10	ⲉⲩⲉⲙⲟⲩϯ] ϧⲣ ⲟⲩⲟϩ
25:11	ⲉⲣϣⲱⲛⲧ] ⲁⲣϣⲟⲛⲧ
25:11	ⲛⲧⲉⲥⲥⲟⲩⲧⲉⲛ] ϧⲣ ⲟⲩⲟϩ
25:12	ⲉⲕⲉϫⲉϫ] ⲉⲕⲉϫⲏϫ
25:13	ⲧⲉⲕⲁⲥⲓⲟⲩⲓⲅ] ⲧⲉⲕⲁⲥⲓⲟⲩⲓ
25:15	ⲛⲁⲗⲏⲑⲓⲛⲟⲛ 2°] ⲁⲗⲏⲑⲓⲛⲟⲛ
25:16	ⲡⲉ ⲛⲧⲉⲛ] ϩⲁⲧⲉⲛ
25:18	ⲛⲏⲉⲧϩⲟⲥⲓ] ⲛⲏⲉⲧⲁⲩϩⲟⲥⲓ
26:1	ϧⲉⲛ ⲟⲩⲕⲗⲏⲣⲟⲥ] om
26:1	ⲛⲧⲉⲕⲉⲣⲕⲗⲏⲣⲟⲛⲟⲙⲓⲛ] ⲛⲧⲉⲩⲉⲣⲕⲗⲏⲣⲟⲛⲟⲙⲓⲛ
26:2	ϧⲉⲛ ⲟⲩⲕⲗⲏⲣⲟⲥ] om
26:2	ⲉⲕⲉϩⲓⲧⲟⲩ ⲉϩⲣⲏⲓ] ⲉⲕⲉⲟⲩⲟⲣⲡⲩ
26:2	ⲉⲟⲩⲕⲁⲣⲧⲁⲗⲗⲟⲛ] ⲉⲡⲓⲕⲁⲣⲧⲁⲗⲗⲟⲥ
26:4	ⲉⲩⲉϭⲓ] ϧⲣ ⲟⲩⲟϩ
26:4	ⲉⲩⲉⲭⲁⲩ] ϧⲣ ⲟⲩⲟϩ
26:5	ⲁⲩϣⲉⲛⲁⲩ] ϧⲣ ⲟⲩⲟϩ
26:5	ⲁⲩϣⲱⲡⲓ 1°] ⲁⲩⲉⲣⲣⲉⲙⲛⲭⲱⲓⲗⲓ
26:5	ⲛⲏⲡⲓ] ⲏⲡⲓ ⲟⲩⲟϩ
26:6	ⲁⲩϯⲙⲕⲁϩ] ϧⲣ ⲟⲩⲟϩ
26:6	ⲟⲩⲉⲛⲧⲉⲛ] ϧⲣ ⲟⲩⲟϩ
26:7	ⲁⲩⲥⲱⲧⲉⲙ] ϧⲣ ⲟⲩⲟϩ
26:7	ⲉⲧⲉⲛⲑⲉⲃⲓⲱ] ⲧⲉⲛⲑⲉⲃⲓⲱ
26:8	ⲟⲩⲛⲓϣϯ ⲛϫⲟⲙ] ⲧⲉⲩϫⲟⲙ ⲛⲟⲩⲛⲓϣϯ
26:10	ⲉⲕⲉⲟⲩⲱϣⲧ] ϧⲣ ⲟⲩⲟϩ
26:12	ⲉⲣⲉⲟⲩⲟⲙⲟⲩ] ⲟⲩⲟϩ ⲉⲣⲉⲟⲩⲱⲙⲟⲩ
26:12	ⲉⲩⲉⲥⲓ] ϧⲣ ⲟⲩⲟϩ
26:14	ⲡⲁⲛⲛⲟⲩϯ] ⲡⲉⲛⲛⲟⲩϯ

26:16	ⲚϨⲢⲎⲒ] ⲚϨⲢⲎⲒ
26:18	ⲚⲀϥⲓ°] ⲚⲀⲕ
26:18	ⲈϥⲞⲚϨ] ⲈϥⲤⲈⲂⲦⲞⲦ
26:18	ⲚⲀⲔ ⲈⲀⲢⲈϨ] ⲚⲦⲈⲔⲈⲀⲢⲈϨ
26:18	ⲈⲚⲈϥⲈⲚⲦⲞⲖⲎ ⲦⲎⲢⲞⲨ] ⲚⲈϥⲈⲚⲦⲞⲖⲎ
27:2	ⲈⲔⲈⲞⲨϪⲞⲨ] ⲡⲣ ⲞⲨⲞϨ
27:3	ⲚϨⲢⲎⲒ Ϩⲓ] ⲈϨⲢⲎⲒ
27:3	ⲚⲒⲰⲚⲒ] ⲚⲀⲒⲰⲚⲒ
27:3	ⲠⲒⲒⲞⲢⲆⲀⲚⲎⲤ ⲈⲘⲎⲢ] ⲈⲘⲎⲢ ⲠⲒⲒⲞⲢⲆⲀⲚⲎⲤ
27:4	ⲚⲀⲒ] ⲚⲎ
27:7	ⲘⲠϬⲞⲒⲤ ⲠⲈⲔⲚⲞⲨϯ°] ⲟⲙ
27:10	ⲈⲔⲈⲒⲢⲒ] ⲡⲣ ⲞⲨⲞϨ
27:13	ⲚⲀⲒ] ⲡⲣ ⲞⲨⲞϨ
27:13	ⲆⲀⲚ] + ⲚⲈⲘ
27:14	ⲈⲦⲈⲈⲢⲞⲨⲰ] ⲡⲣ ⲞⲨⲞϨ
27:14	ⲞⲨⲞϨ] ⲟⲙ
27:15	ⲚⲦⲈϥⲈⲢⲞⲨⲰ] ⲀϥⲈⲢⲞⲨⲰ
27:22	ⲚⲆⲈ ⲠⲒⲤⲢⲀⲎⲖ] ⲠⲒⲖⲀⲞⲤ
27:23	ⲈⲤⲈϢⲰⲠⲒ] + ⲨⲤϨⲞⲨⲞⲢⲦ ⲚϪⲈ ⲪⲎⲈⲐⲚⲀⲈⲚⲔⲞⲦ ⲚⲈⲘ ⲦⲤⲰⲚⲒ ⲚⲦⲈϥ ϨϪⲒⲘⲒ ⲞⲨⲞϨ ⲈⲦⲈϪⲞⲤ ⲚϪⲈ ⲠⲒⲖⲀⲞⲤ ⲦⲎⲢϥ ϪⲈ ⲈⲤⲈϢⲰⲠⲒ
27:25	ⲚⲞⲨⲆⲞⲢⲞⲚ] ⲚⲆⲞⲢⲞⲚ
27:25	ⲈⲦⲀⲔⲞ ⲚⲞⲨⲤⲚⲞϥ ⲚⲀⲦⲚⲞⲂⲒ] ⲈϢⲀⲢⲒ ⲚϮⲮⲨⲬⲎ ⲚⲦⲈ ⲠⲒⲤⲚⲞϥ ⲚⲀⲦⲈⲚϬⲒ
28:1	ⲀⲢⲈⲦⲈⲚϢⲀⲚⲤⲒⲚⲒ ⲈⲘⲎⲢ ⲘⲠⲀⲒⲒⲞⲢⲆⲀⲚⲎⲤ ⲈⲠⲒⲔⲀϨⲒ ⲈⲦⲈ ⲠϬⲞⲒⲤ ⲠⲈⲦⲈⲚⲚⲞⲨϯ ⲚⲀⲦⲎⲒϥ ⲚⲰⲦⲈⲚ] ⲟⲙ
28:2	ⲈⲨⲈⲒ] ⲡⲣ ⲞⲨⲞϨ
28:2	ⲈⲨⲈϪⲈⲘⲔ] ⲈⲨⲈϪⲒⲘⲒ ⲈⲢⲞⲔ
28:2	ⲈϢⲰⲠ ϨⲈⲚ ⲞⲨⲤⲰⲦⲈⲘ] ⲟⲙ

28:3	ⲛⲓⲃⲁⲕⲓ]	ⲧⲃⲁⲕⲓ
28:4	ⲥⲉⲥⲙⲁⲙⲁⲧ]	ⲕⲥⲙⲁⲙⲁⲧ
28:8	ϧⲉⲛ ⲉⲛⲭⲁⲓ]	ⲫⲣ ⲟⲩⲟϩ
28:10	ⲉⲩⲉⲛⲁⲩ]	ⲫⲣ ⲟⲩⲟϩ
28:10	ϥⲧⲟⲃϩ]	ϥⲧⲱⲃϩ
28:11	ⲉⲩⲉⲑⲣⲉⲕⲁϣⲁⲓ]	ⲉⲩⲉⲣⲉⲁϣⲁⲓ
28:11	ⲛⲓⲙⲁⲥ]	ⲛⲓⲙⲓⲥⲓ
28:12	ⲉⲕⲉⲉⲣⲁⲣⲭⲱⲛ]	ⲫⲣ ⲟⲩⲟϩ
28:14	ⲟⲩⲇⲉ]	ⲓⲉ
28:21	ⲉⲩⲉⲑⲣⲉ]	ⲉⲩⲉⲑⲣⲟⲩ
28:24	ⲙⲡⲓϩⲱⲟⲩ]	ⲙⲡⲓⲉϩⲱⲟⲩ
28:24	ϣⲁⲧⲉϥϥⲟⲧⲕ]	ϣⲁⲧⲉⲩⲉⲧⲕ
28:27	ⲛⲧⲉⲕϣⲧⲉⲙϫⲉⲙϫⲟⲙ]	ⲉⲧⲉⲕϣ.
28:33	ⲉⲩⲉⲟⲩⲟⲙⲟⲩ]	ⲉⲩⲉⲟⲩⲱⲙⲟⲩ
28:35	ⲛⲧⲉⲕϣⲧⲉⲙϫⲉⲙϫⲟⲙ]	ⲉⲧⲉⲕϣ.
28:35	ⲛⲗⲟⲁⲕ ⲓⲥϫⲉⲛ]	ⲛⲗⲟⲁⲡ ⲉϫⲉⲛ
28:35	ⲛⲁⲱⲕ]	ϫⲱⲕ
28:38	ⲉⲕⲉⲟⲗⲟⲩ]	ⲉⲕⲉⲱⲗⲟⲩ
28:38	ⲉⲩⲉⲟⲩⲟⲙⲟⲩ]	ⲉⲩⲉⲟⲩⲱⲙⲟⲩ
28:39	ⲉⲕⲉⲉⲣϩⲱⲃ]	ⲫⲣ ⲟⲩⲟϩ
28:39	ⲛⲛⲉⲕⲥⲉ]	ⲛⲛⲉⲕⲉⲥⲉ
28:39	ⲉⲩⲉⲟⲩⲟⲙⲟⲩ]	ⲉⲩⲉⲟⲩⲱⲙⲟⲩ
28:42	ⲉⲩⲉⲟⲩⲟⲙⲟⲩ]	ⲉⲩⲉⲟⲩⲱⲙⲟⲩ
28:44	ⲛⲛⲉⲕϯ ⲛⲁⲩ]	ⲉⲕⲉϯ ⲛⲁⲩ ⲁⲛ
28:45	ⲉⲩⲉⲓ]	ⲫⲣ ⲟⲩⲟϩ
28:45	ⲉⲩⲉⲧⲁϩⲟⲕ]	ⲫⲣ ⲟⲩⲟϩ
28:45	ϣⲁⲧⲟⲩϣⲁⲧⲕ]	ϣⲁⲧⲟⲩϣⲉⲧⲕ

28:48 ⲚⲈⲔⲘⲟⲧ] ⲚⲈⲔⲘⲟⲣⲧ

28:52 Ⲛⲁⲕ] om

28:54 ⲔⲈⲚ ⲩ] ⲔⲈⲚⲔ

28:59 ⲚⲒⲈⲣⲠⲟⲧ] ⲚⲈⲣ.

28:59 ⲈⲧⲈⲚⲌⲟⲧ] ⲈⲧⲈⲚⲌⲟⲧⲒ

28:62 ⲚⲎⲦⲒ] ⲎⲦⲒ

28:64 ⲈⲨⲈⲆⲟⲣⲕ] ⲈⲨⲆⲱⲣⲕ

28:64 ⲚⲎⲈⲦⲈ ⲚⲁⲕⲤⲱⲟⲣⲚ] ⲚⲎⲈⲦⲀⲔⲤⲱⲟⲣⲚ

29:2 ⲚⲈⲘ ⲍ°] om

29:3 ⲈⲐⲚⲀⲀⲨ] ⲈⲐⲚⲀⲈⲨ

29:7 ⲩⲁ ⲡⲁⲒⲘⲁ] ⲈⲡⲀⲒ Ⲙⲁ ⲟⲣⲟⲌ

29:7 ⲚⲐ ⲂⲁⲥⲁⲚ] ⲚⲦⲈ ⲈⲐ ⲂⲁⲥⲁⲚ

29:12 ⲚⲆⲓⲁⲐⲎⲔⲎ] om

29:12 Ⲛⲁⲕ] ⲚⲈⲘⲁⲩ

29:13 ⲚⲦⲈⲨⲤⲈⲘⲚⲎⲦⲕ] — ⲚⲎⲦⲤ

29:13 ⲚⲈⲘ ⲍ°] om

29:15 ⲚⲤⲈ ⲚⲈⲘⲱⲦⲈⲚ ⲁⲚ] om

29:15 ⲘⲡⲀⲒⲘⲁ] + ⲁⲚ ⲟⲩⲦⲈ ⲚⲁⲒ

29:16 ⲈⲦⲀⲚⲤⲒⲚⲒ] ⲈⲦⲈⲚⲤⲒⲚⲒ

29:18 ⲓⲈ ⲟⲩⲡⲁⲧⲣⲓⲁ] ⲟⲩⲘⲈⲦⲒⲱⲦ

29:19 ⲡⲒⲁⲧⲚⲟⲂⲒ] ⲘⲡⲒⲁⲐⲚⲟⲂⲒ

29:20 ⲈⲩⲈⲦⲟⲘⲟⲩ] ⲈⲩⲈⲦⲱⲘⲟⲩ

29:22 ⲧⲄⲈⲚⲈⲁ] ⲧⲔⲈⲄⲈⲚⲈⲁ

29:22 ⲪⲎⲈⲦⲚⲀⲒ] ⲪⲎⲈⲐⲚⲎⲟⲩ

29:22 ⲟⲩⲔⲁⲌⲒ ⲈⲩⲟⲩⲎⲟⲩ] ⲡⲒⲔⲁⲌⲒ ⲈⲩⲎⲟⲩ ⲟⲣⲟⲌ

29:22 ⲈⲆⲱⲦⲈⲚ / ⲚⲆⲈ ⲡⲤⲟⲓⲤ] tr

29:23 ⲈⲩⲆⲈⲩⲆⲱⲩ] ⲈⲩⲆⲈⲣⲆⲱⲩ

29:26 ⲁⲩⲟⲩⲱϣⲧ] ⲫ̄ ⲟⲩⲟϩ

29:28 ⲉⲛⲁⲁⲩ] ⲟⲙ

29:29 ⲛⲉⲧⲉⲛϣⲏⲣⲓ] ⲛⲉⲛϣⲏⲣⲓ

30:2 ⲛⲧⲉⲕⲥⲱⲧⲉⲙ] ⲫ̄ ⲟⲩⲟϩ

30:5 ⲉⲩⲉⲉⲣⲡⲉⲑⲛⲁⲛⲉⲩ] ⲫ̄ ⲟⲩⲟϩ

30:5 ⲉⲩⲉⲑⲣⲉⲕⲁϣⲁⲓ ⲉϩⲟⲧⲉ] ⲉⲩⲉⲁⲓⲧⲕ ⲉⲕⲉⲣϩⲟⲩⲟ ⲉϩⲣⲏⲓ ⲉϫⲉⲛ

30:8 ⲉⲕⲉⲥⲱⲧⲉⲙ] ⲫ̄ ⲟⲩⲟϩ

30:9 ⲛϧⲣⲏⲓ] ⲉϩⲣⲏⲓ

30:9 ⲧⲉⲕⲛⲉϫⲓ] ⲡⲉⲕⲛⲉϫⲓ

30:11 ⲛϩⲟⲩⲟ] ⲛϩⲟⲟⲩ

30:11 ⲥⲟⲩⲏⲟⲩ] ⲥⲟⲩⲉⲓ

30:12 ⲉⲧⲛⲁⲩϣⲉⲛⲁⲩ] ⲉⲧⲛⲁϣⲉⲛⲁⲩ

30:13 ⲛⲧⲉⲩⲑⲣⲉⲛⲥⲱⲧⲉⲙ] ⲫ̄ ⲟⲩⲟϩ

30:14 ⲩ] ⲉⲩ

30:16 ⲉⲣⲉⲧⲉⲛⲉⲁϣⲁⲓ] ϥⲣⲉⲧⲉⲛⲉⲉⲣⲁϣⲁⲓ

30:16 ⲉⲣⲟⲩ] ⲉⲣⲟⲕ

30:17 ⲛⲧⲉⲕⲥⲱⲣⲉⲙ] ⲫ̄ ⲟⲩⲟϩ

30:19 ⲡⲓⲕⲁϩⲓ] ⲙⲡⲓⲕⲁϩⲓ

30:19 ⲡⲱⲛϧ] ⲡⲓⲱⲛϧ

30:19 ⲙⲡⲓⲥⲙⲟⲩ] ⲙⲡⲓⲱⲛϧ

31:2 ⲙⲡⲁⲓⲟⲣⲇⲁⲛⲏⲥ] ⲙⲡⲓⲓⲟⲣ·

31:4 ⲛⲥⲓⲱⲛ] ⲛⲥⲉⲱⲛ

31:5 ⲉⲧⲁⲓϩⲉⲛϩⲉⲛⲑⲏⲛⲟⲩ] ⲉⲧⲁⲓϩⲟⲛϩⲉⲛⲑⲏⲛⲟⲩ

31:6 ϭⲣⲟ] ⲫ̄ ϫⲉ

31:6 ⲛⲛⲉⲩⲭⲁⲕ] ⲛⲛⲉⲩⲉⲭⲁⲕ

31:6 ⲡϭⲟⲓⲥ] ⲫ̄ ϫⲉ

31:6 ⲛⲛⲉⲩⲥⲟϫⲡⲕ] ⲛⲛⲉⲩⲉⲥⲱϫⲡⲕ

31:8 ⲛⲛⲉⲩϫⲁⲕ] ⲛⲛⲉⲩⲉϫⲁⲕ

31:8 ⲛⲛⲉⲩⲥⲟⲇⲡⲕ] ⲛⲛⲉⲩⲉⲥⲱⲇⲡⲕ

31:9 ⲛⲧⲉ ⲡⲓⲥⲣⲁⲏⲗ] ⲛⲧⲉ ⲛⲉⲛϣⲏⲣⲓ ⲙⲡⲓⲥⲗ

31:10 ⲧⲥⲕⲏⲛⲟⲡⲓⲅⲓⲁ] — ⲡⲏⲅⲓⲁ

31:11 ⲡⲓⲧⲟⲡⲟⲥ ⲫⲏⲉⲧⲉ ⲡϭⲟⲓⲥ ⲡⲉⲕⲛⲟⲩϯ ⲛⲁⲥⲟⲧⲡϥ] ⲡⲓⲙⲁ
     ⲫⲏⲉⲑⲛⲁⲥⲟⲧⲡϥ ⲛϫⲉ ⲡⳆⲥ ⲡⲉⲕⲛⲟⲩϯ

31:14 ⲁⲩⲟϩⲓ] ϧⲣ ⲟⲩⲟϩ

31:15 ⲁⲩⲟϩⲓ] ϧⲣ ⲟⲩⲟϩ

31:15 ⲧⲙⲉⲧⲙⲉⲑⲣⲉ] + ⲟⲩⲟϩ ⲁⲩⲟϩⲓ ⲉⲣⲁⲧϥ ⲡⲓⲥⲧⲏⲗⲗⲟⲥ
     ⲛⲉϩⲏⲡⲓ ϩⲓⲣⲉⲛ ⲛⲓⲣⲱⲟⲩ ⲛⲧⲉ ⲧⲥⲕⲏⲛⲏ ⲛⲧⲉ ⲧⲙⲉⲧⲙⲉⲑⲣⲉ

31:20 ⲉⲩⲉⲟⲩⲱⲙ] ϧⲣ ⲟⲩⲟϩ

31:20 ⲉⲩⲉⲟⲩⲱⲙ] + ⲟⲩⲟϩ ⲉⲩⲉⲥⲓ

31:20 ⲟⲩⲟϩ ⲉⲩⲉⲥⲓ] om

31:21 ϫⲉ] om

31:21 ⲁⲣⲓⲣⲓ ⲙⲡⲁⲓⲙⲁ] ⲉⲧⲁⲩⲓⲣⲓ ⲙⲫⲁⲓⲙⲁ

31:28 ϩⲁⲣⲟⲓ] ⲇⲁⲣⲟⲓ

31:29 ⲧⲉⲧⲉⲛⲛⲁⲉⲣⲁⲛⲟⲙⲓⲛ] ⲁⲣⲉⲧⲉⲛⲛⲁⲉⲣ.

31:29 ⲉⲧⲁⲓⲍⲉⲛⲍⲉⲛ] — ⲍⲟⲛⲍⲉⲛ

31:30 ⲛⲙⲁⲩϣⲁ] ⲙⲁⲩϣⲁ

32:5 ⲛⲁⲥⲛⲓ] ⲛⲛⲁⲧⲥⲛⲓ

32:8 ⲁⲩⲥⲉⲙⲛⲓ] ⲁⲩⲥⲉⲙⲛⲏ

32:17 ⲉⲛⲁⲣⲉ ⲛⲟⲩⲓⲟⲧ] ⲉⲛⲁⲉⲣⲉⲛⲟⲩⲓⲟⲧ

32:18 ⲁⲕⲭⲁⲩ] ⲁⲩⲭⲁⲩ

32:20 ⲙⲙⲟⲛ] ⲟⲩⲙⲙⲟⲛ

32:21 ⲫⲏⲉⲧⲉ ⲟⲩⲛⲟⲩϯ] ⲫⲏⲉⲧⲛⲟⲩϯ

32:21 ⲡⲉ 20] ⲛⲉ

32:25 ⲉⲩⲉⲁⲓⲧⲟⲩ] om

32;26 ⲉⲓⲉϫⲟⲣⲟⲩ] ⲉⲓⲉϫⲱⲣⲟⲩ

32:29 ⲉⲕⲁⲧ] ⲕⲁⲧ

32:36 ⲉⲩⲟⲓ ⲛϭⲉⲛⲛⲉ] ⲉⲩϭⲉⲛⲛⲉ

32:38 ⲛⲧⲟⲩⲉⲣⲃⲟⲏⲑⲓⲛ] ⲛⲑⲟⲩⲉⲣ.

32:39 ⲉⲓⲉⲧⲁⲛϩⲟ] — ϩⲱ

32:42 ⲧⲁⲥⲏⲩⲓ] ⲡⲁⲥⲏⲩⲓ

32:42 ⲛϩⲁⲛⲁⲩⲟⲣⲓ] ⲛⲁⲩⲟⲣⲓ

32:46 ⲉⲣⲉⲧⲉⲛⲉϩⲉⲛϩⲉⲛ] — ϩⲟⲛϩⲉⲛ

32:49 ⲛⲁⲃⲁⲣⲓⲙ] ⲁⲃⲁⲣⲓⲙ

33:9 ⲙⲙⲱⲟⲩ] ⲛⲱⲟⲩ

33:10 ⲉⲛⲉⲕⲙⲉⲑⲙⲏⲓ] ⲛⲛⲉⲕⲙⲉⲑⲙⲏⲓ

33:10 ⲟⲩⲥⲑⲟⲓⲛⲟⲩϥⲓ] ⲛⲥⲑⲟⲓⲛⲟⲩϥⲓ

33:10 ⲙⲡⲉⲕϫϥⲟⲓ] — ϫϥⲟ

33:17 ⲉⲩⲉⲧϣⲉⲛϩⲁⲧ] ⲉⲩⲧϣⲉⲛϩⲁⲧ

33:20 ϫⲉ] ⲇⲉ

33:21 ⲉⲧⲉⲩⲁⲡⲁⲣⲭⲏ] ⲧⲉⲩⲁⲡⲁⲣⲭⲏ

33:26 ⲡⲉⲕⲙⲉⲛⲣⲓⲧ] ⲡⲉⲛⲉⲛⲣⲓⲧ

34:6 ⲙⲙⲟⲛ] ⲁⲙⲙⲟⲛ

34:7 ⲛϫⲉ ⲛⲉⲩⲥϥⲟⲧⲟⲩ] ⲛⲛⲉⲩⲥϥⲟⲧⲟⲩ

34:10 ⲥⲟⲩⲱⲛⲩ] ⲥⲟⲩⲱⲛ

These unique readings of Wilkins are significant indicators of his method. The list is too long and the variants too diverse to be explained as accidental. The number of times that ⲟⲩⲟϩ precedes a verb in Bo^W alone is also striking. It is clear that Wilkins used a source other than the extant Coptic mss as the basis for these readings.

The Edition of Lagarde

Bo^L was based on Bo^W and ms D. In the introduction, the editor states that he has corrected what he considers errors in Bo^W, and he also lists the variants between Bo^L and ms D. He questions the truth of Wilkins' claim that he based his edition on three mss. and suggests rather that he most probably used only Huntington 33 = F.

> Die koptische übersetzung des pen-
> tateuchs ist von David Wilkins zu
> London 1731 in kleinem quart her-
> ausgegeben worden, angeblich ex mss
> vaticano, parisiensi et bodleiano,
> in wahrheit wohl nur aus dem 1674
> geschriebenen codex huntingdonianus
> 33, wie schon Woide in Holmes ausgabe
> der LXX im ersten bande auf bogen
> *k4 bemerkt hat.
>   Meine ausgabe dieser übersetzung
> beruht auf dem wilkinsischen drucke
> und nur einem manuskripte, welches
> mir Henry Tattam mit gewohnter
> bereitwilligkeit aus seiner reichen
> sammlung zur verfügung gestellt hat,
> möge mein druck ihm mein dank sein.[11]

In view of the evidence adduced so far, Lagarde's observation concerning the number of mss Wilkins used is inaccurate. Woide's statement applies only to Genesis and cannot be upheld for the entire Pentateuch.[12] Further, the collations of Bo^L which are based on page and line numbers of the edition, are not always trustworthy. It will presently be shown that many readings attested by not only Bo^W and D, but by all the other evidence, have been rejected by Lagarde.

That Bo^L is based on Bo^W can easily be shown. The readings unique to these two editions are listed below as lemma. The variants refer only to mss.

1:19 ⲞⲨⲞⲌ ⲀⲚⲒ ϢⲀ ⲔⲀⲆⲎⲤ ⲂⲀⲢⲚⲎ] om omn

1:40 ⲈⲠⲒϢⲀϤⲈ ⲪⲘⲰⲒⲦ] ϨⲒⲠϢⲀϤⲈ ⲈⲪⲘⲰⲒⲦ   AG'(cvar); ⲠϢⲀϤⲈ ⲈⲪⲘⲰⲒⲦ rell ; D(inc)

3:2 ⲚⲈⲘ ⲠⲈⲨⲔⲀϨⲒ ⲦⲎⲢϤ] om omn

3:2 ⲈⲤⲈⲂⲰⲚ Ị ⲤⲈⲂⲰⲚ   omn

3:12 ⲈⲢⲞⲨⲂⲎⲚ] D(inc) ⲚⲢⲞⲨⲂⲎⲚ rell

3:16 ⲒⲀⲂⲞⲔ] D(inc) ⲀⲂⲞⲔ (c var) rell

3:21 ⲘⲠⲀⲒⲞⲨⲢⲞ] ⲘⲠⲞⲨⲢⲞ omn

3:25 ⲈⲒⲈⲚⲀⲨ] D(inc) ⲚⲦⲀⲚⲀⲨ (c var) rell

4:19 ⲞⲨⲞϨ ⲚⲦⲈⲔϢⲈⲘϢⲒ ⲘⲘⲰⲞⲨ] om omn

4:28 ⲞⲨⲆⲈ ⲘⲠⲀⲨⲞⲨⲰⲘ] om omn

4:38 ⲈϤⲰⲦ] ⲈⲨⲨⲰⲦ omn

4:41 ⲘⲂⲀⲔⲒ] ⲚⲦⲂⲀⲔⲒ B ; ⲦⲘⲂⲀⲔⲒ rell

5:27 ⲚⲎⲈⲦⲈ 1°] ⲚⲦⲈ F ; ⲈⲦⲈ rell

5:27 ⲚⲎⲈⲦⲈ 2°] ⲚⲦⲈ BF ; ⲈⲦⲈ rell

5:31 ⲚⲈⲘⲀⲔ] D(inc) ⲚⲈⲘⲰⲞⲨ rell

6:1 ⲈⲀⲒⲦⲞⲨ] om omn

6:4 ⲚⲎⲈⲦⲈ] D(inc); ⲚⲎⲈⲦⲀ rell

6:4 ⲚⲚⲈⲚϢⲎⲢⲒ] D(inc); ⲈⲦⲈⲚⲚⲈⲚϢⲎⲢⲒ (c var) rell

6:6 ⲚⲎ] ⲚⲀⲒ omn

6:8 ⲞⲨⲞϨ 1°] om omn

6:18 ⲠⲒⲠⲈⲐⲚⲀⲚⲈϤ] ⲘⲠⲈⲐⲢⲀⲚⲀⲨ

6:18 ⲞⲨⲞϨ ⲚⲦⲈⲔϢⲈ ⲈϦⲞⲨⲚ ⲞⲨⲞϨ] om omn

6:22 ⲚⲒⲚⲒϢϮ ⲚⲈⲘ ⲚⲒⲈⲦϨⲰⲞⲨ] ⲈⲚⲀⲚⲈⲨ   omn

6:23 ⲚⲚⲈⲚⲒⲞⲦ] ⲚⲚⲈⲔⲒⲞⲦ omn

6:24 ⲚⲰⲦⲈⲚ] om omn

6:25 ⲞⲨⲞϨ 1°] om omn

7:1 ⲡⲓⲉⲃⲟⲩⲥⲉⲟⲥ] B (inc); ⲡⲓⲉⲃⲟⲩⲥⲉⲟⲥ rell

7:5 ⲛⲓϥⲟⲧⲍ] ⲛⲓϥⲱⲧⲍ

8:4 ⲍⲏⲡⲡⲉ] D (inc); ⲓⲥⲭⲉⲛ H; ⲉ rell

8:7 ⲉⲩⲉⲉⲛⲕ] ⲉⲩⲉϭⲓⲧⲕ Gʹ; ⲉⲩⲉⲥⲟⲧⲡⲕ rell

8:16 ⲛⲉⲕⲉⲍⲟⲟⲩ] ⲛⲓⲉⲍⲟⲟⲩ

8:19 ⲟⲩⲟⲍ ⲛⲧⲉⲕⲟⲩⲱϣⲧ ⲙⲙⲱⲟⲩ] om

9:6 ⲡⲉ] om

9:14 ⲟⲩⲟⲍ ⲛⲧⲁⲭⲉⲣ ⲡⲟⲩⲣⲁⲛ] ⲟⲩⲟⲍ ⲛⲧⲁⲩⲉⲧ ⲡⲟⲩⲣⲁⲛ Gʹ; om rell

9:19 ⲍⲁⲧⲍⲏ ⲙⲡⲓⲭⲱⲛⲧ ⲛⲉⲙ ⲡⲓⲉⲙⲃⲟⲛ] ⲉⲑⲃⲉ ⲡⲭⲱⲛⲧ ⲛⲉⲙ · Gʹ (var); om rell

9:19 ⲟⲩⲟⲍ 2°] om

9:26 ⲟⲩⲟⲍ] om

9:29 ⲛⲉⲙ ⲡⲉⲕⲕⲗⲏⲣⲟⲥ] ⲛⲉⲙ ⲧⲉⲕⲕⲗⲏⲣⲟⲛⲟⲙⲓⲁ Gʹ; om rell

10:15 ⲉⲉⲣⲁⲅⲁⲡⲁⲛ ⲙⲙⲱⲟⲩ] ⲉⲙⲉⲛⲣⲓⲧⲟⲩ

11:16 ⲟⲩⲟⲍ 1°] om

11:24 ϥⲓⲟⲙ ⲉⲧⲥⲁ] om

12:6 ⲛⲉⲙ ⲛⲉⲧⲉⲛϣⲟⲩϣⲱⲟⲩϣⲓ] om

12:6 ⲛⲉⲧⲉⲛⲁⲡⲁⲣⲭⲏ] + ⲛⲏⲉⲧⲉⲧⲉⲛⲛⲁϣϣ ⲓⲙⲙⲱⲟⲩ (c var)

12:6 ⲛⲉⲙ ⲛⲉⲧⲉⲛⲉⲩⲭⲏ ⲛⲉⲙ] ϧⲉⲛ ⲛⲉⲧⲉⲛⲉⲩⲭⲏ

14:21 ⲉⲕⲉⲧ ⲉⲃⲟⲗ] ⲉⲕⲉⲧⲏⲓⲧⲟⲩ Gʹ; om rell

14:25 ⲉⲃⲟⲗ] om

14:25 ⲡⲉⲕⲛⲟⲩⲧ ⲉⲣⲟⲩ] om ⲉⲣⲟⲩ Gʹ; om rell

14:29 ⲛⲏⲉⲧⲉⲕⲉⲓⲣⲓ ⲙⲙⲱⲟⲩ] ⲉⲧⲉⲕⲛⲁⲁⲓⲧⲟⲩ Gʹ; om rell

15:7 ⲟⲩⲓ ⲛⲧⲉ] ⲟⲩⲓ ⲛ Gʹ; om rell

15:7 ϧⲉⲛ ⲡⲓⲕⲁⲍⲓ ϥⲏⲉⲧⲉⲩⲧ ⲙⲙⲟⲩ ⲉⲧⲟⲧⲕ ⲛⲭⲉ ⲡϭⲟⲓⲥ ⲡⲉⲕⲛⲟⲩⲧ] ϧⲉⲛ
ⲡⲓⲕⲁⲍⲓ ⲉⲧⲉ ⲡ̅ϭ̅ⲥ ⲡⲉⲕⲛⲟⲩⲧ ⲛⲁⲧⲏⲓϥ ⲛⲁⲕ Gʹ; om rell

15:8 ϧⲉⲛ ⲟⲩⲟⲩⲱⲙ ⲉⲧⲉⲕⲉⲟⲩⲱⲙ ⲛⲛⲉⲕϫⲓⲝ ⲙⲙⲟⲩ ⲟⲩⲟⲍ] ϧⲉⲛ ⲟⲩⲁⲟⲩⲱⲛ
ⲉⲕⲉⲁⲟⲩⲱⲛ ⲛⲁⲩ ⲛⲧⲉⲕϫⲓⲝ Gʹ; om rell

15:8 ⲌⲰⲤⲞⲚ ⲈⲨⲈⲢⲈⲦⲒⲚ ⲕⲁⲧⲁ] om

15:9 ⲞⲨⲞⲌ] om

15:10 ⲌⲰⲤⲞⲚ ⲈⲨⲈⲢⲈⲦⲒⲚ ⲕⲁⲧⲁ ⲪⲚⲈⲦⲈⲨⲈⲢⲐⲀⲈ ⲘⲘⲞⲨ] ⲘⲪⲚⲈⲦⲈⲨ—
ⲈⲢⲚⲬⲢⲒⲀ ⲘⲘⲞⲨ G' ; om rell

15:10 ⲆⲈ ⲈⲐⲂⲈ ⲠⲀⲒⲤⲀϪⲒ] ϪⲈ ⲞⲨⲎⲒ ⲈⲐⲂⲈ ⲠⲀⲒⲤⲀϪⲒ G' ; om A'

15:11 ⲀⲚⲞⲔ ϯⲌⲞⲚⲌⲈⲚ ⲈⲢⲞⲔ ⲈⲒⲢⲒ ⲘⲠⲀⲒⲤⲀϪⲒ] ⲀⲚⲞⲔ ϯⲌⲞⲚⲌⲈⲚ ⲚⲀⲔ
ⲈⲐⲢⲈⲔⲒⲢⲒ ⲘⲠⲀⲔⲀϪⲒ G'(cvar) ; om A'

15:11 ϦⲈⲚ ⲞⲨⲞⲨⲞⲚ ⲈⲔⲈⲞⲨⲰⲚ ⲚⲚⲈⲔϪⲒϪ] ϦⲈⲚ ⲞⲨⲀⲞⲨⲰⲚ ⲈⲔⲈⲀⲞⲨⲰⲚ
ⲚⲦⲈⲔϪⲒϪ G' ; ⲘⲞⲒ A'

15:11 ⲪⲎⲈⲦϨⲒϪⲈⲚ ⲠⲈⲔⲔⲀϨⲒ] ϦⲈⲚ ⲠⲈⲔⲔⲀϨⲒ G' ; om A'

15:12 ⲚⲢⲈⲘϨⲈ ⲈⲂⲞⲖ ϨⲀⲢⲞⲔ] D inc ; om F ; ⲈⲂⲞⲖ ⲈⲨⲞⲒ ⲚⲢⲈⲘϨⲈ rell

16:12 ⲚⲐⲞⲔ] om

16:12 ⲈⲂⲞⲖϦⲈⲚ 1°] ⲈⲂⲞⲖϦⲞⲨⲚϦⲈⲚ D ; ⲈϦⲞⲨⲚⲈⲂⲞⲖϦⲈⲚ AG' ;
ⲈⲂⲞⲖⲈϦⲞⲨⲚϦⲈⲚ rell

17:8 ⲠϬⲞⲒⲤ ⲠⲈⲔⲚⲞⲨϯ ⲘⲘⲀⲨ] ⲠϬⲞⲒⲤ ⲠⲈⲔⲚⲞⲨϯ ⲈⲘⲞⲨϯ ⲈⲠⲈⲨⲢⲀⲚ
ⲘⲘⲀⲨ G' ; ϥϯ A'

17:11 ⲈⲔⲈⲒⲢⲒ] D inc ; om rell

17:12 ⲈⲨⲞϨⲒ ⲈⲢⲀⲦⲨ ⲈⲨϢⲈⲘϢⲒ ϦⲈⲚ ⲪⲢⲀⲚ ⲘⲠϬⲞⲒⲤ ⲠⲈⲔⲚⲞⲨϯ] ⲪⲚⲈⲦⲞϨⲒ
ⲈⲢⲀⲦⲨ ⲈⲦϢⲈⲘϢⲒ ⲘⲠⲈⲘⲐⲞ ⲠϬⲤ ⲠⲈⲔⲚⲞⲨϯ G' ; om A'

17:14 ⲚⲦⲈⲔϢⲈ] ⲚⲦⲈⲦⲈⲚϢⲦⲈⲘϢⲈ B' ; ⲚⲦⲈⲦⲈⲚϢⲈ rell

17:15 ⲪⲚⲞⲨϯ] ⲠⲈⲔⲚⲞⲨϯ G' ; om A'

17:17 ϨⲒⲚⲀ] ⲞⲨⲆⲈ G' ; om A'

17:19 ⲠⲈⲔⲚⲞⲨϯ] ⲠⲈⲚⲚⲞⲨϯ G' ; om A'

17:19 ⲚⲚⲀⲒⲈⲚⲦⲞⲖⲎ] ⲚⲚⲈⲨⲈⲚⲦⲞⲖⲎ F ; ⲈⲚⲀⲒⲈⲚⲦ. ⲦⲎⲢⲞⲨ G' ; ⲈⲚⲈⲨⲈⲚⲦ. rell

17:20 ϪⲀϬⲎ] ⲈϨⲀϬⲎ G' ; ⲞⲨϪⲀϬⲎ A'

18:14 ⲚⲈⲘ ϨⲀⲚϪⲈⲘⲦⲀⲨ] ⲚⲈⲘ ϨⲀⲚϢⲈⲚϨⲒⲚ G' ; om A'

19:11 ⲛϦⲏⲧⲕ 1°] om

19:11 ⲛⲟⲩϣⲁⲩ] ⲟⲩϣⲁⲩ

19:11 ⲛⲛⲁⲓⲃⲁⲕⲓ] ⲛⲛⲓⲃⲁⲕⲓ

19:13 ⲟⲩⲟϩ 2°] D (inc); om rell

20:3 ⲛⲱⲧⲉⲛ 1°] om

20:5 ⲟⲩⲟϩ ⲛⲧⲉⲩⲕⲟⲧⲩ] om

20:6 ⲟⲩⲟϩ 1° 2°] om

20:6 ⲟⲩⲟϩ ⲛⲧⲉⲩⲕⲟⲧⲩ] om

20:6 ⲛϦⲏⲧⲩ 2°] ⲙⲙⲟⲩ G'; om rell

20:17 ⲉⲣⲉⲧⲉⲛⲉⲁⲓⲧⲟⲩ] ⲉⲣⲉⲧⲉⲛⲁⲓⲧⲟⲩ

21:5 ⲛⲉⲙ ϭⲟϩ ⲛⲓⲃⲉⲛ] om

21:23 ⲉⲣⲉⲧⲉⲛⲉⲕⲟⲥⲩ] ⲁⲣⲉⲧⲉⲛⲕⲟⲥⲩ CF; ⲉⲣⲉⲧⲉⲛⲕⲟⲥⲩ rell

22:7 ⲛⲧⲉⲕⲛⲁⲓ ⲙⲙⲟⲥ ϩⲓⲛⲁ] ϩⲓⲛⲁ ⲛⲧⲉⲕⲁⲛⲁⲓ ⲙⲙⲟⲥ (c var) G';
　　　ϩⲓⲛⲁ ⲛⲧⲉⲕⲛⲁⲓ ⲙⲙⲟⲥ rell

22:7 ϩⲓⲛⲁ ⲛⲧⲉⲩϣⲱⲡⲓ ⲛϫⲉ ⲡⲓⲡⲉⲑⲛⲁⲛⲉⲩ ⲛⲁⲕ] om

22:16 ⲟⲩⲟϩ 2°] deest D; om rell

22:17 ⲛⲗⲱⲓⲭⲓ] om

22:21 ⲛⲧⲉ ⲡⲏⲓ] om

23:9 ⲉⲩϩⲱⲟⲩ] ⲛⲛⲉⲩϩⲱⲟⲩ C; ⲉⲩϩⲱⲟⲩ rell

23:12 ⲟⲩⲙⲁ] D (inc); ⲟⲩⲧⲟⲡⲟⲥ rell

23:19 ⲛⲛⲉⲕϣⲁⲡ] ⲛⲛⲉⲕϣⲉⲧ

23:20 ⲡⲓϣⲉⲙⲙⲟ] + ⲇⲉ

23:20 ⲉⲕⲉϣⲁⲡⲩ] D (inc); ⲉⲕⲉϣⲁⲧⲩ rell

23:20 ⲡⲉⲕⲥⲟⲛ ⲇⲉ ⲛⲛⲉⲕϣⲁⲡⲩ ⲙⲙⲏⲥⲓ] om

24:20 ⲉϭⲱⲗ ⲛⲛⲏⲉⲧϩⲓⲫⲁϩⲟⲩ] ⲉⲥⲣⲓⲧ ⲛⲛⲏⲉⲧϩⲓⲫⲁϩⲟⲩ G';
　　　D (inc); ⲉⲥⲣⲓⲧ ⲛϫⲉ ⲛⲏⲉⲧϩⲓⲫⲁϩⲟⲩ rell

25:19 ⲫⲏⲉⲧⲉ] D inc ; ⲛⲧⲉ F ; ⲉⲧⲉ rell

26:1 ⲫⲏⲉⲧⲉ] ⲛⲧⲉ F ; ⲉⲧⲉ rell

26:12 ⲛⲓⲟⲩⲧⲁⲍ] ⲛⲓⲟⲩⲧⲁⲩⲍ

26:15 ⲫⲏⲉⲧⲁⲕⲧⲏⲓⲩ] ⲧⲁⲕⲧⲏⲓⲩ F ; ⲉⲧⲁⲕⲧⲏⲓⲩ rell

26:16 ⲉⲣⲉⲧⲉⲛⲉⲁⲣⲉⲍ] ⲉⲧⲉⲧⲉⲛⲁⲣⲉⲍ F ; ⲛⲧⲉⲧⲉⲛⲁⲣⲉⲍ rell

26:16 ⲉⲣⲉⲧⲉⲛⲉⲁⲓⲧⲟⲩ] ⲁⲣⲉⲧⲉⲛⲁⲓⲧⲟⲩ BCF ; ⲉⲣⲉⲧⲉⲛⲁⲓⲧⲟⲩ rell

26:17 ⲉⲣⲉⲧⲉⲛⲉⲁⲣⲉⲍ] ⲁⲣⲉⲧⲉⲛⲁⲣⲉⲍ C ; ⲉⲣⲉⲧⲉⲛⲁⲣⲉⲍ rell

26:19 ⲉⲑⲟⲩⲁⲃ] D inc ; ⲉⲩⲟⲩⲁⲃ rell

27:2 ⲫⲏⲉⲧⲉ] ⲉⲧⲉ

27:2 ⲉⲕⲉⲧⲁⲍⲉ ⲛⲟⲩⲛⲓⲩϯ] ⲉⲕⲉⲧⲁⲍⲉ ⲛⲓⲩϯ G ; ⲉⲧⲁⲍⲉ ⲛⲓⲩϯ A'

28:24 ⲟⲩⲟⲍ 1°, 2°] om

28:24 ⲟⲩⲕⲉⲣⲙⲓ] ⲟⲩⲕⲁⲍⲓ

28:24 ⲛϧⲱⲗⲉⲙ] om

28:29 ⲟⲩⲟⲍ 4°] om

28:30 ⲟⲩⲟⲍ 1°] om

28:31 ⲉⲩⲉⲱⲡⲓ 1°] ⲉⲩⲉⲱⲡⲓ

28:31 ⲙⲙⲟⲩ] ⲙⲙⲱⲟⲩ

28:31 ⲡⲉⲕⲉⲱ] ⲡⲉⲕⲟⲓ F ; ⲡⲉⲕⲓⲱ rell

28:32 ⲛⲕⲉⲉⲑⲛⲟⲥ] + ⲛⲣⲱⲙⲓ

28:33 ⲟⲩⲟⲍ] om

28:33 ⲫⲏⲉⲧⲉⲕⲥⲱⲟⲩⲛ ⲙⲙⲟⲩ ⲁⲛ] ⲛⲣⲱⲙⲓ ⲛⲕⲥⲱⲟⲩⲛ ⲙⲙⲟⲩ ⲁⲛ G ; om A'

28:35 ⲛⲁⲕⲉⲗⲓ] ⲛⲉⲕⲃⲁⲗ

28:45 ⲩⲁⲧⲟⲩⲭⲉⲣⲕ ⲩⲁⲧⲟⲩⲧⲁⲕⲟⲕ] ⲩⲁⲧⲉⲩⲧⲁⲕⲟⲕ

28:48 ⲙⲉⲧⲣⲉⲩⲉⲣϣⲁⲉ ⲛⲉⲛⲭⲁⲓ ⲛⲓⲃⲉⲛ] ⲫⲙⲟⲩ

28:53 ⲛⲭⲉ ⲡⲉⲕⲭⲁⲭⲓ] D inc ; + ϧⲉⲛ ⲛⲉⲕⲃⲁⲕⲓ (c var) rell

28:55 ⲍⲱⲥⲧⲉ] ⲍⲱⲥⲇⲉ

28:55 ⲡⲉⲕⲉⲙⲕⲁⲍ] ⲡⲓⲕⲁⲍⲓ

28:55 ⲠⲈⲔⲌⲟⲀⳅⲈⲀ̅] ⲡϪⲟⲀⳅⲈⲀ̅ (ⲥ ⲟⲁⲣ)

28:58 ⲟⲣⲟⳅ] ⲟⲣⲟⳅ ⲧⲱ F ; ⲟⲣⲟⳅ Ⲉⲧⲟⲓ ⲣⲉⲗⲗ

28:59 ⲚⲒⲚⲓⳡⲧ ⲚⲈⲘ] ⲟⲙ

28:60 ⲟⲣⲟⳅ ⲈⳡⲈⲧⲀⲥⲑⲟ] Ⲉ ⲣⲉⲧⲀⲥⲑⲟ

28:63 ⲈⲢⲈⲦⲈⲚⲈⲀ̅ⲱⲣ ⲚⳍⲱⲗⲈⲘ] ⲈⲢⲈⲦⲈⲚⲀ̅ⲱⲣ

28:65 ⲚⲒⲔⲈⲈⲐⲚⲞⲤ] ✝ ⲞⲚ

28:63 ⲚⲚⲈⲦⲈⲚⲦⲞⳓⳅⲞ] ⲚⲚⲈⲦⲈⲚⲔⲈⲐⲎⲚⲞⳓ

28:68 ⲟⲣⲟⳅ ⳍⲟ] ⲟⲙ

29:7 ⲀⲚⳡⲀⲣⲓ Ⲉⲣⲱⲟⳓ] ⲀⲚⲦⲀⲔⲱⲟⳓ

29:9 ⲈⲢⲈⲦⲈⲚⲈⲀⲣⲉⳅ] ⲈⲢⲈⲦⲈⲚⲀⲣⲉⳅ

29:11 ⳡⲀ] ⲟⲙ

29:14 ⲚⲈⲘ ⲚⲀⲓ ⲥⲀⳅⲟⳓⲓ ⳍⲟ] ⲟⲙ

29:18 ⲟⳓⲘⲀⳡⲓ] Ⅾ ⲓⲛⲥ ; ⲟⳓⳡⲀⳡⲓ ⲣⲉⲗⲗ

29:25 Ⲉⳡⲱⲡ] Ⅾ ⲓⲛⲥ ; ⲟⲙ ⲣⲉⲗⲗ

30:9 ⲚⲈⲔⲦⲈⲂⲚⲱⲟⳓⲓ] Ⅾ ⲓⲛⲥ ; ✝ ⲚⲈⲘ ⳆⲈⲚ ⲚⲒⲦⲈⲂⲚⲱⲟⳓⲓ ⲚⲦⲈ ⲠⲈⲔⲔⲀⳅⲓ ⲣⲉⲗⲗ

30:9 ⳆⲈ] Ⅾ ⲓⲛⲥ ; ⲟⲙ ⲣⲉⲗⲗ

31:12 ⲟⲣⲟⳅ ⳍⲟ] Ⅾ ⲓⲛⲥ ; ⲟⲙ ⲣⲉⲗⲗ

32:2 ⲟⳓⲀⲅⲣⲟⲥⲐⲈⲚ] ⲟⳓⲀⲔⲣⲟⲥⲐⲈⲚ

32:4 ⳅⲀⲚⲐⲘⲎⲒ] ⳅⲀⲚⲘⲈⲒ F ; ⳅⲀⲚⲘⲎⲒ ⲣⲉⲗⲗ

32:7 ⲟⲣⲟⳅ ⳍⲟ] ⲟⲙ

32:7 ⲟⲣⲟⳅ ⳍⲟ] ⲟⲙ

32:15 Ⲁⳓⳍⲱⲧ] ⲀⳓⳆⲐⲀⲓ

32:15 ⲟⲣⲟⳅ ⲀⳓⳅⲒⲎⲢⲎⲂ] ⲀⳓⳆⲐⲀⲓ ⲟⲣⲟⳅ ⲀⳓⳅⲒⲑⲢⲎⲂ (ⲥ ⲟⲁⲣ)

32:15 ⲟⲣⲟⳅ ⳍⲟ] ⲟⲙ

32:17 ⲟⲣⲟⳅ ⲈⳓⳆⲀⲉ Ⲁⳓⲓ] Ⲁⳓⲓ ✝ⲚⲞⳓⲚⲎ (ⲥ ⲟⲁⲣ)

32:19 ⲟⲣⲟⳅ ⳍⲟ] ⲟⲙ

32:25 ⲛⲥⲁⲃⲟⲗ] om

32:30 ⲉⲃⲟⲗ] om

32:32 ⲉⲃⲟⲗϧⲉⲛ] ⲟⲩⲉⲃⲟⲗϧⲉⲛ

32:32 ⲛⲭⲟⲗⲏ] + ⲡ F; + ⲡⲉ rell

32:35 ⲉϥϧⲉⲛⲧ] ϥⲁⲧⲩⲉϧⲉⲛⲧ F; ϥϧⲉⲛⲧ rell

32:38 ⲙⲡⲏⲣⲡ] ⲙⲙⲡⲏⲏⲣⲡ F; ⲙⲡⲓⲏⲣⲡ rell

32:39 ϥⲛⲟⲩⲧ] om

32:39 ⲉⲓϧⲱⲧⲉⲃ] ⲉⲧϧⲱⲧⲉⲃ

32:40 ⲉⲓⲉⲱⲣⲕ] ⲛⲧⲁⲱⲣⲕ

32:41 ⲛⲛⲓⲭⲁⲭⲓ] ⲛⲧⲉⲧⲁⲭⲁⲭⲓ F; ⲛⲛⲁⲭⲁⲭⲓ rell

32:47 ϥⲁⲓ ⁱ⁰] ϥⲁⲓ ⲭⲉ ϥⲁⲓ

33:7 ⲉⲕⲉⲓ] ⲉⲧⲉⲓ

33:8 ⲁⲩϧⲱⲟⲩϣ] ⲉⲣϧⲱⲟⲩϣ

33:9 ⲙⲡⲉⲩⲥⲱⲟⲩⲛ] ⲙⲡⲉⲩⲥⲟⲩⲛ F; ⲙⲡⲉⲩⲥⲟⲩⲱⲛ rell

33:13 ⲛⲓⲟⲩⲧⲁϩ] ⲛⲓⲟⲩⲛⲱⲟⲩ Bʹ; ⲛⲓⲟⲩⲛⲟⲩ F; ⲛⲓⲟⲩⲛⲱⲟⲩⲓ rell

33:18 ϧⲉⲛ ⲡⲉⲩⲙⲁⲛϣⲱⲡⲓ] om

33:19 ⲛϩⲁⲛⲉⲑⲛⲟⲥ] + ⲉⲃⲟⲗϧⲉⲛ ⲛⲉⲩⲙⲁⲛϣⲱⲡⲓ

33:21 ⲟⲩⲟϩ ⲁⲩⲛⲁⲩ ⲉⲧⲉϥⲁⲡⲁⲣⲭⲏ] om

33:21 ⲉⲩⲥⲟⲡ] + ⲛⲭⲉ ϩⲁⲛⲁⲣⲭⲱⲛ

33:23 ⲛⲛⲉⲩⲑⲁⲗⲓⲙ] ⲛⲉⲫⲑⲁⲗⲓⲙ

33:24 ⲩⲥⲙⲁⲙⲁⲧ] ⲩⲥⲙⲁⲣⲱⲟⲩ F; ⲩⲥⲙⲁⲣⲱⲟⲩⲧ rell

33:25 ⲙϥⲣⲏⲧ] ⲁⲥⲙϥⲣⲏⲧ

33:26 ϥⲏⲉⲧⲉⲧⲩϣⲓ] ϥⲏⲉⲧⲉⲙⲡϣⲟⲓ

34:1 ⲙⲡⲓⲥⲅⲁ] ⲙϥⲁⲥⲅⲁ

34:1 ΟΥΟϨ 2°] om

34:2 ΝΝΕΥΘΑΛΙΜ] ΝΕΥΘΑΛΙΜ

34:4 ΟΥΟϨ 2°] om

34:6 ΕΤΕΥΚΩϹ] ΕΤΕΥΚΑΙϹΙ

34:6 ΧΑΙ] ΓΕ

34:11 ϪΑΤΕΝ] ϨΕΝ

34:12 ΕΤΑΥΑΙΤΟΥ] ΕΤΑΙΑΙΤΟΥ F ; ΝΗΕΤΑΥΑΙΤΟΥ rell

These readings are based on no known Coptic mss and, while common to Bo[W] and Bo[L], are primarily the work of Wilkins.

There is little doubt that Lagarde used D as he claims. A few places where the reading of Bo[L] and D is unique serve to prove this point.

1:24 ΑΥΜΟΩΥΤϹ = D] ΕΤΑΥΜΟΩΥΤϹ rell

23:1 ΝΤΕ ΠϬΟΙϹ = D] ΜΠϬΟΙϹ rell

25:7 ΜΑϩΡΑΝ = D] ϩϩΡΑΝ G'; ΕϩϩΡΑΝ rell

31:23 ΜΜΟΥ = D] ΕΡΟΥ rell

But Bo[L] also attests many unique readings. These are listed below. An asterisk follows those readings which are not listed in Lagarde's collations.

1:3 ΝϪΕ ΠϬΟΙϹ] D mc; Π͞Ϭ͞Ϲ Ϥ͞Ϯ rell

1:15 ΝϨΑΝΑΝΩϳΟ] ΝϨΑΝΩϳΟ

1:36 ΕΙΕΤ] ΕΤΝΑΤ G'; ΕΥΕΤ rell

1:46 ΑϩΕΤΕΝϨΕΜϹΙ 2°] ΕϩΕΤΕΝϨΕΜϹΙ

2:22 ΜΠΟΥϨΟ] ΜΠΕΥϨΟ Bo[W] ; ΜΠΕΚϨΟ rell

2:34 ΟΥΑΙ ΝϹΑ ΟΥΑΙ] ΟΥΟΝ ΝϹΑ ΟΥΟΝ

2:36 ⲟⲩⲁⲓ ⲛⲥⲁ ⲟⲩⲁⲓ] ⲟⲩⲟⲛ ⲛⲥⲁ ⲟⲩⲟⲛ

3:9 ⲛⲁⲉⲣⲙⲱⲛ] ⲉⲣⲱⲟⲩ

3:9 ⲇⲉ ⲥⲁⲛⲓⲣ] ⲛⲝⲉ ⲥⲁⲛⲓⲣ Bo^W; ⲛⲝⲉ ⲥⲁⲛⲓⲱⲣ B'F; ⲇⲉ ⲥⲁⲛⲓⲱⲣ rell

3:18 ⲟⲩⲟⲛ ⲛⲓⲃⲉⲛ] ⲫⲣ ⲛⲉⲙ

4:3 ⲙⲙⲱⲧⲉⲛ] ⲛⲑⲱⲧⲉⲛ Bo^W; ⲟⲙ rell

4:10 ⲉⲧⲁⲣⲉⲧⲉⲛⲟⲍⲓ] ⲉⲧⲉⲧⲉⲛⲟⲍⲓ Bo^W; ⲉⲧⲁⲧⲉⲛⲟⲍⲓ rell

4:10 ⲍⲁⲧⲍⲏⲓ] ⲍⲁⲧⲁⲍⲏ AG'; ⲍⲁⲧⲍⲏ rell

4:18 ⲛⲧⲉⲃⲧ] ⲛⲧⲉⲃⲛⲏ

4:18 ⲥⲁⲡⲉⲥⲏⲧ] ⲫⲣ ⲛⲉⲙ

4:46 ⲫⲏⲉⲧⲁⲩⲧⲁⲕⲟⲩ] ⲛⲏⲉⲧⲁⲩⲧ· Bo^W; ⲛⲏⲉⲧⲁⲩⲧⲁⲕⲱⲟⲩ (ⲥ var) rell

5:3 ⲛⲉⲧⲁ] Ð inc; ⲛⲛⲉⲧⲁ Bo^W; ⲉⲧⲁ rell

5:3 ⲁⲛ] ⲟⲙ

5:3 ⲉⲣⲉⲧⲉⲛⲟⲛϧ] ⲉⲧⲉⲧⲉⲛⲟⲛϧ C; ⲧⲉⲧⲉⲛⲱⲛϧ rell

6:6 ⲛⲧⲟⲧⲕ *] ⲉⲧⲟⲧⲕ

6:8 ⲉⲕⲉⲙⲟⲩⲣⲟⲩ] ⲉⲕⲉⲙⲟⲩⲣⲟⲩ Bo^W; ⲉⲣⲉⲧⲉⲛⲥϧⲏⲧⲟⲩ (ⲥ var) rell

6:18 ⲙⲡⲓⲡⲉⲑⲛⲁⲛⲉⲩ] ⲙⲡⲉⲑⲣⲁⲛⲁⲩ AG'; ⲟⲙ C; ⲙⲡⲉⲑⲛⲁⲛⲉⲩ rell

6:18 ⲡⲓⲡⲉⲑⲣⲁⲛⲁⲩ] ⲙⲡⲉⲑⲣⲁⲛⲁⲩ Bo^W; ⲟⲙ C; ⲡⲓⲡⲉⲑⲛⲁⲛⲉⲩ rell

7:5 ⲉⲣⲉⲧⲉⲛⲉⲓⲣⲓ] ⲉⲣⲉⲧⲉⲛⲓⲣⲓ

7:5 ⲉⲣⲉⲧⲉⲛⲉⲟⲩⲟⲁⲡⲟⲩ] ⲉⲣⲉⲧⲉⲛⲟⲩⲟⲁⲡⲟⲩ

7:5 ⲉⲣⲉⲧⲉⲛⲉⲕⲟⲣϫⲟⲩ] ⲉⲣⲉⲧⲉⲛⲕ·

7:5 ⲉⲣⲉⲧⲉⲛⲉⲣⲟⲕⲍⲟⲩ] ⲉⲣⲉⲧⲣⲱⲕⲍ B'F; ⲉⲣⲉⲧⲉⲛⲣⲟⲕⲍⲟⲩ rell

7:24 ⲉⲣⲉⲧⲉⲛⲉⲧⲁⲕⲉ *] ⲉⲣⲉⲧⲉⲛⲧⲁⲕⲉ

9:9 ⲛⲍⲙⲉ] ⲛⲍⲙ AD; ⲛⲙ̄ rell

9:12 ⲛⲟⲩⲟⲩⲱⲧⲍ] ⲛⲟⲩ ⲫⲱⲧⲍ G'; ⲛⲟⲩⲱⲧⲍ rell

11:13 ⲛⲓⲉⲛⲧⲟⲗⲏ] ⲛⲉⲩⲉⲛⲧⲟⲗⲏ

12:7 ⲉⲣⲱⲟⲩ ⲛⲉⲙ ⲛⲉⲧⲉⲛⲏⲓ] ⲛⲉⲙ ⲛⲉⲧⲉⲛⲏⲓ ⲉⲣⲱⲟⲩ Bo^W; ⲉⲣⲱⲟⲩ ⲛⲑⲱⲧⲉⲛ
ⲛⲉⲙ ⲛⲉⲧⲉⲛ ⲏⲟⲩ G'; ⲉⲣⲱⲟⲩ rell

12:25 ⲛⲁⲕ] ⲙⲙⲟⲕ

14:6 ⲉⲧⲫⲱⲣⲝ] ⲉⲧⲫⲟⲣⲝ

14:7 ⲛⲏⲉⲧⲫⲱⲣⲝ ⲛⲛⲉⲛϭⲟⲡ] ⲛⲓⲉⲧⲫⲟⲣⲝ ⲉⲛⲉⲛϭⲟⲡ ⲂⲟᵂF ; ⲛⲏⲉⲧⲫⲟⲣⲝ ⲛⲛⲉⲩϭⲟⲡ G' ; ⲛⲏⲉⲧⲫⲟⲣⲝ ⲉⲛⲉⲛϭⲟⲡ rell

14:7 ⲡⲓⲣⲁⲧⲫⲁⲧ] ⲡⲓⲣⲁⲫⲁⲧ

14:8 ⲩⲫⲟⲣⲝ ⳹ⲉⲛ ⲛⲉⲩⲓⲉⲃ] ⲉⲩⲱⲗⲓ ⲛⲉⲩⲓⲉⲃ Ⲃⲟᵂ ; ⲩⲫⲟⲣⲝ ⲛⲛⲉⲩⲓⲏⲃ ⲛⲉⲙ ⲛⲉⲩϭⲟⲡ G' ; ⲉⲩⲩⲱⲣⲝ ⳹ⲉⲛ ⲛⲉⲩⲓⲉⲃ F ; ⲉⲩⲫⲟⲣⲝ ⳹ⲉⲛ ⲛⲉⲩϭⲟⲡ rell

15:7 ⲛⲛⲉⲕⲩⲑⲁⲙ] ⲛⲛⲉⲕⲉⲩⲑⲁⲙ Ⲃⲟᵂ ; ⲛⲛⲉⲕⳋⲟⲇϫⲉⲝ G' ; ⲛⲛⲉⲕⲁⲛⲟⲛⲓ rell

15:7 ⲙⲡⲉⲕⳋⲏⲧ] ⲡⲉⲕⳋⲏⲧ Ⲃⲟᵂ ; ⲡⲉⲕⳋⲟ rell

15:7 ⲛⲛⲉⲕⲛⲁⲩⲧ] ⲛⲛⲉⲕⲉⲛⲁⲩⲧ Ⲃⲟᵂ ; ⲛⲛⲉⲕϥⲉⲛⳋ rell

15:8 ⲉⲟⲩⲩⲁⲡ] ⲙⲡⲟⲩⲩⲁⲡ Ⲃ' ; ⲉⲡⲟⲩⲩⲁⲡ rell

15:10 ⲉⲟⲩⲩⲁⲡ] ⲉⲡⲟⲩⲩⲁⲡ

15:20 ⲥⲁⲙⲉⲛⳋⲏ] ⳋⲁⲧⳋⲏ

16:8 ⲛⲟⲩⲯⲩⲭⲏ] ⲛⲛⲟⲩⲯⲩⲭⲏ

16:13 ⲛⲁⲕ] ⲛⲧⲁⲕ Ⲃⲟᵂ ; om rell

16:19 ⲛⲧⲉ ⲛⲓⲑⲙⲏⲓ *] ⲛⲑⲙⲏⲓ

17:2 ⲉⲭⲓⲣⲓ] ⲉⲩⲓⲣⲓ

17:3 ⲁⲭⲓ] ⲉⲭⲓ Ⲃⲟᵂ ; ⲛⲧⲟⲩⲩⲉⲛⲱⲟⲩ G' ; D inc ; om rell

18:3 ⲉⲃⲟⲗⳋⲓⲧⲉⲛ] ⲉⲃⲟⲗⳋⲉⲛ Ⲃⲟᵂ ; om rell

18:19 ⲉⲓⲉϭⲓⲙⲡⲩⲩⲓⲩ] ⲉⲓⲉϭⲓⲙⲩⲩⲓⲩ

19:6 ⲛⳏⲉ ⲫⲁⲓ ⲙⲙⲟⲛ] ⲟⲩⲟⳋ ⲛⲧⲉ ⲫⲁⲓ ⲙⲙⲟⲛ Ⲃⲟᵂ ; ⲫⲁⲓ ⲙⲙⲟⲛ rell

20:20 ⲉⲕⲉⲕⲟⲧⲩ] ⲉⲕⲉⲕⲱⲧ ADG' ; ⲉⲕⲉⲕⲟⲧ rell

20:20 ⲉⳋⲣⲏⲓ ⲉⲝⲉⲛ] ⲉⳋⲣⲏⲓ ⲉⳉⲉⲛ Ⲃⲟᵂ ; D inc ; om rell

21:20 ⲫⲁⲓ] ⲡⲣ ⲡⲉ

22:25 ⲉⲁⲩⲱⲡ] ⲉⲧⲁⲩⲱⲡ

22:27 ⲉⲁⲩⲱⲡ] ⲉⲧⲁⲩⲱⲡ

23:12 ⲉⲙⲁⲩ] ⲛⲙⲁⲩ

23:18 ⲧⲩⲉⲃⲓⲱ*] ⲩⲉⲃⲓⲱ

24:1 ⲁⲥⲩⲁⲛⲩⲧⲉⲙⲭⲉⲙ] ⲁⲥⲩⲁⲛⲩⲧⲉⲙ– Bo^W (sic!); ⲁⲥⲩⲧⲉⲙⲭⲉⲙ rell

24:6 ⲧⲉ ⲉⲧⲉ] ⲛⲧⲉ Bo^W F ; ⲉⲧⲉ rell

24:15 ⲉⲣⲉⲍⲑⲏⲩ] ⲁⲣⲉ

24:18 ⲁⲩⲥⲟⲧⲕ] ⲁⲩⲥⲱⲧⲕ Bo^W; ⲁⲩⲥⲟⲧⲡⲕ H; ⲁⲩⲥⲟⲛⲧⲕ rell

25:11 ⲉⲣⲩⲱⲛⲧ] ⲁⲣⲩⲱⲛⲧ Bo^W; ⲉⲣⲩⲟⲡⲩ C; ⲉⲣⲩⲟⲛⲧ rell

26:10 ⲛⲉⲣⲱⲧ] ⲉⲣⲱⲧ

26:12 ⲉϭⲓ] ⲉⲕⲉϭⲓ

26:14 ⲙⲡⲓⲧⲁⲗⲉ] ⲙⲡⲓⲧⲁⲗⲟ

27:3 ⲛⲉⲣⲱⲧ] ⲉⲣⲱⲧ

27:4 ⲉⲣⲉⲧⲉⲛⲉⲧⲁⲍⲉ] ⲉⲣⲉⲧⲉⲛⲧⲁⲍⲉ

27:26 ⲉⲁⲓⲧⲟⲩ] ⲉⲧⲁⲓⲧⲟⲩ Bo^W F ; ⲉⲡⲁⲓⲧⲟⲩ rell

27:26 Ϯⲏⲉⲧⲉⲛⲩⲛⲁⲟⲍⲓ] ⲉⲧⲉⲩⲛⲁⲟⲍⲓ Bo^W B'; ⲉⲧⲉⲛⲩⲛⲁⲟⲍⲓ rell

28:10 ⲩⲧⲟⲃⲍ] ⲩⲧⲱⲃⲍ Bo^W; ⲩⲧⲟⲩ rell

28:22 ⲟⲩⲟⲩⲧⲟⲩⲉⲧ] D ms; ⲟⲩⲟⲧⲟⲩⲉⲧ rell

28:25 ⲉⲕⲭⲏⲣ] ⲉⲕⲁⲱⲣ Bo^W F ; ⲉⲭⲁⲱⲣ rell

28:33 ⲉⲕⲉⲉⲣϭⲱⲩⲧ] ⲉⲕⲉϭⲟⲧⲩ Bo^W F; ⲉⲕⲉϭⲟⲧⲡ B'; ⲉⲕϭⲟⲧⲡ rell

28:37 ⲟⲩϤⲓⲣⲓ] ⲉⲩϤⲓⲣⲓ

28:37 ϧⲁ ⲟⲩⲟⲩⲱⲛ ⲛⲥⲁϫⲓ] ϧⲉⲛ ⲟⲩⲱⲛ ⲥⲁϫⲓ

28:40 ⲉⲩⲉⲩⲟⲣⲩⲉⲣ] ⲉⲩⲉⲉⲣⲃⲟⲣⲃⲉⲣ Bo^W AB'F; ⲉⲩⲉⲃⲟⲣⲃⲉⲣ rell

28:45 ⲩⲁⲧⲟⲩⲩⲁⲧⲕ] ⲩⲁⲧⲟⲩⲩⲉⲧⲕ Bo^W; ⲩⲁⲧⲉⲩⲩⲟⲧⲕ G'; ⲩⲁⲧⲉⲩϭⲓⲧⲕ rell

28:46 ϧⲉⲛ] ⲛⲉⲙ ϧⲉⲛ G'; ⲛⲉⲙ rell

28:57 ΝΕΝΧΑΙ] ΝΤΕ ΝΧΑΙ G' ; ΝΤΕ ΕΝΧΑΙ rell

28:58 ϤΑΙΕΤΕ] ϤΑΙ

28:60 ΕϨΡΗΙ] ΕϪΡΗΙ

29:16 ΝΗΕΤΑΡΕΤΕΝΟΕΝΟΥ] —ΡΕΤΕΝΟΙΝΙ Βο^W ; ΜΑΡΗϮ ΕΤΑΡΕΤΕΝΟΙΝΙ (c var) rell

29:19 ΕΙΕΜΟΥΙ] D inc ; ϪΕ ΕΙΜΟΥΙ rell

31:5 ΕΤΑΙϨΕΝϨΕΝΘΗΝΟΥ] ΕΤΑΙϨΟΝϨΕΝΘΗΝΟΥ Βο^W ; ΕΤΑΥϨΟΝϨΕΝΘ· Β'F ; ΕΤΑΥϨΕΝϨΕΝΘΗΝΟΥ rell

31:20 ΝΕΡΩϮ] D inc ; ΕΡΩϮ rell

31:27 ϮΩΤΕΝ] ϮΩΟΡΝ

31:30 ϨΕΝ ΝΙΜΑΥϪ] ϨΕΝ ΜΑΥϪ Βο^W ; ΝΕΜ ΜΑΥϪ F ; ΕΝΕΝΜΑΥϪ rell

32:3 ΝΕΜ] om

32:3 ϮΜΕΤΝΙϢϮ] ΜΕΤΝΙϢϮ

32:6 ΕΤΑΥϪϤΟΚ] ΑΥϪϤΟΚ

32:24 ΟΥΟΠΙΟΘΟΤΟΝΟΟ] ΟΥΕΠΙΟΤΟΤΟΝΟΟ

32:25 ΕϤΕΑΙΤΟΥ] om Βο^W ; ΕΟΑΙΓΟ F ; ΕΟΕΑΙΤΟΥ rell

32:36 ΕΧΕΝ] ΝϪΕ

32:37 ΝϪΕ ϩ°] om

32:37 ΝΗΕΝΑΡΕΤΕΝΧΗ] ΝΗΕΝΑΡΕϨ ΘΗΝΟΥ ΧΗ (c var)

32:41 ΟΝΑϤΜΟΝΙ] ΝΕΟΑΜΟΝΙ Βο^W F ; ΕΟΕΑΜΟΝΙ rell

32:42 ΙΟΧΕΝ] ΕϪΕΝ

32:46 ΝΝΙΟΑϪΙ ϩ°] ΝΝΑΟΑϪΙ Βο^W F ; ΝΝΑΙΟΑϪΙ rell

32:49 ΝΝΑΒΑΥ] ΝΑΒΑΥ

33:4 ϤΗΕΤΑΥϨΕΝϨΩΝΤΕΝ] —ϤϨΕΝϨΩΝ Βο^W Β'F ; —ϤϨΕΝϨΩΝΕΝ rell

33:7 ΜΜΟΥ] ΜΜΩΟΥ

33:8 ΝΗΕΘΟΥΟΝϨ] ΝΙΟΥϨΙ Βο^W F ; ΝΙΟΥΩΝϨ rell

33:9 ΜΜΩΟΥ] ΝΩΟΥ Βο^W ; ΟΥ A ; ΝΟΥ F ; om rell

33:10 ΟΥΟΘΟΙΝΟΥϤΙ] ΝΟΘΟΙ ΝΟΥϤΙ Βο^W ; ΟϤΥΝΟΥϤΙ (c var) rell

33:17 ⲉⲩⲉⲧϣⲉⲛϥⲁⲧ] ⲉⲩⲧϣⲉⲛϥⲁⲧ Bo^W; ⲉⲩⲧϣⲉⲛⲧⲁⲧⲓ rell

33:19 ⲉⲡⲉⲧⲉⲛⲉⲧⲱⲃⲍ] ⲉⲡⲉⲧⲉⲛⲧⲱⲃⲍ

33:19 ⲉⲡⲉⲧⲉⲛⲉϣⲱⲧ] ⲉⲡⲉⲧⲉⲛϣⲩⲱⲧ

33:26 ⲡⲉⲕⲙⲉⲛⲣⲓⲧ] ⲡⲉⲙⲉⲛⲣⲓⲧ Bo^W; ⲛⲧⲉ ⲡⲓⲙⲉⲛⲣⲓⲧ rell

34:7 ⲛⲝⲉ ⲛⲉⲩϭⲫⲟⲧⲟⲩ] ⲛⲛⲉⲩϭⲫⲟⲧⲟⲩ Bo^W; om rell

These unique readings[13] of Bo^L, as well as those of Bo^LW and Bo^W, demonstrate the inadequacy of the Bohairic printed editions. Neither of them utilized all the mss now available, and thus they are not representative of the best possible Bohairic text. Bo^W preserves readings based on a wider manuscript tradition than Bo^L. One should use this text with caution on account of its many spelling mistakes and the large number of unique readings.

Publications After Lagarde's Edition

Since the publication of Bo^L, little has been done to produce a critical edition of the Coptic Pentateuch. A. E. Brooke and N. McLean in their edition of the Old Testament in Greek (1911),[14] collated the text of G for Deuteronomy, along with the texts of Wilkins and Lagarde. In an article in the Journal of Theological Studies,[15] Brooke has also presented a preliminary study of the Bohairic of the Pentateuch. He took samples from each book of the Pentateuch (Gen. 25; Ex. 5, 6; Lev. 16; Num. 28, 29; Deut. 9, 10) and collated the relevant sections from each of the following mss A, C, D, E, F,

G and H. In addition he collated Paris, Bibl., Natl.,
Copte 57, a ms of Genesis and Exodus only. This is a
useful pilot work but too general to be considered de-
finitive. There is an urgent need for a critical edition
of the Bohairic Pentateuch.

References

[1] David Wilkins, S. T. P., _Quinque Libri Moysis Prophetae in Lingua Aegyptia. Ex MSS Vaticano Parisiensi et Bodleiano descripsit ac Latine vertit._ (London: 1731).

[2] Paul de Lagarde, _Pentateuch Koptisch_ . (Leipzig: 1867).

[3] _Ibid._, Neudruck der Ausgabe, 1867. (Osnabrück: Otto Zeller, 1967).

[4] Wilkins, _op. cit._, p. iii

[5] _Ibid._, p. iv

[6] Letter from Mlle. M.-R. Seguy, Conservateur en Chef de la Section Orientale du Département des manuscrits, Bibliothèque Nationale, Paris, February 15, 1974.

[7] Lagarde, _op. cit._, p. iii cf. notes 11 and 12; _Vetus Testamentum Graecum cum variis lectionibus_, ed. R. Holmes, tom. I 1798; H. Hyvernat, "Étude sur les Versions Coptes de la Bible." _Revue Biblique International_, VI. (Paris: 1897), p. 48.

[8] A. E. Brooke, "The Bohairic Version of the Pentateuch." _The Journal of Theological Studies_, 1902, III, p. 261.

[9] See note 5 above.

[10] Brooke, _op. cit._, p. 262.

[11] Lagarde, _op. cit._, p. iii.

[12] The passage in Holmes' introduction runs as follows: "ex collatione facta per Cl. Woidium capitum Geneseos aliquorum in textu Coptico Wilkinsii cum codice Bodleiano, Huntington 33, credibile videtur, Wilkinsium textum codicis, unius scilicet e tribus iis ab ipso nominatis, plerumque in typis expressisse."

[13] For further discussions of these readings see Chapter IV.

[14] A. E. Brooke & N. McLean, Eds., The Old Testament in Greek According to the Text of Codex Vaticanus, Vol. I pt. 3 (Cambridge: 1911).

[15] Brooke, op. cit.

CHAPTER IV

TOWARDS ORIGINAL BOHAIRIC

The Bohairic printed editions have been discussed in
Chapter III. The most significant finding of that chapter
was that many readings appearing in the editions are not
found in any Bohairic mss. The source of these unique
readings must be determined before any further discussion
of the Bohairic mss or editions can proceed. To this
task we now turn.

The unique readings of the editions fall into three
categories: Those unique to (a) Bo^W, (b) Bo^{WL}, (c) Bo^L.

A. <u>Unique Readings of Bo^W</u>

The readings unique to Bo^W are listed on pages 49 to 77.
Almost 50% of these are merely stylistic variants whose
source could not be traced outside the Bohairic tradition.
A sampling of such variants follows. In lists 1-4 below
the variant is that unique to Wilkins.

1. Variations in spelling--itacisms, interchange
of similar consonants, etc.

1:8   ⲚⲚⲈⲧⲉⲛⲓⲟⲧ] ⲚⲚⲈⲧⲉⲛⲓⲟⲣⲧ
1:42   ⲈϨⲞⲘϨⲈⲘ] ⲈϨⲈⲘϨⲰⲘ
2:37   ⲈⲧϮⲐⲞⲩϣ] –ⲐⲰϣ
3:3   ⲈϨⲡϨⲓ] ⲈϪⲡϨⲓ

3:14   ⲡⲓⲙⲟⲅⲁⲑⲓ] ⲡⲓⲙⲁⲅⲁⲑⲓ

4:17   ⲛ̄ϩⲁⲗⲏⲧ] ⲛ̄ϩⲁⲗⲁⲧ

5:28   ϣⲁⲣⲟⲓ] ϩⲁⲣⲟⲓ

6:21   ⲡⲕⲁϩⲓ] ⲡⲓⲕⲁϩⲓ

6:22   ⲛⲓⲉⲧϩⲱⲟⲩ] ⲛ̄ⲏⲉⲧϩⲱⲟⲩ

10:8   ⲛ̄ⲧⲫⲩⲗⲏ] ⲛ̄ⲧⲫⲩⲗⲏ

14:9   ⲉⲣⲉⲧⲉⲛⲉⲟⲩⲟⲙⲟⲩ] ⲉⲣⲉⲧⲉⲛⲉⲟⲩⲱⲙⲟⲩ

19:13 ⲛⲁⲑⲛⲟⲃⲓ] ⲛⲁⲧⲛⲟⲃⲓ

2. Additions or changes of prepositions-- ⲉ for ⲛ , Ⲛ̄ for ⲙ̄, ⲛⲧⲉ for ⲛ̄, etc.

1:7   ⲉⲟⲩⲧⲱⲟⲩ] ϧⲉⲛ ⲟⲩⲧⲱⲟⲩ

3:1   ⲛ̄ⲧⲉ ⲑⲃⲁⲥⲁⲛ] ⲛ̄ⲑⲃⲁⲥⲁⲛ

4:9   ⲛ̄ⲧⲉ ⲛⲉⲕϣⲏⲣⲓ] ⲛ̄ⲛⲉⲕϣ

4:21   ϧⲉⲛ] ⲉⲃⲟⲗϧⲉⲛ

5:9   ⲛ̄ⲧⲉ ⲛⲓⲓⲟⲧ] ⲛ̄ⲧⲉ ⲛⲓⲟⲧ ⲉ-

11:20 ϩⲓ ⲛⲓⲟⲩⲉⲭⲣⲱⲟⲩ] ϩⲓϫⲉⲛ ⲛⲉⲭⲣⲱⲟⲩ

15:7   ⲙ̄ⲡⲉⲕϩⲏⲧ] ⲡⲉⲕϩⲏⲧ

18:3   ⲉⲃⲟⲗϩⲓⲧⲉⲛ] ⲉⲃⲟⲗϩⲉⲛ

19:5   ⲉⲃⲟⲗϧⲉⲛ] ⲉⲃⲟⲗ

21:16 ⲛ̄ⲧ] ⲉⲧ

23:7   ⲛ̄ⲣⲉⲙⲛ̄ϫⲱⲓⲗⲓ] ⲟⲩⲣⲉⲙⲛ̄ϫ

23:13 ⲙⲙⲟⲥ] ⲛ̄ϧⲏⲧⲥ

25:16 ⲛ̄ⲧⲉⲛ] ϧⲁⲧⲉⲛ

28:14 ⲛ̄ⲛⲉⲕϯ ⲛⲁⲩ] ⲉⲕⲉϯ ⲛⲁⲩ ⲁⲛ

3. Changes in verb forms--of tense, person, number, etc.

2:16 ⲁⲥϣⲱⲡⲓ] ⲉⲥⲉϣⲱⲡⲓ

7:2 ⲛⲛⲉⲧⲉⲛⲛⲁⲓ] ⲛⲛⲉⲧⲉⲛⲉⲛⲁⲓ

7:7 ⲧⲉⲧⲉⲛⲉⲣⲕⲟⲩⲝⲓ] ⲧⲉⲧⲉⲛⲕⲟⲩⲝⲓ

7:10 ⲛⲛⲉⲩⲱⲥⲕ] ⲛⲛⲉⲩⲉⲱⲥⲕ

10:16 ⲙⲡⲉⲣⲉⲣⲛⲁϣⲧ] ⲙⲡⲉⲧⲉⲛⲉⲣⲛⲁϣⲧ

15:4 ⲛⲛⲉ ⲟⲩⲟⲛ ϣⲱⲡⲓ] ⲛⲛⲉⲩϣⲱⲡⲓ

15:10 ⲉⲕϯ] ⲉⲕⲉϯ

18:7 ⲉⲑⲣⲉⲩϣⲉⲙϣⲓ] ⲉⲩⲉϣⲉⲙϣⲓ

20:5 ⲛⲧⲉⲩⲕⲟⲧⲩ] ⲙⲁⲣⲉⲩⲕⲟⲧⲩ

27:15 ⲛⲧⲉⲩⲉⲣⲟⲩⲱ] ⲁⲩⲉⲣⲟⲩⲱ

4. Substitution of Coptic synonyms.

1:1 ⲛϩⲁϩ] ⲛϣⲁⲣⲓ

2:10 ⲟⲩⲟϩ] ⲛⲉⲙ

5:8 ⲛⲛⲉⲕⲑⲁⲙⲓⲟ ⲛⲁⲕ] ⲛⲛⲉⲕⲁⲓⲕ

5:14 ⲡⲉⲕⲃⲱⲕ ⲍ·] ⲡⲉⲕⲁⲗⲟⲩ

5:22 ⲥⲛⲟⲩϯ] ⲛⲟⲩⲃ̄

7:19 ϩⲁⲧⲟⲩϩⲏ] ϩⲁⲧⲟⲩϩⲟ

8:17 ⲧⲁⲛⲟⲙϯ] ⲧⲁϫⲟⲙ

11:3 ⲡⲉⲕⲕⲁϩⲓ ⲧⲏⲣⲩ] ⲙⲡⲉⲩⲕⲁϩⲓ ⲛⲓⲃⲉⲛ

14:2 ⲛϩⲉⲧⲭⲏ ⲙⲡⲉⲙⲑⲟ] ⲉⲧϩⲓϫⲉⲛ ⲡϩⲟ

15:4 ⲉⲩⲉⲣϩⲁⲉ] ⲟⲩϩⲏⲕⲓ

28:2 ⲉⲩⲉϫⲉⲙⲕ] ⲉⲩⲉϫⲓⲙⲓ ⲉⲣⲟⲕ

5. Substitution in Wilkins of Coptic equivalents for Greek roots appearing in the mss.

3:29 νάπῃ] †ϩελλοτ Bo^W; ΝΑΠΗ rell

6:16 οὐκ ἐκπειράσεις] ΝΝΕΚΕΡϬωΝΤ Bo^W; ΝΝΕΚΕΡΠΙΡΑϨΙΝ rell

7:19 τοὺς πειρασμούς] ΝΝΙϬωΝΤ Bo^W; ΜΠΙΡΑϹΜΟϹ rell

9:4 ἀγαθήν] ΠΕΘΝΑΝΕϥ Bo^W; ΝΑΓΑΘΟΝ rell

12:21 ὁ τόπος] ΠΙΜΑ Bo^W; ΠΙΤΟΠΟϹ rell

14:7 ἀκάθαρτα] ΕϒϬΑϧΕΜ Bo^W; ϨΑΝΑⲔΑΘΑΡΤΟΝ rell

16:20 τὸ δίκαιον] ΝΘΜΗΙ Bo^W; ΠΑΙ ΔΙΚΕΟΝ rell

19:17 κριτῶν] ΝΝΕϥ†ϨΑΠ Bo^W; ΝΝΙⲔΡΙΤΗϹ rell

21:19 καὶ ἐπὶ τὴν πύλην τοῦ τόπου] ΟϨΟϨ ϨΑ ΝΙΡωΟϒ ΝΤΕ
ΠΙΜΑ Bo^W; ΝΕΜ ϨΑ †ΠΥΛΗ ΝΤΕ ΠΙΤΟΠΟϹ rell

28:14 οὐδέ] ΙΕ Bo^W; ΟϒΔΕ rell

29:18 ἡ πατριά] ΟϒΜΕΤΙωΤ Bo^W; ΟϒΠΑΤΡΙΑ rell

6. Mistakes and minor orthographica in Wilkins

1:17 ΝΝΕΚϨωΠ] ΝΝΕΚϨωτ Bo^W

2:14 †ΠΑΡΕΜΒΟΛΗ] ΠΑΡΕΜΒΟΛΗ Bo^W

2:36 ΜΠΕΒΑΚΙ] ΜΠΕΠΒΑΚΙ Bo^W

3:8 ΝΑΕΡΜωΝ] ΝΤΕ ϙΡΝωΝ Bo^W

5:28 ΝΕΝϹΑϪΙ] ΝΙϹΑϪΙ Bo^W

9:19 ΠΕΜΒΟΝ] ΕΜΒΟΝ Bo^W

9:23 ΕΠΙΚΑϨΙ] ΕΠΟϒΚΑϨΙ Bo^W

11:21 ΝΤΕ ΝΕΤΕΝϣΗΡΙ] ΝΤΕ ΝΕΝϣΗΡΙ Bo^W

14:2 ΕϥωΝϨ] ΕϥϹΕΒΤΟΤ Bo^W

15:8 ΜΜΟϥ] ΝΘΟϥ Bo^W

15:13 ΕϥϣΟϒΙΤ] ΕΤϣΟϒΙΤ Bo^W

15:17 ΜΠΕϥΜΑϣϪ] ΜΠΕⲔΜΑϣϪ Bo^W

20:5 ΝΤΕ ⲔΕΡωΜΙ] ΝΤΕϥⲔΕΡωΜΙ Bo^W

22:28 ⲘⲠⲀⲦⲞⲨⲰⲠ] ⲘⲠⲀⲦⲰⲠ Bo^W

23:8 ⲘⲘⲀⳌ ⲅ̄] ⲘⲘⲀⲨ ⲅ̄ Bo^W

26:18 ⲚⲀⲨ] ⲚⲀⲔ Bo^W

29:12 ⲚⲀⲔ] ⲚⲈⲘⲀⲨ Bo^W

30:9 ⲦⲈⲔⲚⲈⲜⲒ] ⲠⲈⲔⲚⲈⲜⲒ Bo^W

32:18 ⲀⲔⳜⲀⲨ] ⲀⲨⳜⲀⲨ Bo^W

32:42 ⲦⲀⳜⲎⲨⲒ] ⲠⲀⳜⲎⲨⲒ Bo^W

34:10 ⲤⲞⲨⲰⲚ⳨] ⲤⲞⲨⲰⲚ Bo^W

But there remains a large number of readings in the
list of readings unique to Wilkins which are more than
stylistic and which seem to reflect dependence on a
written source. Nearly two hundred readings are
additions of the conjunction ⲞⲨⲟⳌ. A whole phrase is
added or omitted in some instances, e.g., 1:31, 4:20,
9:4(2°), 9:26. In three instances, 27:3, 28:1, and
31:15, the plus or minus in Bo^W is quite substantial.

It seems unusual that Bo^W alone should prepose the
conjunction ⲞⲨⲟⳌ in so many places. The Greek tradition
usually attests ϰαί in these places, and the Coptic mss
often attest a conjunctive verbal form.[1] The possibility
exists that Wilkins could have been influenced by Greek.
If he were, the surest way to determine this would be to
check all of the substantial variants unique to his
edition against all the extant Greek materials. However,
a preliminary indication of the nature of any dependence
on Greek could be obtained if a few of the longer plusses
and minuses of Bo^W were examined against all the Greek

evidence. Such a pilot listing follows. The variant
refers to Bo^W. The Greek support for any of these
variants is also listed.

1:31 εταρετενναγ ερογ Bo] + πιμωιτ ντε πτωογ μπιαμ—
      μορεος Bo^W = B b̲ Sixt

1:45 μπϭοις Bo] + πεκνογ† Bo^W = B C̲" b̲ f̲^-129 s̲
      71'-527 630 407' Compl Sixt

4:11 νεμ ογνιщ† νсмн Bo = B^C C" b̲ d̲ s̲^-343 t̲ 28 55 509
      646 Ald] om Bo^W rell

4:20 αγενθηνογ Bo]+ εβολϩεν πικαϩι νχημι Bo^W = B Sixt

6:5   εβολϩεν πεκϩητ τηρϥ νεμ Bo = 56'] om Bo^W = rell

6:22 ογοϩ εροι νϩοτ Bo] om Bo^W = omn

9:4   αλλα εθβε— f̲in Bo] om Bo^W = B 72 Aeth^C Sixt

27:7 μπϭοις πεκνογ† ι° Bo] om Bo^W = B M O̲' 129-246 54-75'
      71-121-318 z̲ 319 Cyr II 665 Lat_cod 100 Aeth Syh Ald Sixt

27:23 εсεщωπι Bo] + γсϩογορτ νϫε φηεθναενκοτ νεμ τωνι
      ντεγϩιμι ογοϩ εγεχος νϫε πιλαος τηρϥ εсεщωπι Bo^W = B
      f̲^-129 n̲ t̲^-799 Lat_cod 100 Syh Compl Sixt

28:1 αρετενщανсινι εμηρ μπαιιορϫανηс επικαϩι ετε πϭοις πετεν—
      νογ† ναтнιϥ νωτεν Bo] om Bo^W = B b 426 Lat_cod 100 Sixt

31:15 †метмеθρε Bo = 72 C̲-414-422 54 55 Lat_cod 103] + ογοϩ
      αγοϩι ερατγ πιстγλλος νϭηπι ϩιρεν νιρωογ ντε
      †скγνη ντε †метмеθρε Bo^W = rell

These unique readings of Bo^W have one common
feature, they are all attested by the Greek uncial B,
and in one instance only by B. The variants on 1:31,
4:20, 9:4 and 28:1 show that B is the most important

Greek witness in those cases where the unique reading of
Bo^W is supported by a minority of Greek evidence. This
leads one logically to examine the other substantial
unique readings of Bo^W in relation to B. Dependence of
Bo^W on B alone would obviously not be shown if the reading of B is identical to that of the majority of other
Greek mss. A list of minority Greek readings which includes both B and Bo^W would clearly show the nature and
extent of any relationship between these two sources.
Such a list follows. The lemma is the original Greek
text accepted by the writer. The variant presents as
far as possible the reading shared by B and Bo^W together
with any minority Greek support.

2:20 ζομζομμιν Βο] ζοχο(μ)μειν Β; ⲛⲓϫⲟⲭⲟⲙⲙⲓⲛ Bo^W Sixt

2:26 κεδμῶϩ Βο] κεδαιωϩ Β Bo^W Compl Sixt

3:24 κύριε 2° Βο] ο θεος Bo^W B* 527 Sixt

4:45 ἐν τῇ ἐρήμῳ Βο] om Bo^W B 58-707 C" s 392 407' Arab Sixt

5:6 ἐγώ Bo^W B* 963 58 = Ⓜ] + ειμι Bo Sixt rell

5:17 οὐ μοιχεύσεις Bo^W B V 963(vid) b d n t⁻³⁷⁰ 407 509
        Aeth Arm Sa ^Lat_plur Sixt] post φονεύσεις tr Bo rell

9:12 ἐποίησαν Βο] pr και Bo^W B 128 319 ^Lat ClemR 53 Sixt

9:15 πυρί Βο] + εως του ουρανου Bo^W B Sixt

9:22 τὸν θεὸν ἡμῶν Βο] om Bo^W B 58 ^Lat codd 100 104(vid) Sixt

9:26 ἐν τῇ ἰσχύι σου τῇ μεγάλη Βc] om Bo^W B Sa² ³ Sixt

11:31 καὶ κληρονομήσετε αὐτήν Βο] om Bo^W B 963 72 Aeth Sa¹ Sixt

12:14 φυλῶν Bo^W B n ^Lat cod 100 Aeth Sixt] πολεων Bo rell

19:6   καὶ ἀποθάνῃ Bo] om Bo^W B 58-426 <u>C</u>"-131^{mg} 407'
        Lat_{cod} 100 Aeth Arm Sixt

19:10   σου 1° Bo] om Bo^W B 58 <u>f</u>-129 18 Sixt

21:19   καί 3° Bo^W B 414-528 318 Lat_{cod} 100 Arm Sixt] om Bo rell

22:26   τῇ νεάνιδι 2° Bo] om Bo^W B Sa³ Sixt

23:13   ἐν αὐτῷ 2° Bo] om Bo^W B 58-707*(vid) Lat_{cod} 100 Sixt

26:1   ἐν κλήρῳ Bo] om Bo^W B 44-107' Sixt

26:8   ἰσχύι Bo] + αυτου τη Bo^W B Lat_{cod} 100 Sixt

26:18   πάσας Bo] om Bo^W B 71 630^C Sixt

27:3   λίθων Bo] + τουτων Bo^W B Sixt

This list clarifies and strengthens the relationship between Bo^W and B. Three of the variants in
the list are shared by Bo^W and B alone. The other Greek
evidence which shares unique readings with B and Bo^W
consists, with one exception, of cursives and frequently of versional witnesses. Two or three members
of a textual family usually join B, and in the few instances where the minority Greek support is more substantial, the C group and the s group are conspicuous.

The dependence of Bo^W on B should now be clear.
But Wilkins would hardly have had daily access to that
ms in the Vatican. It is more likely that he would have
used the widely known and more readily accessible Sixtine
edition of ms B.[2] This edition of 1587 was based primarily on that great uncial B with its lacunae supple-
mented by other mss.[3] All subsequent Greek editions up
to Largarde (and even beyond) with the exception of

Grabe's,[4] reproduced the text of Sixt. In addition scores
of editions based on Sixt had become available by 1731, so
it is probable that if one owned a copy of the Greek Old
Testament, its text would have been the same as or based
on Sixt. It is reasonable then to assume that if Wilkins
decided to correct his Coptic text on the basis of Greek,
his Greek text would have been the Sixt edition, or at
least one of the several editions based on it. The
following evidence of instances where Bo^W = Sixt against
B validates this assumption.

1:7   μεγάλου Bo (B*)] + ποταμου Bo^W B^c F M 15'-29-82-
       426-707 b̲ 127 130-321'-343' 74'-76 121-318-392
       128-630 407 509 Aeth^{-M} Arab Arm Compl Sixt

2:22   κατεκληρονομήσαν αὐτούς Bo^W Sixt Bo] om αὐτούς
       B 963 c̲I̲$^{,-414}$ ^{422} b̲ n̲ s̲ 71' 28 407 ^{Lat}cod 100 Arm

4:31   fin B* Bo] + κυριος Bo^W B^c 376 C̲'' b̲ 246 s̲$^{-130}$
       z̲$^{-83}$ ^{128} 28 319 407 Aeth Sixt

4:43   Γαδδί Bo^W Sixt] γαδδει B^{txt} V 963 376' 761 129
       85-343 28 407 Sa^2; ⲅⲁⲗⲁⲓⲛ Bo

7:7   ἐξελέξατο B] + κυριος Bo^W 963 o̲I̲ 551* Ald Sixt;
       + ⲡϭⲟⲓⲥ ⲫϯ Bo

7:19   ἡμῶν B*] υμων Bo^W B^c 376 77 b̲ 130^c 799* 18'-83-630
       407 509 ^{Lat}cod 100 Aeth^{-M} Ald Sixt; ⲡⲉⲕ(ⲛⲟⲩϯ) =
       σου Bo Aeth^{ii} Arab Pal

9:15   δύο πλάκες τῶν μαρτυρίων Bo^W Sixt] δυο πλακες Bo B
       G b̲ n̲$^{-127}$ 344^{mg} 318 407 509 ^{Lat}cod 100 104 Aeth Arab
       Arm Sa^1 ^{2} ^{3}

9:27   καὶ ἐπι τὰ ἁμαρτήματα αὐτῶν Bo^W Sixt] και τα αμαρ.

        B V 529 n Aeth Bo$^{G'}$; om Bo$^{A'}$ d^{-106} 346

10:6   Ιακίμ = Bo^W Sixt d t 321' 630'] νακιμ 458 71 = Bo;

        ιακειμ B rell (c var)

11:1   τὰ δικαιώματα αὐτοῦ καὶ τὰς ἐντολὰς αὐτοῦBo^W Sixt]

        τα δικ. αυτουB 52' 646 Aeth^M; και τας εντ. αυτου

        post κρίσεις αὐτοῦ tr 0 407 Arm b Syh; τας εντ.

        αυτου και τα δικ. αυτου= Bo

12:28   τὸ καλὸν καὶ τὸ ἀρεστόν B Bo] το αρ. και το καλ.Bo^W

        75 68'-83-120 Sa^1 Ald Sixt

15:11   τῆς γῆς 1° = Bo B 0 n 30'-343 18'-630'-120 407 509

        Lat$_{cod}$ 100 Arab Syh] + σου Bo^W Sixt rell

19:9   καί 2° B Bo] om Bo^W Sixt

20:17   Ιβουσαῖον καὶ Γεργεσαῖον Bo^W Sixt] γερ. και ιβου.

        Bo B V d^{-44} 127-767 t 407 509

        All the unique readings of Bo^W (excluding the
numerous additions of ⲞⲨⲞⳞ) that are more than stylistic
and do not appear in any of the above lists, are given
below along with the relevant Greek evidence for complete-
ness. These are, in the main, readings of Bo^W based on
majority Greek. The variants in the lists refer, in
general, to the readings of the Bo mss and Bo^L. Any
Greek support for these readings is also listed.

1:21   ὑμῖν 1° Bo^W B] om Bo A F M V 0'' C'' 19 129-246

        y z 55 59 319 407 646 Lat$_{cod}$ 100 Sa$^{1\ 2}$ Syh Ald

        630^C Sixt

2:12 καί 4° Bo^W B Sixt] om Bo

2:14 πολεμιστῶν Bo A*^{vid} 963 F M V 0" n̲ y̲ z̲$^{-122}$ 630
55 59 Aeth^M Arm Sa$^{2\ 3}$ Syh Ald] + αποθνησκοντες
Bo^W B Sixt rell

3:3 αὐτοῦ 1° Bo^W B Sixt] + και πασαν την γην αυτου Bo
77 52-551

3:11 πήχεων 2° Bo^W B Sixt] om Bo 71'-527

3:17 φασγά Bo^W B Sixt] ⲡⲁⲥⲭⲁ Bo

3:21 κύριος ὁ θεός ὑμῶν 1° A 82 707 551* 30-321 799 392
^{Lat}cod 100 Arab] κυριος ο θεος ημων Bo^W B Sixt rell;
Ⲡ̅Ϯ (ο θεος) Bo

3:28 τούτου καί Bo^W B Sixt] om Bo

4:25 καί 1° Bo^W B Sixt] ⲓⲉ (η) Bo

4:38 καί 1° Bo^W B Sixt] om Bo

4:42 φονευτήν Bo^W B^{txt} Sixt] + ος αν φυγη εκει και ζησεται
Bo B^{mg} C" s̲ 18 28 319 509

4:42 τούτων Bo^W B Sixt] om Bo

5:7 πρὸ προσώπου μου Bo^W B M^{txt} 963 376'-707-o̲I̲ 344^{mg}
318-392 83 Ald Sixt] πλην εμου Bo rell

5:22 fin Bo^W A B* F M V 0" 16 f̲$^{-664}$ 54'-75'-767 344 y̲
z̲ 55 59 Iren IV 15 1 ^{Lat}cod 100 Arab Arm Sa$^{1\ 2}$ Syh
Ald Compl Sixt] + κυριος Bo rell

6:11 init Bo^W B Sixt] pr και Bo 376' Arm Aeth Pal

8:20 φωνῆς Bo^W B Sixt] ⲡⲥⲁⲭⲓ Bo

9:6 ὁ θεός σου Bo^W B Sixt] om Bo Sa$^{1\ 3}$

9:28 ἀποκτεῖναι ἐν τῇ ἐρήμῳ Bo] εν τη ερ. απο. αυτους B Bo^{W} 413 Sixt; απο. αυτους εν τη ερ. <u>O</u> (sub ※) Aeth Arm Syh (※)

12:14 σου 3° Bo^{W}] υμων B Arab Sixt; + ⲚⲈⲘ ⲚⲈⲔϢⲞⲨϢⲰⲞⲨϢⲒ Bo

12:31 ὅτι Bo^{W} B Sixt] om Bo 799

13:4 εἰδέναι Bo^{W} B Sixt] ⲈⲚⲀⲨ Bo (ιδειν) 30-85^{mg}-321'^{mg} 407 ^{Lat}cod 100

13:8 ἄκρου 1° 2° Bo^{W} B Sixt] ⲀⲨⲢⲎϪϤ (= αυτου) Bo

13:12 Ἰσραήλ Bo^{W} B Sixt] ⲠⲒⲖⲀⲞⲤ Bo

14:6 δύο χηλῶν Bo^{W} B Sixt] om Bo

14:9 πάντων Bo^{W} B Sixt] om Bo 75

14:16 καί 2° Bo^{W} B Sixt] om Bo

14:21 πᾶν Bo^{W} B Sixt] om Bo

15:13 ἀπό σου Bo^{W} B Sixt] om Bo

15:19 καί ult B Sixt] ⲞⲨⲆⲈ Bo^{W}; om Bo

16:14 ταῖς πόλεσίν σου Bo^{W} B Sixt] ⲦⲈⲔⲂⲀⲔⲒ Bo

17:3 καί 2° Bo^{W} B Sixt] om Bo

17:19 φυλάσσεσθαι Bo] pr και Bo^{W} B F <u>b</u> 58-72 <u>b</u> 527 Aeth Sixt

18:16 ἡμῶν Bo] σου Bo^{W} B 630^{c} Sixt; υμων 53 127* 130 121-527 18-68'-83 Ald

19:2 σου Bo^{W} B Sixt] om Bo <u>b</u> 82-376-618 528 18'-120-630' 319 509 ^{Lat}cod 100 Arm Sa^{3} Arab

19:3 σου 1° Bo^{W} B Sixt] om Bo

19:4 δέ 1° Bo^{W} B Sixt] om Bo V

19:5 συναγαγεῖν ξύλα Bo B Sixt] om Bo^{W}

19:8 ὤμοσεν Bo^{W} B Sixt] + κυριος ο θεος Bo 82 C'' s 28 319 407 509 646 Arm Aeth Sa^{3}

21:5 ἀντιλογία Bo^{W} B Sixt] pr ⲭⲱ ⲉⲃⲟⲗ ⲛⲓⲃⲉⲛ ⲛⲉⲙ Bo

21:6 πᾶσα Bo^{W} B Sixt] om Bo

21:17 υἱόν Bo^{W} B Sixt] om Bo d Arm

22:3 κατά Bo^{W} B Sixt] om Bo 29 Arm

22:16 fin Bo^{W} B Sixt] + ϯⲛⲟⲩ Bo

22:17 νῦν αὐτός Bo^{W} B Sixt] tr Bo A F M oI' f^{-246} 30' y 55 59 319 Lat$_{Aug}$ Deut F

24:16 τέκνων 1° Bo^{W} B Sixt] ϣⲏⲣⲓ Bo; τεκνον 30

26:2 σοί Bo^{W} B Sixt] + εν κληρω Bo A F M V oI' (707 inc) 131^{c} f^{-129} 121-318 z^{-630c} 59 319 Lat$_{cod\ 100}$ Sa^{3}

26:14 τοῦ θεοῦ μου Bo] του θεου ημ. Bo^{W} B Sixt

26:18 εἶπεν = Bo^{W} B 957 n Aeth Sa^{16} Sixt] + σοι Bo rell

27:14 ἐροῦσιν Bo^{W} B Sixt] + ⲟⲩⲟϩ Bo

27:22 ὁ λαός Bo^{W} B Sixt] ⲡⲓⲥⲣⲁⲏⲗ Bo

27:25 πατάξαι ψυχήν Bo^{W} B Sixt] ⲉⲧⲁⲕⲟ Bo

28:3 ἐν πόλει Bo^{W} B Sixt] ⲛⲓⲃⲁⲕⲓ Bo

29:11 σήμερον Bo^{W} B Sixt] pr ⲛⲇⲓⲁⲑⲏⲕⲏ Bo

29:21 ἡ ἑτέρα Bo^{W} B Sixt] om Bo

30:19 τὴν ζωήν 2° Bo^{W} B Sixt] την ευλογιαν Bo A oI b 56' 127 30'-85-343'^{mg} 18'-120-630' 55 407 509 646

31:6 ὅτι Bo^{W} B Sixt] om Bo

31:9 τῶν υἱῶν Ισραήλ Bo^{W} A B 413 71-527-630^{c} Sixt] om υἱῶν Bo 58 Lat Luc Athan I 96 om τῶν rell

32:15 καὶ ἐνεπλήσθη Bo^{W} B Sixt] tr post κορήσουσιν Bo

B. Unique Readings of Bo[LW]

The 179 readings unique to both editions are listed
on pages 79 to 86 . Sixty-one of these cannot be shown to
derive from a source outside Bohairic, being merely
stylistic in nature. Seventy-five of the remaining 118
readings consist of variant forms of readings attested by
the Bohairic mss. But there remain 43 readings in the
editions which are based on no known Bohairic mss.

All the unique readings to both editions are
essentially unique readings of Wilkins since Lagarde's
edition is based on Wilkins. It has been demonstrated
that the basis of the unique readings of Bo[W] is the
Sixtine edition of the text of B. One can thus assume
that that source was also the Greek basis for the readings
unique to both editions. A comparison of those 43 unique
readings of Bo[LW] not found in the Bohairic mss is given
below, together with all the Greek evidence .

1:19   ⲚⲀⲚ Bo] + ⲞⲨⲞⲌ ⲀⲚⲒ ⲰⲀ ⲔⲀⲀⲎⲤ ⲂⲀⲢⲚⲎ Bo[LW] = omn

3:2   ⲠⲈⲨⲖⲀⲞⲤ ⲦⲎⲢⲨ Bo = 130-321-346] + ⲚⲈⲘ ⲠⲈⲨⲔⲀⲌⲒ
        ⲦⲎⲢⲨ Bo[LW] = B Sixt rell

4:19   ⲘⲘⲰⲞⲨ 1° Bo] + ⲞⲨⲞⲌ ⲚⲦⲈⲔⲰⲈⲘⲰⲒ ⲘⲘⲰⲞⲨ Bo[LW] = omn

4:28   ⲘⲠⲀⲨⲤⲰⲦⲈⲘ Bo] + ⲞⲨⲆⲈ ⲘⲠⲀⲨⲞⲨⲰⲘ Bo[LW] = omn (c var)

6:1   ⲈⲢⲰⲞⲨ Bo] + ⲈⲀⲒⲦⲞⲨ Bo[LW] = omn

6:8   ⲈⲔⲈⲚⲞⲢⲞⲨ Bo = d[-106]] pr ⲞⲨⲞⲌ Bo[LW] = B Sixt rell

6:18   ⲚⲀⲔ Bo] + ⲞⲨⲞⲌ ⲚⲦⲈⲔⲰⲈ ⲈⲂⲞⲨⲚ ⲞⲨⲞⲌ Bo[LW] = omn
        (c var)

109

6:24   ⲀⲨⲌⲞⲚⲌⲈⲚ Bo = 46^{II}-52-313-615 767 319 646] +
       ⲚⲰⲧⲈⲚ Bo^{LW} = B Sixt rell

6:25   init Bo] pr ⲞⲨⲞⲌ Bo^{LW} = omn

8:19   ⲚⲦⲈⲔⲰⲈⲘϢⲒ ⲘⲘⲰⲞⲨ   Bo = B* C'' s^{-343} 630 28 319
       Lat$_{cod}$ 104] + ⲞⲨⲞⲌ ⲚⲦⲈⲔⲞⲨⲰⲰⲦ ⲘⲘⲰⲞⲨ Bo^{LW} = B^{c}
       Sixt rell

9:19   ⲀⲨⲤⲰⲦⲈⲘ Bo] pr ⲞⲨⲞⲌ Bo^{LW} = omn

11:16 ⲚⲦⲈⲔⲒ Bo] pr ⲞⲨⲞⲌ Bo^{LW} = omn

11:24 ϢⲀ 2° Bo] + ϤⲒⲞⲘ ⲈⲦⲤⲀ Bo^{LW} = omn

12:6   ⲚⲈⲦⲈⲚⲊⲗⲓⲗ Bo = B(deest) F^{txt} (c F^{mg}) V b 75'
       669 txt] + ⲚⲈⲘ ⲚⲈⲦⲈⲚϢⲞⲨϢⲞⲨϢⲒ Bo^{LW} = rell

15:8   ⲈⲞⲨϢⲀⲠ Bo] + ⲌⲞⲤⲞⲚ ⲈⲨⲈⲢⲈⲦⲒⲚ ⲔⲀⲦⲀ Bo^{LW} = omn
       (c var)

15:9   ⲈϤⲈϢϢ Bo] pr ⲞⲨⲞⲌ Bo^{LW} = omn

16:12 ⲆⲈ 1° Bo = omn] + ⲚⲐⲞⲔ Bo^{LW}

19:11 ϢⲰⲠⲒ ⲚⲒϨⲏⲦⲔ Bo^{LW} = B 121 68'-83-630^{c} Ald Sixt]
       ϢⲰⲠⲒ Bo = rell

20:3   ⲈⲨⲈϪⲞⲤ Bo] + ⲚⲰⲦⲈⲚ Bo^{LW} = omn

20:5   ⲘⲀⲢⲈϤϢⲈⲚⲀϤ Bo] + ⲞⲨⲞⲌ ⲚⲦⲈϤⲔⲞⲦϤ Bo^{LW} = omn (c var)

21:5   ⲀⲚⲦⲒⲗⲞⲄⲒⲀ ⲚⲒⲂⲈⲚ Bo] + ⲚⲈⲘ ϬⲞⲌ ⲚⲒⲂⲈⲚ Bo^{LW} = omn

22:7   ⲈⲔⲈϬⲒⲦⲞⲨ ⲚⲀⲔ Bo] + ⲌⲒⲚⲀ ⲚⲦⲈϤϢⲰⲠⲒ ⲚϪⲈ ⲠⲒⲠⲈⲐⲚⲀⲚⲈϤ
       Bo^{LW} = omn

22:17 ⲚⲌⲀⲚⲤⲀϪⲒ   Bo] + ⲚⲗⲰⲒϪⲒ Bo^{LW} = omn

22:21 ⲚⲒⲢⲰⲞⲨ Bo = B b n 68'-120 407 509 Lat$_{cod}$ 100 Arm]
       + ⲚⲦⲈ ⲠⲎⲒ Bo^{LW} = Sixt rell (c var)

23:20 ⲈⲔⲈϢⲀⲠϤ ⲘⲘⲏⲤⲒ Bo = 58 314 W^{I}-458 509] + ⲠⲈⲔⲤⲞⲚ
       ⲆⲈ ⲚⲚⲈⲔⲰⲀⲠϤ ⲘⲘⲏⲤⲒ Bo^{LW} = B Sixt rell

28:24 ⲟⲩⲕⲉⲣⲏⲓ Bo] pr ⲟⲩⲟ︦ Bo[LW] = omn

28:24 ⲛⲧⲉⲩⲧⲁⲕⲟⲕ Bo = b̲. Lat_Isid Fid II 10 7] pr ⲟⲩⲟ︦ Bo[LW] = B Sixt rell

28:24 ⲛⲧⲉⲩⲧⲁⲕⲟⲕ Bo] + ⲛ︦ⲭⲱⲗⲉⲙ Bo[LW] = B Sixt

28:29 ⲛ︦ⲛⲉⲩϣⲱⲡⲓ Bo = 16] pr ⲟⲩⲟ︦ Bo[LW] = B Sixt rell

28:30 ⲉⲕⲉⲟⲗⲥ Bo] pr ⲟⲩⲟ︦ Bo[LW] = omn

28:33 ⲉⲕⲉⲉⲣϭⲱⲩⲧ Bo] pr ⲟⲩⲟ︦ Bo[LW] = omn

28:59 ⲉⲣⲟⲓ Bo] + ⲛ︦ⲛⲓϣϯ ⲛⲉⲙ Bo[LW] = omn

28:68 ⲉⲣⲉⲧ Bo] pr ⲟⲩⲟ︦ 2° Bo[LW] = omn

29:11 ⲛ︦ⲧⲱⲧⲉⲛ ⲛⲉⲙ Bo] + ϣⲁ Bo[LW] = omn

29:14 ⲛ︦ⲧⲁⲓⲇⲓⲁⲑⲏⲕⲏ Bo] + ⲛⲉⲙ ⲛⲁⲓⲕⲁϩⲟⲩⲓ Bo[LW] = omn (c var)

32:7 ϥⲛⲁⲧⲁⲙⲟⲕ Bo] pr ⲟⲩⲟ︦ Bo[LW] = omn

32:7 ⲥⲉⲛⲁϫⲟⲥ Bo] pr ⲟⲩⲟ︦ Bo[LW]

32:15 ⲁⲩϣⲉⲛⲁϥ Bo] pr ⲟⲩⲟ︦ Bo[LW] = omn

32:19 init Bo] pr ⲟⲩⲟ︦ Bo[LW] = omn

32:25 init Bo] pr ⲛ︦ⲥⲁⲃⲟⲗ Bo[LW] = omn c var

32:39 ⲕⲉⲟⲩⲁⲓ Bo] + ϥⲛⲟⲩⲧ Bo[LW] = omn

33:18 ⲓⲥⲁⲭⲁⲣ Bo] + ϧⲉⲛ ⲡⲉϥⲙⲁⲛϣⲱⲡⲓ Bo[LW] = omn (c var)

33:21 init Bo] pr ⲟⲩⲟ︦ ⲁⲩⲛⲁⲩ ⲉⲧⲉϥⲁⲡⲁⲣⲭⲏ Bo[LW] = omn (c var)

34:1 ⲁⲩⲧⲁⲙⲟⲩ Bo] pr ⲟⲩⲟ︦ Bo[LW] = omn

34:4 ⲁⲓⲧⲁⲙⲉ Bo = A M F* V 29-376' f̲ 767 71-121-392 319 646* Lat_cod 100 Arm Compl] pr ⲟⲩⲟ︦ Bo[LW] = B Sixt rell

The above list shows that the majority of these readings of Bo[LW] is based on all the Greek evidence.

There are a few significant minority readings, however,
which further demonstrate that Bo[LW] depended on Sixtine,
e.g., 8:19, 19:11, 22:21 (here Sixt attests the reading
while B omits it), 28:24. The omission by the Bohairic
mss is supported in a few instances by some Greek mss,
but these are usually minority readings, and the families
are not consistent. See for example, 3:2, 6:8, 6:24, 8:19,
12:6, 23:20, 28:24, 34:4.

The 75 readings of Bo[LW] which have some support
in the Bo mss were checked, and in every instance the
reading of the editions was the equivalent to Sixt. A
few typical examples from that list follow. The variant
refers to the Bohairic mss.

2:37 ⲓⲁⲃⲟⲕ (c var) Bo[LW] B Sixt] pr ⲉⲁⲡⲛⲱⲛ Bo

3:2 ⲉⲥⲉⲃⲱⲛ Bo[LW] Sixt] ⲥⲉⲃⲱⲛ Bo = 53 630

3:16 ⲓⲁⲃⲟⲕ (c var) Bo[LW] B Sixt] ⲁⲃⲟⲕ Bo D inc

3:21 ⲙⲡⲁⲓⲟⲩⲣⲟ Bo[LW] Sixt] ⲙⲡⲓⲟⲩⲣⲟ Bo = 630

5:31 ⲛⲉⲙⲁⲕ Bo[LW] B Sixt] ⲛⲉⲙⲱⲟⲩ Bo = 619 D(inc)

6:22 ⲛⲓⲱⲧ ⲛⲉⲙ ⲛⲓⲉⲧⲍⲱⲟⲩ Bo[LW] B Sixt] ⲉⲛⲁⲛⲉⲩ Bo

6:23 ⲛⲛⲉⲛⲓⲟⲧ Bo[LW] B Sixt] ⲛⲛⲉⲕⲓⲟⲧ Bo; (ⲛⲛⲉⲧⲉⲛⲓⲟⲧ)
      414[c] 54 799 55 59

8:4 ⲍⲏⲡⲡⲉ Bo[LW] B Sixt] D(inc); ⲓⲥⲭⲉⲛ Ꜧ; ⲉ Bo

8:16 ⲛⲉⲕⲉⲍⲟⲟⲩ Bo[LW] = B* ⲥ'·-551 ⲥ-730 28 319 ₒ46 Aeth[-c]
      Compl Sixt] ⲛⲓⲉⲍⲟⲟⲩ Bo = 53'-56' 75' 72; om rell

9:29 ⲛⲉⲙ ⲡⲉⲕⲕⲗⲏⲣⲟⲥ Bo[LW] B Sixt] ⲛⲉⲙ ⲧⲉⲕⲕⲗⲏⲣⲟⲛⲟⲙⲓⲁ G' =
      b 71'-527 59 Sa[2] 3 12 Compl; om A'

12:6   ⲛⲉⲧⲉⲛⲁⲧⲁⲣⲭⲏ ⲃⲟ[LW] ⲃ Sixt] + ⲛⲏⲉⲧⲉⲧⲉⲛⲛⲁϣⲩ ⲙⲙⲱⲟⲩ ⲃⲟ

14:25   ⲡⲉⲕⲛⲟⲩϯ ⲉⲣⲟⲩ ⲃⲟ[LW] ⲃ Sixt] ⲡⲉⲕⲛⲟⲩϯ ⲅ' = 381' b 246
        407 Arm Arab Syh; om Λ'

15:10   ϩⲟⲥⲟⲛ ⲉⲩⲉⲣⲉⲧⲓⲛ ⲕⲁⲧⲁ ⲫⲏⲉⲧⲉⲩⲉⲣϩⲁⲉ ⲙⲙⲟⲩ ⲃⲟ[LW] = ⲃ b
        d t Sixt] ⲙⲫⲏⲉⲧⲉⲩⲛⲭⲣⲓⲁ ⲙⲙⲟⲩ ⲅ' = rell; om Λ'

17:8   ⲡϬⲟⲓⲥ ⲡⲉⲕⲛⲟⲩϯ ⲙⲙⲁⲩ ⲃⲟ[LW] = ⲃ Cyr I 331 [Lat]cod 100
        Sixt] ⲡϬⲟⲓⲥ ⲡⲉⲕⲛⲟⲩϯ ⲉⲙⲟϣⲧ ⲉⲡⲉⲩⲣⲁⲛ ⲙⲙⲁⲩ ⲅ' = rell;
        ⲫϯ Λ'

17:12   ⲉⲩⲟϩⲓ ⲉⲣⲁⲧⲩ ⲉⲩϣⲉⲙϣⲓ ϧⲉⲛ ⲫⲣⲁⲛ ⲙⲡϬⲟⲓⲥ ⲡⲉⲕⲛⲟⲩϯ ⲃⲟ[LW]
        ⲃ Sixt] ⲫⲏⲉⲧⲟϩⲓ ⲉⲣⲁⲧⲩ ⲉⲩϣⲉⲙϣⲓ ⲙⲡⲉⲙⲑⲟ ⲡϬⲟⲓⲥ ⲡⲉⲕⲛⲟⲩϯ
        ⲅ'; om Λ'

17:19   ⲡⲉⲕⲛⲟⲩϯ ⲃⲟ[LW] = ⲃ b ⲱ[I] 54'-75 321'[mg] 407' [Lat]cod 100
        Luc Athan I 7 Arm Sa[3] Sixt] ⲡⲉⲛⲛⲟⲩϯ ⲅ'; om Λ'; τον
        θεον αυτου (ⲡⲉⲩⲛⲟⲩϯ) rell

19:11   ⲛⲛⲁⲓⲃⲁⲕⲓ ⲃⲟ[LW] Sixt] ⲛⲛⲓⲃⲁⲕⲓ ⲃⲟ

28:24   ⲟⲩⲕⲉⲣⲙⲓ ⲃⲟ[LW] Sixt] ⲟⲩⲕⲁϩⲓ ⲃⲟ

28:33   ⲫⲏⲉⲧⲉⲕⲥⲱⲟⲩⲛ ⲙⲙⲟⲩ ⲁⲛ ⲃⲟ[LW] ⲃ Sixt] ⲛⲣⲱⲙⲓ ⲛⲕⲥⲱⲟⲩⲛ
        ⲙⲙⲟⲩ ⲁⲛ ⲃⲟ

28:35   ⲛⲁⲕⲉⲗⲓ ⲃⲟ[LW] ⲃ Sixt] ⲛⲉⲕⲃⲁⲗ ⲃⲟ

C.   Unique Readings of Bo[L]

The list of readings unique to Bo[L] appears on pages
86 to 91. Sixty-six of the 111 readings are merely stylistic in nature--inner Bohairic variants which cannot be
traced to a Greek source. The following 20 of the remaining 45 consist of instances where the reading of Bo[L] is
a slight variant of that of Bo[W], and would seem to be

based on it: 3:9(2°), 6:8, 6:18(1° & 2°), 12:7, 15:7(1°, 2° & 3°), 16:13, 17:3, 18:3, 20:20, 24:18, 27:26, 28:10, 28:45, 31:5, 33:9, 33:17, 34:7.

Another 15 of the unique readings of Bo^L are clearly based on Greek because, in these instances, Bo^W and the Bo mss attest a different reading from Bo^L and the Greek mss. The variant refers to the reading of Bo^W and Bo. Any Greek support for such readings is also listed.

1:3   NΧE ΠϬOIC Bo^L] ΠϬC ΦϮ Bo D(inc)

2:22   MΠOYϪO Bo^L] MΠEЧϪO Bo^W = 528* (c pr m) 125; MΠEKϪO
       Bo

3:9   NΑEPMWN Bo^L] EPWOY Bo

3:18   OYON NIBEN   Bo^L] pr OYOϨ Bo

4:18   NTEBT Bo^L] NTEBNH Bo

4:18   CΑΠECHT Bo^L] pr NEM Bo

4:46   ΦHETAЧTAKOЧ Bo^L B Sixt] NHETAЧTAKOЧ Bo^W = B*
       963 426 d^{-125} n 74'-76 Arm Sa^2 Syh; NHETAЧTAKWOY
       Bo (c var)

11:13 NIENTOΛH Bo^L = B Aeth Sixt] NEЧENTOΛH Bo = rell

16:19 NTE NIΘMHI Bo^L] NΘMHI Bo

28:46 ϦEN Bo^L = B 75' 71-527 646 Sixt] NEM ϦEN
       G' = rell; NEM Bo^W Bo^Λ'

31:30 ϦEN NIMAЩϪ Bo^L= B Sixt] ϦEN MAЩϪ Bo^W; NEM MAЩϪ
       F: ENENMAЩϪ Bo

32:36 EϪEN Bo^L] NΧE Bo

32:42   ⲓⲥⲭⲉⲛ Bo^L] ⲉⲭⲉⲛ Bo

32:46   ⲛⲛⲓⲕⲁⲝⲓ 2° Bo^L] ⲛⲛⲁⲕⲁⲝⲓ Bo^W F; ⲛⲛⲁⲓⲕⲁⲝⲓ Bo

33:7   ⲙⲙⲟⲩ Bo^L] ⲙⲙⲱⲟⲩ Bo

    This list reveals that most of the unique readings
of Bo^L which are based on Greek are based on the unified
Greek tradition. There are two instances (11:13, 28:46)
where the text of Lagarde is in agreement with B and
Sixt against the majority tradition. This similarity of
reading seems purely coincidental.

    Eight significant unique readings of Bo^L remain,
and these appear to be mistakes of Lagarde in some cases,
but in others to be deliberate changes on the part of the
editor. The variant is the unique reading of Bo^L.

17:2   ⲉⲩⲓⲣⲓ Bo] ⲉⲣⲓⲣⲓ Bo^L

    Largarde used the third plural apparently for sty-
listic reasons. He conceived of the man or the woman
"doing evil" not as two separate personalities either of
which could function as subject of the sentence, but
rather as a plural entity (the man and the woman), hence
the plural verb.

20:20   ⲉⲕⲉⲕⲟⲧ Bo] ⲉⲕⲉⲕⲟⲧⲩ Bo^L

    A resumptive particle ⲩ is added to complete the
sense.

29:16   ⲙⲁⲫⲏϯ ⲉⲧⲁⲡⲉⲧⲉⲛϭⲓⲛⲓ   Bo (ⲛⲏⲉⲧⲁⲡⲉⲧⲉⲛϭⲓⲛⲓ   Bo^W)
        ⲛⲏⲉⲧⲁⲡⲉⲧⲉⲛϭⲉⲛⲟⲩ Bo^L

    A resumptive particle ⲟⲩ is again added to complete
the sense.

29:19 ⲬⲈ ⲈⲒⲘⲞⲱⲒ Bo D(inc)] ⲈⲒⲈⲘⲞⲱⲒ Bo^L 509 ^{Lat}codd 92
94 96

Lagarde considered the use of a second ⲬⲈ redundant.

31:27 ⲦⲤⲰⲞⲨⲚ Bo] ⲦⲤⲰⲦⲈⲚ Bo^L

Lagarde uses ⲤⲰⲦⲈⲚ "to hear" for ⲤⲰⲞⲨⲚ "to know."
A possible orthographical mistake, but either reading can
make sense. No reason for the editor's choice is obvious.

32:3 ⲘⲈⲦⲚⲒⲱϯ Bo] ⲚⲈⲘ ⲦⲘⲈⲦⲚⲒⲱϯ Bo^L

Lagarde supplies the conjunction and definite
article, for reasons not clearly obvious. No Coptic or
Greek manuscript supports this emendation.

32:6 ⲀⲨⲬⲀϥⲞⲔ Bo] ⲈⲦⲀⲨⲬⲀϥⲞⲔ Bo^L = ^{Lat}cod 330 Psalt Moz
Verec Cant II 6 Aeth Arm

The extra relative "ⲈⲦ" supplied by Lagarde seems
unnecessary. The meaning "father who created you" is
absent in the Greek or Coptic mss.

33:26 ⲚⲦⲈ ⲦⲒⲘⲈⲚⲢⲒⲦ Bo (ⲦⲈⲘⲈⲚⲢ. Bo^W)] ⲦⲈⲔⲘⲈⲚⲢⲒⲦ Bo^L

The reading of the Bohairic mss is identical with
all the Greek evidence. The addition of the possessive
prefix by Lagarde could have been a mistake.

It should now be clear that the Bohairic of the
printed editions was influenced by Greek. Since our
objective is first of all to arrive at original Bohairic,
and thereafter to assess its value as a witness to the
Greek of the third-fourth century A.D., all those unique
readings of the editions based on Greek will have to be

disregarded. In fact, the critic is advised, in the absence of a critical edition, to consult the oldest and
most complete ms of the Bohairic Pentateuch, G, for an
accurate picture of Bohairic.

Certain broad guidelines for reconstructing original Bohairic from the editions may, however, be drawn.
For practical reasons, the edition of Lagarde may serve
as a point of departure, but only as corrected on the
basis of manuscript evidence. Readings unsupported by
mss are to be closely scrutinized and only to be allowed
credence when the text of the mss is clearly corrupt.
In Deuteronomy, no such reading has been found which
must be called corrupt.

No rule of thumb can be followed concerning the
original text when the ms evidence is divided; as every
text critic knows, the majority rule or counting heads
is an irrelevancy in textual decision. The mss divide
into two families and the writer believes that the better
text is in most cases to be found in the group G'. Each
instance must, of course, be studied by itself in the
light of such standards as the syntactical patterns of
Bohairic in general, the style of Bohairic in Deuteronomy,
and what is particularly the case in Deuteronomy of
parallel passages.

A number of difficult decisions have to be made
where the manuscript evidence is divided. Examples of

such instances are listed below with the accepted reading
underlined. The reasons for the decision are given after
each variant.

1:36 δώσω] ειετ Bo^L; ε̱τ̱ν̱α̱τ G'; εγετ rell

The reading of the G' group is chosen not only
because it is the oldest, but because it alone preserves
a future. The reading of the A' group ("rell") makes
poor sense in this context, since Caleb would hardly
have given the land to himself. Then too, a similar
translation of δώσω is attested in vs 39.

6:18 τ̱ὸ̱ ̱ἀ̱ρ̱ε̱σ̱τ̱ὸ̱ν̱ ̱κ̱α̱ὶ̱ ̱τ̱ὸ̱ ̱κ̱α̱λ̱ό̱ν   B 963 426 551 ḇ
      54'-75'-767 ẕ Arm Sa Ald Sixt = A G'] αρεστον et
      καλον tr rell = Bo^{LW}; ΜΠΕΘΝΑΝΕϤ ΝΕΜ ΠΙΠΕΘΝΑΝΕϤ
      Bo rell

The reading of the G' group is again chosen be-
cause, in context, it is the only one which makes sense.
The majority of Bohairic mss attests a dittography of
ΠΕΘΝΑΝΕϤ = καλόν

8:7 εἰσάξει σε] ΕϤЕΕΝΚ Bo^{LW}; Ε̱Ϥ̱Е̱Ϭ̱Ι̱Τ̱Κ̱ G'; ΕϤΕСΟΤΠΚ A'

The G' reading is best suited to the context. The
A' reading makes poor sense here.

9:12 χώνευμα] ΝΟΥΟΥΩΤ2 Bo^L; ΝΟΥϤΩΤ2 G'; Ν̱Ο̱Υ̱Ω̱Τ̱2̱ rell

The A' reading is chosen because it better fits
the Greek. The verb χοανεύω describes the action of
casting (metal) into a mould. The Coptic verb ΟΥΩΤ2
describes the same action. The reading of the G' group,

ϥⲱⲧⲍ, means to engrave or to carve. The meanings over-
lap and either verb could be original. It seems likely
that the error was a copyist's somewhere in the Bohairic
transmission history.

12:7 ὑμεῖς καὶ οἱ οἶκοι ὑμῶν = G'] ⲛⲉⲙ ⲛⲉⲧⲉⲛⲏⲓ Bo^{LW};
om A'

The G' reading is certainly original Bohairic.
The later Bohairic mss tended to shorten the text for
reasons not always obvious.

15:8 καθότι ἐνδεεῖται] ⲕⲁⲧⲁ ϥⲛⲉⲧⲉⲩⲉⲣⲣⲟⲁⲉ Bo^{LW}; ⲕⲁⲧⲁ
ⲙϥⲏⲉⲧ. G'; ⲕⲁⲧⲁ ⲉϥⲏⲉⲧ. A'

The difference in the reading of G' and A' is
slight, and that of G' was chosen simply because of its
age.

17:8 κύριος ὁ θεός σου ἐπικληθῆναι τὸ ὄνομα αὐτοῦ ἐκεῖ
= G'] κυριος ο θεος σου εκει B Sixt = Bo^{LW}; ⲫϯ A'

The dependence of the editions on Sixt is obvious
here, whereas the G' group alone preserves original
Greek. The reading of the A' group is again shorter than
G'.

22:7 καί] ⲛⲧⲉⲕⲛⲁⲓ ⲙⲙⲟⲥ ⲍⲓⲛⲁ Bo^{LW}; ⲍⲓⲛⲁ ⲛⲧⲉⲕⲁⲛⲁⲓ
ⲙⲙⲟⲥ G' (c var); ⲍⲓⲛⲁ ⲛⲧⲉⲕⲛⲁⲓ ⲙⲙⲟⲥ A'

This addition by the Bohairic is present (c var)
in all the mss. The reading of the G' group is almost
certainly a scribal error; accordingly, the reading of
the A' group is accepted.

24:20 καλαμήσασθαι τὰ ὀπίσω σου] ⲈⲤ̄ⲱⲗ ⲚⲚⲎⲈⲦⲌⲒⲪⲀⲌⲞⲨ Bo[LW]

ⲈⲤⲢⲒⲦ ⲚⲚⲎⲈⲦⲌⲒⲪⲀⲌⲞⲨ G'; D(inc); ⲈⲤⲢⲒⲦ ⲚⲆⲈ ⲚⲎ-

ⲈⲦⲌⲒⲪⲀⲌⲞⲨ rell

    The difference in the reading of the G' group and
the A' group is minimal, and that of G' was again chosen
on account of its age.

27:2 στήσεις σεαυτῷ . . . μεγάλους] ⲈⲔⲈⲦⲀⲌⲈ ⲚⲞⲨⲚⲒⲱϯ

Bo[LW]; ⲈⲔⲈⲦⲀⲌⲈ ⲚⲒⲱϯ G'; ⲈⲦⲀⲌⲈ ⲚⲒⲱϯ A'

    The reading of the A' group was probably the result
of parablepsis on ⲉ.

28:46 καὶ ἐν = G'] εν B 75' 71-527 646 = Bo[L]; ⲚⲈⳘ rell

    Only the G' group preserves original Greek, whereas
the A' group is again witness to a shorter reading.

    Only after one has arrived at original Bohairic
can one proceed to analyze its meaning for original Greek.
We now proceed in the following chapters to an evaluation
of and description of the textual place of Bohairic
within the Greek tradition.

References

[1] This term refers to the verbal prefixes ΝΤϵ- ΝΤⲹ
cf. A Mallon, Grammaire Copte (Beruit 1926) p.117f. These
forms are often used without a preceding conjunction in
Bohairic. In Deut, they occur with and without free conjunctions (see Chapter 5). Wilkins also preposes ⲟⲩⲟϩ to
all the other verbal prefixes.

[2] The following edition by van Ess was used. Vetus
Testamentum Graecum iuxta Septuaginta Interpretes ex autoritate Sixti Quinti Pontificis Maximi editum iuxta Exemplar Originale Vaticanum. Romae: editum Studio. Leandri
van Ess, Lipsiae, (1835). Comparison of this printed
edition with a photocopy of the original Sixt was made
possible thanks to Prof J. W. Wevers.

[3] The mss which were probably used are discussed by
H. B. Swete, An Introduction to the Old Testament in Greek.
Cambridge Univ. Press (1914) p. 181. A short list of edi-
tions based on Sixt appears in this work also.

[4] Septuaginta Interpretum, Tomus I, continens Octa-
teuchum quem ex Antiquissimo Codice Alexandrino Accurate
Descriptum . . . edidit Johannes Ernestus Grabe. S. T. P.
Oxonii e theatro Sheldoniano MDCCVII.

Chapter V

TRANSLATION TECHNIQUE

This chapter discusses some elements of Bohairic
as a translation from Greek in order to facilitate inter-
pretation of the subsequent discussion of the place of
Bohairic within the Greek textual tradition. A knowledge
of elementary Coptic and an extensive knowledge of Greek
is assumed throughout.

The differences in the grammatical and syntactical
structures of Greek and Bohairic create problems for the
translator and for the text critic. Greek is a highly
developed inflectional language and Coptic much less so.
Translation of Greek into Bohairic inevitably means that
in several areas where distinctions are made in Greek
they are not made in Coptic; and even if it were theore-
tically possible to show them, the translator(s) sometimes did not. For example, the negative οὐ with the
indicative cannot be differentiated from οὐ μή with the
subjunctive in Bo translation, since Bo shows only the
indicative mood and negates verbs in a different manner
from Greek. Bo can therefore not be used as support for
a Greek ms or text group which omits μή in an οὐ μή
construction.

121

The list of these kinds of distinctions will not
be recorded in every detail, but such features which
frequently recur in the text of Deut and which are
essential for an understanding of it are discussed below.
The discussion is divided into two interdependent sections.
The first describes such elements of the Greek language
which Bo, as a language, is incapable of reproducing
because its "coding system" differs from Greek. The
second discusses aspects of Greek which Bo is fully
capable of reproducing, but which the translation of Deut
takes lightly or disregards.

A. Grammar and Syntax

1. The Verb

(a) Tense. The differences between the Greek
Perfect, Pluperfect first and second Aorists cannot be
shown in Bo. The present, future, and imperfect tenses
can be shown, and so differences of this kind will, as
far as possible, be recorded.

(b) Mood. Bo shows only the Indicative, Impera-
tive, and Optative moods. The subjunctive is not distinguished from the indicative in Bo, therefore Greek
variants of this kind are disregarded.

(c) Voice. The Bo verb has no particular form
for the passive; passivity is usually indicated by means
of the third person plural of the Active forms. Greek
variant readings based on middle and passive conjugations

are therefore recorded only when a clear equation with the Bo translation can be established.

2. The Noun

(a) Gender. There is no gender correspondence between Greek and Bo. Greek has three genders, masculine, feminine and neuter, Bo has two--masculine and feminine. Nouns which are masculine or feminine in Greek are not necessarily masculine or feminine in Bo; and further, most Bo nouns do not inflect for gender in the plural, being marked by a common plural article Nι- or Νєν. These morphological differences affect several areas of grammar. Any similarity of the genders of Greek and Bo nouns is only fortuitous.

(b) Number. Bo and Greek usually correspond as to the singular number. The majority of Bo nouns have a common plural form. Only a few Bo nouns have Coptic masculine and feminine plural endings. Variant readings of Greek nouns are therefore only recorded when Bo can support them.

(c) Case. Case endings are not shown in Bo, but the function of Greek cases is usually assumed by certain preposed Bo morphemes, e.g., Nχє often precedes word functioning as subject; N·, Νєν-, or Ɔєν- precedes the Bo noun which translates a Greek noun in the Dative case; NTє- or N· before a Bo noun indicates a genitive relationship, and the object of a clause can be marked by a preposed Μ.

(d) Transliteration of Greek nouns. Only the roots
of Hellenized Greek names transliterated into Bo can be
used as evidence for dependence. Bo tends to use the
nominative masculine singular form of the Greek noun
(usually second declension) as a root form and then to
prepose the appropriate Bo article throughout, e.g., των
χανανεων becomes ΝΙ ΧΑΝΑΝΕΟϹ. Variants involving inflectional changes in Hellenized Greek nouns are therefore
disregarded.

3. Pronouns

Pronouns in Bo and Greek correspond only within
the limits established under the noun above. The limi-
tations of gender and number of the Bo nominal system
produce parallel changes in the demonstrative and relative pronouns and in all other areas of grammar
affected by number and gender. There exists, for
example, only one form in Bo for the respective plurals
of demonstrative and relative pronouns--ΝΑΙ for the near
demonstrative, ΝΗ for the distant, and ΝΗ (ετε) for the
relative. This means that words like οὗτοι , αὗται , and
ταῦτα cannot be distinguished from each other in Bo,
neither can οὕς be distinguished from ἅ etc. The lack
of correspondence of gender of Bo and Greek, and the Bo
tendency towards a common plural must be remembered when
one compares their texts.

4. The Article

The comments under nouns and pronouns particularly
affect the article. Only one form of the plural article
exists and two forms of the singular, i.e., masculine and
feminine. The article as a marker of definiteness is
usually shown in Bo. Other uses and forms of the Greek
article are recorded only when Bo is able to show them.

5. Prepositions

The precise semantic range of the prepositions of
one language is difficult to duplicate in the prepositions of another. This is especially true with respect
to Greek and Bo. The spatial categories of up, down, in,
out, and around are represented adequately by the prepositions of both languages. Distinctions between ἄνω and
ἐκ, for example, can therefore be clearly shown in Bo.
Differences between ἐν and εἰς, ἐκ and ἀπό, παρά and
περί, πρό and ἀπό, by contrast, are more difficult to
determine in Bo and are recorded only when a correspondence with or divergence from Bo prepositions can be
determined with certainty. The Greek prepositions κατά
and ἐν are usually transliterated into Bo--the former
without modification and the latter with an aspirate ɔ.

The difficulty in making one-to-one equivalences
in the prepositions of Greek and Bo is illustrated by
the preposition ἐν. One would presume that the range
of Greek ἐν was substantially covered by Bo ɔɛN, but

126

this is not the case. For example, in the first six
verses of Deut, ἐν is translated by three different pre-
positions--ⲛ̀ϧⲏⲓ ⳨ (1:1), ⲆⲈⲚ (1:4), and ⳨ (1:6). This
condition is symptomatic of the case with prepositions,
in general, throughout Deut; therefore, only indisputable
equivalences and deviations are listed.

Bo usually translates a Greek pronoun in the Dative
case by preposing ⲛ-, ⲚⲈⲘ, or ⲆⲈⲚ to its Bo equivalent.
When the Greek pronoun is preceded by a preposition, Bo
does not use an extra preposition to show this. Accordingly, both σοί and ἐν σοί are usually translated ⲚⲀⲔ,
αὐτῷ, and ἐν αὐτῷ are translated ⲚⲀⳝ, etc. Greek differences of this kind cannot be shown.

6. Participles

The Greek participles are translated into Bo as
verbs or as nouns with prepositions. As verbs they
usually take the number and person of the logical subject
in the clause (usually the subject of the main verb), and
may or may not be joined to what follows by a conjunction,
e.g.:

8:11 πρόσεχε σεαυτῷ μη ἐπιλάθῃ κυρίου . . .(12) μὴ
        φαγὼν καὶ ἐμπλησθεὶς καὶ οἰκίας καλὰς οἰκοδομήσας
        καὶ κατοικήσας ἐν αὐταῖς is translated ⲘⲀ⳨ⲐⲎⲔ ⲈⲢⲞⲔ
        ⲘⲠⲈⲢⲈⲢⲠⲱⲂⳝ ⲘⲠϬⲞⲒⲤ· · · ⲘⲎⲠⲰⲤ ⲚⲦⲈⲔⲞⲨⲰⲘ ⲚⲦⲈⲔ⳨Ⲓ ⲞⲨⲞ⳨
        ⲀⲔⳝⲀⲚⲔⲰⲦ Ⲛ⳨ⲀⲚⲎⲒ ⲈⲚⲀⲚⲈ⳨ ⲞⲨⲞ⳨ ⲚⲦⲈⲔⳝⲰⲠⲒ Ⲛ⳨ⲎⲦⲞⲨ

The participles in this verse are all translated into
second person singular verbs.

21:15 ἐὰν δὲ γένωται . . . μία αὐτῶν ἠγαπημένη . . .

μισουμένη becomes ⲉϣⲱⲡ ⲇⲉ ⲁⲣⲉⲩⲁⲛ . . . ⲩϣⲱⲡⲓ ⲟⲩⲓ

ⲙⲏⲱⲟⲩ ⲉⲩⲙⲉⲓ · · · ⲉⲩⲙⲟⲥⲧ

As a noun the participle is often marked by the indefinite
article, e.g.,

6:17 φυλάσσων φυλάξῃ becomes Ⲇⲉⲛ ⲟⲩⲁⲣⲉⲍ ⲉⲕⲉⲁⲣⲉⲍ

13:9 ἀναγγέλλων ἀναγγελλεῖς becomes Ⲇⲉⲛ ⲟⲣⲧⲁⲙⲟ ⲉⲕⲉⲧⲁⲙⲱⲟⲩ

A Greek variant which substitutes a verb for a participle
is thus impossible to distinguish in those instances where
Bo translates participles as verbs. When Bo translates
the participle as a noun, Greek variants which show a
noun are also disregarded.

7. Infinitives

    Differences between the Present and Aorist Greek
infinitives cannot be shown in Bo. Differences between
the marked (by an article) and the unmarked infinitive
are recorded only where it is possible to determine
certain correspondence with the Bo reading.

8. Numerals

    Since Bo cardinal and ordinal numbers are usually
written as numerals in Deut and not spelled out as words,
variants on the spelling of Greek numbers are irrelevant.
Accordingly, declension differences (εἷς μία ἕν, etc.)
cannot be shown either.

9. Conditional Clauses

    Distinctions between ἐάν and ἄν and their
respective uses in Greek cannot be shown.

10. Comparison

    Degrees of comparison of the adjective can usually
be shown but the meanings of words like ὥς, ὡσεί, κατά,
καθότι, καθώς, etc., and other such Greek words of comparison tend to fall together in Bo and are translated
by ⲙ̅ⲫⲣⲏⲧ or a composite form of this word. Such Greek
differences are therefore not recorded.

B. Bohairic as a Translation

    Bohairic is, in general, a faithful translation
from Greek. There are some components of Greek, however,
which the Bo of Deut translates inconsistently, or ignores,
even though Bo as a language is able to reproduce them
accurately. Some of these will now be examined.

1. Word Order

    Bo does not follow Greek word order. The order of
subject, modifiers and predicate is often mixed in Bo.
Transpositions including these elements cannot be shown
to derive from a Greek Vorlage and are to be ignored.
Naturally, transposition of nouns or nominal elements
in a series, transpositions of verses or across verse
divisions, etc., are followed in Bo and are recorded.
Adverbs like ⲉⲙⲁϣⲱ / σφόδρα, ⲙ̅ⲫⲟⲟⲩ / σήμερον, Greek

loan words, and adjectives can be fairly accurately
placed in the word order; their omissions, additions or
transpositions are recorded.

2. Conjunctions

        The Bohairic of Deut is inconsistent in its trans-
lation of Greek καί. The situation is complicated by the
fact that Bohairic can and often does utilize a double
marker for the conjunction, i.e., the free conjunctions
ΟⲨΟⳘ or ⲚⲈⲘ , and the bound conjunctive tense markers
ⲚⲦⲈϥ-, ⲚⲦⲈⲔ-, etc. If one or the other or both of these
markers were consistently used to translate καί, it
would be simple to determine when the Greek parent text of
Bo omits καί. But this is not the case. The use of the
free conjunction before the conjunctive tense markers is
widely attested in Deut. There are many instances, on
the other hand, where Bo alone omits καί attested by all
extant Greek mss. The Bo verb which follows the conjunction is not conjunctive in some of these cases, and in
others the conjunction does not even precede a verb.
This is demonstrated in the following list of unique Bo
readings chosen at random. The list shows the way Bo
deals with καί in Chapter 24. The tense marker of the
following Bo verb (if any) is indicated in parentheses.

        24:1 καί 1°] om Bo (ⲚⲦⲈϥ-)
        24:3 καὶ ἐξαποστελεῖ] om καί Bo (ⲚⲦⲈϥ-)

24:4   καὶ οὐ] om καί Bo (ⲚⲚⲈⲦⲈⲚ-)

24:5   καὶ οὐκ] om καί Bo (ⲚⲚⲞⲨ-)

24:13 καὶ εὐλογήσει] om καί Bo (ⲈⲨⲈ-)

24:15 καὶ ἐν αὐτῷ] om καί Bo (ⲀⲠⲈ-)

24:15 καὶ ου] om καί Bo (ⲚⲚⲈⲨ-)

24:15 καὶ ἔσται] om καί Bo (ⲚⲦⲈⲨ-)

24:19 καί 1°] om Bo (ⲚⲦⲈⲔ-)

This evidence indicates that the translator considered
the ideas expressed more important than the connectives
used to link them. In four of the nine readings above,
καί is translated into Bo by means of a conjunctive
tense marker and thus may not be omitted at all. No
such explanation is possible for the other five readings.
It may be concluded, then, that the presence or absence
of the co-ordinating conjunction in Bo is of little
textual significance.

The Bo treatment of conjunctions is also worthy
of note in the following cases. The word ⲚⲈⲘ functions
both as a conjunction translating Greek καί and as a preposition translating a Greek noun in the dative case.
The conjunction οὐδέ is always transliterated, but μηδέ
is usually rendered by οὐδέ followed by the negative
Bo prefix ⲘⲠⲈ⸗.

3. Possession

The Bo translation of Greek possessive pronouns
is haphazard. Bo is equipped to translate Greek

accurately in this respect, but the translator seems
to have taken little care to do so. It often happens
that Bo adds a possessive prefix to a noun, the Greek
equivalent of which is not followed by a possessive
pronoun; or, on the other hand, Bo may lack a possessive
attested by all the Greek mss.

The noun πλησίον may serve as an example. The Bo
translation of this word in Deut always attests a possessive
prefix--ⲡⲉϥϣⲫⲏⲣ , ⲡⲉⲕϣⲫⲏⲣ, etc. The Greek evidence
normally supports the absence of a possessive pronoun
with a few mss adding it. Bo alone adds the possessive
in 19:21. Omissions of the possessive are less frequent
than additions in Bo, but they exist, as the following
two examples, unsupported by any Greek mss show.

4:47 αὐτοῦ] om Bo

19:3 σου 1°] om Bo

It seems clear from the above, and several other instances throughout Deut, that the addition or omission
of the possessive prefix is in keeping with the style
of the Bo translator and does not necessarily indicate
Greek influence. Variants involving Greek possessive
pronouns, though recorded, do not constitute strong
evidence for dependence.

4. The Article

The Bo use of the definite article is usually
precise, but there are some instances where its presence
may be misleading. Bo shows possession by means of the

possessive suffixes ⲡⲉϥ- , ⲡⲉⲕ-, ⲡⲟⲩ- , etc., when the
noun is definite. When the noun is indefinite, Bo uses
the following circumlocution: the Genitive prefix ⲛⲧⲉ
the indefinite article ⲟⲩ /ⲍⲁⲛ, and the preposition ⲛⲧⲁ ⲍ
with the appropriate suffix. For instance, τοῦ υἱοῦ σου
would properly be translated ⲛⲧⲉ ⲡⲉⲕϣⲏⲣⲓ, while υἱοῦ
σου would be translated ⲛⲧⲉ ⲟⲩϣⲏⲣⲓ ⲛⲧⲁⲕ . In practice,
however, the Bo translator rarely if ever makes a dis-
tinction between the presence or absence of the article
in these Greek constructions but usually translates them
as having the definite article. Accordingly, Greek
variants which show the omission of the definite article
before a noun with a possessive pronoun, though theore-
tically possible in Bo, are not recorded. The omission
of the possessive pronoun by contrast is usually shown
in Bo and is thus recorded.

The Bo indefinite article is usually used with
Bo nouns to translate indefinite Greek nouns, but
especially when the Bo translator wishes to distinguish an indefinite from a definite noun (cf participle
above). This practice is not consistent; indefinite
Greek nouns are sometimes translated with the Bo definite
article, e.g., 1:17 ἐν κρίνει becomes ϧⲉⲛ ⲡϩⲁⲡ;
πρόσωπον becomes ⲙⲡϩⲟ ; 2:8 ὁδὸν ἔρημον becomes ⲉⲡⲓⲙⲱⲓⲧ
ⲛⲧⲉ ⲡϣⲁϥⲉ ; 2:4 υἱῶν Ἠσαύ becomes ⲛⲓϣⲏⲣⲓ ⲛⲧⲉ ⲏⲥⲁⲩ , etc.
This seems to be the translator's style and need not
indicate the article in the Greek Vorlage. Accordingly,

such readings are recorded only when attested by a substantive amount of Greek evidence.

5. Resumptive Particle/Suffix after Relative

The construction exemplified by the phrase ⲡⲓⲙⲁ
ⲉⲧⲉ ⲡⲈⲤ ⲡⲉⲕⲛⲟⲭⲧ ⲛⲁⲥⲟⲧⲡⲩ ⲉⲙⲟⲭⲧ ⲙⲡⲉⲩⲣⲁⲛ ⲙⲙⲁⲥ is extremely
frequent in Coptic and does not necessarily indicate a
Greek parent text with a resumptive pronoun. It is
difficult to show in the example above whether or not
Bo ⲛⲁⲥⲟⲧⲡⲩ reflects the Greek verb ἐκλέξηται followed
by αὐτόν/αὐτό or without the pronoun, since Bo usually
shows the resumptive particle in such constructions.
When original Greek attests the resumptive pronoun Bo
is cited along with it; elsewhere, Bo is cited as a
witness to the resumptive pronoun only if there is substantive Greek support. In any event the Bo support of
the resumptive pronoun in Greek is of little textual
significance.

A similar statement may be made for ⲙⲙⲁⲥ / ἐκεῖ
in the example above. Bo adds words like ⲙⲙⲁⲥ, ⲧⲏⲣⲩ,
ⲛⲓⲃⲉⲛ, etc., to complete the sense of some passages,
often without extant Greek support. If there is little
or no Greek support for Bo in these instances, it may be
assumed that Bo is simply acting in character and is
making no comment on its Greek parent text. Such instances, though recorded, should be understood in this
light.

6. Verbs Doubly Marked for Person

Both Bo and Greek are equipped to mark verbs for person. Both languages have independent personal pronouns which may be used to intensify the person of the verb. Bohairic is erratic in its translation of Greek independent pronouns in this kind of construction. The probability of omission of the pronoun in Bo is strongest if the verb is in a relative construction. The popular phrase ὅσα ἐγὼ ἐντέλλομαι may be used to illustrate this point. In Chapters 11 and 12 (which were chosen at random) the phrase occurs eight times. Bo translates the phrase ΝΗ ⲀΝⲞⲔ ⲈϯⲌⲞⲚⲌⲈⲚ in five of these instances but omits ⲀΝⲞⲔ in the other three. This pattern was observed throughout the book, and it seems clear that the absence of ⲀΝⲞⲔ does not necessarily indicate the omission of ἐγώ in the Greek parent text, and further, that the free personal pronoun, especially in relative constructions, was added at the discretion of the translator and does not necessarily indicate Greek dependence.

The verb "to be" can be expressed in Bo either by ⲰⲰⲡⲓ or ⲡⲉ. It is not always expressed, so omissions of ἐστιν, etc., though recorded, are not strong evidence for dependence.

7. Faulty Translations

The translator's knowledge of Greek seems to be generally sound, but there are a few instances where the

Bo translation reflects a misreading of the Greek. In
21:5, ἄφη meaning "assault, striking" is read as ἄφη
a form of ἀφίημι "to forgive, to leave," and is thus
translated as ⲭⲱ ⲉⲃⲟⲗ = forgiveness. In 5:26, the
relative ἥτις is read as the conjunction ἤ plus τις
and is accordingly translated into Bo as ⲓⲉ ⲛⲓⲙ .

   The treatment of translation techniques in this
chapter is not exhaustive but is adequate to assist in
the forthcoming investigation. The following chapter
deals specifically with the place of Bohairic within the
Greek textual tradition.

Chapter VI

THE PLACE OF BOHAIRIC WITHIN THE GREEK TEXTUAL TRADITION

The purpose of this chapter is to determine the place of Bohairic within the larger complex of witnesses to the Greek of Deut. The materials available to the Göttingen Septuaginta-Unternehmen for the Greek Deut are listed elsewhere.[1] J. W. Wevers arranged these materials into textual families similar to those he established for his edition of the Greek Genesis.[2] Membership in each family has changed slightly for Deut, but the families remain essentially the same.

Bo will initially be compared with each textual family to determine a possible relationship. Scattered agreement of Bo with individual members of a group, or with codices mixti, will be regarded as irrelevant.

A. The Hexaplaric recension is represented by mss which, although they often bear no hexaplaric signs, preserve readings based on the fifth column of Origen's Hexaplar. The nature of his work is well known. He indicated by the obelus (÷) passages in Greek not present in his Hebrew text. Words or phrases in Hebrew which had no equivalent in his Greek text were supplied by Origen from the "three" but placed under the asterisk (※).

A metobelus (⌐) followed both kinds of readings. Most
mss whose texts contain hexaplaric materials have lost
these signs in transmission. In the main, only G and Syh
preserve a number of them in Deut. The other hex mss
can be identified by their witness to plusses and transpositions based on the Hebrew text. Such plusses under
the asterisk give the clearest indication of hex activity.
A list of the asterisked plusses in Deut with all Greek
support follows. Those instances where Bo supports the
hex reading are marked by a star before the chapter and
verse number.

List 1   Asterisked plusses

1:1 Φαράν] + (※ Syh) και ανα μεσον F^a $\underline{0}$-82-58 $\underline{d}$-106
     ^{125} 246 $\underline{t}$ 18'-669 646 Arab Syh Barh 224 = Ⓜ

1:15 καὶ ἔλαβον] + (※ Syh) τους αρχιφυλους $\underline{0}$-82 108^{mg}
      $\underline{d}$ $\underline{t}$ Arm Syh = Ⓜ

1:25 ἡμᾶς] + (※ Syh) και επεστρεψαν ημιν ρημα $\underline{0}$-82-15
      $\underline{d}$ 767 $\underline{t}$ Arab Arm Syh = Ⓜ

1:30 fin] + (※ Syh) κατ' οφθαλμους υμων A^c $\underline{0}$-82-15-58
      $\underline{d}$ $\underline{t}$ 121 Arm Syh = Ⓜ

1:35 τούτων] + (※ Syh) η γενεα η πονηρα αυτη M^{mg} $\underline{0}$-82
      108^{mg} $\underline{d}$ 767 $\underline{t}$ Syh = Ⓜ

1:36 ἐπέβη] + (※ Syh) εν αυτη (επ' 376) $\underline{0}$-82 Syh = Ⓜ

2:2 fin] + (※ Syh) λεγων $\underline{0}$-82 108^{mg} $\underline{d}$ $\underline{t}$ Syh = Ⓜ

2:5 βῆμα] + (※ Syh) ιχνους $\underline{0}$-82 108mg Syh Barh 224 = Ⓜ

2:25 τοῦ] pr (※ Syh) παντος $\underline{0}$-82 $\underline{d}$ $\underline{t}$ Syh = Ⓜ

3:11 ἀπό] + (※ Syh) λειμματος (c var) $\underline{0}^{-82}$-58 Syh = Ⓜ

4:11 τοῦ] pr (※ G Syh) καρδιας $\underline{0}^{-82}$ Syh = Ⓜ

4:15 ὁμοίωμα] pr (※ G Syh) παν $\underline{0}^{-82}$-58 $\underline{b}^{-537}$ $\underline{f}^{-129}$ $\underline{t}$ 318 $\underline{z}$ Syh = Ⓜ

4:19 τοῦ 2°] pr (※ G Syh) παντος $\underline{0}^{-82}$ $\underline{d}$ $\underline{t}$ Or Cels III 36 Syh = Ⓜ

4:21 γῆν] + (※ G Syh) την αγαθην (+ ταυτην 246) $\underline{0}^{-82}$-15 $\underline{d}$ $\underline{f}^{-129}$ $\underline{t}$ 128-630' Arab Syh = Ⓜ

*4:21 θεός ult] + (※ G Syh) σου B M $\underline{0}^{-82}$-15 417 $\underline{d}^{-44}$ 125 129 $\underline{t}^{-799}$ Arm Bo Syh = Ⓜ

4:26 ἀπολεῖσθε] + (※ G Syh) ταχυ $\underline{0}^{-82}$-58 108^{mg} $\underline{f}^{-129}$ 767 128-630' Syh = Ⓜ

4:34 ἐποίησεν] + (※ Syh) υμιν (pr in ^{Lat}cod 100) F M V $\underline{0}^{,-82}$ (707 inc) 52'-77-417-551-616 53' $\underline{s}^{-30'}$ 28 59 ^{Lat}cod 100 Syh = Ⓜ

4:49 ἡλίου] + (※ Syh) και εως θαλασσης της Αραβα $\underline{0}^{-82}$-15-58 85^{mg} 28 Arm Syh = Ⓜ

5:3 ὧδε] pr (※ Syh) αυτοι $\underline{0}^{-82}$-15-58 Syh = Ⓜ

5:3 πάντες] + (※ Syh) υμεις $\underline{0}^{-82}$ Syh = Ⓜ

5:14 προσήλυτος] + (※ Syh) σου $\underline{0}^{-82}$ Aug $\underline{C}$ $\underline{Adim}$ 16 Syh = Ⓜ

*5:22 ἔδωκεν] + (※ Syh) αυτας $\underline{0}^{-82}$ $\underline{d}$ $\underline{t}$ Bo $Sa^{1\ 2}$ Syh = Ⓜ

5:24 αὐτοῦ 1°] + (※ Syh) και την μεγαλωσυνην αυτου $\underline{0}^{-82}$-58 108^{mg} 106 767 85^{mg} $\underline{t}$ 28 Arab Arm Syh = Ⓜ

5:26 σάρξ] pr (※ Syh) πασα $\underline{0}^{-82}$-58 108^{mg} 767 CyrHier 740 Syh = Ⓜ

5:29 τάς 1°] pr (✕ Syh) πασας 0̲-15-58 106 t̲-799 Arm^ap
Syh = Ⓜ

5:31 τάς] pr (✕ Syh) πασας 0̲^-82-15 d̲-107 t̲ Arab Syh = Ⓜ

7:10 πρόσωπον 1°] + (✕ Syh) αυτου 0̲^-82-15-58 Sa² Syh
= Ⓜ

7:10 μισοῦσιν 2°] + (✕ Syh) αυτον M 15-426 106 t̲ Lat_cod
100 Sa² 3 Syh = Ⓜ

7:10 πρόσωπον 2°] + (✕ Syh) αυτου 58-426 Syh = Ⓜ

*7:11 ποιεῖν] + (✕ Syh) αυτα 0̲^-82-58 d̲ t̲ Aeth^CG Syh = Ⓜ

*7:15 ἐπιθήσει 1°] + (✕ G Syh) αυτα 0̲^-82-58 108^mg d̲-125
30 t̲ Arab Arm Bo Syh = Ⓜ

7:25 μή] + (✕ G 108) ποτε (-ται376) 0̲-82 108^mg d̲-125
246 t̲ z̲ Syh

7:26 προσοχθειῖς] + (✕ G Syh) αυτο 0̲ d̲ t̲ Syh = Ⓜ

7:26 βδελύξη] + (✕ G Syh) αυτο 0̲-58 d̲ t̲ Lat_spec 44 Aeth
Syh = Ⓜ

8:2 θεός σου] + (✕ G Syh) τουτο τεσσαρακοστον ετος
0̲ 108^mg d̲^-44 f̲-56txt 767 85^mg t̲ 128-630 Procop 961
Tht I 240 Arab Sa Syh Barh 228 = Ⓜ

8:9 φάγη] + (✕ G Syh) εν αυτη 0̲^-82-15 108^mg Syh = Ⓜ

8:11 μή] + (✕ G Syh) ποτε 0̲-58 108^c d̲ 246 t̲ 128-630*-
669 Syh = M

*8:11 κρίματα] + (✕ G Syh) αυτου V 0̲ d̲ W¹-127-767 t̲
Aeth Arab Bo Sa² Syh = Ⓜ

8:12 μή] + (✕ G) ποτε 0̲'-58 108^mg d̲ 246 t̲ 83-128-630'
Aeth Syh

9:21 κονιορτόν] + (※ G Syh) αυτου (-των 426) 0-15-58
108ᶜ d⁻¹²⁵ t Syh = Ⓜ

*9:28 ἀποκτεῖναι] + (※ G Syh) αυτους B 0 Aeth Arm Bo Syh
= Ⓜ

10:4 πυρός] + (※ G Syh) εν τη ημερα της εκκλησιας
M 0 108ᵐᵍ d⁻⁴⁴ 125 n⁻¹²⁷ 767 t Arab Syh = Ⓜ

10:8 λειτουργεῖν] + (※ G) αυτου 0-58 d t Syh = Ⓜ

10:9 εἶπεν] + (※ G) κυριος ο θεος σου (om 125) 0 d t
Syh = Ⓜ

10:10 ὄρει] + (※ G) ως ημεραι αι πρωται 0-58 108ᵐᵍ d
767 85ᵐᵍ t Arab Syh = Ⓜ

*11:2 χεῖρα] + (※ G) αυτου 0-15-58 d 75' t Bo Syh = Ⓜ

*11:2 βραχίονα] + (※ G) αυτου 0-15-58 d t Bo Syh = Ⓜ

11:10 σπόρον] + (※ G Syh) σου 0⁻⁸² Syh = Ⓜ

11:10 ποσίν] + (※ G Syh) σου 0⁻⁸² 376 Syh = Ⓜ

11:11 ἥν] + (※ G) υμεις 0 d t Arab Arm Pal Syh = Ⓜ

11:18 ῥήματα] + (※ G Syh) μου 0 Syh = Ⓜ

11:19 καθημένους] + (※ G) σου G*-58; -μενου σου B 0⁻ᴳᶜ
Pal Syh = Ⓜ

11:19 πορευομένους] + (※ G) σου G*; -μενου σου B 0⁻ᴳᶜ-58
Pal Syh = Ⓜ

11:19 κοιταζομένους] + (※ G) σουG*; -μενου σου B 0⁻ᴳᶜ-58
Syh = Ⓜ

11:19 διανισταμένους] + (※ G) σου G*; -μενου σου B
0⁻ᴳᶜ-58 Syh = Ⓜ

*11:22 ποιεῖν] + (✳ G Syh) αυτας του 0̲-15 d̲ t̲ Bo Syh = Ⓜ

11:24 ποδὸς ὑμῶν] + (✳ G Syh) εν αυτω 0̲ Syh = Ⓜ

*12:2 δὲνδρου] pr (✳ G Syh) παντος Fᵃ 0̲-15-58 b̲ d̲ 246
n̲ t̲ z̲⁻⁶³⁰ᶜ Bo Syh = Ⓜ

12:3 ἐκκόψετε] + (✳ G) πυρι G Syh = Ⓜ

12:6 θυσιάσματα ὑμῶν] + (✳ G) και τας δεκατας υμων 0̲-58
108ᵐᵍ d̲ 85ᵐᵍ t̲ 28 Arab Arm Syh = Ⓜ

12:6 ἀπαρχάς] + (✳ G) των χειρων 0̲-58 85ᵐᵍ 28 Arab Syh
= Ⓜ

12:13 μή] + (✳ G Syh) ποτε 0̲-58 d̲ t̲ Eus VI 12 Syh

12:15 ἐπιθυμία] + (✳ G Syh) ψυχης (-χη 82) 0̲ Procop 908
Syh = Ⓜ

12:15 πόλει] + (✳ G Syh) σου 0̲ d̲ t̲ Saˡ 3 Syh = Ⓜ

12:17 εὐχάς] + (✳ G) σου 0̲ C̲" s̲ t̲ 28 319 509 Eus VI 13
Pal Syh = Ⓜ

12:19 μή] + (✳ G Syh) ποτε (-ται 376) 0̲ d̲ t̲ Syh

12:21 τήν] pr (✳ G) πασαν 0̲ d̲ t̲ Arab Syh = Ⓜ

12:22 fin] + (✳ G) αυτο 0̲⁻⁸²-15 C̲"⁻⁷³' 551 b̲ d̲ 246 n̲ s̲
t̲ z̲⁻⁶⁸' 83 28 55 319 509 Aeth Syh = Ⓜ

*12:24 φάγεσθε] + (✳ G) αυτο 0̲ d̲ 246 130-321' t̲ z̲⁻⁶³⁰ᶜ
Aethᴹ Bo Sa Syh = Ⓜ

*12:28 λόγους] + (✳ G)τουτους 0̲-58 d̲ t̲ Bo Syh = Ⓜ

12:28 υιοῖς σου] + (✳ G Syh) μετα σε 0̲ d̲ Wˡ t̲ Syh = Ⓜ

12:30 μή 1°] + (✳ G Syh) ποτε (πω.376) 0̲ d̲ t̲ Syh

12:30 μή 2°] + (✳ G) ποτε 0̲-58 d̲ t̲ Syh

12:30 ποιήσω] + (✳ G) ουτως (c var) 0̲-58 d̲ t̲ Syh = Ⓜ

13:3　ἀγαπᾶτε] pr (✗ G Syh) υμεις $\underline{0}$ Syh = Ⓜ

13:8　αυτόν] pr (✗ G) επ´ $\underline{0}^{-82}$-58 730 Syh = Ⓜ

13:15　fin] + (✗ G) και τα κτηνη αυτης εν στοματι μαχαι-ρας $\underline{0}$ $\underline{d}$ $\underline{t}$ Arab Arm Syh = Ⓜ

14:12　init] pr (✗ G Syh) και τον ιξον $\underline{0}^{-82}$-15-58 54-458 Syh = Ⓜ

14:20　φάγεται] + (✗ G) αυτο (c var) $\underline{0}$-58 $\underline{d}$ $\underline{t}$ Sa¹ ³ Syh = Ⓜ

14:26　σου 1°] + (✗ G Syh) ουκ εγκαταλειψεις αυτον Fᵃ $\underline{0}$-58 $\underline{d}$ $\underline{t}$ Arab Arm Syh = Ⓜ

14:28　ἔργοις] + (✗ G) των χειρων $\underline{0}$-58 $\underline{b}$ $\underline{d}$ $\underline{t}$ Syh = Ⓜ

*15:2　πλησίον] + (✗ Syh) σου 58 Cyr I 504 Aeth Bo Sa¹ ³ Syh

15:2　ἀπαιτήσεις] + (✗ G) τον πλησιον σου $\underline{0}$ $\underline{d}$ $\underline{t}$ Arab Arm = Ⓜ

15:8　δανιεῖς αὐτῷ] + (✗ G Syh) ικανον $\underline{0}$-58 $\underline{d}$ $\underline{t}$ Syh = Ⓜ

15:9　μή] + (✗ G Syh) ποτε (bis scr 376) $\underline{0}$-58 $\underline{b}$ $\underline{d}$ 246 $\underline{t}$ 128-630*-669 Cyr I 568 Or III 320 Syh

15:11　πένητι] + (÷ G: mend pro ✗ ; ✗ Syh) σου $\underline{0}$-58 Syh = Ⓜ

15:11　ἐπιδεομένω] + (✗ G Syh) σου $\underline{0}$-15-58 Aeth Syh = Ⓜ

*15:12　ἑβδόμω] pr (✗ Syh) ετει τω (c var) $\underline{0}$-58 106 $\underline{n}$ $\underline{t}$ Cyr VI 685 Aeth^CG Arm Bo Syh = Ⓜ

15:15　fin] + (✗ G Syh) σημερον (post εντελλομαι tr 376) $\underline{0}$-15-58 $\underline{d}$ $\underline{t}$ Aeth^M Arab Syh = Ⓜ

16:15　ἔση] + (✗ G Syh) πλην $\underline{0}^{-82}$ Syh = Ⓜ

17:4 σοί] + (✳ G) και ακουσης 0̲-15-58 d̲ t̲ Syh = Ⓜ

17:8 θεὸς σου] + (✳ G) εν αυτω 0̲ d̲ t̲ Syh = Ⓜ

17:11 νόμον] + (✳ G Syh) ον φωτιουσιν σοι 0̲ d̲ 246 t̲ 128-
      630' Arab Syh = Ⓜ

18:6 παροικεῖ] + (✳ Syh) εκει και ελευσεται 0̲ Arm (om
      εκει) Syh = Ⓜ

18:15 προφήτην] + (✳ G Syh) εκ μεσου σου 0̲-15 Arab Syh
      Barh 234 = Ⓜ

18:16 ἀκοῦσαι] pr (✳ G Syh) του 0̲-82 426 Syh

19:2 fin] + (✳ G Syh) του κληρονομησαι αυτην 0̲-15-58
      d̲ t̲ Arab Syh = Ⓜ

20:8 ὥσπερ ἡ] + (÷ Syh: mend pro ✳) καρδια Mᵐᵍ 0̲'-58
      30'-85ᵐᵍ-343-344ᵐᵍ-346ᵐᵍ z̲-68' 120 646 Syh = Ⓜ

21:21 ἄνδρες] pr (✳ Syh) παντες 0̲-15-58 d̲ t̲ Arab Syh = Ⓜ

22:25 βιασάμενος] + (÷ Syh: mend pro ✳) αυτην ο ανθρωπος
      0̲-15-58 Or Cels I 170 Syh = Ⓜ; + αυτην t̲ Aeth Bo

23:2 fin] + (✳ Syh) και γενεα δεκατη ουκ εισελευσεται
      εις εκκλησιαν κυριου 0̲-376 630' Arab Syh = Ⓜ

23:5 θεὸς σου 2°] + (✳ Syh) σοι 0̲-376 246 128-630*-669
      Syh = Ⓜ

23:16 τόπω] + (✳ Syh) ου αν εκλεξηται εν μια των πυλων
      σου 0̲ C" d̲ 85ᵐᵍ t̲ Syh = Ⓜ

25:1 κρίνωσιν] + (✳ Syh) αυτους 0̲-15-58 d̲ t̲ Sa³ Syh = Ⓜ

25:6 ὀνόματος] + (✳ Syh) του αδελφου αυτου 0̲ d̲ 344ᵐᵍ
      t̲ Lat_Or Matth XVII 30 Syh Barh 240 = Ⓜ

28:15 αὐτοῦ] + (※ G) και τα ηκριβασμενα αυτου 0̲-15 106
t Lat_Mart I 12 Syh = Ⓜ

28:26 τοῖς 1°] pr (※· G; pr τοις 376) πασιν 0̲⁻⁴²⁶ d̲ t̲
121 Syh = Ⓜ

28:32 αὐτά] + (※ G) ολην την ημεραν 0̲ t̲ Arab Syh = Ⓜ

28:33 ἔση] + (※ G) ποτε 0̲-58 d̲ t̲ Syh = Ⓜ

*28:48 επαποστελεῖ] + (※ G Syh) αυτους 0̲ t̲ Bo Syh = Ⓜ

28:51 γῆς σου] + (※ G) εως αν εκτριψη σε 0̲-58 106 t̲
Arab Syh = Ⓜ

28:52 ἔδωκεν] pr (※ G) εν παση τη γη σου η 0̲-58 106 t̲
Arab = Ⓜ

28:54 init] pr (※· G; ÷ Syh: mend pro ※·) ο ανηρ 0-58
Arab Sa³ Syh = Ⓜ

28:63 ἐξολεθρεῦσαι υμας] + (※ G Syh) και του εκτριψαι
υμας F 0̲-15-58 d̲⁻¹²⁵ t̲ Syh = Ⓜ

28:66 κρεμαμένη] + (※· Syh) σοι 0̲⁻ᴳᶜ 32 Or VI 144 Syh = Ⓜ

29:5 ἱμάτια ὑμῶν] + (※ G) επανωθεν υμων F 0̲-15-58 d̲ t̲
Arab Syh = Ⓜ

29:11 προσήλυτος] + (※ G) υμων 0̲ Syh cf Ⓜ

29:13 στήσῃ] + (※· G Syh) σημερον 0̲ 106 t̲ Syh = Ⓜ

29:15 σήμερον 1°] pr (※· G) εστωσι 0̲⁻⁸² Syh = Ⓜ

29:18 διάνοια] + (※· G) αυτου 0̲ d̲⁻¹²⁵ t̲⁻⁷⁹⁹ = Ⓜ

29:18 ἐξέκλινεν] + (※· G) σημερον 0̲-58 106 t̲ Syh = Ⓜ

29:26 αὐτοῖς] + (※· G Syh) θεοις (θεους 82) 0̲-58 Syh = Ⓜ

30:2 σήμερον] + (※· G) συ και οι υιοι σου 0̲ d̲ 767 t̲
Arab Syh = Ⓜ

*30:7 τὰς ἀρὰς ταύτας] pr (⋇ G Syh) πασας 0$^{-426txt}$-58 Bo Syh = Ⓜ; sub ⋇ G (mend)

30:8 τάς] pr (⋇ G) πασας 0 d t 128 Lat$_{cod}$ 100 Aeth^{-M} = Ⓜ

30:9 γῆς σου] + (⋇ G Syh) εις αγαθον 0-58 d t Syh = Ⓜ

30:18 Ἰορδάνην] + (⋇ G Syh) εισελθειν 0-15-58 d^{-125} t Syh = Ⓜ

31:2 ἑκατόν] pr (⋇ M) υιους M^{mg} 426 = Ⓜ

31:5 αὐτοῖς] + (⋇ G) κατα πασαν την εντολην ην 0^{-82}-58 d t = Ⓜ

31:8 κύριος] + (⋇ G Syh) αυτος 0-58 Syh = Ⓜ

31:8 μετὰ σοῦ] pr (⋇ Syh) αυτος εσται 0^{-82}-58 d t Syh; sub ⋇ Syh (mend)

31:15 κύριος] + (÷ Syh: mend pro ⋇) εν τη σκηνη 0-58 d t Syh = Ⓜ

32:25 φόβος] + (⋇ Syh) και γε 376 Arm^{ap} Syh = Ⓜ

32:27 ὑπεναντίοι] + (⋇ Syh) ημων (υμων 376) 376' Syh = Ⓜ

Only 16 of these 134 plusses (12%) are supported by Bo and of these 16, 12 involve the addition of a pronominal element--either as a marker of possession or as object. Bo tends to add pronoun objects to the verb ad sensum freely, especially after relative clauses. These twelve readings are probably mere coincidence. Only four significant readings (12:2, 12:28, 15:12, 30:7) remain; these could also be explained as ad sensum additions. A form of the adjective πας appears before a noun in two instances, and the pronoun ταυτας is added in another. The

fourth instance is the repetition of ετει τω before the
ordinal ἑβδόμω in a context where "year" is clearly understood. The translation of ταυτας into Bohairic is achieved
by the addition of only an ⲁ to the articulated noun i.e.,
Nⲓ becomes Nⲁⲓ etc. It is possible then that this reading
though equivalent to that of the hex mss was simply due
to inner Coptic activity. It appears from this list that
the hex recension had no influence on Bo.

The relationship of the hex recension to Bo may
be further investigated by a list of those instances in
Deut where the O group attests an addition supported by
Ⓜ , but from which the asterisk appears to have been lost
in transmission. The plusses included in the list are
supported by at least one O ms.

List 2   Hexaplaric plusses without the asterisk

1:7   περιοίκους] + αυτου O-82 = Ⓜ

1:8   ὤμοσα] ωμοσε κυριος O-82-58 d t Arab Syh = Ⓜ

1:22   πάντες] + υμεις O-82-15-58 b d 246 t 128-669 Sa[1] [2]
       Syh = Ⓜ

1:35   ὤμοσα] + (+ του 426) εουναι O-82 767 Arm Syh = Ⓜ

1:40   ἐπιστραφέντες] + εαυτοις O-82 d t Syh = Ⓜ

2:14   ἐκ] + μεσου O-82-58 d t Aeth Syh = Ⓜ

2:20   κατῴκουν] + εν αυτη O-82 Syh = Ⓜ

2:21   κατεκληρονόμησαν] + αυτους O-82-58 d-610* f-56*
       t Syh = Ⓜ

3:5 πᾶσαι] + αυται 0̲⁻⁸²-15 f̲⁻¹²⁹ Syh = Ⓜ

*3:8 Ἀερμών] pr ορους F Mᵐg 0̲'·⁻⁸²-15 d̲ f̲⁻¹²⁹ 767 t̲ 121 83-128-669 59 Lat_Cassiod Ps XLI 7 Arab Bo Syh = Ⓜ

3:11 Βασάν] pr της 426 d̲ t̲ = Ⓜ

*3:24 θεράποντι] + σου 0̲⁻⁸² 16-529 53'-129 85-343-344 c pr m 28 55 Bo Syh = Ⓜ

*3:24 χεῖρα] + σου F 58-426 f̲⁻¹²⁹ 54-75 71' Aeth Bo Sa¹ Syh = Ⓜ

3:26 λαλῆσαι] + προς με 0̲⁻⁸²-58 56' Syh = Ⓜ

*4:6 σύνεσις] + υμων 0̲⁻⁸²-15-58 d̲ f̲⁻¹²⁹ t̲ Aeth (vid) Arab (vid) Bo Sa¹ ² Syh = Ⓜ

*4:39 διανοίᾳ] + σου 0̲⁻⁸²-58-707 414 Cyr IX 901 Bo Sa² Syh = Ⓜ

*4:42 πλησίον] + αυτου 0̲⁻⁸²-29-58 d̲ 767 t̲ 407 Lat_cod 100 Aeth Arm Bo Syh = Ⓜ

*5:22 θύελλα] pr και 72 Lat_cod 100 Aeth Arab Arm Bo Sa¹ ² ³ = Ⓜ

*6:1 fin] + αυτην Bᶜ 0̲'⁻⁸² b̲ d̲ t̲ 630ᶜ Aeth Bo Syh = Ⓜ

*6:7 οἴκω] + σου 963 0̲⁻⁸²-58 414 b̲ Nil 828 Lat_Spec 4 Arab Bo Pal Sa¹ ² ³ Syh = Ⓜ

6:17 δικαιώματα] + αυτου F 0̲⁻⁸²-58-381' 73' b̲ 106 53' t̲ z̲ Aeth Pal Sa² ³ Syh = Ⓜ

6:22 τῷ οἴκῳ] pr ολου 0̲⁻⁸²-58 106 t̲ Syh = Ⓜ

7:1 εἰσπορεύῃ] pr σου 426 d̲ t̲ Arm Pal = Ⓜ

*7:10 μισοῦσιν 1°] + αυτον 0̲'⁻⁸²-58 83 Lat_cod 100 Arm Bo Syh = Ⓜ

*7:19 τὰ σημεῖα] pr και G-58-426 52 246 Aeth Arab Bo Syh
= Ⓜ

7:19 τὴν χεῖρα] pr και 963 O⁻⁸²-58 ᴸᵃᵗcod 100 Sa² ³ Pal
Syh = Ⓜ

7:20 ἀπό] + προσωπου O⁻⁸² d̲ t̲ 509 Pal Syh = Ⓜ

9:5 κύριος 1°] + ο θεος σου O-376 344ᵐᵍ ᴸᵃᵗcod 104
Arm Saˡᵗᵉ Syh = Ⓜ

9:10 ἡμέρα] pr εν (+ τη d̲ t̲) O̲ 73' b̲ d̲ 343-344 c pr m
n̲ t̲ CyrHier 1045 Syh = Ⓜ

9:27 ἀσεβήματα] + αυτου O̲ d̲ 730 t̲ Syh = Ⓜ

11:28 ὑμῖν 2°] + σημερον O̲ d̲⁻¹²⁵ 610 t̲ 128-630' Aeth
Arab Syh = Ⓜ

12:12 οἱ παῖδες] pr και O̲-381' 129 71' z̲ ᴸᵃᵗcod 100 Aeth
Arm Saˡ ³ Syh = Ⓜ

12:18 ὁ παῖς σου] pr και 426 Cyr I 880 ᴸᵃᵗcod 100 Aeth
Arab Pal Saˡ = Ⓜ

12:31 τά] pr παν O̲ d̲ t̲ 128-630' Syh = Ⓜ

13:2 fin] + και λατρευσωμεν αυτοις O̲ d̲ t̲ Or Cels I 410
= M

13:8 οὐκ 2°] pr και O̲-58-618 313 Cyr VI 969 ᴸᵃᵗcod 100
Luc Parc 2 Arm Pal Saˡ ³ Syh = Ⓜ

14:1 οὐκ] pr και O̲⁻⁸² d̲ 246 n̲⁻⁷⁵ t̲ 128-630' Tht I 421
Aeth Pal Syh = Ⓜ

*14:7 χοιρογρύλλιον] pr τον 58-426 44' 246 Bo = Ⓜ

14:12 ταῦτα] + α O̲⁻⁸² Arm Aeth = Ⓜ

*14:14 γλαῦκα] pr τον O̲⁻⁸² Bo = Ⓜ

14:14 λάρον] pr τον 0^{-82} = Ⓜ

14:14 ἱέρακα] pr τον 0^{-82} = Ⓜ

14:15 ἐρωδιόν] pr τον 426 = Ⓜ

14:15 κύκνον] pr τον 426 = Ⓜ

14:16 πορφυρίωνα] pr τον 426 = Ⓜ

14:16 νυκτικόρακα] pr τον 426 = Ⓜ

14:18 init] pr και 0^{-426}-58 b d n 343 t Arm = Ⓜ

15:8 init] pr οτι 0^{-376}-58 d t = Ⓜ

*16:18 φυλάς] + σου 0-58 $Bo^{A'}$ Sa^{3} Syh = Ⓜ

17:5 καὶ λιθοβολήσετε] pr τον ανδρα η την γυναικα 0 106 t Arab Syh = Ⓜ

17:10 τόπου] + εκεινου 0-58 d t ^{Lat}Luc Athan I 6 Syh = Ⓜ

18:3 αὕτη] + εσται 0^{-82} Syh = Ⓜ

18:8 πράσεως] + αυτου V 0^{-G}-58 d f^{-129} t 319 Cyr I 877 Syh = Ⓜ

18:9 ἐισέλθῃς] pr συ 0 Syh = Ⓜ

19:1 θεός σου 2°] pr κυριος 0 d n 85^{mg}-346^{mg} t $z^{-630^{c}}$ Arm Syh = Ⓜ

*19:5 πλησίον 2°] + αυτου 0 d t 319 Aeth Bo Syh = Ⓜ

19:9 ταύτας 1°] + αυτας 0 Syh = Ⓜ

19:9 πορεύεσθαι] pr και 0-58-72 d^{-125} n t Aeth Arm Syh = Ⓜ

20:14 ἀπαρτίαν] + αυτης (αυτων 799) 0 d t Syh = Ⓜ

*21:1 κληρονομῆσαι] + αυτην 0 d t Aeth Bo Syh = Ⓜ

*21:1 πατάξαντα] + αυτον 0 d f^{-56*} t Arm Bo Syh = Ⓜ

*21:6 χεῖρας] + αυτων 0-58 d t Aeth Arab Arm Bo Syh = Ⓜ

*21:13 πατέρα] + αυτης A V 0-15 19 106 n t 319 407 Aeth Arab Bo Sa^{8} Syh Barh 234 = Ⓜ

*21:13 μητέρα] + αυτης V 0̲-15-58 d̲ 54-75' t̲ 319 Aeth Arm
       Bo Sa⁸ Syh Barh 234 = Ⓜ

*22:15 μήτηρ] + αυτης 0̲ Aeth Bo Sa³ Syh = Ⓜ

22:15 γερουσίαν] + της πολεως 0̲-15-58 d̲ 85ᵐᵍ t̲ 28 Arab
       Syh = Ⓜ

22:24 init] pr και 0̲ 417 Or Cels I 170 = Ⓜ

22:24 ὅτι 1°] pr επι λογου 0̲⁻³⁷⁶ ᵗˣᵗ-15 Or Cels I 170
       Syh = Ⓜ

22:24 ὅτι 2°] pr επι λογου 0̲-15 Or Cels I 170 Syh = Ⓜ

23:8   εἰσελευσονται] + αυτοις (c var) 0̲-58 = Ⓜ

23:20 εἰσπορεύῃ] pr συ (σοι 799) 0̲-58 d̲ t̲ = Ⓜ

*23:21 ἐκζητησει] + αυτην 0̲ d̲ t̲ Bo Syh = Ⓜ

24:2   καὶ ἀπέλθουσα] pr και εξελθη εξ οικιας αυτου 0̲ d̲
       767 t̲ Arab Syh = Ⓜ

24:4   λαβεῖν αὐτήν] + του ειναι 0̲ 106 t̲ Or VI 333 335
       Syh = Ⓜ

*24:7   ἀποδῶται] + αυτον 0̲⁻⁸² d̲ t̲ Aeth Bo Syh = Ⓜ

*24:10 ἐνέχυρον] + αυτου B 0̲ d̲ t̲ Bo Syh = Ⓜ

24:14 προσηλύτων τῶν] + εν τη γη σου 0̲ Syh = Ⓜ

24:15 ἔχει] pr αυτος 0̲-15 106 t̲ Syh = Ⓜ

*24:15 ἐλπίδα] + αυτου 0̲-15-58 Bo Sa³ Syh = Ⓜ

25:7   γυνή] + του αδελφου αυτου 0̲⁻⁸²-58 106 t̲ Or VI 678f
       685 Syh = Ⓜ

25:14 οὐκ ἔσται] + σοι 426 Aeth = Ⓜ

26:2   τῶν καρπῶν] pr παντων 0̲ Syh = Ⓜ

26:2   γῆς σου] + οσα αν ενεγκης απο της γης σου 0̲-58
       d̲⁻¹⁰⁶ 344ᵐᵍ t̲ Syh = Ⓜ

26:11 οἰκία σου] + συ O^{-82}-58 Arm Syh = Ⓜ

26:14 οὐκ ἐκάρπωσα] pr και 376 18 Aeth Arm = Ⓜ

*26:17 δικαιώματα] + αυτου V O 106 53' n$^{-127\ 767}$ t 319 Aeth Bo Sa^{16} Syh = Ⓜ

26:19 εἶναι 2°] pr και O-58 n t Sa^{16} Syh = Ⓜ

27:1 Ἰσραήλ] + τω λαω O-58 d t Arab Syh = Ⓜ

27:13 Ζαβουλών] pr και 376 630 Aeth Arab = Ⓜ

27:14 παντί] + ανδρι 58-82-426^{mg} Lat$_{cod}$ 100 Syh = Ⓜ

*27:17 πλησίον] + αυτου O 106-107 t Arm Bo Syh = Ⓜ

*27:22 ἀδελφῆς] + αυτου F O-58 d t Lat$_{PsAmbr}$ Lex 6 Arm Bo Syh = Ⓜ

*27:22 πατρός] + αυτου V O 106 n t^{-799} 121 68'-83 Aeth Bo Syh = Ⓜ

*27:24 πλησίον] + αυτου B V O-58-72-618 529 d 54-75' t 318-527 319 Aeth Bo Syh = Ⓜ

28:4 γῆς σου] + και καρπος κτηνων σου O Lat$_{Aug}$ C Adim 18 Hi Ezech 14 Syh = Ⓜ

28:8 χεῖρά σου] + και ευλογησαι σε O-58 d t Arab Syh = Ⓜ

28:27 κνήφῃ] pr εν O^{-82}-58 = Ⓜ

28:54 τέκνα] + αυτου O-58 Syh = Ⓜ

*28:56 υἱόν] + αυτης O 106 t 318 Lat$_{Aug}$ Leg I 50 Aeth Arab Arm Bo Sa Syh = Ⓜ

29:23 θυμῷ] + αυτου O-58 106 f^{-129} t Aeth Syh = Ⓜ

*29:27 κατάρας] + της διαθηκης B O^{-82}-707 b d n t 407 509 Aeth Arab Bo Sa^3 Syh = Ⓜ

30:6 κύριος] + ο θεος σου (om 58) O-58 Syh = Ⓜ

*30:16 φυλάσσεσθαι] + τας εντολας αυτου και A <u>O</u> ^{Lat}cod 104
Arab Bo Syh = Ⓜ

31:24 fin] + αυτων <u>O</u>-58 <u>d</u> <u>t</u> Sa³ Syh = Ⓜ

31:25 ἐνετείλατο] + μωυσης <u>O</u> <u>d</u> <u>t</u> Syh = Ⓜ

32:41 ἐχθροῖς] + μου F^b 58-376-707 414 246 54'-75 c pr m
83* 59 407 Tht II 1464 Aeth Arab Arm Bo Sa³ ⁶ Syh = Ⓜ

32:52 ἐισελεύσῃ] + προς την γην ην εγω διδωμι τοις υιοις
ισραηλ <u>O</u>⁻⁸² <u>d</u> 767 85 <u>t</u> 28 = Ⓜ

33:7 εἰσάκουσον] pr και ειπεν <u>O</u>⁻⁸² <u>d</u> <u>n</u> <u>t</u> 59 = Ⓜ

33:24 βάψει] pr και <u>O</u>⁻⁸²-58 <u>d</u> <u>t</u> Aeth Arm = Ⓜ

33:28 ἐπί 2°] + γης <u>O</u>⁻⁸²-58-707 <u>d</u> <u>n</u> <u>t</u> 59 Aeth Sa³ ¹⁶ = Ⓜ

34:3 περίχωρα] + πεδιου <u>O</u>⁻⁸²-58 <u>d</u> <u>t</u> = Ⓜ

34:4 ἔδειξα] + σοι 426 <u>d</u> W^I <u>t</u> Aeth = Ⓜ

*34:11 τοῖς θεράπουσιν] pr πασιν <u>O</u>⁻⁸²-707 85 28 55 Bo = Ⓜ

The pattern observed in the first list of asterisked
plusses is also present here. Thirty five of these 113
plusses without the asterisk (30%) are supported by Bo,
but again the significant variants seem to be much fewer.
Twenty one of these 35 plusses are the addition of the
possessive pronoun to a noun. It has been shown that Bo
treats the Greek possessives loosely; we may conclude
therefore that few if any of these readings had a genuine
hexaplaric basis. Six plusses in the list are the addition
of the personal pronoun as object. This again is typical
of Bo and does not indicate hex influence. The article

is placed before a noun in two instances; this may be coincidence. The remaining six variants (3:8, 5:22, 7:19,
29:27, 30:16, 34:11) include the preposing of και in two
instances. The presence or absence of ογο2 in Bo has
been shown to be no substantive evidence for Greek και.
A third instance is the preposing of the noun ορους to
the name Ἀερμών, and a fourth is the addition of the
adjective πασιν before a noun. Two significant plusses
(29:27, 30:6) remain, but in a total of 247 readings this
is hardly convincing evidence of influence or dependence.

A list of transpositions based on the Hebrew word
order could not show hex influence on Bo since Bo tends
to transpose the order of Greek words without a pattern;
thus any occurrence of transpositions based on Hebrew
would probably be mere coincidence. It is now established
that Bo is not hexaplaric.

The affinity of the d and t groups to the 0 group
is evident in the above lists. All but 98 of the 247 hex
readings above are also attested by the d and/or t groups.
The possible relationship of each of these to Bo will now
be considered.

B. The following list of unique readings to the d
group includes only such readings which could have been
shown in Bo. Readings attested by fewer than three of the
five members of the group are not included. A star will
again precede those readings supported by Bo in this and
all subsequent lists.

List 3 Unique readings of the d̲ group

1:8   παραδέδωκα] + υμιν 29 d̲⁻¹⁰⁶ 53' Sa¹⁶

1:8   om ὑμῶν 1° d̲⁻¹⁰⁶ 53'

1:16 om ἀνὰ μέσον ἀδελφοῦ αὐτοῦ d̲⁻¹⁰⁷'

1:17 τὸν μικρόν] om τον d̲⁻⁴⁴

1:27 σκηναῖς ὑμῶν] σκηναις ημων 72 d̲⁻¹⁰⁶ ¹²⁵ 630

1:39 om καὶ αὐτοὶ κληρονομήσουσιν αὐτὴν d̲⁻¹⁰⁶ 458

1:41 κατά] και d̲⁻¹⁰⁶

1:41 θεὸς ἡμῶν] om ημων d̲⁻¹⁰⁶ 319

1:44 om ὡς εἰ ποιήσαισαν αἱ μέλισσαι d̲⁻¹⁰⁶

1:44 σιηρ 376ᶜ 19 d̲ 664 59

1:45 om κύριος d̲⁻¹⁰⁶

2:1   σιηρ 376 57 19 d̲⁻¹⁰⁶ 799

2:4   σιηρ (σηηρ 610) 376 19 d̲ 59

2:5   σιηρ 376 19 d̲⁻¹⁰⁶ 59

2:7   om ἐκείνην d̲⁻¹⁰⁶ 619 Arm

2:11 om ὥσπερ οἱ ʼΕνακίμ d̲⁻¹⁰⁶

2:12 σιηρ 19 d̲⁻¹⁰⁶ 59

2:16 om ἀποθνήσκοντες ἐκ μέσου τοῦ λαοῦ (17) καὶ d̲⁻¹⁰⁶

2:18 Ἀροήρ] pr γην σιρ (c var) d̲

2:26 Κεδμώθ] κηδεμων d̲⁻¹⁰⁶

2:27 om πορεύσομαι d̲⁻¹⁰⁶

2:29 σιηρ 82 19 d̲⁻¹⁰⁶ 56* 59

2:30 om Σηὼν βασιλεὺς ʼΕσεβών d̲⁻¹⁰⁶

2:30 om καὶ κατίσχυσεν τὴν καρδίαν αὐτοῦ 413 d̲⁻¹⁰⁶

2:30 σου] ημων d̲⁻¹⁰⁶ Aeth

3:2   om ἐποίησας d⁻¹⁰⁶

3:2   om ὅς — fin 72 d⁻¹⁰⁶

3:6   om ὥσπερ — ἐξωλεθρεύσαμεν d⁻¹⁰⁶

3:18   om ὑμῖν τὴν γῆν d⁻¹⁰⁶

3:21   ὑμῶν 1°] ημων 313-413 d⁻¹⁰⁶ 619* (vid) 55

3:24   om συ ult F* 426 d 18 Sa¹ ²

4:24   om κύριος ὁ θεός σου d⁻¹⁰⁶

4:29   om καὶ ἐξ ὅλης τῆς ψυχῆς σου d⁻¹⁰⁶

4:30   φωνῆς αὐτοῦ] φωνης σου d⁻¹⁰⁶ 318

4:32   om τὸ μέγα 72-376ᵗˣᵗ c pr m 528ᶜ d Tht I 408 Aeth

4:41   om πέραν d

4:45   om init — Ἰσραήλ d⁻¹⁰⁶

4:47   om κατά — fin d⁻¹⁰⁶

5:21   om αὐτοῦ 1° 72 d⁻¹⁰⁶

5:21   οὐδε τὸν παῖδα] η τον παιδα d⁻¹⁰⁶

5:21   οὔτε τοῦ βοός] η τον βουν d⁻¹⁰⁶

5:28   om κύριος 2° 417 d⁻¹⁰⁶

5:28   om ἤκουσα — τούτου d⁻¹⁰⁶

5:28   σε] + ο λαος ουτος d⁻¹⁰⁶

5:28   om πάντα ὅσα d⁻¹⁰⁶

5:30   om ὑμεῖς d⁻¹⁰⁶ Aeth Arab

*6:1   om ἐκεῖ 72 d⁻¹⁰⁶ Aeth Arm Bo

6:2   ἐντολὰς αὐτοῦ] om αυτου 381' d⁻¹⁰⁶ 125

6:2   om πάσας — fin d⁻¹⁰⁶

6:4   om init — Αἰγύπτου 381'-426 d⁻¹⁰⁶ Arab = ⑪

6:7   om καὶ λαλήσεις ἐν αὐτοῖς d⁻¹⁰⁶

6:8   om init — σου 1° d⁻¹⁰⁶

6:9   om καὶ τῶν πυλῶν ὑμῶν 963* $\underline{d}^{-106}$ 127 ^{Lat}cod 100

6:12   om ἐξ οἴκου δουλείας $\underline{d}^{-106}$

6:13   om καὶ πρὸς αὐτὸν κολληθήσῃ 58 $\underline{d}^{-44'}$ Arab Barh 228

            = Ⓜ

6:15   om μή — fin $\underline{d}^{-106}$

6:20   ἔσται] + σοι $\underline{d}^{-106}$

6:20   om σε 376 $\underline{d}^{-106}$

6:20   om ἡμῶν 707 $\underline{d}$ 54-75 730

6:21   om καί 1° 72 $\underline{d}^{-106}$

6:21   om ἐν χειρὶ — fin $\underline{d}^{-106}$

6:22   om κύριος 58-72-82 $\underline{d}^{-106}$ 59

6:23   om ἡμῖν $\underline{d}$

6:24   om ἐνετείλατο — ταῦτα $\underline{d}^{-106}$

7:2   om ἀφανισμῷ ἀφανιεῖς αὐτούς $\underline{d}^{-106}$ 56^{txt}

7:9   om θεός ὁ θεὸς ὁ πιστός $\underline{d}^{-106}$

7:10   om τοῖς 2° — fin $\underline{d}^{-106}$

7:12   om ἔσται $\underline{d}^{-106}$ Aeth

7:12   om ἄν — καί 1° $\underline{d}^{-106}$

7:12   om καὶ ποιήσητε $\underline{d}^{-106}$

*7:12   καὶ διαφυλάξει] om και $\underline{d}^{-106}$ Aeth^{-M} Arm Bo Pal

7:19   om init — σου 1° $\underline{d}^{-106}$

7:21   om init — (22) προσώπου σου $\underline{d}^{-106}$

7:24   om αὐτούς $\underline{d}^{-106}$

8:1   om τοῖς πατράσιν — (2) κύριος $\underline{d}^{-44}$ 106^{mg}

8:3   ἀναγγείλῃ] pr μη $\underline{d}^{-44}$ 106^{c}

8:12   om καὶ οἰκίας — fin $\underline{d}^{-106}$

*9:1   om καί 1° d̲ Aeth Bo

9:2   om υἱῶν d̲$^{-106}$ Arab

9:3   om αὐτούς 1° d̲$^{-106}$

9:3   om οὗτος 707 d̲$^{-106}$

9:3   om καὶ ἀπολεῖς — fin d̲$^{-106}$

*9:5   om κύριος 2° B 376 16 d̲$^{-106}$ 458 59 509 Lat$_{Ambr}$ <u>Cain</u> I 28 Bo$^{A'}$ Sa^{13}

*9:5   ὑμῶν] σου 72 d̲$^{-106}$ 121 407 Arab Bo$^{A'}$ Sa^1 ap = Ⓜ

9:5   om Ἀβραάμ — fin d̲$^{-106}$ 30'

9:7   om μνήσθητι d̲$^{-106}$

9:7   om τὸν θεόν σου d̲$^{-106}$

9:7   om ἀφ' ἧς — fin d̲$^{-106}$

*9:16   om τοῦ θεοῦ ὑμῶν d̲$^{-106}$ Bo$^{A'}$ Sa^{1ap} 13

9:16   om ὑμῖν ἑαυτοῖς d̲$^{-106}$

9:20   om κύριος d̲$^{-106}$

9:21   om καὶ ἐγενήθη d̲$^{-106}$ Arm = Ⓜ

9:25   om ἔναντι κυρίου d̲$^{-106}$

*9:27   om καὶ ἐπὶ τὰ ἁμαρτήματα αὐτῶν d̲$^{-106}$ 346 Bo$^{A'}$

10:3   om init — κιβωτόν G^{txt} d̲ 68'

10:7   om comma d̲

10:11   om κύριος 417 d̲ 630

10:18   om δοῦναι — (19) προσήλυτον 72 d̲$^{-106}$

10:20   om καί ult — (21) καί 1° d̲$^{-44'}$

10:22   om τά ult d̲$^{-44'}$

11:3   om αὐτοῦ 1° d̲$^{-107'}$ 767 669

11:3   om πάσῃ — (4) ἐποίησεν d^{-106}

11:6 σκηνὰς αὐτῶν] om αυτων 72 d$^{-44'}$ 71'

11:10 om γῆ 2° 550* c pr m d^{-106}

11:10 om ὅθεν ἐκπορεύεσθε ἐκεῖθεν d^{-106}

11:11 ἡ δέ] αλλ η d^{-106}

11:11 om ἐκεῖ κληρονομῆσαι αὐτήν d^{-106} Lat$_{cod}$ 100

11:11 ἐξ 1°∩2° V d^{-106} 107 321

11:17 om ὁ κύριος ὑμῖν d

11:19 om καθημένους — fin d^{-106}

11:21 om αἱ ἡμέραι d^{-106} 125

11:21 τοῦ οὐρανοῦ] om του d^{-107}

11:26 δίδωμι] + υμιν d 53 767 Lat$_{cod}$ 100

11:28 om ὅσας ἐγὼ ἐντέλλομαι ὑμῖν d^{-610}

11:28 om πλανηθῆτε d^{-125} 610

11:31 om πάσας — αὐτήν d^{-106} Lat$_{cod}$ 100

12:3 τοὺς βωμοὺς αὐτῶν/καὶ συντρίψετε] tr d^{-106}

12:3 τάς] pr και d^{-106} Sa^3

12:3 στήλας αὐτῶν] om αυτων d^{-106}

12:5 ὑμῶν 1°] ημων 376-618^c 52'-528 d^{-44} 107* 68'

12:6 τὰς ἀπαρχάς] om τας d

12:6 om καὶ τὰ ἑκούσια ὑμῶν d^{-106}

12:9 κληρονομίαν] + αυτων d

12:11 τῶν δώρων] δωρον d^{-106} 59 (το δ.)

12:12 παῖδες ὑμῶν] om υμων d^{-125} 71 Lat$_{cod}$ 100

12:17 om τὰ πρωτότοκα— εὐχάς d

12:21 τὴν ἐπιθυμίαν] πασαν επ. d^{-106}

*12:29 om καί ult — fin d^{-106} Bo$^{A'}$

13:2 om τὸ σημεῖον ἢ τὸ τέρας d⁻¹⁰⁶

13:3 καρδίας ὑμῶν] om υμων 72 d⁻¹⁰⁶ Anast 525

13:3 om ἐξ ὅλης d⁻¹⁰⁶ Anast 529

13:4 om καὶ τὰς ἐντολας αὐτοῦ φυλάξεσθε B d⁻¹⁰⁶

13:5 om σου 1° d⁻⁴⁴' 630

13:5 om τοῦ λυτρωσαμένου σε ἐκ τῆς δουλείας d⁻¹⁰⁶

13:5 om καί ult — fin d⁻¹⁰⁶

13:6 om ἡ ἐν τῷ κόλπῳ σου 75 d⁻¹⁰⁶

13:6 ὁ φίλος] om ὁ B 15 d⁻¹⁰⁶ Or VI 247

13:6 om ὁ ἴσος τῆς ψυχῆς σου d⁻¹⁰⁶

13:8 om αὐτῷ 1° d⁻106 125

13:10 om ὅτι — fin d⁻¹⁰⁶

13:14 om init — ἐρωτήσεις d⁻¹⁰⁶

*13:15 om ἀναθέματι 58 d⁻¹⁰⁶ 246 75' 392 Bo = Ⓜ

13:16 om πάντα 1° d⁻¹⁰⁶

13:16 διδόους αὐτῆς] om αυτης d⁻106 Pal³

13:16 πόλιν] + αυτων d

13:16 σκῦλα αὐτῆς 2°] σκελη αυτου (c var) d

*13:18 om ὅσας ἐγὼ ἐντέλλομαι σοὶ σήμερον d⁻¹⁰⁶ Boᴬ'

*14:2 om κύριος ὁ θεός σου d⁻¹⁰⁶ 71' Bo

14:7 om καὶ ὁπλην οὐ διχηλοῦσιν d⁻¹⁰⁶

14:8 ὃν] υιων (c var) d⁻⁴⁴

*14:8 κρεῶν αὐτῶν] κρεων αυτου d⁻106 125 Bo Sa¹

*14:12 om καί 2° d⁻¹⁰⁷' Bo

*14:12 om καί 3° d⁻¹⁰⁷' Bo

*14:13 καὶ τὸν γύπα] om καί d⁻¹⁰⁷' Boᴬ'

*14:13 καὶ τὸν ἰκτῖνα] om καὶ d$^{-107'}$ Bo^A'

 14:17 om καί ult d$^{-107'}$

 14:21 ἀγροῦ] αγιου d^{-106}

 14:22 τῶν βοῶν] om των d^{-125}

 14:23 om σε d^{-106} 59 Aeth^F

 14:28 om οὐδε κλῆρος d^{-106}

 15:3 ἄφεσιν] pr οτι επικεκληται d^{-106}

 15:5 om φυλάσσειν καί d^{-106}

 15:5 om πάσας 16 d^{-106}

 15:9 om τὸ ἔτος d

 15:11 om ἐγώ d^{-106} Lat$_{Spec}$ 24

 15:11 om ποιεῖν τὸ ῥῆμα τοῦτο λέγων d^{-106}

 15:12 om αὐτόν d^{-106} 75

 15:15 om ἐγώ d^{-106} Sa^3

 15:20 φάγῃ] σφαγη 616 d^{-106}

 15:22 om ὁ ἀκάθαρτος — fin d^{-106}

 16:2 om κυρίῳ τῷ θεῷ σου d^{-106}

 16:3 om ἐπ' αὐτοῦ 2° d^{-106} 107 246 Tht I 424 Sa^1 3(vid)

 16:8 om ἡμέρᾳ τῇ d^{-106} 107

 16:9 fin] + ολοκληρους d^{-106}

 16:11 κυρίου τοῦ θεοῦ σου] αυτου d^{-106}

 16:12 om γῇ 618* 414 d^{-106}

 16:12 om καὶ φυλάξῃ 29 d^{-106}

 16:13 init] pr εις d^{-106}

*16:13 om σεαυτῷ d^{-106} Bo^{BE}

 16:14 om init — (15) αὐτόν d^{-106}

16:16 om ἐν τῇ ἑορτῇ 2° d⁻¹⁰⁶

16:18 om αἷς — σοί d⁻¹⁰⁶

16:18 κατὰ φυλάς / καὶ κρινοῦσι τὸν λαόν] tr d⁻¹⁰⁶

16:20 om καί — fin d⁻¹⁰⁶

*17:5 om ἐκείνην d⁻¹⁰⁶ Aethᴹ Arm Boᴬ'

17:8 om ἀνὰ μέσον ἀντιλογία ἀντιλογίας d⁻¹⁰⁶

17:9 σοί ⌒ (10)1° d⁻¹⁰⁶ᵐᵍ

17:11 τοῦ ῥήματος οὗ ἐὰν ἀναγγείλωσι σοί] τουτων d⁻¹⁰⁶

17:14 om καὶ κατακληρονομήσῃς αὐτήν d⁻¹⁰⁶

17:15 om καθιστῶν d⁻¹⁰⁶

17:15 om καθαστήσεις ἐπὶ σεαυτὸν ἄρχοντα 72 d⁻¹⁰⁶

*17:17 καὶ ἀργύριον] om καί d⁻¹⁰⁶ Bo

17:18 om ἔσται B d⁻¹⁰⁶ Aeth Sa³

17:19 om καὶ ἔσται μετ' αὐτοῦ d⁻¹⁰⁶

17:19 φυλάσσεσθαι πάσας] και d⁻¹⁰⁶

17:19 om ταύτας d⁻¹⁰⁶ 125

17:19 ποιεῖν] + και φυλαττειν d⁻¹⁰⁶

17:20 ἵνα μή 2°] και d⁻¹⁰⁶

17:20 om ἀπό d⁻¹⁰⁶

17:20 παραβῇ / τῶν ἐντολῶν] tr d⁻¹⁰⁶

18:3 ἐάν τε] η d⁻¹⁰⁶

18:5 εὐλογεῖν] + αυτω (αυτον 125) d⁻¹⁰⁶

13:7 λειτουργήσει] λειτουργει σοι d

18:7 om ἐκεῖ d 53' 18 Lat_cod 100

18:10 om φαρμακός d⁻¹⁰⁶

18:14 om κληδονισμῶν καί d⁻¹⁰⁶ Lat_cod 100

18:18 λαλήσει] -σω d̲⁻¹⁰⁶ 125ᶜ

18:21 om οὐκ 15 d̲⁻¹⁰⁶ 458 509

19:9 om ἃς ἐγὼ ἐντέλλομαι σοί d̲⁻¹⁰⁶ 125

19:13 om σοὶ ἔσται d̲⁻¹⁰⁶ᶜ 125

19:15 om κατὰ πᾶν d̲⁻¹⁰⁶

19:15 om καταλέγων αὐτοῦ ἀσέβειαν d̲⁻¹⁰⁶

19:17 om ἔναντι 2° d̲⁻¹⁰⁶

19:17 om ἔναντι τῶν 2° d̲⁻¹⁰⁶ 125

19:17 om οἱ ult — fin d̲⁻¹⁰⁶

19:18 om ἀκριβῶς d̲⁻¹⁰⁶

19:18 om ἀντέστη κατὰ τοῦ ἀδελφοῦ αὐτοῦ d̲⁻¹⁰⁶

*19:19 om αὐτῶν 58 d̲⁻¹⁰⁶ 458-767 Arm(vid) Bo

19:20 om ἀκούσαντες d̲⁻¹⁰⁶

19:20 ἔτι] + τουτο d̲⁻¹⁰⁶

19:20 om κατά — fin d̲⁻¹⁰⁶

20:3 πόλεμον] pr τον B M d̲⁻¹⁰⁶ Cyr I 369

20:3 om μηδὲ θραύεσθε d̲⁻¹⁰⁶

20:5 ἐγκαινιεῖ] ληψεται d̲⁻¹⁰⁶

20:6 τίς ∩ (3) d̲⁻¹⁰⁶

20:12 ποιήσωσιν] ποιησω d̲⁻¹⁰⁶

20:14 om πάντα τά d̲⁻¹⁰⁶

20:14 om πάντα 2° d̲⁻¹⁰⁶

20:17 om καί 1° d̲ 71'

20:17 καὶ Εὐαῖον] om καί d̲ 71' = ☺

20:17 om καὶ Γεργεσαῖον d̲

20:18 om ὅσα ἐποίησαν τοῖς d̲⁻¹⁰⁶

20:19 μή] και d$^{-44'}$

21:2 σου 2°] + οι πρωτιστοι d^{-106}

21:3 om ἥτις d^{-106}

21:5 om ὅτι — fin d^{-106}

21:6 om οἱ ἐγγίζοντες τῷ τραυματίᾳ d^{-106}

21:8 αὐτοῖς] αυτης 72 d^{-106} 610 75*

21:14 om αὐτήν 2° d^{-106}

21:15 om αὐτῶν 2° 58 46 d^{-106} Phil I 209^{ap} ^{Lat}Ambr Cain I 13 Aeth Arm Sa^{8} = (M)

*21:16 om τον υἱόν d^{-106} Bo

21:16 om τὸν προτότοκον d^{-106} ^{Lat}Ambr Cain I 13 Aeth

*21:17 om υἱόν d Arm Bo

21:18 καὶ φωνήν] η d^{-106} 71'

21:19 om αὐτοῦ 1° 72-426 d^{-106} 71' Arm

21:10 om ἐρεθίζει d^{-106}

21:21 αὐτοῦ] αυτων 616* d 767 30 799 120

21:23 οὐκ] και d^{-106c}

21:23 om τοῦ 376 529 19' d^{-106} 509

21:23 om αὐτόν d^{-106}

21:23 om σου 58 d^{-106} 30 799

22:3 om οὕτως ποιήσεις 2° 72 d 458 Arab

22:3 om αὐτοῦ καὶ οὕτως ποιήσεις 2° d^{-106}

22:4 om ὄψη — fin d^{-106}

22:6 om ἐπὶ παντί d^{-106}

22:6 om τῆς d^{-106}

22:6 om ἐπὶ τῶν 2° d^{-106}

22:9 τόν] παν d⁻¹⁰⁶

22:14 om αὐτῇ 1° d⁻¹⁰⁶ Armᵗᵉ

22:18 om ἡ γερουσία τῆς πόλεως ἐκείνης d⁻¹⁰⁶

22:20 om οὗτος 73' d⁻¹⁰⁶ Arm

*22:21 om καί init 72 d⁻⁴⁴' Arm Bo

*22:21 τὴν νεᾶνιν] αυτην d⁻¹⁰⁶ Bo

22:25 om τήν 1° d⁻¹⁰⁶

22:25 om τήν 2° d⁻¹⁰⁶

22:25 om τὸν κοιμώμενον μεθ' αὐτῆς μόνον d⁻¹⁰⁶

22:27 om comma d⁻¹⁰⁶

22:29 om ὁ ἄνθρωπος ὁ κοιμηθεὶς μετ' αὐτῆς d⁻¹⁰⁶

22:29 τῆς νεάνιδος] αυτης 72 d⁻¹⁰⁶ Arab

23:3 om init — κυρίου 1° 58 414ᵗˣᵗ 314 d⁻¹⁰⁶ᶜ

23:4 om μετά d⁻¹⁰⁶

23:4 om τῆς F d⁻¹⁰⁶

23:5 om ὅτι — fin d⁻¹⁰⁶

23:6 om αὐτοῖς 2° d⁻¹⁰⁶ 53'

23:10 τὴν παρεμβολήν] αυτην d⁻¹⁰⁶

*23:12 ἐκεῖ ἔξω] tr 72 d⁻¹⁰⁶ Bo

23:13 om σου ult d

23:17 καὶ οὐκ ἔσται 1°] ουτε d⁻¹⁰⁶

*23:17 καὶ οὐκ 2°] om καί V 72 d⁻¹⁰⁶ Bo

23:20 om ἵνα — ἔργοις σου d⁻¹⁰⁶

23:21 θεός σου] om σου d⁻¹⁰⁶ 630 Fulg Ep I 11 Latcod 100

24:3 om ὁ 1° d⁻⁴⁴ 106ᶜ 610 71 Cyr I 584

24:3 om καὶ δώσει εἰς τὰς χεῖρας αὐτῆς d⁻¹⁰⁶

24:3 om ἐκ τῆς οἰκίας αὐτοῦ $\underline{d}^{-106}$

24:3 ὁ ἀνήρ 2°] om ὁ $\underline{d}^{-44'}$

24:3 om ἑαυτῷ γυναῖκα $\underline{d}^{-106}$

24:4 ἑαυτῷ γυναῖκα] εις γυν. $\underline{d}^{-106}$

24:4 om μετὰ τὸ μιανθῆναι αὐτήν $\underline{d}^{-106}$

24:4 θεὸς ὑμῶν] om υμων $\underline{d}^{-106}$ 767 799 18 Arm

24:7 om αὐτῶν $\underline{d}^{-106}$ 458

24:8 om φυλάξῃ σφόδρα $\underline{d}^{-106}$

24:8 ὑμῖν 1°] υμεις $\underline{d}^{-44}$

*24:10 om ὀφείλημα 2° 528 $\underline{d}^{-106}$ 407 ^{Lat}cod 100 Ambr

Tob 57 69 Spec 11 Bo Sa^3

24:12 om ὁ ἄνθρωπος $\underline{d}^{-106}$

24:13 om καὶ σοί — fin $\underline{d}^{-106}$

24:15 om init — αὐτοῦ $\underline{d}^{-106}$

24:15 ὅτι — ἐλπίδα] post σου tr $\underline{d}^{-106}$

24:15 κατὰ σοῦ / πρὸς κύριον] tr $\underline{d}^{-106}$

24:15 om καὶ ἔσται ἐν σοὶ ἁμαρτία $\underline{d}^{-106}$

24:19 τῷ ἀγρῷ σου] αυτω $\underline{d}^{-106}$

24:19 ἵνα — (20)καλαμήσασθαι] post (22)fin tr $\underline{d}^{-106}$

24:21 οὐκ ἐπανατρυγήσεις — (22)fin] ομοιως σοι εσται $\underline{d}^{-106}$

25:2 αὐτόν 2° ⌒ (3)1° 528 $\underline{d}^{-106}$

25:3 om ὑπερ ταύτας τὰς πληγάς $\underline{d}^{-106}$ Tht I 432

25:7 om ἐπι τὴν πύλην $\underline{d}^{-106}$ 75 ^{Lat}Aug Quaest VI 7 Arab

25:7 om οὐκ — (8)καί init $\underline{d}^{-106}$

25:9 om καί init $\underline{d}^{-106}$

25:11 om ἐκ χειρὸς τοῦ τύπτοντος αὐτόν$\underline{d}^{-106}$

25:11   fin] + του τυπτοντος τον ανδρα αυτης $\underline{d}^{-106}$

25:15   καί 1°⌒ 2° $\underline{d}^{-44'}$

25:15   om ἀληθινὸν καί $\underline{d}^{-44'}$

25:16   om πᾶς 1° — fin $\underline{d}^{-106}$

25:17   σου] ημων $\underline{d}^{-106}$ 318 120

25:19   κύριος ὁ θεός σου / δίδωσιν σοί] tr $\underline{d}^{-106}$

25:19   om κατακληρονομῆσαι αὐτήν $\underline{d}^{-106}$ 75 71

26:1   om ἐν κλήρῳ $\underline{B}$ 72 $\underline{d}^{-106}$

26:1   om καὶ κατοικήσῃς ἐπ᾽ αὐτῆς $\underline{d}^{-106}$

26:2   καὶ ἐμβαλεῖς] om και $\underline{d}^{-44'}$

26:3   om κύριος V $\underline{d}^{-106}$ 509

26:5   εἰς ἔθνος] ως εθνος $\underline{d}^{-106}$ 125

26:6   οἱ Αἰγύπτιοι / καὶ ἐταπείνωσαν ἡμᾶς] tr $\underline{d}^{-106}$

26:6   om καί ult — fin $\underline{d}^{-106}$

26:7   om καί ult — fin $\underline{d}^{-106}$ 125 458 799

26:8   om καὶ ἐν ὁράμασι — fin $\underline{d}^{-106}$

26:10   σου 1°⌒ 2° 426 73'-551 $\underline{d}$ 129^{txt} 458 30 134^{txt} 630'

26:11   om ὁ θεός σου $\underline{d}^{-106}$ 610

26:12   ἔτει] ορει $\underline{d}^{-106}$

26:15   om comma $\underline{d}^{-106}$

26:16   om καί ult — fin 52 $\underline{d}^{-106}$ 53' 799 630

26:17   om καὶ τὰ κρίματα αὐτοῦ $\underline{d}^{-106}$ Aeth^{M}

26:19   εἶναι 1°⌒ 2° $\underline{d}^{-125}$

27:3   om σου 1° $\underline{d}^{-106}$

27:3   om ὃν τρόπον — (4)᾽Ιορδάνην $\underline{d}^{-106}$

27:4   στήσετε] pr και $\underline{d}^{-106}$ 134

27:4   om οὓς ἐγὼ ἐντέλλομαί σοι σήμερον d⁻¹⁰⁶

27:4   om καί ult — fin d⁻¹⁰⁶

27:5   σου ⌒ (6)1° 528 d⁻⁴⁴' 53' 458ᵗˣᵗ 71

27:6   om ἐπ' αὐτοῦ d⁻⁴⁴ Wᴵ

27:8   τῶν λίθων] τον λιθον τουτον d

27:10   om κυρίου τοῦ θεοῦ σου 72 d⁻¹⁰⁶ 71

27:10   om ἃ ἐγὼ ἐντέλλομαί σοι σήμερον d⁻¹⁰⁶

27:12   om καί 426 d⁻¹⁰⁶ 107

27:13   καὶ Ἀσήρ] om καί 58-72-82 320 537 d^Lat cod 100 Arm

27:19   om καί ult — (20)fin d⁻¹⁰⁶ᵐᵍ

27:21   om καί — fin d⁻¹⁰⁶ 527

27:22   ἐκ παρτός] η πατρος αδελφης d⁻¹⁰⁶

27:22   om ἤ — (23)fin d⁻¹⁰⁶

27:24   om καί — fin d 527

27:25   om καί — fin d(sed hab καί 106)

27:26   om τοῦ ποιῆσαι — fin d⁻¹⁰⁶

28:1   θεοῦ ὑμῶν] θεου ημων V 72 46-52-551* 19 d 30 59 Arm

28:2   om πᾶσαι 761 d⁻¹⁰⁶ 458 30 121-318 68' ᴸᵃᵗcod 104 Arab

28:3   om εὐλογημένος συ 2° d⁻¹⁰⁶ 71

28:4   εὐλογημένα] και d⁻¹⁰⁶

28:4   om καί 1° d⁻¹⁰⁶

28:4   om καί ult d⁻¹⁰⁶

28:5   om εὐλογημέναι d⁻¹⁰⁶

28:5   om καί d⁻¹⁰⁶ 83

28:6   om εὐλογημένος σου 2° 72 d 767

28:11   om καὶ επι τοῖς ἐκγόνοις τῶν κτηνῶν σου d⁻¹⁰⁶

28:13   om ἐάν — (14)fin d⁻¹⁰⁶

28:15   om τῆς φωνῆς κυρίου τοῦ θεοῦ σου d⁻¹⁰⁶

28:15   om καὶ ποιεῖν πάσας d⁻¹⁰⁶

28:15   ἐντολὰς αὐτοῦ] εντολας του κυριου σου (cvar) d⁻¹⁰⁶

28:15   ὅσας ἐγὼ ἐντέλλομαί σοι σήμερον καί] και πορευεσθε
        οπισω θεων ετερων λατρευειν αυτοις d⁻¹⁰⁶ 125

28:16   om ἐπικατάρατος σύ 2° d 71 Aeth

28:18   om ἐπικατάρατος d⁻¹⁰⁶

28:18   om καί 1° d⁻¹⁰⁶ 125

28:18   om καί ult d⁻¹⁰⁶

28:19   om ἐπικατάρατος σύ 2° 58 413 d 246

28:20   ἀπολέσῃ σε] om σε 72 d⁻¹⁰⁶

28:21   om σε 2° d⁻¹²⁵

28:22   om καί 1° d⁻¹⁰⁶

28:22   om καί 2° d⁻¹⁰⁶ 71

28:22   om καί 3° d⁻¹⁰⁶ 71

28:22   om καί 4° d⁻¹⁰⁶

28:27   om καί 1° d⁻¹⁰⁶ Aeth

28:27   om σε 2° 16-616 d⁻¹⁰⁶ 125 664 75* Aeth

28:28   om καὶ ἐκστάσει διανοίας d⁻¹⁰⁶

28:29   ἔσῃ 2°] εκ d⁻¹²⁵

28:32   om καὶ οἱ ὀφθαλμοί — fin d⁻¹⁰⁶

28:34   om init — (35)fin d⁻¹⁰⁶

28:38   om ὅτι — fin d⁻¹⁰⁶

28:39   om καὶ κατεργᾷ d⁻¹⁰⁶ 799

28:39   om οὐδέ — fin d⁻¹⁰⁶

28:40   om ὅτι — fin d⁻¹⁰⁶

28:43 om ὅς ἔστιν ἐν d⁻¹⁰⁶

28:43 om ἄνω 2° 16-528 d⁻¹⁰⁶ 53' 318 Tht I 437 Lat_codd
       100 103

28:43 om κάτω 2° d⁻¹⁰⁶ 53' 68 Tht I 437 Lat_cod 103 Ambr
       Tob 66

28:44 om οὗτος ἔσται — fin d⁻¹⁰⁶

28:45 om σε 2° d 71

28:45 om καὶ ἔως ἄν ἀπολέσῃ σε 426 d⁻¹⁰⁶ 246 458 669ᵗˣᵗ
       Arab Sa³ = Ⓜ

28:45 om αὐτοῦ 1° d⁻¹⁰⁶ 125 71

28:45 om ὅσα ἐνετείλατό σοι d⁻¹⁰⁶ 125

28:47 om διά — fin d⁻¹⁰⁶ 71

28:48 om καί 2° 707 d⁻⁶¹⁰

28:48 om καὶ ἐν ἐκλείψει πάντων d⁻¹⁰⁶

28:48 om ἔως ἄν ἐξολεθρεύσῃ d⁻¹⁰⁶

28:50 om ἔθνος ἀναιδὲς προσώπῳ d⁻¹⁰⁶

28:51 om ὤστε — (52) καί 1° d⁻¹⁰⁶

28:52 om αἷς 2° — fin d⁻¹⁰⁶ 71

28:53 ἐν 1°⌒2° d⁻¹⁰⁶

28:53 om ἤ θλίψει σε ὁ ἐχθρός σου d⁻¹⁰⁶

28:54 om τὴν ἐν τῷ κόλπῳ d⁻¹⁰⁶

28:56 om init — (57) fin d⁻¹⁰⁶

28:58 τό 1°⌒2° d⁻¹⁰⁶

28:60 ὀδύνην] οδον d⁻¹⁰⁶

28:61 τοῦ νόμου τούτου] τουτω d 55 Lat_cod 100

28:62 om τά 15* d⁻¹⁰⁶ 71

28:64   οἷς] ης 376 d̲

28:65   om ἐν d̲$^{-106}$

28:65   σοι κύριος ἐκεῖ] κ̅ς̅ ο θ̅ς̅ σου επι σοι d̲$^{-106}$

29:2   om καὶ πᾶσι τοῖς θεράπουσιν αὐτοῦ   72 d̲$^{-44'}$

29:3   om init — (4) καί init d̲$^{-44'}$

29:10   κριταὶ ὑμῶν] om υμων   72 d̲$^{-106}$

29:13   om ὃν τρόπον 2° d̲$^{-106}$

29:13   ὤμοσε / τοῖς πατράσι σου] tr d̲$^{-106}$

29:13   om Ἀβραάμ   — fin d̲$^{-106}$

29:15   σήμερον   1°∩ 2° 618^{txt} cprm 46-500 d̲$^{-106}$ 53' 321* cprm

29:16   om ὡς 2° d̲$^{-106}$

29:16   om οὓς παρήλθετε   d̲$^{-106}$

29:17   om αὐτῶν   1° 426 d̲$^{-106}$ 127 71

29:19   om τῇ 1° d̲$^{-106}$

29:20   om καὶ ὁ ζῆλος αὐτοῦ d̲$^{-106}$

29:20   om αἱ γεγραμμέναι — τούτου d̲$^{-106}$ 71

29:21   om διαστελεῖ — κατά d̲$^{-106}$

29:21   om τῆς διαθήκης d̲$^{-106}$ Arab

29:22   om τῆς γῆς 72 d̲$^{-106}$ 527

29:23   om οὐ σπαρήσεται οὐδὲ ἀνατελεῖ d̲$^{-106}$ Sa^3

29:23   ἐπ᾽ αὐτῆς] επ᾽ αυτοις   d̲$^{-106}$ 610

29:23   om Ἀδαμά — fin d̲$^{-106}$

29:26   om καί 2° — fin d̲$^{-106}$

29:28   om καὶ παροξυσμῷ μεγάλω σφόδρα   d̲$^{-106}$

30:3   om εἰς d̲

30:6   σου 1°∩ 2° d̲$^{-106}$

30:6   ἐξ 1° ⌒ 2° $\underline{d}^{-106}$

30:9   om ἐν τοῖς ἐκγόνοις $\underline{d}$ 55

30:10   καί 2° ⌒ 3° $\underline{d}^{-106}$ 343 ^{Lat}cod 100 = Ⓜ

30:10   om ἐπί 16* $\underline{d}^{-106}$ 125

30:15   πρὸ προσώπου σου / σήμερον] tr $\underline{d}$ Arm

30:16   καί 1° ⌒ 4° $\underline{d}^{-106}$ 71

30:18   κληρονομῆσαι] pr καὶ $\underline{d}^{-44}$ 125

31:4   κύριος] + ο θεος (+ σου Β 44) Β $\underline{d}^{-106}$

31:4   om αὐτοῖς $\underline{d}^{-106}$ 68'

31:14   τῆς σκηνῆς τοῦ μαρτυρίου 2°] αυτος $\underline{d}^{-106}$ 125

31:16   om κύριος $\underline{d}^{-106}$ 458

31:17   om ἔσται κατάβρωμα καί $\underline{d}^{-106}$

31:18   om ἃς ἐποίησαν $\underline{d}^{-106}$ 125 246

31:20   γάλα μέλι] tr 72 $\underline{d}^{-44}$'

31:20   om κορήσουσιν $\underline{d}^{-106}$ 318

31:21   στόματος 2°] σπερματος 707 $\underline{d}^{-125}$ 75

31:21   σπέρματος] στοματος 707 $\underline{d}^{-44}$ 125

31:25   κυρίου ⌒ (26) $\underline{d}^{-125}$

32:5   οὐκ] επ' $\underline{d}$

32:43   θεοῦ 1° ⌒ 2° $\underline{d}^{-106}$ 318 Sa^{6}

32:44   om Μωυσῆς 2° $\underline{d}^{-125}$ 610

32:45   om τούτους 72 $\underline{d}^{-125}$ 74-76 318

32:46   πάντας 2° → fin] ταυτα $\underline{d}^{-106}$

32:49   om τοῦτο ὅρος $\underline{d}^{-106}$

33:2   om ἄγγελοι $\underline{d}$

33:5   ἅμα] ανα $\underline{d}^{-106}$ 107

33:8   om εἶπεν — αὐτοῦ 1° d

33:14   μηνῶν] βουνων d^{-106}

33:21   om γη d^{-106} 120

34:4   om καί ult d

34:10   om προσωπον 1° 19 d 392

Only 26 of these 466 readings (5.5%) are shared by Bo or
any Bo ms. Eight of these 26 readings are the omission of καί
and since Bo's translation of καί is erratic, these cannot be
used as evidence for dependence on a Greek source. The remaining 18 readings include one addition, one omission, and
one substitution of the possessive pronoun. This kind of
variant has been shown to be typical of Bo. Fifteen substantial readings remain, seven of which are supported by only
a part of the Bohairic evidence. These seven are all omissions
and are frequently the result of parablepsis due to homoioteleuton. The identity of reading of the d group and some Bo
mss in these instances is therefore probably mere coincidence.
The remaining eight readings include one transposition (23:12)
and one substitution of a pronoun for a noun (22:21) ad sensum.
These are also coincidence. Six omissions remain but they too
can be attributed to coincidence. The noun υἱόν is twice
omitted from the phrase τὸν υἱὸν πρωτότοκον and in context
this not only makes sense, but may also have been the result
of parablepsis. The four remaining omissions are not enough
to justify further comment. It is clear that Bo is not a
witness to the d group, and any similarity of reading is due
to mere coincidence.

C. The following is a list of those instances where the <u>d</u> group and one other group attest a reading. Those readings listed before under the hexaplaric recension are not again included.

List 4   Readings attested by <u>d</u> and one other group

1:15   om καὶ πεντηκοντάρχους B* 550-552 <u>d</u> 664* 767 <u>t</u> 71'

1:25   ὁ θεός ἡμῶν] om ημων 618 46-761 <u>d</u> 767 <u>t</u> 120 509 Arm^{te}

1:39   ἔσεσθαι] εσονται <u>d</u> <u>t</u> ^{Lat}codd 91 92 94 96 Arm

1:43   καὶ παρέβητε] ουδε εποιησετε κατα (c var) <u>d</u> <u>t</u>

2:6   μέτρω] pr εν <u>d</u>⁻¹⁰⁶ <u>t</u>

2:8   Αἰλών] ανατολων <u>d</u> <u>t</u>^{-370c}

2:10   ·Ομμίν 64^c <u>d</u>⁻¹²⁵ 321' <u>t</u>^{-370 799} 18'-669 55^c

2:11   Ὀμμίν] νοομμιν (-μμην 799) <u>d</u>⁻¹²⁵ <u>t</u>

2:28   om καὶ φάγομαι καὶ ὕδωρ ἀργυρίου ἀποδώσῃ μοι <u>cI</u> (c var) <u>d</u> 68'-120

2:29   om ἡμῶν 58 <u>d</u> 75'-767 799 71' 18 59 ^{Lat}cod 100 Arm

2:37   γῆν] pr την 58-72 d <u>f</u>⁻¹²⁹ 59

3:3   σπέρμα] καταλειμμα (c var) <u>d</u> <u>t</u>

3:4   ἐν Βασάν] εκ Βασαν <u>d</u> <u>t</u> 68

*3:6   τὰ παιδία] + αυτων V 417 <u>d</u> 30 <u>t</u> Aeth Bo Sa^{1 2}

3:17   τὴν φασγά] της φαραγγος <u>d</u> <u>t</u> Sa²

4:25   τὸ πονηρόν] om το B^c 52-615 <u>d</u> <u>t</u>⁻⁷⁹⁹

4:27   om πᾶσιν 82 56* <u>d</u> <u>t</u> = ⑪

4:33   ἐκ] post πυρος tr <u>d</u> <u>t</u>

4:43   Γαλαάδ] pr γη <u>d</u>⁻¹⁰⁷ <u>t</u>

4:43   Γαυλών] αυλων <u>d</u> <u>t</u> 392

4:43 ρασάν] pr γη d̲ t̲

4:48 ἐπί 2°] εως d̲ t̲ Aeth Arm

4:49 ἡλίου] + και εως θαλασσης των δυσμων ηλιου d̲ 767 t̲ Arab

5:10 τὰ προστάγματα] τας εντολας d̲ t̲

5:27 om ὅσα 2° — πρὸς σέβ̲ d̲$^{-106}$

5:32 οὐδέ] η 376 C̲'' d̲ 85 18 28 319

6:5 ψυχῆς] ισχυος M^{mg} d̲ 767 t̲

6:5 δυνάμεως] διανοιας 376 d̲ t̲ 59

6:7 οἴκῳ] οικοις d̲ t̲$^{-370}$

7:2 οὐδέ] ουτε V d̲ 30' t̲ Cyr III 80 Sa^{3}

7:7 κύριος] + ο θεος 414 d̲ 458 t̲$^{-370}$

7:10 πρόσωπον 1°] + αυτων d̲ t̲ Aeth

7:12 τὸ ἔλεος] τον ελαιον d̲$^{-125}$ n̲$^{-75}$ 127

*7:15 αὐτά] + επι τους εχθρους σου και d̲$^{-125}$ t̲ Aeth Arm Bo Sa

7:24 ἐκ τοῦ τόπου ἐκείνου] υποκατωθεν του ουρανου d̲ t̲ Arab = Ⓜ

8:6 τὰς ἐντολάς] pr πασας d̲$^{-44}$ t̲ Aeth

8:9 ὀρέων] οριων 46 d̲ t̲

8:13 om ἀργύριου καὶ χρυσίου πληθυνθέντος σοι 417-552^{txt} 19 d̲ 458 t̲ 318-527 55 509

8:17 ἡ ἰσχύς] pr οτι d̲ t̲

8:18 πατράσιν σου] + τω αβρααμ και ισαακ και ιακωβ (c var) d̲ t̲

8:18 σήμερον] η ημερα αυτη (c var) d̲ t̲ = Ⓜ

9:4   κύριος] + ο θεος σου d t⁻⁷⁹⁹

9:10   ἡμέρα] pr εν τη d⁻⁴⁴ t

9:10   ἐκκλησίας] pr της d⁻⁴⁴ t

9:12   ἐποίησαν] + γαρ d⁻⁴⁴ t

9:23   om κύριος d⁻¹⁰⁶ s⁻³⁴³ᵐᵍ 28

9:26   θεόν] κυριον d t ᴸᵃᵗcod 100 Arm

10:4   πλάκας] pr δυο 58 d t 59 Arm

10:6   βηρώθ] pr Μακηδωθ και παρενεβαλον εις d 767 t

10:6   υἱῶν] εν υιοις d t

10:6   ἐκεῖ 1° — fin] post (7)fin tr d 767 t

10:7   fin] + κακειθεν απηραν και παρενεβαλον εις Εβρωνα
       εκειθεν απηραν και παρενεβαλον εν Γασιων Γαβερ
       εκειθεν απηραν και παρενεβαλον εν τη ερημω Σιν
       αυτη Καδης εκειθεν απηραν και παρενεβαλον εν τω
       ορει Ωρ (c var) d 767 t

*10:10 om κύριος ult 72-381' 16-529 d⁻¹⁰⁶ 30 71'-527 Arm Bo

10:15 υἱῶν] σου 72* c pr m d t

10:16 σκληροκαρδίαν] ακροβυστιαν της καρδιας d t = Ⓜ

*10:17 καὶ ἰσχυρός] ο ισχυρος A 58 761 d t Phil V 249ᵃᵖ
       Bo = Ⓜ

11:7   τὰ μεγάλα] + εκεινα d t

11:9   init] pr και d t = Ⓜ

11:15 fin] + τοις εν αγρω σου d t

*11:24 om ποταμοῦ 2° V 82 d 246 Μⁱ⁻⁴⁵⁸ 392 z⁻⁸³ 669ᵐᵍ
       509 ᴸᵃᵗcod 100 Aeth Boᴬ' Pal

11:29 ὄρος 1°] ορους 376-707 19 d̲ f̲⁻⁵⁶ ¹²⁹ 619 Procop 905

12:7   ἐπιβάλητε / τας χεῖρας ὑμῶν] tr B d̲ t̲

12:7   οἶκοι] οικεται d̲ t̲

12:11 δόματα ὑμῶν] + και τας ευχας υμων d̲ (om τας 125) t̲

12:17 ταῖς πόλεσιν] pr πασαις d̲ t̲ Eus VI 13 Aeth Sa

12:18 om καὶ ὁ προσήλυτος d̲ t̲ Arab = Ⓜ

12:19 τὸν χρόνον] + σου d̲ t̲ Arm Barh 225 = Ⓜ

*12:21 μακρότερον] μακραν B̲ d̲ 344ᵐᵍ t̲ Bo

*12:21 ἀπέχῃ] + απο d̲ 85 t̲ Bo

12:31 βδελύγματα] pr τα d̲ t̲

13:2   καὶ λατρεύσωμεν] οπισω d̲ t̲ = Ⓜ

13:4   αὐτῷ ult] + μονω d̲⁻¹²⁵ 127 t̲⁻³⁷⁰

13:6   οἱ πατέρες] ο πατηρ d̲ t̲

*13:14 om σαφῶς b̲⁻¹¹⁸ᵐᵍ 314 537ᵐᵍ d̲⁻¹⁰⁶ Bo Sa³

13:17 ἀπο θυμοῦ / τῆς ὀργῆς] tr d̲ 53 t̲ 527

13:18 σου ult] υμων d̲⁻¹⁰⁶ ¹²⁵ t̲

14:9   φάγεσθε 1°] pr ου d̲⁻¹⁰⁶ᶜ ¹²⁵ t̲

14:9   λεπίδες] + ταυτα A d̲⁻¹²⁵ t̲

14:16 αὐτῷ] αυτων d̲⁻¹⁰⁶ 127 t̲⁻³⁷⁰

15:3   ἐάν] δαν d̲ t̲

15:7   θεός σου] om σου 72' C"⁻¹⁶ 77' 417 528' d̲⁻¹⁰⁶ 85 28 Syh

15:12 δουλεύσει σοι / ἓξ ἔτη] tr d̲ t̲ Cyr VI 685 Aeth

15:17 om τό 1° d̲ t̲

15:17 το οὖς / αὐτοῦ] tr V d̲ t̲ 121

15:18 ἔσται] + σοι d̲ 54-75 t̲

*15:20 om τοῦ θεοῦ σου B b̲ d̲⁻¹⁰⁶ Lat_cod 100 Aeth⁻ᶜ Arm
Bo^A'

16:7 τοὺς οἴκους] τον οικον 58 551 d̲ 458 t̲ Lat_cod 100
Arm Sa³

17:8 ῥήματα] ρημα 414 d̲ W^I 85 t̲ Arm

17:11 οὐδέ] η C-73'-414 d̲⁻¹⁰⁶ 75 18 407

17:14 καθά] καθαπερ d̲ t̲

17:19 ταῦτα] αυτου C̲" d̲⁻¹⁰⁶ ¹²⁵ 407 Aeth

18:7 om οἱ Λευῖται o̲I̲-72 d̲⁻¹⁰⁶

18:21 fin] + ο ὗς d̲ t̲⁻⁷⁹⁹

18:22 ἀφέξεσθε] ακουσεσθε d̲ t̲ Syh^mg

19:5 συναγαγεῖν] εκκοψαι d̲ t̲ Aeth Arm

19:9 om πάσας 1° d̲⁻¹⁰⁶ ¹²⁵ 54-75'

20:3 μή 2°] + δε 552* d̲ 75' t̲

20:13 πᾶν ἀρσενικόν / αὐτῆς] tr V 19 d̲ t̲

20:14 κύριος ὁ θεός σου / δίδωσιν] tr d̲ t̲

20:17 om καὶ τὸν Χαναναῖον d̲ t̲

*20:17 Ἰεβουσαῖον / Γεργεσαῖον] tr B V d̲⁻⁴⁴ 127-767 t̲ 407
509 Bo

20:18 om πάντα 72 d̲⁻¹⁰⁶ z̲⁻⁸³ 630

21:3 εἴργασται] + εν αυτη d̲ t̲ = Ⓜ

21:22 κρίμα] pr η 58 d̲ t̲

21:23 τῇ ἡμέρα/ ἐκείνη] tr d̲ t̲

22:5 κυρίῳ τῷ θεῷ σου / ἐστιν] tr V 82 d̲ t̲ 318 Arm

22:15 γερουσίαν] + της πολεως εκεινης d̲ t̲

22:18 λήψεται] ληψονται d̲ t̲

22:26 om ὅτι B oI d^{-106} 630^{c}

23:16 om κατοικήσει 2° b d^{-106}

24:5 om αὐτοῦ ult b d^{-106}

24:17 κρίσιν / προσηλύτου] tr d t

25:6 παιδίον] + το πρωτοτοκον d t

25:9 τὸ ὑπόδημα / αὐτοῦ] tr d t

25:9 om ἀποκριθεῖσα F 29-72 d^{-106} f^{-129} 246 59 Or Matth 113 Sa^{3}

25:16 σου] + εστιν A b d 71 ^{Lat}cod 100

26:4 om τοῦ θυσιαστηρίου A*(vid) d 54-75' 730

26:5 πλῆθος] ισχυρον d t

26:5 πολύ] pr και d t^{-199}

26:8 om αὐτός 72 b d^{-106} 125 75 71 Arab Sa^{3} = Ⓜ

26:8 om καὶ ἐν χειρὶ κραταιᾷ 72 d^{-106} W^{I} $z^{-68'}$ 83 59

26:10 om γῆν 2° — fin 72 413-528 b d^{-106} 53' Arab = Ⓜ

27:3 om τῶν πατέρων 58-381' d^{-106} z^{-18} 68' = Ⓜ

27:6 om κυρίῳ τῷ θεῷ σου 2° 72 b $d^{-44'}$ 71 Aeth

27:12 διαβάντες] διαβαντων υμων d t Aeth Arm = Ⓜ

28:9 ὤμοσεν] + κ̅ς̅ d 127 t ^{Lat}cod 104 $Aeth^{-M}$ Sa^{16}

28:10 σοί] pr επι d t Aeth Arm Syh

28:11 om ἐπί ult — fin b d^{-106} 53'

28:12 om πολλῶν d t 318 Arab

*28:20 om ἕως ἂν 2° d^{-125} $z^{-68'}$ 83 646 Bo Sa^{3}

28:20 με] κ̅ν̅ d^{-125} t

28:24 om ἕως 1° — fin $C^{-131^{mg}}$ d^{-106}

28:25 om ἐν 2° 707 d t

28:25 om ἐν 4° F 58-72 d̲ 129 t̲ 59

28:36 λατρεύσεις] -σετε d̲ t̲ Lat_cod 100

28:41 om γάρ 82 b̲ d̲⁻¹²⁵ 527

28:59 πιστάς] πλειστας (c var) d̲⁻¹²⁵ t̲ 55 Sa³ ¹⁶

28:67 τοῦ φόβου] om του 376 d̲ t̲

29:15 μεθ' ὑμῶν / σήμερον 1°] tr A d̲⁻¹⁰⁶ t̲ Aeth

30:3 διεσκόρπισεν σέ] om σε 618 77 d̲ z̲⁻¹⁸' 630'

30:4 θεός σου (5) ο̲ι̲ d̲⁻¹⁰⁶ 458 30 71-392 630' 55

30:9 εὐφρανθῆναι] pr του d̲⁻¹⁰⁷' t̲

30:10 ἐπιστραφῇς] -φηση d̲⁻¹²⁵ t̲⁻⁷⁹⁹ 55

30:11 om ἐστιν 2° B 72-426 d̲⁻¹⁰⁶ 107 n̲⁻¹²⁷ 767 Tht I 441
       Arm

30:16 πολλοί]εν πολλοις d̲⁻¹²⁵ t̲

30:18 om σου V 82 529 d̲⁻⁴⁴ ¹²⁵ t̲⁻¹³⁴

30:19 Ἀβραάμ] pr τω 15 d̲ t̲

30:19 αὐτοῖς] υμιν d̲ t̲

31:8 κύριος] + ο θεος σου d̲ t̲ Sa³

31:11 om τοῦτον d̲ t̲ 318 68

*31:15 om καὶ ἔστη 2° — fin 72 C̲-414-422 d̲⁻¹⁰⁶ 54 343 318
       55 Lat_cod 103 Aeth⁻ᶜᴳ Bo

*31:16 εἰσπορεύεται] -ρευονται 376 d̲ 75 t̲ 55 Lat_codd 100
       103 104 Aeth Bo

31:20 αὐτῶν] + δουναι αυτοις B d̲⁻¹²⁵ t̲

31:21 αὐτόν] αυτους 414 d̲⁻¹²⁵ t̲

31:21 στόματος 2°] pr του V 707 417 d̲⁻¹²⁵ t̲⁻⁷⁹⁹ 392 407

31:21 ἐγὼ γὰρ οἶδα] οιδα γαρ 426 d̲⁻¹²⁵ t̲

31:22 om ἐν d⁻⁴⁴ᶜ 125 610 t

31:22 om ἐν $\underline{d}^{-44c}$ 125 610 $\underline{t}$

31:24 γράφων] λαλων $\underline{d}^{-125}$ $\underline{t}$

31:27 σκληρόν] + ει $\underline{d}$ $\underline{t}$

31:28 πάντας τούς] tr $\underline{d}^{-125}$ $\underline{t}$

32:25 ταμιείων] + αυτων 529 $\underline{d}^{-44}$ $\underline{f}^{-56}$ 129 75 59 Lat_codd
330 416

32:44 ἐδίδαξεν] εδειξεν $\underline{d}$ $\underline{t}^{-799}$

33:8 πείρα] περασμω $\underline{d}$ $\underline{t}$ 318

33:13 οὐρανοῦ] pr του $\underline{d}^{-125}$ $\underline{t}$

33:15 κορυφῆς 1°⌒2° $\underline{d}$ W^I $\underline{t}$ 120 59 646

33:18 Ἰσσαχάρ] τω ισαχαρ ειπεν (om τω 76 125) $\underline{d}$ $\underline{t}$ Arm

33:20 βραχίονα] βασιλεα (-λεις 799) 29 $\underline{d}$ $\underline{t}$

33:21 κρίσιν] κριματα $\underline{d}$ $\underline{t}$

33:24 ἀπο τέκνων] αποκτενων 376 $\underline{d}^{-106c}$ $\underline{t}$

34:4 Ἀβραάμ] pr προς $\underline{d}$ $\underline{t}$

34:7 οὐκ] pr και b d^{-106} Aeth Arm

34:9 πνεύματος] + σοφιας και $\underline{d}$ $\underline{t}$

34:11 πάσῃ] pr εν $\underline{d}$ $\underline{t}$ Arm

34:11 φαραώ] pr και εν $\underline{d}$ $\underline{t}$

34:12 κραταιάν] + και παντα (om και 799) $\underline{d}$ $\underline{t}$

The textual picture changes but slightly with the broader base of the $\underline{d}$ group and one other text group. Only 13 of these 175 readings (7%) include Bo. Six of these 13 readings are not significant one being an addition of a posessive pronoun, one a substitution of o for καί , one a substitution of η for οὐδέ , another a substitution of

the positive for the comparative form of an adjective,
one a change of number and person of a verb, and one a
transposition of nouns in a series. The remaining seven
significant readings include two (11:24 and 15:20) which
are attested only by Bo$^{A'}$. This identity of the readings
of a sub-group of Bo and that of two groups of Greek mss
is merely coincidence. The remaining five readings (7:15,
10:10, 12:21, 13:14, 28:20) include the omission of
κύριος, of σαφῶς, and of ἕως ἄν, and the addition of απο.
These are probably mere coincidence. The remaining plus
(7:15) is an ad sensum expansion of the object of a preposition. The Lord will place evils "upon (your enemies
and) those who hate you." The expansion may well be coincidental; in any event it is fully clear that the parent
text of Bo was not related to the d group.

   D. It is obvious from the evidence presented so far
that the t group is closely related to the d group. All
but 37 of the 175 readings above are shared by d and t.
It may even be more accurate to describe the t group in
Deut as a sub-group of a larger d group.[2] The next two
lists will in turn show the unique readings of the t
group, and the unique readings of t joined by one other
group. Because the group joining t is so frequently d,
and since the full list of d readings joined by one other
group has just been presented, only those few instances
where the group joining t is not d are listed. The

statistics are based on the full evidence.

List 5   Unique readings of the t group

*1:44   Σηίρ 64^c 321' $\underline{t}^{-370}$ 18'-669 Bo

*2:4   Σηίρ 64^c 321 $\underline{t}$ 18'-669 Bo

*2:5   Σηίρ 107 321' $\underline{t}$ 18'-669 Bo

*2:8   Σηίρ 64^c 107 321' $\underline{t}$ 18'-669 Bo

 2:9   Ἀροήρ] σηιρ $\underline{t}^{-370c}$ 799

*2:12   Σηίρ 321' $\underline{t}$ 18'-669 Bo

*2:22   Σηίρ 321' $\underline{t}$ 128-669 Bo

 2:26   Κεδμώθ] κηδεμωθ 106 $\underline{t}$

*2:29   Σηίρ 64^c 321' $\underline{t}$ 18'-669 Bo

 3:14   τὴν Βασάν] ιαιρ $\underline{t}^{-370}$ 799

 4:25   γεννήσῃς] γεννηση $\underline{t}^{-799}$

 8:8   om ἐλαίας 106-610 $\underline{t}$

11:19   om καὶ διανισταμένους 106 $\underline{t}$

11:25   θεὸς ὑμῶν] θεος ημων 72 52'-417-739 246 $\underline{t}^{-134}$ 68'

13:14   ἐτάσεις] εκζητησης (c var) $\mathbb{M}^{mg}$ 106 $\underline{t}$

15:11   ἐντέλλομαι] + σημερον 376 106 $\underline{t}$ Aeth

15:22   φάγεται] + αυτο 106 $\underline{t}$

16:14   om οὖσα 106 53' 75' $\underline{t}$

16:15   αὐτὸν ἐπικληθῆναι τὸ ὄνομα αὐτοῦ ἐκεῖ] εν αυτω 106
         W^I-54-458 $\underline{t}$ 509 Arm

17:8   ῥήματα] pr και 106 $\underline{t}$ Arm^{ap}

18:5   λειτουργεῖν] + αυτω 106 $\underline{t}$

19:21   ὀφθαλμόν] pr και 106 $\underline{t}$ Aeth

22:4   αὐτοῦ 1°] + η παν κτηνος αυτου 106 $\underline{t}$

22:17   om αὐτός 125 t^{-134} 799 Lat_{cod} 100 Aeth Arm

23:13   om καὶ ὀρύξεις ἐν αὐτῷ t

26:4   θυσιαστηρίου] + εναντι t

26:15   om τόν 2° 552^{txt} 106 246* t

27:18   om Γένοιτο t^{-799}

27:20   αὐτοῦ 1°⌒2° t Lat_{PsAmbr} Lex 6

27:23   om init — Γένοιτο 1° 707^{txt} t Aeth Arm

28:1   ἐάν] pr και εσται (om 106) 58-82-376 106 t Syh

28:11   ἐπί ult] pr και 106 321 t 59

28:65   κύριος] + ο θεος σου 106 t

29:3   σου] υμων 106 t Arm

29:28   παροξυσμῷ] pr εν G-376 106 t Syh

30:3   τας ἁμαρτίας] ταις αμαρτιαις 106 t

30:10   τὰ] pr παντα 707 106 t

33:2   ἄγγελοι] + αυτου t

List 6

Unique readings of t and one other group (d excluded)

2:11   οἱ Ἐνακίμ] pr και $οI^{-15}$ 64* 106 t^{-799}

*7:12   φυλάξητε] + αυτα 106 n t $Aeth^{-II}$ Arab Bo $Sa^{2\ 3\ 16}$

7:21   θεός] pr o 106 n t

7:21   μέγας] pr o 106 n t

7:21   κραταιός] pr o 106 54'-75 t

9:5   τῷ Ἀβραάμ BV 73'-413 b 106 767 343 t 630 55 407 509]
        om τω rell

11:28   om σήμερον 0^{-426} 344^{mg} t

13:5 ἐκ τῆς δουλείας] εξ οικου δουλειας 106 85^{mg}-321-346^{mg}
      t̲-370 y̲-121 392 Lat_{cod} 100 Pal = Ⓜ

13:14 ἐρωτήσεις ἐξερευνήσεις] tr 0̲ 106 t̲ Syh

17:10 τό] παν n̲ t̲

19:18 οἱ κριταί / ἀκριβῶς] tr V 106 54'-75'-767 t̲ ^{Lat}Luc
      Athan I 7

20:15 fin] + ων κυριος ο θεος σου διδωσι σοι κληρονομειν
      την γην αυτων (c var) 44 n̲-767 t̲-134

28:11 σοί] αυτους 106 n̲ t̲

28:53 ᾗ] pr εν 106 n̲ t̲

29:21 διαθήκης] + ταυτης 82-707 106 n̲ t̲

29:23 ὀργῇ] pr εν 0̲ 106 t̲

31:20 κορήσουσιν] pr και b̲ 106 53' W^I t̲

The 38 unique readings of the t̲ group (List 5) include seven which are shared by Bo. All seven readings
are identical--the spelling of the place name Σηίρ--and,
being support for the lemma, are thus irrelevant.

The 17 readings in List 6 must be augmented for
statistical purposes by the 138 readings (in List 4 above)
where the d̲ group is joined by its congener t̲. Only
nine of the total of 155 readings are shared by Bo. Eight
of these nine have already been shown to be coincidence.
The ninth (7:12) is the addition of a pronoun object, a
phenomenon typical of Bo. Clearly t̲ was not related to
the parent text of Bo.

E. One further possibility may be explored in connection with the hexaplaric recension and the textual
groups related to it. Wevers showed[4] that for Genesis the
textual relations of the O̲ group where it is non-hexaplaric are different from those where Origen's activity is
evident. The relationship of Bo to the O̲ group as a
representative of the hex recension in Deut has already
been examined. The possible relationship between Bo and
the O̲ group when it is not hexaplaric will be examined in
the next two lists. The first presents the unique readings of the O̲ group (including sub-groups) and the second
the unique readings of O̲ joined by one other group.

List 7

Non-hexaplaric unique readings of the O̲ group
(including sub-groups)

1:8	αὐτοῖς] + αυτην o̲I̲$^{-15}$ 83
1:12	τὰς ἀντιλογίας] την αντιλογιαν o̲I̲$^{-15}$ = Ⓜ
1:15	καὶ κατέστησα] καταστησαι o̲I̲ 128-669
1:16	om αὐτοῦ ult o̲I̲ 318 18'-669 Aeth Sa$^{1\ 2\ 16}$
1:30	om ὑμῶν 1° o̲I̲$^{-15}$ 108
3:10	Ἐδραΐν] εδραι o̲I̲$^{-64^C}$
4:18	ἐν] επι o̲I̲
4:41	Μωυσῆς] pr o Μ o̲I̲$^{-15}$
4:45	om αὐτῶν o̲I̲ 19'
*5:21	οὔτε 4°] ουδε 963 o̲I̲ 127 Bo^{-F}

5:26   λαλοῦντος] pr και o‾I⁻¹⁵

*5:32   δεξιά] pr εις A B F M oI-58 55 59 319 Lat‾Hi I‾s 16
       Ma‾l 2 PsHi Bre‾v 26 Opt App‾l Or Matt‾h 33 Ruf E‾x VI
       14 Nu‾m III 2 Arm Bo

\ 6:14   οὐ] και ου μη M o‾I

6:19   om σου 1° o‾I⁻¹⁵ 246 Arm

7:7   ἐξελέξατο] + κυριος 963 o‾I 551 Bo

7:13   εὐλογήσει 1°] et πληθυνεῖ tr o‾I 392

7:25   αὐτό] τουτο o‾I 54-75 83

8:9   om καί 1° 0‾⁻⁸²-72 343¹ Lat‾cod 100 = Ⓜ

8:18   om ὡς o‾I-707 75¹

9:1   ἰσχυρότερα] ισχυρα o‾I-707 83

9:2   Ἐνάκ 1° 2°] αινακ o‾I W‾I-127 18

9:12   ἐκ γῆς] εξ o‾I 33 Arab = Ⓜ

9:27   πρὸς τὸν θεόν] pr τα 0‾-58 Syh

10:22   πεντε] pr και o‾I 83

11:1   om καὶ τὰς κρίσεις αὐτοῦ o‾I

11:24   ὅρια ὑμῶν] ορια σου B 0‾⁻ᴳᶜ Pal

11:25   τὸν φόβον] pr και oI-29 18-83 Aeth Armᵃᵖ

11:32   ταῦτα   (÷ G Syh) 963 0‾⁻⁸² Saˡ 3 Syh] αυτου rell

12:1   καί 2°] α o‾I

12:5   ὑμῶν 1° ⌒ 2° o‾I 16

12:19   ζῆς] ζη A 426-o‾I 127 Cyr I 880

*12:29   om δέ 0‾⁻³⁷⁶ 53 Bo

12:29   εἰς οὖς] ου 0‾⁻³⁷⁶ 57 Armᵗᵉ

12:29   om ἀπὸ προσώπου σου o‾I⁻⁶⁴ Cyr IX 696

14:1   om οὐκ ἐπιθήσετε o̲I̲

14:22   σίτου σου] om σου 82-o̲I̲ 414-422-528-550*

14:25   προβάτοις] pr τοις o̲I̲

15:4   τῇ γῇ] om τη o̲I̲

15:6   συ δέ] και συ O̲$^{-376}$ Syh

15:15   om γῇ o̲I̲

15:21   μῶμος 1°] μοσχος o̲I̲ 19' 53

15:21 om καί o̲I̲ 131 44 W^{I}-127 130 83 ^{Lat}Aug Loc in hept
       44 Bo = ⊙

16:19   καθότι] καθα O̲$^{-376}$ Eus VI 14

16:17   om σου o̲I̲$^{-618*}$ 730

17:1   om ἐν 2° o̲I̲ 75

17:2   om σου 1° o̲I̲ Arm

17:11   κρίσιν] εντολην o̲I̲

*17:13 ἀσεβήσει] -σουσιν O̲ Bo

18:1   om Λευί o̲I̲ 19 730 318 83

18:15   θεός σου] om σου o̲I̲-72 528 Chr II 803 X 824 XIII
       104 XVI 645 Did 844 Epiph II 136 159 Eus VI 96
       Isid 797 Tht IV 1393 Titus 1225

18:19   τῶν λόγων αὐτοῦ] παντα O̲ Eus V 427 430 Syh

19:13   καί 2°] ινα o̲I̲ 127 83

20:16   ἰδοὺ δέ] ουδε o̲I̲ 83

20:16   ἐθνῶν] λαων O̲$^{-82}$-15

20:19   περικαθίσῃς] pr μη o̲I̲ 83

22:4   μή] και o̲I̲$^{-15*}$ 54 59' 76-370 Arm Sa^{3} = ⊙

22:11   om κίβδηλον o̲I̲ Cyr X 773

22:21 οἴκου] pr του F M 72-426-o̲I̲ 44 53' 18ᶜ-83-630ᶜ 319

22:22 ἀποκτενεῖτε] pr και 0̲-58 619 Syh

24:7 ψυχήν] + αυτου o̲I̲⁻¹⁵ 83

*24:11 om σου 426-707-o̲I̲ 77 407 Bo

25:1 κρίσιν] + και προσελθωσι o̲I̲⁻¹⁵

25:5 σπέρμα δέ] και σπερμα 0̲ Syh

25:5 ᾗ] αφη 0̲-58 Syh (+ αφη 82)

26:3 μου] σου F*(corr Fᵇ) M 29-82-426-o̲I̲ 53'-56* 767
71-318 83 Syh = Ⓜ

26:5 om ἐν o̲I̲

28:32 σφακελίζοντες] pr και 0̲

28:35 om τῆς 0̲ 75

*28:43 om ἐπὶ σέ B o̲I̲-29 630ᶜ Bo

28:52 om κύριος o̲I̲ 53'

28:53 θλίψει σου] om σου o̲I̲-58 83 Sa³ = Ⓜ

28:66 om τῶν οφθαλμῶν 0̲⁻ᴳᶜ 32 Syh = Ⓜ

28:68 παιδίσκας] pr εις o̲I̲ 646 ᴸᵃᵗcod 100 Arm

29:7 fin] + εν τω πολεμω M o̲I̲ 83

29:9 om ποιεῖν 0̲ Syh = Ⓜ

29:15 ὧδε] post σήμερον tr o̲I̲

29:27 om πάσας o̲I̲

29:28 ὀργῇ] pr εν 0̲-58 414 Syh

30:1 ἔλθωσιν] εισελθωσιν M o̲I̲-72 44 83

30:4 οὐρανοῦ 1°∩ 2° 0̲ 44 54 68'-120 509 Phil II 267ᵃᵖ
Aeth = Ⓜ

30:16 τὰς ἐντολάς] της φωνης 0̲⁻⁴²⁶-32 319 Aeth Syh

31:8   om ὁ o͟I 30 71-527

31:21   αὐτῶν 1°] αυτου O͟-58 = Ⓜ

32:45   παντί] pr παντας (sic) o͟I 83

32:47   om ἐκεῖ o͟I 55 Arm Sa³ ¹⁶

33:9   om καὶ τοὺς υἱους αὐτοῦ 72-82^txt c pr m_-o͟I 56^txt
        71-527 68'-83 55 319 Chr I 80 Isid 489

34:2   καί 1°∩ 2° o͟I-72 68-83-669

List 8

Non-hexaplaric unique readings of the O͟ group

(including sub-groups) joined by one other group

1:7   λίβα] pr νοτον o͟I-58 130-321' z͟^-68' 630

2:4   λαῷ] + τουτο o͟I 18'-83-669

2:11   οἱ Ενακίμ] pr και o͟I^-15 64* 106 t͟^-799

3:7   om τά 28 o͟I 71'-527

5:7   πρὸ προσώπου μου B M^txt 963 O͟'-707 344^mg y͟^-121 83
        Arm Sa¹ ² ³ ¹⁶] πλην εμου rell

5:14   ὁ υἱός] οι υιοι B* O͟^-82-707 767 y͟ 59 509

6:21   κύριος] + ο θεος o͟I 414-417 W^I-767 71'527 83 Arm
        Pal

8:11   om αὐτοῦ ult o͟I b͟^-103c Lat_cod 100

9:27   om οἷς ὤμοσας κατὰ σεαυτοῦ A* G-58-426-707^txt
        344^mg 121-318-392 Arab = Ⓜ

10:9   αὐτῶν] αυτου O͟ 71'-527 18 Aeth^F = Ⓜ

10:9   κύριος] + ο θεος M 376-o͟I^-15 C" 730 83 55 319 646
        Lat_Ambr Ps 118 VIII 4 Cassiod Ps CXVIII 57 Hil Ps
        CXVIII 3

10:21 init] pr και o̲I̲ b̲ Arm

*10:21 σοί] pr εν B V 0̲'-426-58-707 129 y̲ 407 509
Lat_cod 100 Bo

11:3 τέρατα] εργα 0̲ 130^mg-321'^mg-344^mg 509 Arm^ap Pal
Syh = Ⓜ

11:4 τὰ ἅρματα] pr και o̲I̲^-15 68'-83-630 Aeth Sa^3

11:23 om πάντα o̲I̲^-15-72 z̲ Aeth^-M Arm^te

11:28 om σήμερον 0̲^-426 344^mg t̲

11:30 γῆ] pr τη 0̲^-426-58 b̲

12:7 χεῖρας A B o̲I̲^-15-58-707 129 121-392 z̲^-83] + υμων
rell

*12:17 τας εὐχάς] om τας A B M 0̲'-376 618-58 129 y̲ 55
Bo

12:21 om κύριος 2° A F M o̲I̲ 57 n̲ 121 55 Lat_cod 100
Arm^te Pal Syh

12:23 ἡ ψυχή] + αυτου o̲I̲ 127 85^mg-321'^mg-344^mg

*13:4 ἀκούσεσθε B o̲I̲^-15-707 129 n̲ 318-392 407 509 Ath II
476 Lat_cod 100 Spec 6 Luc Parc 2 Aeth Arm^ap Bo
Pal] + και αυτου δουλευσετε rell

13:14 ἐρωτήσεις] et ἐξερευνήσεις tr 0̲ 106 t̲ Syh

*14:25 ἐπὶ οἴνω A F M V 0̲' 56 y̲^-318 59 Bo Syh] pr η rell

16:16 τῷ τόπῳ] om τω o̲I̲ C̲'-414'-551 664 71'

*17:1 om ὅτι 0̲ b̲ 246 128-630' 319 Aeth Bo Sa^1 3 11 Syh

*18:4 om καί 1° 0̲-72 b̲ Lat_cod 100 Bo Syh

18:7 om οἱ Λευῖται o̲I̲ 72 d̲^-106

19:8 om σου 1° o̲I̲^-64-58-72 552 b̲ 799 319

19:14   om ἐν κλήρῳ O'-707 b 319 Lat_cod 100 Syh = Ⓜ

22:8   om δέ B O b W^I Cyr I 585 Lat_cod 100

22:26   om ὅτι B oI d^{-106} 630^c

*23:9   om καί O f^{-129} 128-630' 55 319 Aeth Arm Bo Syh

23:23   om κυρίῳ B oI 54-75' Lat_cod 100 Spec 65 Fulg Ep 11
        Arm

26:17   θεόν 1°] κυριον O^{-82} 246 767 120-122-630' Phil V
        324^{ap} Syh = Ⓜ

27:2   σοί] + εν κληρω oI b 83 (vid) Arab

*27:26 om ἐν 426-oI 528 z^{-68'} 120 Chr IX 188 X 335 XIII
        96 Cyr VI 649 X 965 Epiph I 331 Bo

28:54   καταλειφθῇ B O^{-82}-707* n 407 Sa^3 Syh = Ⓜ] + αυτω rell

28:56   τρυφερά B 963 O^{-82} n Chr II 892 Lat_cod 103 Aeth
        Sa^3 Syh = Ⓜ] + σφοδρα rell

29:2   κύριος A B 963 O^{-82} 129 y^{-619} Lat_cod 100 Aeth^{-CM}
        Arab Arm Sa^3 16 Syh = Ⓜ] + ο θεος υμων (c var)
        rell

29:7   πολέμῳ] pr τω A M oI 46 18'-120-630*-669

29:23   ὀργῇ] pr εν O 106 t

30:4   θεός σου ∩ (5) oI d^{-106} 458 30 71-392 630' 55

31:10   ἀφέσεως] pr της oI 246 z^{-68'}

31:21   καί 1°∩ 2° M V oI-58 56 54-75 z^{-18} 55 Lat_codd 100
        103 104 Aeth Arm Sa^3 (vid)

31:23   ἐνετείλατο B 963 O b Lat_codd 100 103 Arab Sa^3 Syh
        = Ⓜ] + μωυσης rell

33:16   τῷ] pr εν 376-oI z^{-68'} 55

List 7 contains 87 readings of which only eight (9%)
are supported by Bo. Six of these (5:21, 5:32, 12:29,
15:21, 17:13, 24:11) are not significant and are probably
simply coincidence. The remaining two (7:7 and 28:43)
consist of an ad sensum addition of κυριος and omission
of ἐπὶ σέ. These two readings alone are not enough to
show dependence by Bo on the non-hexaplaric O group but
are also probably mere coincidence.

The expanded base of investigation provided by the
O plus one other group (List 8) produces similar results.
Eight of the 48 readings (16.5%) include Bo. Seven of
these are insignificant and the similarity of reading
with Bo is probably coincidence. In the eighth instance
(13:4) oI and Bo constitute support for the original
text. It is now clear that neither the hexaplaric nor
the non-hexaplaric O group was the parent text of Bo.

F. The Catena group C" together with its congener the s group will now be examined in relation to
Bo. The next four lists will in turn show unique readings of C including its sub-groups, unique readings of
C joined by one other group, unique readings of the s
group, and unique readings of s joined by one other
group (excluding C). Readings attested by fewer than
four of the eight members of the s group are not included.

List 9

Unique readings of the C̲ group (including sub-groups)

1:1   Λοβόν] λωβον C̲

1:7   εἰς ὄρος] pr και C̲" 458 646

1:16   om init — ὑμῶν 1° 618* c pr m C̲" 664* 59 319 407
       Aeth[II]

1:16   ὑμῶν 2°] αυτου C̲"-417 422 552 319

1:16   om καὶ κρίνετε — ἀδελφοῦ αὐτοῦ C̲"-417 422 552 319

1:19   om ἤλθομεν ἔως Καδὴς Βαρνή (20)καὶ εἶπα πρὸς ὑμᾶς c̲I

1:23   om δώδεκα C̲'-550'-414-422

1:27   κύριον ἡμᾶς] κυριον υμας C̲-77-46-52'-57-73'-414
       19 318 122* 59 319

1:45   καθίσαντες] + εκει C̲

2:8   τὴν Ἀραβά] om την C̲" 125 319 646 Sa[2]

2:13   Ζάρεδ 1°] ζαδερ C̲" 730 319

2:13   Ζάρεδ 1°] ζαδερ C̲'-529-414-422

2:14   Ζάρεδ] ζαδερ C̲" 319

2:34   πόλιν] pr την C̲"

2:36   οὐκ] pr και 72 C̲'-414-422

2:36   om οὐκ C̲

2:37   om τάς 2° C̲" 319

3:16   Γάδ] γαδδει (c var) B[c] C̲"

4:9   σου 3°⌒4° C̲" 319

4:27   ἔθνεσιν 1°⌒2° 707[txt] c̲I' 83 319

4:31   θεός 1°] pr κυριος   F V 29 C̲"-500 616 85 28 59 319

4:34   om ὁ θεός 2° C̲-77

4:34 ἐποίησεν] + ημιν C"-52' 77 417 616* 56' 30' 319

4:35 πλήν] φερειν την απειλην C-551ᶜ

5:23 φωνήν] + κυριου C"-414' 615 730 319

5:23 φυλῶν] αλλοφυλων C'-77 528-414'-551

5:28 λόγων 1°∩ 2° cI-551 68'-120

5:28 μέ 1°∩ 2° C-414 458ᵗˣᵗ c pr m

6:2 φυλάσσεσθαι] pr και 381' C-414 44 458 799 318 Aeth

6:4 κύριος 1°] + ο θεος 376 C" 30' 319 646

6:11 ἀμπελῶνας] pr και C" 319 646 Aeth Arab Arm Sa¹ ² ³

6:11 om καί ult C 19

6:16 ἐν τῷ] αυτον C'-414'-417-422 85 28

6:17 τὰ δικαιώματα] + και τα κριματα C"-52' 30' 319

7:6 ἔθνη ∩ (7)1° C

7:10 πρόσωπον 1°∩ 2° 376 C"-16 57 422 314 59 319

7:13 om κύριος C'-414'-422 Arab = Ⓜ

7:14 οὐκ ἔσται] pr και C"-550

7:19 om σύ C-131

7:24 οὐδείς] + το ονομα κυριον C

7:25 οὐδέ] η 15-82 C" 55 319 Pal³ ⁵

8:13 om καὶ πάντων — fin C'-551

9:15 om αἱ C'-414 106

9:17 om καί 2° — fin C" 53' 319 646

9:20 om ἐν C" 646

9:23 om ὑμᾶς κύριος C" 319 646

10:9 om αὐτός C" 319 646 ᴸᵃᵗAmbr Ps 118 VIII 4 Cassiod Ps CXVIII 57 Hil Ps CXVIII 3

10:15 ὑμῶν] ημων c̲I̲ʼ⁻⁴¹⁴ʼ 19ʼ 246 75-767ᶜ 30ʼ-130ᵐᵍ 83*
59 319

10:17 πρόσωπον] + ανθρωπον c̲"⁻⁵² 730 319 646

11:5 ὑμῖν] ημιν B 376-618* c̲-46ʼ 610 246 68ʼ-120 646*

11:6 Ἐλιάβ] -αμ c̲-46-422-528ʼ-550ʼ-551 53ʼ

11:8 om τῆν γῆν — fin c̲I̲-551

11:10 om ἡ 1° c̲"⁻⁵²⁹ 319 646 Procop 904

11:12 om ἐνιαυτοῦ καί c̲⁻¹³¹ᵐᵍ-422

11:21 κύριος] + ο θεος c̲

11:27 om init — (28)κατάρας c̲I̲-551 85-343 134

11:27 om τὰς ἐντολάς c̲

12:3 καί 2°∩3° c̲ʼ⁻⁵⁵¹

12:3 om συντρίψετε — θεῶν αὐτῶν c̲I̲-551

12:17 οἴνου σου] om σου c̲"⁻⁷³ʼ 85 83 28 319 ᴸᵃᵗcod 100

12:18 τῷ τόπῳ] om τω c̲" 19-314 129 75 85 318 28 319 Eus
VI 13

12:20 κρέα 1°∩2° 19 c̲

12:23 πρόσεχε] + σεαυτω 618 c̲" 730 134 319 ᴸᵃᵗcodd 91 92
94-96 Saˡ 3

12:23 om μή 15ᵗˣᵗ c̲I̲ʼ 319

13:5 τῆς δουλείας] γης αιγυπτου και απο δουλειας c̲

13:12 ἀκούσῃς] -ση c̲"⁻⁵⁰⁰ 83 319

13:14 ἐτάσεις] + και ερευνησεις (c var) c̲

13:14 ἐξερευνήσεις] ερευνησεις και εξερευνησεις (c var)
c̲I̲ʼ

13:18 σοί] υμιν c̲-52

14:1 ὀφθαλμῶν] αδελφων c̲"⁻⁴⁶ʼ 52ʼ 417 71ʼ

14:7 om init — φάγεσθε C'$^{-528}$-414-422

14:22 τῷ τόπῳ] om τω A 64^{txt}-72'-376 C" 19 129-246 85
28 319 Eus VI 13

15:5 om τῆς φωνῆς C"-131^{mg} 319

15:7 om σου ult C"-16 528 30'-85 28 319

*15:13 om ἀπὸ σου C Bo

16:6 om ἑσπέρας C 53 134^{txt} 318

*16:7 om καί 1° C" 18 319 646 Aeth^M Bo

16:7 αὐτόν] εκει C

16:8 ἑορτῇ] pr και cI-551 106^c

16:17 κατά 2°] pr και C" 68' 73 646

17:1 ῥῆμα] βρωμα C"

17:2 θεός σου] om σου 707 cI'$^{-46}$ 761* 610 619

17:9 ταῖς ἡμέραις / ἐκείναις] tr C"

17:12 ποιήσῃ] + εν υμιν (ημιν C^{-77}) C"

17:13 ὁ λαός] ισραηλ 29 C

17:14 om τήν C'$^{-16}$-414'

17:19 om καὶ ἀναγνώσεται ἐν αὐτῷ πάσας C" 646

18:5 αὐτός] αυτοι C"-52' 414

18:5 αὐτοῦ] αυτων C-417

18:15 om ἀναστήσει σοὶ κύριος ὁ θεός σου C^{-131c}

18:22 κυρίου] μου C

18:22 το ῥῆμα 1°] om το C'-551

19:9 ἐάν] + δε C^{-16} 799 509 Arm

19:9 om ταύτας 1° 72 C 71'

20:14 σεαυτῷ] εαυτω cI'$^{-414}$ 417 246 767

20:14 om σου ult 707 C"-16 130 392

20:17 om καὶ τὸν Φερεζαῖον καὶ Εὑαῖον C"-131

21:2 om καί 2° C"-16 413 414 344

21:8 σου] του C"-413 552 wI

21:11 γυναῖκα 2°] pr εις C" 318 646

21:15 om καί ult — fin C-131ᶜ-52

21:16 om ὑπεριδὼν τὸν υἱὸν τῆς μισουμένης C"

21:17 τέκνων] pr των C" 646

21:18 ᾖ υἱός / ἀπειθής] tr C" 646

22:22 om κοιμώμενος F C" 318 83

22:23 παῖς] πας C 19 44 619

23:3 om καί 2° 82 C"-422 Procop 2101 2113 Tht I 180
    Lat_cod 104 Arm Sa³

*23:6 καί] ουδε C" Bo

23:7 om init — ἐστιν C"-46' 52' 417 125

23:9 ῥήματος πονηροῦ] πονηρου πραγματος και ρηματος C

23:18 om καί Fᶜ V 426 C-551 318 Aeth Arm Bo

23:21 om τῷ θεῷ cI' 75 85-344ᵗˣᵗ 28 407 509

24:11 om ἐξοίσει — (12)πένηται C-77

24:14 om καί C"-46' 52' 85* Aeth

24:17 κρίσιν] pr εις C

24:18 om σου C'-414'

24:18 ποιεῖν / το ῥῆμα τοῦτο] tr C"

24:22 διά] pr και C Aeth

24:22 om ποιεῖν 15-58 C"-417 75 83 Lat_Pel Vita 8

25:2 τῶν κριτῶν] αυτων B C" 85* c pr m 59

25:7 ἀνδρός 1°⌒2° C"

26:3 αὐτόν] τον ιερα C"-500 615 616

26:3 κύριος] + ο θεος 707 C-417

26:11 om init — σου 1° C-131mg

27:3 σοί 2°] pr διδωσι C-73'

27:6 θυσιαστήριον] post σου 1° tr C-77

27:6 καί — fin] post (7)σωτηριου tr C'-77 413 500-414'-417-422

27:9 Ἰσραήλ 1°] τω λαω C"

27:16 om comma C'-414'-417

28:18 τὰ βουκόλια] pr και C" 106 370 68'-128 646 Aeth Arm

28:19 ἐπικατάρατος 1°⌒2° C'-413-414'-422

28:27 om ἐν 1° B C"-52' 313 417 767 630c

28:27 om καί 2° C'-528-422-551

28:32 βλέψονται] pr ουκ C"

28:35 om σε ἰαθῆναι C-131mg

28:45 καί 2°⌒3° 610 C-131mg Latcod 103

28:52 ἐν πάσῃ] pr και C" 85'-321 28 646

28:53 om σοί C"-131 550 509

28:63 ὑμῖν εὖ ποιῆσαι ὑμᾶς] υμας ποιησαι ευ υμιν C

29:2 ἐν] pr παντα C"-73' 313

29:7 om βασιλεύς 1° C'-131mg 413-422-551

29:11 om ἀπό — fin C-131mg

30:2 κατά] και C'-414'-422 53' Aethii

30:17 om καί 1° C-77

30:20 καὶ Ἰσαάκ] om και 58 C-16 125 246-664 Latcod 100

   = ⒒

31:3   προσώπου 1°⌢2° C̲ 246 767

31:12   om τόν 2° C̲"⁻⁵⁵¹ 646

31:12   om ταῖς C̲"

31:13   om καὶ μαθήσονται C̲" 44 130 646

31:15   om καὶ ἔστη 1° C̲ Lat_cod 103

32:21   om παρεζήλωσάν με ἐπ᾽ οὐ θεῷ C̲᾽⁻⁷⁷ ¹³¹₋₅₅₀'

32:46   om ἐπί C̲ 319

32:47   om τοῦ λόγου C̲"⁻¹³¹ᶜ 85 28 646

32:49   ὄρος 2°] pr το C̲" 129 767 130 527 59 509

32:49   ὅ] οτι C̲⁻⁷⁷

34:1   om τό C̲"⁻⁵²' 550' 53'

34:5   οἰκέτης] pr ο Β C̲"⁻⁴⁶' 417 500 615 ₆₃₀ᶜ

34:8   Ἀραβώθ] αβωθ C̲⁻⁵⁰⁰ᶜ

List 10

Unique readings of the C̲ group (including sub-groups)

joined by one other group

1:30   αὐτός] pr και C̲" s̲⁻⁷³⁰ 28 319 646 Arab

2:7   θεός σου] om σου 72 C̲" s̲⁻³⁰' 343 28

2:20   om καί 2° Βᶜ (vid) 963 C̲" s̲ 28 319 407 509

2:24   om οὖν 72-426 C̲" s̲⁻³⁰' 343' 28 319 Arab = Ⓜ

2:28   μοί 1°⌢2° c̲I (c var) d̲ 68'-120

2:33   αὐτόν 1°] αυτους C̲" s̲⁻³⁰' 343' 28 319 646 Lat_cod 100

2:33   om πρὸ προσώπου ἡμῶν 963 c̲I 71'-527 120-669
        Lat_cod 100 Aeth Arm Sa²

3:19   ταῖς πόλεσιν] pr πασαις C̲" s̲ 28 319 646

4:32   om προτέρας 1° C̲" s̲⁻³⁰' 343' 76 318 28 319 509
        Ath II 244

4:39   καί 1°⌒ 2° c̲I̲-551* n̲$^{-127}$

*4:42   φονευτήν] + (+ καὶ Bo) ος αν φυγη εκει και ζησεται
        B^{mg} C̲" s̲ 18 28 319 407 509 Bo

4:45   om καὶ τὰ κρίματα C̲" s̲

4:45   om ἐν τῇ ἐρήμῳ B 58-707 C̲" s̲ 28 319 407 509 Arab
        Arm = Ⓜ

5:8   οὐδέ] ουτε C̲" s̲ Sa^3

*5:23   προσήλθετε] -ηλθον C̲" s̲ 28 319 407 646 Arab Arm Bo

5:28   κύριος 1°] + ο θεος C̲" 458-767 s̲$^{-30'}$ 343' 28 319
        646

5:32   οὐδέ] η 376 C̲" d̲ 85 18 28 319

7:5   om τῶν θεῶν B^c C̲" 44 s̲ 318 28 319 407 509 ^{Lat}Spec
        44 Arm = Ⓜ

7:7   om ἐξελέξατο ὑμᾶς C̲$^{-131mg}$ s̲$^{-85}$ 343' 730 68'

7:12   om σου 72 C̲"$^{-414'}$ 422 528 b̲ 129 30'-85 28 319

8:14   καρδία B C̲" s̲ 630^c 28 55 319 407 509 646 Phil I
        224] + σου rell

8:19   αὐτοῖς 1°⌒ 2° B C̲" s̲$^{-343'}$ 630 28 319
        ^{Lat}cod 104 Bo

9:1   μᾶλλον ἢ ὑμεῖς] σου C̲" s̲ 28 319 407 509 Arab

9:4   om τὰ ἔθνω ταῦτα C̲" s̲ 28 319 407 509

9:5   τῶν ἐθνῶν τούτων] αυτων C̲" s̲ 28 319 646

9:5   ὑμῶν] ημων V 618 C̲$^{-739}$ 318 z̲ Phil I 225te Arm

9:12   παρέβασαν] pr και 707 C̲" s̲$^{-85}$ 76' 28 319 646

9:16   om μόσχον B C̲" W^I s̲$^{-344mg}$ 630^c 28 319 407 646 509
        ^{Lat}codd 100 104 Aeth Arm Sa^{1te} 2 3

9:17 om καί 1° C" 53' s̲ 28 319 407 646

*9:19 om καί ult M V 58-72-707ᶜ C"-528 44-125 129 s̲ 28
59 319 407 509 Lat_codd 100 104 Aeth Arm Bo Sa¹ 2 3 13

10:9 κύριος] + ο θεος M 376-o̲I̲⁻¹⁵ C" 730 83 55 319 646
Lat_Ambr P̲s̲ 1̲1̲8̲ VIII 4 Cassiod P̲s̲ CXVIII 57 Hil P̲s̲
CXVIII 3

10:12 αἰτεῖται] ζητειται C"-46' s̲-130ᵐᵍ 344ᵐᵍ 346ᵐᵍ 28
55 319 646

10:14 ἡ γῆ] pr και C" b̲⁻¹⁹ 319 646 Tht I 416 Aeth Arab
Arm Pal

11:6 Ἀβιρών A B C"-761 106 75-767 s̲⁻³⁰' 343' 28 319 509
646] pr τω rell

*11:7 om ὅτι C" s̲ 28 319 407 509 646 Bo

11:7 ὑμῖν] ημιν 82 C̲'-77 761-313-417 108 f̲⁻⁵³ 129 75
68'-120 319 646

11:12 om σου 1° C" 246 s̲ 319 646 Lat_cod 100

11:12 om σου 2° 58-72 C" s̲ 319 646

*11:12 om καί 72 c̲I̲'·⁻⁴²² s̲ 319 646 Lat_cod 100 Aeth Arm
Bo Pal Syh

*11:13 σοί] υμιν C" s̲⁻³⁴³ 344ᵐᵍ Aeth Arab Boᴬ' = Ⓜ

11:29 om εἰς 2° A V 72-376 C" n̲⁻⁷⁶⁷ 319

11:31 om καί 1° C" s̲ 54-75' 28 319 407 509

12:8 om σήμερον C" s̲⁻³⁴³' 28 319 407

*12:15 φάγεται] -γονται (c var) C" b̲ 85 28 319 Aeth Arm Bo
Sa¹ 3

12:17 om σου 2° 72 C" s̲⁻³⁴⁴ᵐᵍ 28 319

12:17 om καί 4° C" s 28 319

13:1 om ἧ 1° V C-551-761 54 71'-527 Chr II 854 Cyr X 677 Tht I 240

13:1 τέρας ⌒ (2) F^txt C"-46' 52' 458 s^-30' 343' 319 Anast 529 Lat_cod 100

13:7 om τῶν θεῶν C" s 28 319 407

13:16 εἰς 1°] επι C" s^-30 28 319 407

13:17 τῆς ὀργῆς] pr και C" s 28 319

13:17 om ὂν τρόπον ὤμοσεν 707^mg C" s^-346mg 28 319

14:10 αὐτοῖς] pr εν C" b 30 319 509

14:21 το γένημα] pr και C" 30'-85^mg-321'^mg 319

15:6 om σου 1° 58 C"-551 53' s^-343 799 28 59 319 407

15:7 om σου 3° 72' C"-16 77 417 528' d-106 35 28 Syh

15:11 om καί 426 C" z^-83 55 59 319 646

15:23 ἐκχεεῖς] εκχεειτε C" 54-75 s^-30' 343 28 319

*16:3 Αἰγύπτου 1°] pr γης C"-616 19 129 s^-85mg 321'mg 28 319 646 Lat_cod 100 Arab Bo Sa^1 = ⊕

16:4 εἰς τό] εως C" s^-30' 343 28 319 646

16:14 om ἐν τῇ ἑορτῇ σου A F M^txt 29-72 C" 56^txt s^-85mg 321'^mg 121-318 18 28 59 319 407 646

16:16 om τῷ ol C'-414'-551 664 71'

17:4 τοῦτο] αυτου C" s 646

17:11 οὐδέ] η C-73'-414 d^-106 75 18 407

17:16 τῇ ὁδῷ / ταύτῃ] tr C"-52 414 s^-30' 407

17:19 ταῦτα] αυτου C" d^-106 125 407 Aeth

18:2 om αὐτοῦ C"-52 s Lat_cod 100

*18:10   κληδονιζόμενος B 72 C" W^I s 28 407 509 Anast 529
         Cyr III 464 X 724 Lat$_{cod}$ 100 Spec 55 Bo = Ⓜ] pr και
         rell

18:14   οὗτοι] αυτοι C" s 28 407

18:19   om ὁ 1° C" W^I-75 s$^{-30'}$ 28 407 509 Cyr IX 892

19:6   om τήν B C"$^{-77}$ 414 529 552 s$^{-321'mg}$ 28 407

19:6   om καὶ ἀποθάνη B 58-426 C"$^{-131mg}$ s$^{-321'mg}$ 28 407
         509 Lat$_{cod}$ 100 Aeth Arm Syh = Ⓜ

*19:8   ὤμοσεν] + κυριος ο θεος 82 C" s 28 319 407 509 646
         Aeth Arm Bo Sa^3

19:11   αὐτόν 1° ∩ 2° C" d^{-106} 646 Arab

20:4   om μεθ' 707^{mg} C" s 28 Aeth

*20:14   om καὶ πάντα 2° C" s 28 646 Bo

20:20   om τόν 72 C" s 318 28 646

21:1   οἴδασιν] οιδας C" s$^{-30'}$ 28 407

21:21   ἐξαρεῖς] -ρειτε (c var) C" s 28 407 646 Cyr I 509
         Arm

22:17   παρθένια 1°] pr τα C" s 28

22:26   om αὐτοῦ C b

24:12   om αὐτοῦ B C" s 28 509

25:7   ὁ ἄνθρωπος / λαβεῖν] tr C" b

25:11   χειρός] pr της 72 C" s 76' 28^c

*26:11   εὐφρανθήση] + εκει cI' s 28 407 509 Arm Bo

26:16   αὐτά] ταυτα C" 767 s 28 Arm

26:17   om αὐτοῦ 2° B V C" s 630^c 28 Lat$_{cod}$ 100

27:1   om πάσας 707 C" s^{-321mg} 344^{mg} 28 407 Aeth^{ii} Arab

28:7　παραδῷ] + σοι M 58 C̲'-16' 73' 550 616 761₋52'₋417₋

422 s̲⁻⁸⁵' 68' 646 Sa¹⁶

28:9　λαόν] pr εις C̲" s̲ 28 407 646

28:9　om ἐν C̲"-413 s̲-30' 28 407 509 646

28:20　ἐπιτηδεύματά σου] tr C̲" s̲ 28 646

28:24　om ἕως 1° — fin C̲-131ᵐᵍ d̲-106

28:35　om σε 2° c̲I' s̲ 28

28:56　om αὐτῆς 2° C̲" s̲ 28 646 Arm Sa³

28:67　om τό 2° C̲-761 18'-630' 407

29:13　Ἀβραάμ] pr τω C̲" b̲ 458 730

29:18　om ἐν ὑμῖν 1° 72 C̲" s̲⁻³⁴⁴ᵐᵍ 28 407

30:9　ἐπιστρέψει] + σε 58 C̲"-414 s̲ 28 646 Arm Syh

*30:12　οὐρανῷ] + ανω Aᶜ B 376 C̲"-528 s̲ 28 407 Bo

30:14　αὐτὸ ποιεῖν B C̲" s̲⁻³⁰' 28 407 509 Latcod 100] tr rell

30:18　τὸν Ἰορδάνην / ἐκεῖ] tr C̲" s̲⁻³⁰' 28 407 646

31:11　om τῷ 2° 707 C̲⁻⁵⁰⁰ 44-125 75 s̲⁻⁸⁵' 630' 407

31:14　κάλεσον] + ουν 58 C̲" s̲ 407 646

*31:15　om καὶ ἔστη 2° — fin 72 C̲-414-422 d̲⁻¹⁰⁶ 54 343

318 55 Latcod 103 Aeth⁻ᶜᴳ Bo

*31:16　om αὐτός 2° 58 C̲" 75 s̲ 71 319 407 646 Aeth Bo

*31:16　om ἐκεῖ 72' C̲"-77 s̲-30 407 509 646 Latcodd 100 103

104 Iust D̲i̲a̲l̲ LXXIV 1 Aeth Arm Bo

*31:26　om ἐν 963 C̲"-320 s̲ 799 55 Aeth Bo

32:44　Μωυσῆς / τὴν ᾠδὴν ταύτην] tr C̲"-46' 52' 417* s̲⁻³⁰'

83 28

33:5　Ἰσραήλ] ιακωβ C̲"-131ᵐᵍ s̲-30' 85ᵐᵍ 344ᵐᵍ 28

*33:13 ἀπὸ ὡρῶν] pr και C" s 18 28 646 Aeth Bo

33:22 om Δάν 2° F* (corr Fᵃ) 72 C"-615 75' s-130 346 28

407 Procop 988

33:25 om ἔσται καί C" s-343 28 407

33:28 om αὐτῷ C" s 28 509 646

34:11 om γῆ 1° 618* C"-615 s 28 319 646

List 9 shows that there is no relation between
the variants of the C group and Bo. Only four of the 158
unique readings of C are supported by Bo. Three of these
involve καί--two omissions and one substitution by οὐδέ.
The fourth is the ad sensum omission of the prepositional
phrase ἀπό σου. The agreement on these four readings is
simply due to coincidence.

The pattern changes somewhat when C is joined by
another group (List 10). Bo supports 19 of the 115
(16.5%) unique readings. Fourteen of these 19 may be
explained as coincidence--three omissions and one addition
of καί, three changes of number, omissions of ὅτι,
οὗτος, ἐκεῖ and ἐν, the preposing of γη before Αἰγύπτου,
additions of ανω to οὐρανοῦ and the adverb εκει to a
verb. The remaining five variants (4:42, 8:19, 19:4,
20:14, 31:15) could be of more interest. The long omission in 31:15 is obviously due to parablepsis on και and
that in 8:19 to parablepsis on αὐτοῖς. The identity of
the reading of Bo and C in these instances is probably
coincidence but it could point to a common parent. The
third omission (20:14) concerns καὶ πάντα as specified

antecedent for ὅσα. The phrase is recurrent in Deut and
its omission by Bo and C̲ is probably independent in
origin. The two remaining variants are plusses. The
addition of ος αν φυγη εκει και ζησεται in 4:42 is
borrowed from 19:4 and was probably transmitted indepen-
dently by Bo and C̲. The addition of κυριος ο θεος in
19:8 cannot be used as evidence for relationship since
the divine name recurs so frequently in Deut. In any
event, 23 agreements of Bo and C̲ out of a total of 273
readings are hardly sufficient to conclude that the parent
text of Bo was related to C̲.

      G. The s̲ group appears as an independent family
only rarely in Deut. It is most often seen in connection
with another group especially C̲. The following list of
unique readings of s̲ is therefore not extensive. The
subsequent list of readings of s̲ joined by one other
group (cf. d̲ and t̲ above) includes only such instances
where the group joining s̲ is not C̲. The statistical
analysis of this list will again be based on all the
evidence.

      List 11 Unique readings of the s̲ group
*2:24   αὐτόν] αυτους 30'-85^{mg}-321'^{mg} Bo
 8:11   om σου 52'-313-417 s̲$^{-30'}$ 344^{mg} 392 28
*9:5   om αὐτῶν 30'-343' 407 Bo$^{A'}$
 9:17   om αὐτάς 2° B 376 s̲ 28 407 509 Arm
11:2   παιδείαν] φωνην 11^{mg} 130^{mg}-321'^{mg}-344^{mg} 55

11:25 om πάσης 458 s⁻⁸⁵' 321' 344ᵐᵍ

11:25 om πάσης 458 $\underline{s}^{-85'}$ 321' 344^{mg}

12:6 ἑκούσια ὑμῶν] om υμων 106 $\underline{s}^{-30'}$ 343' 28

12:11 το ὄνομα αὐτοῦ / ἐκεῖ] tr 422 $\underline{s}$ Tht I 417

12:18 om τοῦ θεοῦ σου 30'-343'

15:14 om κύριος $\underline{s}^{-343'}$ 28 407 509

16:18 om σου 2° 707 53' $\underline{s}^{-30}$ 344 128-669 28

20:4 διασῶσαι B $\underline{s}^{-30'}$ 28 407 509 Cyr I 369 ^{Lat}cod 100
       Arm = Ⓜ] pr και rell

21:15 μισουμένη 1°⌒ 2° $\underline{s}^{-30'}$ 343' 18-28 Aeth

22:6 om ἤ 1° 82 30'-343' 319 = Ⓜ

25:7 om τοῦ ἀδελφοῦ ult A 58-82 75 $\underline{s}$ 71' 28 407 Syh

27:13 Δάν] pr και $\underline{s}^{-85}$ 346 730

28:1 θεὸς ὑμῶν] θεος ημων 52-551 53' $\underline{s}^{-344mg}$ 630' 28
       55-59

28:1 om τῆς γῆς $\underline{s}^{-85}$ 130 630' 407 509

List 12

Unique readings of $\underline{s}$ and one other group ($\underline{C}$ excluded)

2:18 Ἀροήρ] γην σηειρ (c var) $\underline{n}^{-767}$ 85'ᵐᵍ-321'ᵐᵍ

6:6 om ταῦτα $\underline{b}$ 85'-321'

9:23 om κύριος $\underline{d}^{-106}$ $\underline{s}^{-343mg}$ 28

10:2 πλάκας] pr δυο Mᵐᵍ $\underline{f}^{-129}$ 30'-85ᵐᵍ-130-321'ᵐᵍ 55 Arab

11:3 τέρατα] εργα $\underline{o}$ 130ᵐᵍ-321'ᵐᵍ-344ᵐᵍ 509 Armᵃᵖ Pal
       Syh = Ⓜ

12:23 ἡ ψυχή] + αυτου $\underline{oI}$ 127 85ᵐᵍ-321'ᵐᵍ-344ᵐᵍ

16:19 om κρίσιν $\underline{b}$ 85'-321'

Two of the 18 readings in List 11 have Bohairic
support. One is the change in the number of a pronoun
object, the other is the omission of a pronoun as a
marker of possession. This kind of change is typical of
Bo and the agreement with the s̲ group is coincidental.

The seven readings in List 12 must be augmented
by the 91 in List 10 above where C̲ is joined by s̲. The
17 readings in List 10 where Bo supports the joint reading of C̲ and s̲ have already been discussed. Bo supports
no reading in List 12. The s̲ group obviously had minimal influence on Bo.

H. The unique readings of the f̲ group and of f̲
joined by one other group appear below.

List 13 Unique readings of the f̲ group

1:19 om τήν 3° f̲⁻¹²⁹ 71'

1:28 καρδίαν ἡμῶν 426 528-761 f̲⁻¹²⁹ 30-321 669 319
646 = ⑩] καρδιαν υμων rell

1:29 πρὸς ὑμᾶς] + εν τω καιρω εκεινω λεγων 376 f̲⁻¹²⁹
Lat
    cod 100 Aeth⁻ᶜ

2:6 λήμψεσθε παρ᾽ αὐτῶν / ἀργυρίου] tr f̲⁻¹²⁹ Arm

2:11 ῾Ραφαΐν] -φειν f̲⁻¹²⁹

*2:36 χειμάρρου] pr του f̲⁻¹²⁹ Bo

3:1 ᾿Εδράϊν] -ειμ B f̲⁻¹²⁹

4:10 τὸν λαόν] + τουτον 58-376 f̲⁻¹²⁹ Latcod 100

4:21 ἵνα 2°] ου 58 f̲⁻¹²⁹

4:35 οὐκ ἔστιν] + ο θεος 58 f̲⁻¹²⁹

*4:39 τῇ διανοίᾳ] pr εν f⁻¹²⁹ 246 Bo

4:45 init] pr και f⁻¹²⁹

*5:16 om ἵνα 2° 73' f⁻¹²⁹ 246 Or IV 47 Lat_cod 100 PsAug
        Ep XI 1 Aeth Arm^ap Bo

*5:24 om ἡμῶν 72-376 f⁻¹²⁹ 509 Arm Bo

6:24 κύριος] + ο θεος f⁻¹²⁹ 121

*8:16 om σου 2° 72 f⁻¹²⁹ 75' Bo

9:9 πλάκας 1°] pr δυο f⁻⁵⁶ Aeth Bo Sa¹ 2 13

9:19 fin] + και ουκ ηθελησεν εξολοθρευσαι υμας (c var)
        f⁻¹²⁹

10:17 ὑμῶν] ημων 413 19 106 f⁻⁵⁶ 129 75 Arm

11:23 om ταῦτα f⁻¹²⁹

12:6 om καὶ τὰς ἀπαρχὰς ὑμῶν f⁻¹²⁹ 246

12:11 om ὑμῶν 2° 509 f⁻⁵⁶ 129 71' Lat_cod 100 Spec 59

12:28 ἀρεστόν] ευαρεστον f⁻¹²⁹ Phil III 164

*13:5 ἐν αὐτῇ] επ' αυτη f⁻¹²⁹ 246^c Bo

*13:11 τὸ πονηρόν / τοῦτο] tr f⁻⁵⁶ 129 Bo

16:12 τὰς ἐντολάς] pr πασας f⁻¹²⁹ 799 Aeth Sa³

16:14 om σου 1° f⁻⁵⁶^mg 129

16:18 om τὸν λαόν f⁻⁵⁶ 129

17:4 γεγένηται] pr και f⁻⁵⁶' 318 Arm Syh^G

17:8 ἀπὸ σοῦ / ῥῆμα] tr F 29-58-72 f⁻¹²⁹ 30'

18:1 καρπώματα] -μα A 72-82 417* f⁻¹²⁹ 321-343 318 319
        407

18:6 πάντων] + των πολεων f⁻⁵⁶ 129

18:22 om τοῦτο V 72 552 f⁻⁵⁶ 129

19:10 om σου 1° B 58 f^{-129} 18

21:22 om ἐν F 29-72 $f^{-56\ 129}$ 318 59 319 Arm

21:22 καὶ ἀποθάνη] post ξυλου tr $f^{-53\ 129}$

22:5 om ἐστιν $f^{-56\ 129}$ 527 55 Aeth = Ⓜ

22:20 παρθένια] pr η $f^{-56\ 129}$

23:3 Ἀμμανίτης / Μωαβίτης] tr F 29 73' f^{-129} 30' 59

23:4 Μεσοποταμίας] + συριας f^{-56*}

23:13 ἔξω] + της παρεμβολης 19 44 f^{-129}

23:14 παρεμβολή σου 2°] om σου f^{-129}

25:3 τεσσαράκοντα / μαστιγώσουσιν αὐτόν] tr f^{-129}

25:3 πληγάς] bis scr f^{-56*}

*26:11 ἔδωκεν σοί / κύριος ὁ θεός σου] tr f^{-129} Bo

26:15 λαόν] δουλον $f^{-129\ 246}$

27:6 αὐτό] αυτους f 318-392 Cyr II 665 Aeth

28:7 om σου 1° 72 f^{-246}

28:55 στενοχωρίᾳ] + σου B 376 f^{-56*} Arm Sa^3

31:30 fin] + λεγων f^{-129}

*33:1 om καί 1° F 29-707 $f^{-129\ 246}$ 121 407 509 Arab Arm Bo

33:3 om καί 3° 72 $f^{-129\ 246}$

33:5 φυλαῖς] -λης 537* $f^{-56\ 129}$ W^I 120 59

33:10 ἐν ὀργῇ] ενωπιον $f^{-129\ 246}$

33:15 ἀρχῆς] δαμις $f^{-129\ 246}$

33:29 αὐτῶν] αυτου 707 $f^{-56c\ 129}$ 54 71-527 799 669

34:6 Φογώρ] φογορ 414 44 f^{-129} PsClem 74

List 14 Unique readings of f̲ and one other group

2:8   Αἰλών] ελων f̲⁻¹²⁹ 343 527-619 68'-83-120

*2:37   γῆν] pr την 58-72 d̲ f̲⁻¹²⁹ 59 Bo

*3:24   τον βραχίονα] + σου 58-72-376 f̲⁻¹²⁹ 71'-527
         Lat_cod 100 Aeth Bo Sa¹ 2

4:24   θεός 2°] pr αυτος 0̲⁻⁸²-58 f̲⁻¹²⁹

10:2   πλάκας] pr δυο Μ^mg f̲⁻¹²⁹ 30'-85^mg-130-321'^mg 55
         Arab

11:29   ὄρος 1°] ορους 376-707 19 d̲ f̲⁻⁵⁶ ¹²⁹ 616
         Procop 905

12:11   θεῷ] κυριω 0⁻⁴²⁶ f⁻¹²⁹ 246

12:31   om ἐν F 29 b̲ f̲⁻¹²⁹ 59

13:1   om σοί 72-618 44 f̲⁻⁵⁶ ¹²⁹ 54-75'-767 527 509
         Chr II 854 935 Lat_cod 100 Luc Parc 2 Aeth⁻ᶜ

16:16   om σου 1° F V 29 f̲⁻¹²⁹ 71'-318 Or II 344 Phil I
         115 Lat_cod 100 Aeth^M Sa³

18:22   om ὅ F 29-707 b̲ f̲⁻¹²⁹ 318 Aeth

19:9   ὁδοῖς] εντολαις f̲⁻⁵⁶ ¹²⁹ z̲-68' 83

*23:9   om καί 0̲ f̲⁻¹²⁹ 128-630' 55 319 Aeth Arm Bo Syh

23:14   om σου 2° A F* (corr Fᵇ) b̲ f̲⁻¹²⁹ 246 75'

24:20   init — καλαμήσασθαι] post (22)fin tr F 29-72 f̲⁻¹²⁹
         n̲⁻⁷⁶⁷ 30' 59 319 407 Aeth⁻ᶜ Arm

28:40   om σοί F 29-707 414 f̲⁻¹²⁹ n̲ 318-527 59 Arm

32:25   ταμιείων] + αυτων 529 d̲⁻⁴⁴ f̲⁻⁵⁶ ¹²⁹ 75 59 Lat_codd
         330 416

33:6   ἔστω] pr συμεων A M V 82 b̲ f̲⁻¹²⁹ 127 121 68'

The 56 unique readings of f (List 13) include nine
supported by Bo. Eight of these nine variants are the
kinds determined above to be typical of Bo; the agreement
with f is therefore of no serious consequence, but probably mere coincidence. These include two omissions of
the possessive pronoun (5:24, 8:16), one transposition
of subject and object (26:11) and one of noun and modifier
(13:11), one omission of καί (33:1), one omission of ἵνα
(5:16), one instance of the preposing of the definite
article (2:36) and one of εν to a noun in the dative case
(4:39), and one substitution of επι for ἐν (13:5). The
ninth reading (9:9) involves the preposing of δυο before
πλάκας, a phrase common throughout Deut and thus of no
significance.

The 18 readings of f joined by one other group
(List 14) contain three instances of insignificant agreements of Bo and f. These include one preposing of the
definite article (2:37), one addition of the possessive
pronoun (3:24) and one omission of καί (23:9). These
agreements are most likely due to coincidence. The f
group seems to have exerted little influence on Bo.

I. The b group is a cohesive and consistent group
in Deut. The readings unique to that group are listed
below. Readings supported by fewer than three of its five
members are not included.

List 15   Unique readings of the b̲ group

1:15   συνετούς] + εις τας φυλας υμων b̲ 56-664 343

1:22   om ἡμῖν 72 b̲

1:26   om κυρίου 72 b̲ 509

*1:28   καὶ πολύ] om και 16 b̲ Bo

1:31   εἴδετε] + οδον ορους του αμορραιου B b̲

1:35   τὴν γῆν] om την B b̲

1:38   Ναυή] pr ο του b̲

1:43   καὶ παρέβητε] κατα παρεβητε b̲

1:46   fin] + εκει B b̲ Aeth Arm Bo

2:1   ἀπήραμεν] απηλθομεν b̲

2:13   Ζάρεδ 1°] ζαρετ A B b̲ 509 Latcod 100

2:13   Ζάρεδ 2°] ζαρετ B b̲ Aeth⁻C

2:14   Ζάρεδ] ζαρετ A B b̲⁻¹⁹ 44 W^I 121 509 Latcod 100

2:18   Ἀροήρ] pr γην b̲

2:19   κλήρῳ 1°⌒2° 707^txt 57* c pr m b̲

2:20   om αὐτούς 761* b̲ Latcod 100

2:22   ὥσπερ] ως γαρ b̲

2:24   κληρονομεῖν] pr κληρω (-ρον 537) b̲

2:26   Κεδμώθ] καιδαμωθ b̲

2:28   παρελεύσομαι] + δια της γης σου b̲ Sa²

2:31   γῆν 1°⌒2° b̲ 799 669^txt

*2:34   om αὐτῶν 1° 58-72 b̲ Arab Bo = ⑪

3:4   Ἀργόβ] αρβουκ b̲⁻¹⁹

3:5   ὀχυραί] ισχυραι b̲⁻¹⁹

3:12   Γαλαάδ] pr του b̲ 610 W^I 318

*3:14   αὐτό] αυτας B b̲ Lat cod 100 Bo

3:14   τὴν Βασάν] γην βασαν b̲

3:22   om ὅτι b̲

3:28   διαβήσεται] + εμπροσθεν b̲

4:2   τὸ ῥῆμα] + τουτο 963 c pr m b̲ Lat Ruf R̲e̲g̲ S̲ B̲a̲s̲ 12
Spec 84 Bo

4:19   om σου V 414 b̲ Lat cod 100 Spec 44 Arm

4:23   συνέταξεν] pr ου V b̲⁻¹¹⁸*

4:28   ἀκούσωσιν] + τοις ωσιν b̲

4:28   οὐδέ 2°] ουτε B b̲ 407 509

4:32   σου] υμων b̲

4:34   om ἐν 3° 72 551 b̲ 106-125 71' 18 Bo

4:34   om ὑμῶν 58-72 529 b̲ 129 75

4:38   ἔχεις] εχει Fᶜ b̲ 53 767 619 128-630'

4:48   ἐπὶ τοῦ χείλους] παρα το χειλοςB* b̲

*5:8   ἐν τῇ γῇ] επι της γης 58-376 txt b̲ 53' 75 Bo

5:10   om τοῖς 2° 15-72 b̲ 392 55

5:15   om καί 1° b̲

5:16   ἵνα 2°] εση b̲

5:16   om γένῃ b̲

5:22   ὑμῶν] υιων ισραηλ b̲ Iren IV 15:1

5:25   μή] + ποτε b̲

5:27   om πάντα 2° b̲

5:28   om τῶν λόγων 72 b̲ 509 Arab

5:29   om ἐν αὐτοῖς b̲

5:31   init] pr και b̲

5:31   om δέ b

5:33   om σοί 1° b

5:33   σου] ημων 963 b⁻⁵³⁷* = Ⓜ

6:6   σου 1° ∩ 2° b = Ⓜ

6:7   οἴκω] pr τω b Nil 822

6:7   πορευόμενος] εν τω πορευεσθαι σε b = Ⓜ

6:7   ὁδῷ] pr τη b

6:10   τὴν γῆν] + την αγαθην b

6:15   om ἐν σοί 2° b 55 Arm

6:20   om αὔριον b

6:22   τῷ οἴκῳ] τοις θεραπουσιν b

6:23   ἐξήγαγεν] + κυριος b Arab

6:25   om πάσας 417ᶜ b

7:1   καὶ ἰσχυρότερα] προ προσωπου b

7:8   σε] + κυριος ο θεος σου b

7:9   om ὁ θεος ὁ 500 b

7:9   om ὁ ult b 71' 509ᶜ Tht I 412

7:9   τὰς ἐντολάς] τα προσταγματα b

7:11   τὰς ἐντολάς] + αυτου B b Aeth Bo Pal Sa¹⁶

7:12   om ταῦτα b

7:18   om μνείᾳ 72 b⁻¹⁰⁸ᶜ Aethᴹ Arab

7:22   τὰ ἄγρια] της γης b⁻¹⁰⁸ᵐᵍ

7:26   προσοχθίσματι] pr και 57 b

8:2   om καὶ πειράσῃ σε b⁻¹⁰⁸ᵐᵍ 246 Anast 412

8:11   κρίματα] et δικαιώματα tr V 707 422 b Aeth

8:13   om σου 1° 500-529 b ᴸᵃᵗTert Ieiunio 6 Marc IV 15
       Aethᴹ Armᵗᵉ

8:15   οὗ οὐκ]om ου <u>b</u> 127-767 59 509

*8:18   init] pr και γνωση τη καρδια <u>b</u> Bo (om και) Sa¹

8:18   στήσῃ] + κυριος <u>b</u>

9:4   τὰ ἔθνη ταῦτα] + τα κυκλω σου <u>b</u>

9:6   διά] κατα <u>b</u>

*9:6   κληρονομῆσαι] + αυτην <u>b</u> ^{Lat}codd 100 104 Hi <u>C</u> <u>Pal</u>
      I 36 Bo Sa^{2 13} = Ⓜ

*9:15   ἐπί] εν <u>b</u> 75 392 ^{Lat}cod 100 Arm Bo

9:21   om αὐτόν 1° 77 <u>b</u> Arm = Ⓜ

9:23   δίδωμι] διδωσιν 82 <u>b</u>; + κυριος ο θεος υμων
      (ημων 19) <u>b</u>

9:26   θεῶν] αιωνων 707 <u>b</u>

9:26   κληρονομίαν σου] + και την μεριδα σου <u>b</u>

*9:29   om ἐν τῇ ἰσχύι — fin <u>b</u>-108^{mg} 30 Bo^{Λ'}

10:3   om τάς 1° <u>b</u> 767

10:3   om τάς 2° B <u>b</u> 767

10:7   χείμαρρου] pr ου <u>b</u>

10:8   κυρίου 1° ⌒ 2° <u>b</u> 56^{txt}

10:10   om καί ult F^c 376 <u>b</u> = Ⓜ

10:12   καρδίας] et ψυχῆς tr <u>b</u>

*10:13   δικαιώματα αὐτοῦ] + και τα κριματα <u>b</u> Bo

10:15   παρὰ πάντα τὰ ἔθνη / κατὰ τὴν ἡμέραν ταύτην] tr <u>b</u>

10:17   κυρίων] κυριευοντων <u>b</u>

10:17   δῶρον] δωρα <u>b</u> ^{Lat}cod 100

10:18   fin] + περιβαλεσθαι <u>b</u>

11:2   om κυρίου <u>b</u>

11:3   καί ult ⌒ (4)1° 707 <u>b</u>-118 537

11:4 ὡς] pr και b

11:8 φυλάξεσθε] + ποιειν b

11:8 σήμερον] + ποιειν b

11:8 om καί ult B 376 b Arm

11:8 om ἐκεῖ b 458 Arm

11:13 om πάσας b⁻¹⁰⁸ᵐᵍ Arab = ⓜ

11:13 fin] + και εξ ολης της δυναμεως σου b

11:14 τῇ γῇ] επι της γης (bis scr 19) b

11:15 χορτάσματα] χορτον b Aeth

11:16 πρόσεχε] προσεχετε b Arm Pal = ⓜ

11:16 σεαυτῷ] εαυτοις b⁻⁵³⁷ᶜ Arm Pal = ⓜ

11:18 εἰς τὴν καρδίαν] επι των καρσιων b Pal

11:18 ὑμῶν 1°⌒2° b 75'

11:18 om πρό 72 b

11:20 γράψετε] γραψεις b

11:20 τῶν οἴκων ὑμῶν] του οικου σου b Pal

11:20 τῶν πυλῶν ὑμῶν] εν ταις πυλαις σου (om 509) b 407
     509 Pal

11:24 om τόν V 72 615 b 53'

11:28 ὑμῖν 1°] σοι b 318

11:30 Γολγόλ] σολγολ b

12:5 ἐν μιᾷ] εκ πασων b

12:5 om ἐκεῖ 1° 618 b Arm

12:6 ὑμῶν 1°⌒2° Fᵗˣᵗ V b⁻¹⁰⁸ᵐᵍ 75' 669ᵗˣᵗ 407

12:10 ἐχθρῶν] εθνων 529 b

12:10 ὑμῶν / τῶν κύκλῳ tr b 59

12:11 om ἐκεῖ 2° B 15-72-82 b 128-630' 59 Eus VI 12
Lat_cod 100 Spec 59 Aeth

12:11 δόματα] ολοκαυτωματα των υιων b

12:12 ἐπι τῶν πυλῶν] εν ταις πολεσιν b Aeth^M

12:18 πόλεσιν σου] πολεσιν υμων B b Aeth

12:19 τὸν χρόνον] om τον b

*12:21 ἐνετειλάμην] ενετειλατο V b 407 509 Lat_cod 100 Bo
Pal Sa^l

12:21 σοί 2°] + κυριος b

*12:24 ἐπι τὴν γῆν / ἐκχεεῖτε αὐτό] tr b Bo Sa^l 3

12:26 ἥξεις] οισεις b

12:26 om αὐτῷ B 73' b W^I 55 Aeth Bo

12:27 καί 1°] ουτως b

*12:27 πρός] επι 72 b^-314 Bo = 𝔐

12:28 ἐὰν ποιήσῃς] και ποιησης b Arm

12:29 om αὐτῶν 1° b

12:30 om προσώπου b

13:4 αὐτού] τουτον B b Cyr I 426

13:5 πλανῆσαι] αποστησαι b Arm

*13:5 ἀφανιεῖς B b 630^C 509 Bo = 𝔐] αφανιειτε rell

13:6 om σου 1° 72 b

13:7 τῶν θεῶν] pr παντων b

13:7 τῶν ἐγγιζόντων] pr η V b

13:14 λόγος] + ουτος b

13:16 σκῦλα αὐτῆς 2°] εν αυτη b

13:16 ἀνοικοδομηθήσεται] + εις τον αιωνα b^-314

13:18 init] pr οτι <u>b</u>

13:18 εἰσακούσητε] ακοη ακουσητε <u>b</u>

13:18 καλόν] et ἀρεστόν tr B <u>b</u>

14:5   om καί 2° <u>b</u> 127

*14:5   om καί 4° <u>b</u> Bo^{A'}

14:7   διχηλούντων] pr μη 381 <u>b</u>⁻³¹⁴ 527

14:7   ὀνυχιζόντων] pr μη <u>b</u>⁻³¹⁴ Arm Sa

14:7   τὸν κάμηλον] των καμηλων <u>b</u>⁻³¹⁴ 537

14:9   φάγεσθε 1°] pr α V <u>b</u> 68-120 Aeth Arm

14:17 καὶ νυκτερίδα] pr και παντα κορακα και τα ομοια αυτω <u>b</u>

14:20 θεῷ σου] θεω υμων <u>b</u>

14:22 ἐπικληθῆναι] pr ἐκεῖ <u>b</u>

14:24 om αὐτόν 381' <u>b</u> 246 407 Arab Arm Syh

14:25 ἐπί 2°] εν <u>b</u> ^{Lat}cod 100

14:25 ἐπί 3°] εν <u>b</u> ^{Lat}cod 100

14:26 αὐτῷ] pr εν <u>b</u>

14:27 om ἐν 1° M <u>b</u>

14:28 om ὅτι — μετὰ σοῦ 72 <u>b</u>

*14:28 om οἷς ἄν ποιῇς <u>b</u> 75 Sa¹ Bo^{A'}

15:4   om κύριος ὁ θεός σου δίδωσιν σοί <u>b</u> 71' Sa³

15:8   om καθότι — fin <u>b</u> 75' 509 Aeth^{CH}

15:9   ἔτος 2°] pr το <u>b</u>

15:9   τῷ ἀδελφῷ] pr εν <u>b</u>

15:9   βοήσεται] κατανοησεται <u>b</u>

15:13 om ἐλεύθερον <u>b</u> Arm Syh

15:13   ἀπο σοῦ] post κενόν tr b̲

15:13   om αὐτόν 2° b̲ 53'

15:18   init] pr και b̲ Lat_cod 100 Aeth Arm

*15:23 φάγῃ] φαγεσθε B b̲ Lat_cod 100 Arm^ap Bo

16:2   om αὐτόν 58-426 b̲ 75 318 Lat_cod 100 Aeth Arm

16:6   om κύριος — αὐτοῦ b̲

16:6   om πρός b̲

16:6   ἐξῆλθες] εξηλθετε b̲ 85^mg

16:9   ὁλοκλήρους ἐξαριθμήσεις] tr b̲

*16:11 om ἐν τῷ τόπῳ — fin b̲ Bo^A'

16:13   om ἑπτὰ ἡμέρας b̲

16:13   ἐκ 1°] pr τα b̲

16:15   om καί 1° b̲

16:20   σου] υμων (ημων 19) b̲ Aeth^M

16:20   σοι] υμιν b̲ Arm^te Aeth^M

*17:10 om ἐκ τοῦ τόπου — ἐκεῖ b̲ Bo^A'

17:12   ποιήσῃ] + χειρι b̲

17:12   κριτοῦ] + σου b̲

17:14   om ἐπ᾽ 2° F 72'-426 529*-550'-551 b̲ 54-458 134
        Cyr III 81 Aeth

17:14   om τά ult b̲ 30' 134

17:19   μάθῃ] μαθης 528 b̲

17:19   φυλάσσεσθαι] pr και B F^b 58-72 b̲ 127 527 Aeth

17:19 ταύτας] αυτου F 29-72 16-761*(vid) b̲ 125 53'
        75-458* 30' 527 Aeth Bo^A'

18:4   δώσεις] pr και b̲

18:5　εὐλογεῖν] επευχεσθαι b

18:5　fin] + κυριω 376' b Arab Syh (÷)

18:6　om τῶν 2° b⁻¹⁹

18:7　λειτουργήσει] + κω̄ b

18:7　om κυρίου 1° b

18:17　ἐλάλησαν] ελασησας b 106 53 392 59

18:22　om ὁ προφήτης 1° b

19:5　om τόν b

*19:6　καὶ τούτῳ] om και b Bo

*19:7　ἐντέλλομαι] + ποιειν b Aeth Bo

19:8　σου 3°⌒ 4° b

19:9　om ἀγαπᾶν — τὰς ἡμέρας b

19:10　om ᾗ — κλήρῳ 72 b

19:14　πατέρες] προτερον b

19:15　καὶ ἐπὶ στόματος] η 72 b 44-125 53' 75 799 319 = Ⓜ

19:15　om μαρτύρων ult 72 b 53' 799 319

19:21　πόδα] pr και b Aeth

20:3　εἰς πόλεμον / ἐπὶ τοὺς ἐχθροὺς ὑμῶν] tr b 799

*20:7　μεμνήστευται] + εαυτω b Bo

20:8　ὥσπερ] + και b

20:15　αἵ] και 376 b 610 767

20:16　om ἀπ᾿ αὐτῶν B 58 b 630ᶜ Latcodd 91 92 94-96 100
　　　　Aug Ios XXI 2 = Ⓜ

20:17　om σοι b Armᵗᵉ

21:1　om ἣν κύριος — κληρονομῆσαι b⁻¹⁰⁸ᵐᵍ

21:2　init] pr και b Latcod 100

21:4   om ἡ γερουσία τῆς πόλεως ἐκείνης b̲ Arab

21:6   ἡ γερουσία] om ἡ b̲

21:7   om καί 2° b̲

21:10   κύριος B b̲ 767 407 509 Lat_cod 100] pr αυτους rell

21:13 σου 2°] σοι A 46'-52' b̲ 767 343 318 319 646
        Aeth Bo Sa⁸ 10(vid) Syh = Ⓜ

21:14   διότι] pr ου b̲

21:21   om αὐτοῦ 414 b̲ 75 318

21:21   fin] + και ουκ ασεβησουσιν b̲

21:22   κρίμα] pr και b̲ Lat_Hi G̲a̲l̲ II 3

*22:1   καὶ ἀποδώσεις αὐτῷ A^mg B V 72-707^mg b̲ 509 Aeth Bo]
        om rell

22:6   om ἤ 2° b̲ 799

22:12   ἃ ἄν] και b̲

22:14   αὐτῆς ult] εν αυτη b̲

22:18   om τῆς πόλεως ἐκείνης b̲

23:9   σου] υμων b̲

23:10   om ἐν b̲

23:17   οὐκ ἔσται 3°] pr και b̲ 71 120 Cyr I 904 Lat_cod 100
        Aeth⁻ᴹ

23:18   init] pr και b̲

*23:18 βδέλυγμα] βδελυγματα 82 b̲⁻¹⁹' Aeth Bo Syh

23:23   τά] + γαρ b̲

23:23 τῷ 2°] pr εν b̲ 370 55 Bo

23:24   om δέ b̲ Eus VIII 2 225

23:25   ψυχήν] pr την b̲ 127* (vid)

24:3   om αὐτῆς 1° b̲⁻⁵³⁷

24:3   om ὅς — fin b 75

24:4   om καὶ οὐ — fin 58 b 527

24:7   ἀποδῶται] pr και b

24:7   ἀποθανεῖται] pr και b

24:8   ἐνετειλάμην ὑμῖν] tr b

24:19 ἀμητόν] pr τον b

24:19 ἐν τῷ ἀγρῷ σου] και b

25:5   αὐτῇ] αυτω b 527

25:14 καί] η b⁻³¹⁴ 54

25:15 om ἔσται 2° — σου b

25:19 om ἐν — κατακληρονομῆσαι 72 b 125

25:19 ἐξαλείψεις] pr και b 71 Aeth^M

26:2   om ἧς κύριος ὁ θεός σου δίδωσι σοί b

26:10 om ἔναντι — fin b 53'

*26:11 καί 2°] pr συ b 319 Lat_cod 100 Aeth Bo

26:12 ἔτει] επι b

26:13 μου] σου b

26:17 init] pr και 552 b

26:17 καί 2° ⌒ (18)1° 72 b

27:3   om ὡς ἄν — fin 72 b 53' 71

27:6   init] pr και b

27:20 ὁ 1°] pr πας V 82 413-529-761 b 75' 392 120

27:22 om ἐκ 2° B b 75' 646

27:25 αἵματος ἀθώου] tr b

28:1   ἔσται B 426 b Lat_cod 100 Aeth Arm = Ⓜ] + ως αν
       διαβητε τον Ιορδανην εις την γην ην κυριος ο θεος
       υμων διδωσιν υμιν rell

28:1 om ἃς ἐγὼ ἐντέλλομαι σοὶ σήμερον b

*28:10 om καί 1° b Bo

28:11 ἐπί 1°] εν B b

28:12 init] pr και b

28:12 κύριος] + ο θεος (+ σου 19) 707 b

*28:13 καταστήσαι] ποιησαι b Bo

28:13 ἀκούσης] ακουσητε 963 b Aeth

28:13 θεοῦ σου] θεου υμων 963 b⁻³¹⁴ᶜ ᴸᵃᵗAmbr Tob 62 Aeth
     Arab

28:13 σοί] υμιν 963 b Aeth⁻ᴹ Arab

28:13 φυλάσσειν] et ποιεῖν tr b

28:14 τῶν λόγων ὧν ἐγω ἐντέλλομαι σοὶ σήμερον] τουτων b

28:15 om φυλάσσειν — σήμερον b 71

28:19 om ἐπικατάρατος συ ἐν τῷ 2° 72 b 44-125 71

*28:20 κύριός σοι] tr V 58-72 73' b 767 319 ᴸᵃᵗcod 100
     Luc Athan I 8 Aeth Arm Bo

28:21 ἀπό] επι b 799

28:22 φόνῳ] φοβω b Aeth Arm

28:24 init] pr και b ᴸᵃᵗcod 100 Aeth

*28:24 om καί 2° b ᴸᵃᵗIsid Fid II 10:9 Bo

28:25 ἐπικοπήν] pr εις b

28:28 om καί 1° B 963 b

28:28 om καί 2° 963 vid 707* b 630ᶜ 407 509

28:30 οὐκ οἰκήσεις] ετερος οικησει b

28:30 οὐ] ετερος b

28:30 τρυγήσεις] τρυγησει b

28:36 om ἐκεῖ b 664* c pr m Arab

28:41 ἀπελεύσονται] pr καὶ b

28:53 om ὁ θεός σου 963 707 b⁻¹⁹ Lat_cod 100 Arab Arm Sa³

28:53 ᾗ θλίψει] καὶ εθλιψε b

28:54 fin] + σοι b 509

28:56 ἐν 1°] pr η 618 b 127 Arm

28:56 om διὰ τήν 2° B 376-381' b⁻¹⁹ 71-318

*28:57 om αὐτῆς 1° b 55 Arm Bo

28:63 om εὐφράνθη b

28:65 τῷ [χνει] τοις ιχνεσι b Arm

28:67 ἑσπέρα] οψε b

29:11 om ὁ 2° 610 b 76

29:12 om ἐν 1° A b 121 68'

29:13 ὃν 1°⌒2° b⁻¹⁹

29:13 καὶ Ἰσαάκ] om καί F b 106 246 318 509 = ⑪

29:18 om ἔστιν 2° b

29:18 ἐν ὑμῖν / ῥίζα] tr b

29:22 om ὁ 761* b 344* 59* 319

29:25 om τοῦ θεοῦ 72 b

30:3 om κύριος 2° b 458 Aeth

30:5 om κύριος ὁ θεός σου 72 b 106 509

30:5 ποιήσει 1°⌒2° b 56ᵗˣᵗ 120 55 509 Lat_cod 100

30:10 ἐάν 1°⌒2° 72 b

30:13 om ἡμῖν 1° b Lat_cod 100 Aug Perf 22 Arab Arm

30:16 τά] pr παντα b 319

30:16 δικαιώματα αὐτοῦ B 58-707ᵗˣᵗ b 630ᶜ Lat_cod 100 Aeth
       Sa] + και τας εντολας αυτου rell

30:18 σοί 2°] υμιν <u>b</u>

30:18 om εἰς — fin <u>b</u> 125

31:6 πτοηθῇς] φοβηθης (c var) <u>b</u> 318

31:13 οἳ οὐκ] pr και <u>b</u>

31:14 om τῆς 2° — fin <u>b</u>

31:16 om τῆς γῆς — αὐτήν <u>b</u> 53'

*31:17 ἔσται] εσονται V 707 <u>b</u> W^I-127 Aeth Arm Bo

31:21 ποιοῦσιν] + μοι A <u>b</u> 121 68'

31:23 ἐνετείλατο B 963 82-376 <u>b</u> ^{Lat}codd 100 103 Sa^3 Syh] +
       μωυσης rell (c var)

31:23 αὐτός] ουτος <u>b</u>

31:24 λόγους] + τουτους 376 <u>b</u> Aeth

31:25 om τούτου 376 <u>b</u>$^{-19}$ Aeth

31:26 om τούτου <u>b</u> 71 ^{Lat}cod 100

31:27 σου 1°] αυτων <u>b</u>

31:27 σου 2°] αυτων <u>b</u>

32:10 αὐτόν 1°] αυτους b 44 75 319 ^{Lat}codd 300 460 Brev
       Goth 53 B Aeth Syh^G

33:1 ἄνθρωπος] pr ο 82 16 <u>b</u> 106 59^c

33:3 ὑπό 1°] επι <u>b</u>

33:7 διακρινοῦσιν] διακονλυσαι <u>b</u>

33:10 θυμίαμα] + μοι <u>b</u>$^{-19}$

33:10 ὀργῇ] εορτη A^c F <u>b</u> 319 Chr I 80 ^{Lat}cod 100

33:13 εὐλογίας] ευλογιαις <u>b</u> 129 318

33:18 αὐτοῦ] σου V <u>b</u> ^{Lat}cod 100 Aeth = Ⓜ

33:20 om εὐλογημένος <u>b</u>

33:20 ἄρχοντα] αρχοντας 707 <u>b</u> 129 799 ^{Lat}Ambr <u>Patr</u> 36 Arm Sa^3 ^{5} ^{16}

33:27 Ἀπόλοιο] απολοις <u>b</u> 75

34:8 οἱ υἱοὶ ᾽Ισραήλ / τὸν Μωυσῆν] tr 376 <u>b</u>

Thirty eight of these 350 <u>b</u> readings (11%) are supported by Bo or some Bo mss. Twenty seven of these consist of agreements of Bo and <u>b</u> due to coincidence and/or the nature of the Bohairic translation. These include five omissions of καί (1:28, 14:5, 19:6, 28:16 28:24); as for pronouns, there are three omissions (2:34, 12:26, 28:57), four additions (4:2, 7:11, 9:6, 26:11), and three substitutions (3:14, 17:19, 21:13); instances involving prepositions include one omission (4:34), one addition (23:23), and three substitutions (5:8, 9:15, 12:27); three instances of change in number (13:5, 15:23, 23:18), one of change in person (12:21), one transposition of verb and modifier (12:24) and one of noun and modifier (28:20), and one substitution of the third person plural verb for its infinitive (31:17).

The remaining eleven variants include four which are supported only by Bo$^{A'}$ (9:29, 14:28, 16:11, 17:10). All four are omissions of details which add little to the meaning of the text; in one instance (9:29) however the omission is simply the result of parablepsis. The variants in 16:11 and 17:10 consist of the omission of the recurrent phrase in Deut "in the place which the Lord our God has chosen to call his name there" (c var).

Because this phrase appears so often in the text, its omission here shows no particular dependence of the sub-group of Bo on the b group. The omission of οἷς ἄν ποιῇς in 14:28 is ad sensum and the agreement of Bo and b may be coincidence. The seven remaining readings include three which are easily explained. The additions of εκει in 1:46, of ποιειν to ἐντέλλομαι in 19:7 and of εαυτω to μεμνήστευται in 20:7 are all in keeping with the sense of their respective contexts so the reading of Bo and b may be independent in origin.

Four readings (8:18, 10:13, 22:1, 28:13) remain. The variant in 10:13 shows the addition of και τα κριματα in a list of divine requirements. Lists of this kind frequently appear in the text of Deut, e.g., 4:8, 4:45, 6:3, 6:20, 7:11, 8:11, so this addition may well be ex par. The fact that it is here attested only by Bo and b cannot however be ignored, and the possibility of influence remains open. A similar phrase και γνωση τη καρδια is preposed to the beginning of 8:18. This plus, borrowed from 8:5 init, is attested only by b Bo and Sa. It seems likely that the parent of b and of the Coptic versions preserved this variant reading from an early date. The variant in 28:13 is interesting; only b and Bo witness to ποιησαι for καταστήσαι. This variant may well have been exegetical and independent in origin, but its distinct character tends to suggest relationship between these two sources. The reading in 22:1 shows both b and Bo as witnesses to original Greek and, though interesting, is not relevant in a discussion of possible dependence. It appears from this list that there is some slight textual connection between the b group and Bo.

The relationship of Bo to b may be investigated further by a list of instances where b is joined by one other group. Such a list follows.

List 16 Readings of b and one other group

1:29 εἶπα] ειπον b n

4:28 οὐδὲ 3°] ουτε B b z 407'

4:43 Γαδδί] γαδ 58 414 b n 121 59 ^{Lat}cod 100 Arm Syh

5:27 om ὅσα 2° — προς σέ b d^{-106}

5:30 εἰπόν] ειπεν 551 b n

6:6 om ταῦτα b s$^{-30'}$ 343' 28 55

*6:6 ἐν τῇ καρδίᾳ] επι της καρδιας b z Bo = Ⓜ

7:9 om τήν B* b n Tht I 412

7:9 om τό B* 963 b n Tht I 412

7:12 om σου 72 c"-414' 422 528 b 129 30'-85 28 319 Arm

7:14 εὐλογητος ἔσῃ] ευλογησει σε b 54'-75

7:15 om πάντας F b n 407 Aeth^{11}

7:20 om οἱ 2° b 767 z

8:11 om αὐτοῦ 2° oI b^{-108}^{C} ^{Lat}cod 100

9:5 τῷ Αβραάμ B V 73'-413 b 106 767 343 t 630 55 407'] om τῷ rell

*9:10   ὄρει B b̲$^{-108mg}$ n̲$^{-127}$ 121^{txt} 55 407' Lat$_{codd}$ 100
        104 Aeth Arm Bo Sa$^{1\ 2\ 3\ 13}$] + εκ μεσου του πυρος
        rell

9:15   πλάκες B G b̲ 246 n̲$^{-127}$ 344^{mg} 318 407' Lat$_{codd}$ 100
        104 Aeth Arab Sa$^{1te\ 2\ 3}$] + των μαρτυριων rell

9:26   ἐν 2°⌒3° b̲ 54-75' Arab = Ⓜ

9:29   κλῆρος] κληρονομια (-μιας 118 314) b̲ 71'-527 59
        Sa$^{2\ 3\ 12}$

10:14   ἡ γῆ] pr και C̲" b̲$^{-19}$ 314 Tht I 416 Aeth Arab Arm
        Pal

10:21   init] pr καιο̲I̲ b̲ Arm

11:10   ὑμεῖς εἰσπορεύεσθε] εισπορευη (c var) B b̲ 54'-75-
        767 Aeth

11:21   om πλουημερεύσητε καί b̲ z̲ 407' Lat$_{codd}$ 91 92 94-96

11:23   ἰσχυρότερα] + υμων 72 b̲ 246 134 z̲$^{-83}$

11:27   ὑμῖν] σοι b̲ y̲$^{-121}$ 392

11:30   γῆ] pr τη ο̲$^{-426}$-58 b̲

*12:15 φάγεται] φαγονται (c var) C̲" b̲ 85 28 318 Aeth Arm
        Bo Sa$^{1\ 3}$

12:21   om σου 2° G*-72-82-381' b̲ n̲ Lat$_{cod}$ 100 Arm

12:31   om ἐν F 29 b̲ f̲$^{-129}$ 59

13:9   om καί 1° B b̲ z̲$^{-83}$ 407' Lat$_{cod}$ 100 Cypr Fortun 5
        Firm M̲at XXIX 1 Luc Parc 2 Tert Scorp 2 Aeth^{-CG}
        Arm^{te}

*13:14 om σαφῶς b̲$^{-118mg}$ 314 537^{mg} d̲$^{-106}$ Bo Sa^{3}

14:4   om ἅ 72 b̲ 75' z̲

14:7 om ταῦτα 2° B b⁻³¹⁴ n 30'-343 407' Lat_cod 100 Aeth

*15:20 om τοῦ θεοῦ σου B b d⁻¹⁰⁶ Lat_cod 100 Aeth⁻C Arm
Bo^A'

16:19 om κρίσιν b s⁻³⁰' 343'

*17:1 om ὅτι O b 246 128-630' 319 Aeth Bo Sa¹ ³ ¹¹ Syh

*17:18 om τοῦ δίφρου B V b n 407' Lat_Luc Athan I 7 Aeth
Arm Bo Sa³

17:19 θεὸν αὐτοῦ] θεον σου B b n 321'ᵐᵍ 407' Lat_Luc Athan
I 7 Arm Sa³

17:20 om τοῖς b n

*18:2 αὐτῶν B 82 52 b 458 z⁻⁶⁸' 83 646 Cyr I 361 Aeth
Bo] αυτου rell (c var)

*18:4 om καί 1° O-72 b Lat_cod 100 Bo Syh

*18:12 om ὁ θεός σου B 16-422 b n 630ᶜ 407' Lat_cod 100
Spec 55 Hes 5 Aeth Arm Bo

18:18 ἀναστήσω αὐτοῖς / ἐκ τῶν ἀδελφῶν αὐτῶν] tr V b
z⁻⁶⁸' 83 Eus VI 100 Eus VI 427

18:22 om ὅ F 29-707 b f⁻¹²⁹ 318 Aeth

*19:2 om σου 1° 82-376-618 528 b z⁻⁶⁸' 83 319 509 Lat_cod
100 Arm Arab Bo Sa³

19:5 μετὰ τοῦ πλησίον / εἰς τὸν δρυμόν] tr b 54-75'

19:8 om σου 1° oI⁻⁶⁴-58-72 552 b 799 319

19:14 om ἐν κλήρῳ O'-707 b 319 Lat_cod 100 Syh = Ⓜ

22:8 om δέ B O b W^I Cyr I 585 Lat_cod 100

22:21 om οἴκου B b 610 n 68'-120 407' Lat_cod 100 Arm

22:26 om αὐτοῦ C b

23:4　ἐξ] εκ γης <u>b</u> 71'-527 Aeth[M] Arab

23:14　om σου 2° A F* (corr F[b]) <u>b</u> <u>f</u>$^{-129}$ 246 75'

23:14　ὀφθήσεται] ευρεθησεται <u>b</u> <u>n</u> Tht I 429 Sa^3

23:16　om κατοικήσει 2° <u>b</u> <u>d</u>$^{-106}$

24:5　om αὐτοῦ 2° <u>b</u> <u>d</u>$^{-106}$

25:7　ὁ ἄνθρωπος / λαβεῖν] tr <u>C</u>" <u>b</u>

25:16　σου] + εστιν A <u>b</u> <u>d</u> 71 ^{Lat}cod 100

*26:8　om αὐτός 72 <u>b</u> <u>d</u>$^{-106}$ 125 75 71 Arab Bo Sa^3 = Ⓜ

26:10　om γῆν ῥέουσαν γάλα καὶ μέλι 72 413-528 <u>b</u> <u>d</u>$^{-106}$

　　　　53' Arab = Ⓜ

27:2　σοί] + εν κληρω <u>oI</u> <u>b</u> 83 (vid) Arab

27:6　om κυρίῳ τῷ θεῷ σου 2° 72 <u>b</u> <u>d</u>$^{-44'}$ 71 Aeth

28:11　om ἐπί ult — fin <u>b</u> <u>d</u>$^{-106}$ 53'

28:13　οὐκ ἔσῃ] ουχ 761 <u>b</u> <u>n</u>$^{-767}$ 319 Tht I 436 ^{Lat}Ambr

　　　　<u>Tob</u> 62 Luc <u>Conven</u> 2 Arm Bo

28:36　κύριος σέ] tr <u>b</u> <u>n</u> Arm

28:41　om γάρ 82 <u>b</u> <u>d</u>$^{-125}$ 527

29:13　Ἀβραάμ] pr τω <u>C</u>" <u>b</u> 458 730

31:5　ἐνώπιον ὑμῶν] υμιν B 707 <u>b</u> <u>n</u>$^{-75}$ 344^{mg} 630^c

　　　　^{Lat}cod 100 Aeth

31:15　στύλῳ νεφέλης] νεφελη B <u>b</u> <u>n</u>$^{-458}$ 630^c 407 ^{Lat}codd

　　　　100 103

31:20　κορήσουσιν] pr και <u>b</u> 106 53' W^I <u>t</u>

31:21　πρόσωπον B 707 <u>b</u> <u>n</u>$^{-127}$ 59 ^{Lat}codd 100 103 104 Arm]

　　　　+ αυτων rell

33:6　ἔστω] pr συμεων A M V 82 <u>b</u> <u>f</u>$^{-129}$ 127 121 68'

33:28   γῆς] pr της b z 407

*34:5   om ἐκεῖ B 72' b n 318 55 59 407' PsClem 74 Lat_cod
        100 Lib geneal 496 Aeth Arm Bo

34:7   οὐκ] pr και b d^{-106} Aeth Arm

This list of 75 readings includes 14 (19%) supported wholly or partly by Bo. Again, nine of the 14
agreements of Bo and b probably do not indicate influence
or dependence. These consist of one omission of καί
(18:4), two omissions (19:2, 26:8) and one substitution
(18:2) of pronouns, one change of number (12:15), one
substitution of prepositions (6:6), and omissions respectively of ὅτι (17:1), ἐκεῖ (34:5) and of ἔσῃ repeated
in the context (28:13).

The variants in 9:10, 13:14, 15:20, 17:18 and 18:12
are of a different nature and must be further examined.
The divine name occurs so frequently in the text of Deut
that its omission (15:20, 18:12) by two presumably related sources is, by itself, of little significance. The
adverb σαφῶς in 13:14 follows ἀληθής and its omission
in context takes little away from the meaning. The
group joining Bo and b is in this instance d and again
the only other evidence is Sa. This also appears to be
an early variant reading now extant only in Coptic and
in these two textual groups. The omission of τοῦ δίωρου
(17:18) alters the sense of the text only slightly. It
should be noted that Sa again supports the reading of

Bo and <u>b</u> together with two early witnesses. No external explanation for the omission is evident; it clearly seems to be an early variant reading. The reading in 9:10 shows Bo and <u>b</u> as witnesses to original Greek and is therefore not relevant.

The influence of the <u>b</u> group on Bo appears to have been minimal. Few readings seem to show relationship of some kind between these two sources. The majority of instances where the reading of the <u>b</u> group is unique proves, however, that Bo did not depend on the <u>b</u> group or on its parent.

J. The <u>n</u> group which for Genesis consisted of only two mss is composed of six members in Deut. The readings supported mainly by that group are listed below. Readings attested by fewer than three of the six mss in the group are not included.

List 17: Readings supported mainly by the <u>n</u> group

1:1   Μωυσῆς] μωσης 58-72-376 54'-75'-767

This abbreviated spelling of Μωυσῆς is attested by at least five members of the <u>n</u> group in 36 other instances in Deut. Two or three other mss, usually from <u>O</u>, often join <u>n</u>. Bo never supports the shorter (<u>n</u>) spelling. The remaining instances will therefore not be listed but will be included in the statistical analysis.

3:7   om πάντα n̲

3:19   ὑμῶν 2°⌒ 3° M n̲ 121 Aeth

4:3   om πάντα 72 n̲ Lat_cod 100 Arm = Ⓜ

4:42   πρό] απο 54'-75'-767 Arm

6:17   τά 1° B V 963 72 761 106 54'-75 407' Lat_cod 100
       Luc Athan I 6 Arm] pr και rell

7:15   fin] + και επι παντας τους εχθρους σου 54'-75'

*9:16 παρέβητε B V 58 n̲ 509 Lat_codd 100 104 Aeth Arm
       Bo Sa^1 2 3 13] + ταχυ rell

*9:27 om ἐπί ult B V 529 n̲ Aeth Bo

11:2   οὐδέ] ουτε n̲^{-75}

11:17 τὸν καρπόν] τα εκφορια n̲

11:19 om αὐτά 1° 58 417^{txt} n̲ 509 Lat_cod 100 Arm

11:32 om πάντα 54-75'

12:14 φυλῶν B n̲ Lat_cod 100 Aeth = Ⓙ] πολεων rell

12:25 καλόν] et ἀρεστόν tr 58 551 n̲

12:26 γένηται] + και τας απαρχας σου 54-75'-767

12:31 κύριος / ἐμίσησεν] tr n̲ Lat_cod 100 Arm

*13:8 om καί 2° 72 n̲ 55 Lat_Luc Parc 2 Tert Scorp 2 Bo^{A'}

13:14 om καὶ ἐτάσεις B n̲^{-75} 318 407' Lat_cod 100 Aeth

13:14 ἐρωτήσεις] + και εκζητησεις n̲^{-75}

*13:14 ὑμῖν] ιηλ n̲ Bo

13:15 om πάντας 58 n̲^{-127} Pal3 = Ⓜ

13:16 πάντα / τὰ σκῦλα αὐτῆς 2°] tr n̲

*14:5 καὶ δρυγα] om καί B n̲ 407' Lat_codd 91 92 94-96 100
       Bo

14:8   om ὁπλήν A n̲

14:14   πάντα] τον n̲⁻⁷⁵ 30 Aeth Arm

15:7   τῶν B n̲-ᵂᴵ 509] pr εκ rell

15:7   ἀποστέρξεις B n̲ 85ᵐᵍ-321'ᵐᵍ Latcod 100 Barh 230
        = Ⓜ] αποστρεψεις rell

17:7   om παντός B 54-75'-767

*17:10   ῥῆμα] προσταγμα n̲⁻⁷⁵' Latcod 100 Luc Athan I 6 Arm
        Bo

*17:12   om καί 2° 72 54-75'-767 LatCypr Ep passim Luc Athan
        I 6 Spec 19 34 77 Aeth Arm Bo

17:16   προσθήσεσθε] προσθησεται (c var) B̲ 72-82-426
        n̲⁻¹²⁷ 134* 799

18:8   om τῆς πράσεως 54-75'-767

18:12   κύριος / ὁ θεός σου ἐξολεθρεύσει αὐτούς] tr n̲ Aeth
        Arm

18:12   om προσώπου B V n̲ Latcod 100 Spec 55 Hes 5 Hi Numb
        XVI 7 Aeth

18:16   οὐδέ] ινα 54-75'-767 Latcod 100 Aeth Arm cf Bo (ⲭⲉ)

18:19   om ὁ προφήτης 58-72 54-75'-767

18:20   προφήτης 2°] ανθρωπος n̲ 121

19:7   om σοί 54-75'

19:8   om κύριος 2° 58-72 n̲ Latcod 100 Arab = Ⓜ

19:15   καί 1°⌒2° 46'-52' n̲ 646 LatLuc Athan I 7 Aeth
        Sa³

*19:20   om κατά n̲ Latcod 100 Luc Athan I 7 Aeth Bo

20:3   om εἰς πόλεμον 54-75' 128-630'

20:17   om τόν 1° B 125 54'-75-767

20:17   om τόν 2° n^{-458}

21:9   καλόν] et ἀρεστόν tr V 381' 551 n

22:1   om αὐτοῦ 376 n Arm

22:6   ὀρνέων] ορνεου V n^{-75} Lat$_{Aug}$ Loc in hept V 52

22:15   παιδός] γυναικος n

22:23   om παῖς 54-75' Cyr I 540 Lat$_{Ambr}$ Ps XLIII 74 76:2

22:27   οὐκ ἦν / αὐτῇ] tr 73' n

*23:3   εἰσελεύσεται] -σονται 54'-458 Phil I 131 Lat$_{cod}$
        104 Arm Bo

*23:6   εἰρηνικὰ αὐτοῖς] tr n 392 Arm Bo

24:8   om πάντα 54-75'

24:14   om ἐκ 2° n

24:21   τῷ ὀρφανῷ καί] post σου 2° tr n

25:5   om αὐτῆς n

26:12   om τό 1° 54-75' 85* (vid)

26:13   om αὐτά 72 414 54-75'

26:14   om καί 1° V n

*26:14 om μου 1° 19 n Arm Bo

26:15   τοῦ ἁγίου / σου] tr n

26:18   εἶπεν B 957 n Aeth Sa^{16}] + σοι rell

27:4   om σήμερον 54-75'

27:21   ὁ 1°] pr πας 529 n^{-127} 767 120 Lat$_{Aug}$ Loc in hept
        V 59

27:24   comma] post (25)fin tr n

28:1   om ἐάν — σου 1° n^{-127}

28:2 ἐάν 963 58 n⁻¹²⁷ Lat_cod 104 Aeth Arm Sa³ (vid) =
Ⓜ] + ακοη rell

28:12 πάντα] post χειρῶν σου tr n⁻¹²⁷ 767

28:14 λατρεύειν]pr και 376 54-75'-767

28:35 om ἐν V 72-426* 46-413-414-417 n 71-527 319

28:54 ἀδελφόν B 963 707 125 n Lat_cod 100] + αυτου rell

28:60 ἥν] ων n⁻¹²⁷

29:5 οὐ κατετρίβη / ἀπὸ τῶν ποδῶν ὑμῶν] tr n

29:7 τὴν γῆν / αὐτῶν] tr n

29:17 om αὐτῶν 2° n⁻¹²⁷

*30:1 κύριος B 707 129ᵗˣᵗ n Lat_cod 100 Aeth Arm Bo Sa³] +
ο θεος σου rell

30:11 ἐστιν / οὐδὲ μακράν] tr n⁻¹²⁷ 767 Tht I 441

30:18 om ἧς — σοί B 58-426-707 129 n Lat_codd 100 104
Aeth Arm = Ⓜ

*30:19 καὶ ἐκλέξαι] om καί B 46'-52' n⁻¹²⁷ Lat_cod 104 Bo

*31:10 αὐτοῖς Μωυσῆς B 963(vid) 58-72 n⁻⁵⁴ 59 Lat_Luc Athan
I 9 Arm Bo] tr rell

31:21 ἐπιλησθῇ ἀπό B 963 426 53' n⁻¹²⁷ 59 Lat_codd 100
103 Sa Syh = Ⓜ] + στοματος αυτων και απο rell

31:23 om αὐτῷ B V 963 58 n 59 Lat_codd 100 103 104 Arm
Sa³ = Ⓜ

*32:3 θεῷ] pr κυριω W^I-54' 59 509 Lat_codd 100 300 330
Psalt Moz Brev Goth 53A Arm Bo

32:46 καρδία B 707 n 59 Lat_cod 100] + υμων rell

*33:2 ἐκ Σηίρ / ἡμῖν] tr V 707 54'-75'-767 Tht I 449
Barh 246 Arm Bo

33:5   om ἀρχόντων W^I-75-458^{txt}-767 59 Tht I 449

33:10   om σου ult 376 54-75'-767

33:18   αὐτοῦ] αυτων n^{-127} 344^{mg} 120 59 Arm

34:2   τῆς θαλάσσης] om τῆς 528 125 n^{-75} 59

34:7   ἐωθάρησαν]εωθαρη F^c M^{mg} n 59 Arab

34:11   αὐτοῦ ult] αιγυπτου (c var) n^{-54} 59

    This list of 128 n readings contains 17 (13%) at-
tested by Bo. The pattern observed in several of the
previous lists is again evident here. Eleven of these
seventeen readings may not be used as proof of dependence
or influence. These include four omissions of καί (13:8,
14:5, 17:12, 30:19), two omissions of prepositions (9:7,
19:20), three transpositions of nouns and modifiers
(23:6, 31:10, 33:2), one change in number (23:3) and one
omission of a possessive pronoun (26:14).

    The remaining six readings (9:16, 11:32, 13:14
17:10, 30:1, 32:3), though of a different kind, are not
enough to show any marked influence by n on Bo. These
consist of an omission of πάντα supported only by Bo$^{A'}$
and three n mss (11:32), the preposing of κυριω to θεῷ
(32:3), a phrase so common this variant is not significant,
the substitution of ισραηλ for ὑμῖν (13:14) and of
προσταγμα for ῥῆμα (17:10). The last two variants cannot
lightly be dismissed. Only n and Bo attest ισραηλ in
13:14, and while the possibility that the agreement is
coincidental is always open, this reading seems to indicate

a link, however tenuous, between these two sources. The
evidence for προσταγμα (17:10) is not as convincing but
it does help to show some connection between n̠ and Bo.
Both Bo and n̠ are evidence for original Greek in 9:16 and
30:1.

The relationship between n̠ and Bo may be further
tested by a list of readings of n̠ joined by one other
group.

List 18   Readings of n̠ and one other group

1:29   εἶπα] ειπον b̠ n̠

2:18   Ἀροήρ] γην σηειρ (c var) n̠$^{-767}$ 85^{mg}-130^{mg}-321'^{mg}

2:29   om ἡμῶν 58 d̠ 75'-767 799 71' 18 59 Lat$_{cod}$ 100 Arm

3:22   om ἀπ' αὐτῶν B 54'-75'-767 344 71'-527 630 407
       Lat$_{cod}$ 100 Arm Bo

4:39   καί 1°⌒ 2° c̠I-551* n̠$^{-127}$

4:43   Γαδδί] γαδ 58 414 b̠ n̠ 129 59 Lat$_{cod}$ 100 Arm Syh

5:30   εἶπόν] ειπεν 551 b̠ n̠

7:9   om τήν B* b̠ n̠ Tht I 412

7:9   om τό B* 963 b̠ n̠ Tht I 412

*7:12   φυλάξητε] + αυτα 106 n̠ t̠ Aeth^{-11} Arab Bo Sa^2 3 16

7:12   τὸ ἔλεος] τον ελαιον d̠$^{-125}$ n̠$^{-75}$ 127

7:15   om πάντας F b̠ n̠ 407 Aeth^M

7:21   θεός 2°] pr o 106 n̠ t̠

7:21   μέγας] pr o 106 n̠ t̠

7:21   κραταιός] pr o 106 54'-75 t̠

*9:10   ὄρει B b̲⁻¹⁰⁸ᵐᵍ n̲⁻¹²⁷ 121ᵗˣᵗ 55 407' ᴸᵃᵗcodd 100

104 Aeth Arm Bo Sa¹ 2 3 ¹³] + εκ μεσου του πυρος

rell

9:15   πλάκες B G b̲ 246 n̲⁻¹²⁷ 344ᵐᵍ 318 407' ᴸᵃᵗcodd 100

104 Aeth Arab Saᛁᵗᵉ 2 3] + των μαρτυριων rell

9:26   ἐν 2°⌒ 3° b̲ 54-75' Arab = Ⓜ

11:10   ὑμεῖς εἰσπορεύεσθε] εισπορευη (c var) B b̲ 54'-75-

767 Aeth

11:29   om εἰς 2° A V 72-376 C̲" n̲⁻⁷⁶⁷ 319

12:21   θεός 2° A F M o̲I̲ 57 n̲ 121 55 ᴸᵃᵗcod 100 Armᵗᵉ

Pal Syh] pr κυριος rell

12:21   om σου 2° G*-72-82-381' b̲ n̲ ᴸᵃᵗcod 100 Arm

*13:4   ἀκούσεσθε B o̲I̲⁻¹⁵-707 129 n̲ 318-392 407' Ath II

476 ᴸᵃᵗcod 100 Spec 6 Luc Parc 2 Aeth Armᵃᵖ Bo

Pal] + και αυτου δουλευσετε rell

13:11   ἔτι ποιῆσαι] tr 426 n̲ z̲⁻¹⁸' 630'

17:10   τό 1°] παν n̲ t̲

17:20   om τοῖς b̲ n̲

18:6   ἡ ψυχὴ / αὐτοῦ]tr V n̲ z̲ ᴸᵃᵗcod 100

*18:12 om ὁ θεός σου B 16-422 b̲ n̲ 630ᶜ 407' ᴸᵃᵗcod 100

Spec 55 Hes 5 Aeth Arm Bo

18:18   ὥσπερ] + και 53 n̲⁻¹²⁷ 458 71'-527

*18:20 λαλῆσαι / ῥῆμα ἐπὶ τῷ ὀνόματί μου] tr B V n̲⁻ᵂᴵ z̲

Arm Bo

19:3   καταωυγὴ ἐκεῖ] tr n̲ z̲ 646 Aeth Arm

19:5   μετὰ τοῦ πλησίον / εἰς τὸν δρυμόν] tr b̲ 54-75'

19:9   om πάσας 1° $\underline{d}^{-106}$ 125 54-75'

19:18   οἱ κριταί / ἀκριβῶς] tr V 106 $\underline{n}^{-WI}$ $\underline{t}$ ^{Lat}Luc Athan
        I 7

20:15   fin] + ων κυριος ο θεος σου διδωσι σοι κληρονομειν
        την γην αυτων (c var) 44 $\underline{n}^{-767}$ $\underline{t}^{-134}$

22:21   om οἴκου B $\underline{b}$ 610 $\underline{n}$ 68'-120 407' ^{Lat}cod 100 Arm

23:14   ὀφθήσεται] ευρεθησεται $\underline{b}$ $\underline{n}$ Tht I 429 Sa^3

23:23   om κυρίῳ B $\underline{oI}$ 54-75' ^{Lat}cod 100 Spec 65 Fulg Ep
        I 11 Arm

24:20   init — καλαμήσασθαι] post (22)fin tr F 29-72 $\underline{f}^{-129}$
        $\underline{n}^{-767}$ 30' 59 319 407 Aeth^{-C} Arm

26:4   om τοῦ θυσιαστηρίου A* (vid) $\underline{d}$ 54-75' 730

28:11   σοί] αυτοις 106 $\underline{n}$ $\underline{t}$

28:13 οὐκ ἔσῃ] ουχ 761 $\underline{b}$ $\underline{n}^{-767}$ 319 Tht I 436 ^{Lat}Ambr
        Tob 62 Luc Conven 2 Arm Bo

28:36   κύριός σε] tr $\underline{b}$ $\underline{n}$ Arm

28:40   om σοί F 29-707 414 $\underline{f}^{-129}$ $\underline{n}$ 318-527 59 Arm

28:53   ᾗ] pr εν 106 $\underline{n}$ $\underline{t}$

28:54   καταλειφθῇ B $\underline{o}^{-82}$-707* $\underline{n}$ 407 Sa^3 Syh = ☺] + αυτω
        rell

28:56   τρυφερά B 963 $\underline{o}^{-82}$ $\underline{n}$ Chr II 392 ^{Lat}cod 103 Aeth
        Sa^3 Syh = Ⓜ] + σφοδρα rell

29:21   διαθήκης] + ταυτης 82-707 106 $\underline{n}$ $\underline{t}$

30:11   om ἔστιν 2° B 72-426 $\underline{d}^{-106}$ 107 $\underline{n}^{-127}$ 767 Tht I 441
        Arm

31:5   ἐνώπιον ὑμῶν] υμιν B 707 $\underline{b}$ $\underline{n}^{-75}$ 344^{mg} 630^c ^{Lat}cod
        100 Aeth

31:15 στύλῳ νεφέλης] νεφελη B b̲ n̲$^{-458}$ 630^c 407 ^{Lat}codd
100 103

31:21 πρόσωπον B 707 b̲ n̲$^{-127}$ 59 ^{Lat}codd 100 103 Arm] +
αυτων rell

*34:5 om ἐκεῖ B 72' b̲ n̲ 318 55 59 407' PsClem 74 ^{Lat}cod
100 Lib geneal 496 Aeth Arm Bo

These 53 readings of n̲ joined by another group
include eight supported by Bo. Six of these eight (7:12,
9:10, 13:4, 18:12, 28:13, 34:5) have already been discussed
and the agreement with Bo is not of much significance.
The remaining two consist of a transposition of an infinitive and its modifier (18:20) and an omission of the
prepositional phrase ἀπ' αὐτῶν (3:22). The n̲ group seems
from this evidence to have barely influenced Bo.

K. The possible relationship of Bo to the y̲ group
will now be considered. The y̲ group is not overly
coherent in Deut but often divides into what may be considered two sub-groups--71-527-619 and 121-318-392.
Unique readings of the entire y̲ group are rare, and
unique readings of the second sub-group occur occasionally.
The majority of distinct y̲ readings appears in the
first sub-group 71'-527. Although these three mss constitute only one half of the group, their readings will
be included in the lists below. The following is a list
of y̲ readings.

List 19: Readings supported mainly by y

1:5   γῇ] pr τη 528 71'-527

1:6   ἡμῶν] υμων 71'-527

1:12   om καὶ τὴν ὑπόστασιν ὑμῶν 376 71'-527 128 Arab(vid)

1:15   fin] + και εις τας φυλας υμων 71'-527 (om και 71 527)

1:16   τοῖς κριταῖς ὑμῶν] υμιν 71'-527

1:19   om κύριος 71'-527

1:19   ἡμῶν] υμων 30 71'-527 83 59

1:20   om ὁ κύριος 71'-318-527 (sed hab κυριος 318)

1:21   om κύριος 1° 53' 71'-527

1:21   om κύριος 2° 71'-527

*1:24 εἰς] επι 71'-527 59 Bo

1:25   τοῦ καρποῦ] των καρπων 71'-527

*1:36 om τά 71'-527 630 407 Arm Bo

1:41   καὶ εἴπατε / μοί] tr B V W^I y^{-121} 392 Lat$_{cod}$ 100 Arm

1:41   om κυρίου τοῦ 71'-527

1:41   αὑτοῦ] αυτων 71'-527

2:6   λήψεσθε] πιεσθε 71'-527

2:7   om ὁ γάρ 71'-527

2:12   om αὑτούς 2° 71'-527

2:13   om Ζάρεδ 1° 71'-527

2:17 πρὸς μέ] προς μωυσην F 29 56 71'-527 68'-120 Aeth^F Bo

2:25   om ἐν 71'-527

2:25   om σου 2° V 963 426 71'-527

2:30   ἡμᾶς] υμας 376 71'-527

2:31   om τὸν Ἀμορραῖον 71'-527 ^{Lat}cod 100 Arab

*2:31   κληρονομῆσαι] pr κληρω W^I-54 71ᐟ527 Aeth Bo

2:36   om τήν 1° 71'-527

3:5   πλήν] πασων 71'-527

3:9   init] pr και 71'-527

*3:11   om πήχεων 2° 71'-527 Bo

3:11   om αὐτῆς ult B 71'-527 Bo

3:13   βασιλείαν] pr την y^{-121} 392

3:16   χειμάρρου 1°⌒2° 56* c pr m vid 71'-527

3:17   om ἔως θαλάσσης 71'-527

3:17   θαλάσσης 2°] pr εως 71'-527

3:17   ἀνατολῶν] pr εως 71'-527

3:19   πολλά] pr τα 71'-527

3:21   ὑμῶν 2°] σου 71'-527 Arm

3:24   om καί ult 29-376 71'-318 55 ^{Lat}cod 100 Arm

4:23   ποιήσητε] pr ου 71'-527

4:35   οὗτος] pr ο 71'-527

4:43   om ἐν Γαλαάδ 71'-527

*5:21   οὔτέ 1°] ουδε A 29-82 75 130-321' y^{-318} Bo^{-F}

*5:21   οὔτέ 2°] ουδε A 29 y^{-318} 55 Bo^{-F}

6:15   θεός 1°] κυριος 71'-527

6:15   om ἐν σοί 1° 77 71'-527

6:15   om σου 2° 963^c 321 71'-527

7:22   om κατά 71'-527

8:2   σε 2°] + χς 71'-527

8:6   om ἐν B* V 71'-527

8:12   μή] και 71'-527

9:4   εἰσήγαγεν] εξηγαγεν 71'-527

9:5   ἵνα στήσῃ] αναστησει 71'-527 509

9:6   om τὴν ἀγαθήν 125 53' 71'-318 Aeth[M] Sa[1] 3

9:16   ἰδών] ειδον y[-121] 392

*10:3   εἰς] επι 71'-527 Bo

10:7   Γαδγάδ 1° 2°] γαλδαδ 71'-527

10:17   θεός 2°] pr o V 71'-527 646

11:1   om καὶ τὰ δικαιώματα αὐτοῦV 458 71'-527

12:2   ἐπί 2°] υπο 72 528 y[-121] 318 509

12:14   om αὐτόν 72-381' 75 Lat[PsAug] Fulg I 18 Aeth

12:17   ἐπιδέκατον] επιλεκτον 71'-527

12:21   βοῶν σου] om σου 53' 71'-527

13:3   τῶν λόγων] τον λογον 72-376 53 75 799 71'-527

13:8   φείσεται] φοβηθησεται 71'-527

13:14   βδέλυγμα] pr δε 71'-527

13:15   om καὶ πάντα τὰ ἐν αὐτῇ V 707 71'-527

14:12   om init — φάγεσθε 71'-527

15:9   om ἔτος 2° V 381' 414 246 76-134 71'-318

15:20   ὁ οἶκος] οι υιοι 71'-527

16:15   ἑορτάσεις] εορτασει 71'-527

17:6   om μάρτυσιν 1° y[-121] Lat[cod] 100 Arm

*17:6   om ἐπί 2° F 72 19 y[-121] 120-630 319 Aeth Bo = Ⓜ

17:20   om ἐν F 29-72 77-500 129 30' y 59 319 Lat[cod] 100

18:19   ἐκδικήσω] + αυτον 71'-527

18:20   om 8 οὗ 71'-527

18:21 δ] οτι 71'-527

20:8   om ὁ 2°] 71'-527

21:3   om ἐκ 29 71'-527 = ⑪ (vid)

21:23 θεοῦ] κυριου y⁻³¹⁹ 392

22:4   αὐτοῦ 2°] σου 71'-527

*22:8 καὶ οὐ] om και 71'-527 Bo

23:6   om σου F 44 76-370 71'-527 55 Lat_cod 100

30:9   ἐκγόνοις 1°⌒2° y⁻¹²¹

31:8   om σε 2° F 29 129 y⁻³¹⁸

The percentage of agreement of Bo and y is as in the preceding lists very small. Eleven of these 85 y readings (12%) are supported by Bo but only three (2:17, 2:31, 3:11) of these may indicate dependence. The remaining eight consist of two substitutions of prepositions (1:24, 10:3) and two of conjunctions (5:21 1° & 2°), and omissions, respectively, of καί (22:8), ἐπί (17:6), αὐτῆς (3:11), and τά (1:36).

The more interesting variants include a substitution of the noun μωυσην for the pronoun μέ (2:17). The agreement of Bo and y is not exclusive, so a strong case for dependence cannot be made; some relationship is, however, indicated. The infinitive κληρονομῆσαι is intensified by the preposing of its cognate noun in the dative case κληρω in 2:31. The evidence includes Bo, the dominant sub-group of y, and two n mss. Again, this reading indicates some relationship between y and Bo, but not a strong one. The omission of πήχεων in 3:11 is attested only by Bo and 71'-527. The agreement need not indicate dependence, since the noun is being repeated in context. It could be simply coincidence, but the possibility of dependence must be left open.

The following list includes readings shared by y and one other textual group.

List 20: Readings of y and one other group

2:33   om πρὸ προσώπου ἡμῶν 963 cI 71'-527 120-669 Lat_cod 100 Aeth Arm Sa^2

3:7   om τά 2° 28 oI 71'-527

3:22   om ἀπ' αὐτῶν B 54'-75'-767 344 71'-527 630 407 Lat_cod 100 Arm Bo

*3:24   τὸν βραχίονα] + σου 58-72-376 f^{-129} 71'-527 Lat_cod 100 Aeth Bo Sa

5:7   πρὸ προσώπου μου B M^{txt} 963 O'-707 344^{mg} y^{-121} 83 Arm Sa$^{1 2 3 16}$] πλην εμου rell

5:14   ὁ υἱός] οι υιοι B* O^{-82}-707 767 y 59 509

6:21   κύριος] + ο θεος oI 414-417 W^I-767 71'-527 83 Arm Pal

7:8   om σε B* y^{-318} 392 z^{-18} 83 319 509

7:11   om ταῦτα F 58 71'-527 z^{-83} 630^c 646 Arab Arm = Ⓜ

9:27   om οἷς ὤμοσας κατὰ σεαυτοῦ A* G-58-426-707^{txt} 344^{mg} 121-318-392 Arab = Ⓜ

9:29   κλῆρος] κληρονομια (—μιας 118 314) b 71'-527 59 Sa^2 3 12

10:9   αὐτῶν] αυτου 0 71'-527 18 Aeth^F = Ⓜ

*10:10 om κύριος 2° 72-381' 16-529 d^{-106} 30 71'527
        Arm Bo

*10:21 σοι] pr εν B V 0'$^{-426}$-58-707 129 y 407 509 ^{Lat}codd
        100 Bo

11:27   ὑμῖν] σοι b y^{-121} 392

*12:17 εὐχάς A B M 0'$^{-376}$ ^{618}-58 129 y 55 Bo] pr τας rell

13:1   om ἡ 1° V C-551-761 54 71'-527 Chr II 854 Cyr X 677
        Tht I 420

13:5   ἐκ τῆς δουλείας] εξ οικου δουλειας 106 85^{mg}-321-
        346^{mg} t^{-370} y^{-121} 392 Lat$_{cod}$ 100 Pal = Ⓜ

*15:6   om συ ult C 72 71'-527 z^{-83} ^{Lat}cod 100 Bo Sa^1 ^{3} = Ⓜ

16:16   om σου 1° F V 29 f^{-129} 71'-318 Or II 344 Phil I
        115 ^{Lat}cod 100 Aeth^{M} Sa^3

18:18   ὥσπερ] + και 53 n^{-127} 458 71'-527

23:4   ἐξ] εκ γης b 71'-527 Aeth^M Arab

29:2   κύριος A B 963 0^{-82} 129 y ^{Lat}cod 100 Aeth^{-C} ^{M}
        Arab Arm Sa^3 ^{16} Syh = Ⓜ] + ο θεος υμων (c var)
        rell

        The 23 readings above include six (26%) which are
supported by Bo. All but one of these have been already
discussed above under various groups, and they all fall
into the category of insignificant agreements. The
sixth (15: 6) is an omission of συ. This single reading
is hardly enough to show influence or dependence.
Bohairic was influenced very little by the y group.

L. The only remaining textual group is z. The
family is closely knit and distinct, the most aberrant
member being 83. The possible relationship of Bo to
this group will be explored in the following lists.
Readings attested by fewer than four of the eight members in the group are not included.

List 21   Readings attested mainly by z

4:1   fin] + εν κληρω 246 z

4:5   κύριος] + ο θεος ημων 246 z^{-83}

4:10   ἥν] εν η z 646

4:17   ὁμοίωμα 2°] pr και z

4:19   om καί init $z^{-128\ 630'}$ 646

4:20   ἔγκληρον] και κληρον $z^{-128\ 630'}$

4:40   τὰ δικαιώματα] et τας ἐντολάς tr 57* c pr m z

4:45   μαρτύρια] δικαιωματα 963* z^{-83} 407

4:45   δικαιώματα] κριματα z^{-83}

4:45   κρίματα] μαρτυρια z^{-83}

4:46   γῆ] pr τη 129 z

5:3   ὑμεῖς] + δε 19' 246 54 z

5:27   om καί 2°—λαλήσῃ 413 76 527 $z^{-128\ 630'}$ Lat$_{cod}$ 100

*5:28 σέ] με $z^{-83\ 128\ 630'}$ Bo

5:28   om ὅσα 413-414 53' z 646 ^{Lat}cod 100 Arm

5:29   ᾖ] γενηται z

5:33   ᾖ] γενηται 121 z

6:3   om ὁ θεός $z^{-18\ 83}$

6:14   πορεύσεσθε] πορευθεις (c var) 246 z 646

6:15   om προσώπου z̲ Sa³

6:18   om καί 4° 246 458 z̲

7:13   τὸν σῖτον] pr και 15-72-376 131 19 458-767 z̲⁻⁸³ Aeth Arm

8:18   om σου 1° z̲⁻⁶³⁰' Phil I 225ᵃᵖ

9:4   init] pr και z̲⁻⁸³

9:5   ἀσέβειαν] + και ανομιαν z̲

9:11   πλάκας ult] της 71' z̲⁻⁸³ 630ᶜ

9:15   ἐκ] απο z̲⁻⁸³ 630ᶜ

*9:29   οὗτοι] ουτος (c var) 58-376 246 321'ᵐᵍ z̲ 407' Bo Sa² 3

10:8   ἐπεύχεσθαι] + και ευλογειν 246 z̲

11:5   ὑμῖν] pr εν z̲⁻⁶³⁰ᶜ

11:16   προσκυνήσητε] προσκυνησης (c var) 376 z̲⁻⁶⁸' 83

11:21   ὑμῶν 2°] σου 321'ᵐᵍ z̲ 407' Latcod 100 Arm

11:21   αὐτοῖς] σοι z̲⁻⁸³ 407' Latcod 100 Arm Sa³

11:22   om πάσας 619* c pr m z̲⁻⁸³ Arab

11:25   τρόμον B 426 z̲⁻⁶⁸' 83 Latcod 100 Pal Syh] et φόβον tr rell

*12:1   om ὑμεῖς z̲⁻⁸³ Latcod 100 Bo

12:26   θεός σου] + αυτον z̲

12:28   καλόν] et ἀρεστόν tr 75 z̲⁻¹⁸' 630' Sa¹

13:3   om ὑμῶν 1° z̲⁻⁶⁸' 83

13:3   καρδίας] et ψυχῆς tr 72 z̲⁻⁶⁸' 83 669

13:5   ἐκ 2°∩ 3° z̲⁻⁸³ 128 630'

*13:6   om σου 2° 75 318 z̲⁻¹⁸' 83 630 LatLuc Parc 2 Tert Scorp 2 Arm Bo

13:8 om μή $\underline{z}^{-83}$ 55

13:9 παντός / τοῦ λαοῦ] tr $\underline{z}^{-83}$

13:10 om ἐν G-72 $\underline{z}^{-83}$

*13:11 φοβηθήσεται] -σονται M 30' $\underline{z}^{-83}$ 630^{c} 55 407' Lat$_{cod}$ 100 Bo = Ⓜ

14:2 om σου 2° $\underline{z}^{-83}$ Sa^{1}

14:2 γενέσθαι σε αὐτῷ / λαόν] tr $\underline{z}$

14:4 κτήνη] κρεα 246 $\underline{z}^{-83}$

14:10 ὑμῖν ἐσται B 376 106 129 121 $\underline{z}^{-83}$] tr rell

14:23 om ἀπο σοῦ 1° $\underline{z}^{-83}$

14:28 ἐν πᾶσιν] επι $\underline{z}$

15:4 om ὅτι $\underline{z}^{-18'}$ 83 669

15:15 om ποιεῖν 29-58 $\underline{z}^{-83}$ Aeth^{F} Arab = Ⓜ

*15:18 om ἀπο σου 72 $\underline{z}^{-83}$ Bo$^{A'}$

16:1 Αἰγύπτου] pr γης 246 $\underline{z}$ Lat$_{cod}$ 100 Hiln Pasch 11 Aeth Bo Sa^{1} 3

16:10 ἰσχύει / ἡ χείρ σου] tr B V $\underline{z}$ Lat$_{cod}$ 100

16:10 καθότι 2°] κατα 72-376 $\underline{z}^{-83}$

17:12 ἀποθανεῖται] απολειται $\underline{z}^{-68'}$ 83

17:12 ἐξαρεῖς] εξαρειτε (c var) F 53' 318 $\underline{z}^{-68'}$ 83 630^{c} 646 Lat$_{Spec}$ 34 Aeth^{-M}

17:17 αὐτοῦ ἡ καρδία] την σεαυτου καρδιαν (εαυτ. 128-630') $\underline{z}^{-83}$

17:20 ἀρχῆς] γης $\underline{z}^{-18}$ 83

18:12 ἀπό] προ $\underline{z}^{-68'}$ 83

19:6 om ἤ 376-707* 52 44 75-767 799 $\underline{z}^{-68'}$ 83 407 Syh

19:6   om πρό 2° 730 619 z⁻⁶⁸' 83 Bo

19:11   γένηται] + εν σοι B 68'-83-630ᶜ

19:12   τῷ ἀγχιστεύοντι] των αγχιστευοντων B z ᴸᵃᵗLuc Athan
        I 7

20:13   om τάς z

21:4   τὴν δάμαλιν / εἰς φάραγγα τραχεῖαν] tr z⁻⁶⁸' 83

*21:19 om καί 1° 72 537 53' z⁻⁶⁸' 83 509 646 Arm Bo

22:2   om σου 2° 120-128-630'

22:11   κίβδηλον] κιβδηλα z⁻⁸³ 630ᶜ 407

22:13   om δέ 82 z⁻⁶³⁰ᶜ

22:21   om έν 1° 767 z⁻⁶³⁰ᶜ

24:8   om ὑμῖν 2° z⁻⁶⁸' 83

26:8   μεγάλη] κραταια z⁻⁶⁸' 83

26:12   γενημάτων] + σου και 664*(vid) z⁻⁸³ 630ᶜ

26:16   init] pr και 121 68'-83-630

26:16   om ταῦτα B 618 30 z⁻⁶⁸' 83 55 Sa¹⁶

26:17   δικαιώματα] + και τας εντολας 246 121 z 407'
        ᴸᵃᵗcod 100

27:3   διαβῆτε] διαβης 246 z⁻⁶⁸' 83 = ⑪

*27:5   αὐτούς] αυτο(c var) B 58-72-426 246 458 30' 121-
        318 z⁻⁸³ 407' Bo

27:6   om τὸ θυσιαστήριον 376 246 z⁻⁸³

27:22   om αὐτοῦ z⁻⁶⁸' 83 ᴸᵃᵗPsAmbr Lex 6 Arm

28:8   έν 2°] επι 376 321* z⁻⁶⁸' 83

*28:14 οὐδέ B F V 246 z⁻⁶⁸' 83 407' 646 Phil II 22
        ᴸᵃᵗcod 100 Arm Bo] η rell

28:15 εἰσακούσῃς] pr ακοη 85^mg-321^mg-344^mg z^{-68}.' 83 407

28:15 ἐπι σέ / πᾶσαι αἱ κατάραι αὗται] tr z^{-68'} 83 646

28:20 ἐξολεθρεύσῃ] et ἀπολέσῃ tr z^{-68'} 83 646

28:22 ἀπορίᾳ] pr εν B 761 z^{-68'} 83

28:35 ἕως] pr και z^{-68'} 83 Aeth^M = Ⓜ

28:37 om εἰς z^{-83}

28:49 init] pr και 318 68'-83-120 646 Aeth Arab

28:49 κύριος / ἐπὶ σέ] tr 68'-83-120

28:56 om τῷ 2° B 30' z^{-83}

28:58 τά 2°] pr και 246 z^{-68'} 83 630^c

28:64 ξύλοις] et λίθοις tr z^{-68'} 83 Aeth^{-M}

30:11 ἐντέλλομαι / σοί] tr 120-128-630'

30:11 μακράν] + εστιν 127 z^{-68'} 83

30:16 ὁδοῖς] εντολαις 120-128-630'

30:20 om σε 29-426 30 z^{-68'} 646 Lat_codd 100 104 Arm = Ⓜvid

31:8 om μετὰ σου 82 71 z^{-68'} 83 120

33:22 Δάν / σκύμνος λέοντος] tr 130-346 z^{-68'} 83 120
      646 Hipp Ant 11 (1°)

33:24 τὸν πόδα] τους ποδας z^{-68'} 83 120 646 Aeth

33:25 om καί 2° B 550 344 318 z^{-68'} 83 509 646 Arm Bo

34:1 om γῆν z^{-83} 509

34:4 Ἀβραάμ] pr τω 413 246 799 z^{-18'} 630'

34:5 Μωάβ ⌒ (6) 72-618^{txt c} pr m 53' 458 z^{-83} 128 630'

The readings in List 21 clearly show that z
followed a different path from Bo. Eleven of the 108
readings in the list have Bohairic support, but all are

of the type repeatedly shown above to be of no great
significance. These include two omissions of καί (21:19,
33:25), one substitution of conjunctions (28:14), three
changes (5:28, 9:29, 27:5) and two omissions of pronouns
(12:1, 13:6), one change in number (13:11), an omission
of the preposition πρό (19:6), and of the prepositional
phrase άπο σου supported only by Bo$^{A'}$ (15:18).

All the readings of z and one other textual group
are scattered throughout previous lists, and any agreements with Bo have already been discussed. They are
brought together for convenience in the following list.

List 22   Readings of z joined by one other group

1:7   λίβα] pr νοτον o**I**-58 130-321' z$^{-68'}$ 630

2:4   λαῷ] + τουτο o**I** 18'-83-669

2:8   Αἰλών] ελων f^{-129} 343 527-619 68'-83-120

4:28   οὐδέ 3°] ουτε B **b** z 407'

*6:6   ἐν τῇ καρδίᾳ] επι της καρδιας **b** z Bo = Ⓜ

7:8   om σε B* y^{-318} 392 z^{-18} 83 319 509

7:11   om ταῦτα F 58 71'-527 z^{-83} ^{630c} 646 Arab Arm = Ⓜ

7:20   om οἱ 2° **b** 767 z

9:5   ὑμῶν] ημων V 618 **c**$^{-739}$ 318 z Phil I 225te Arm

11:4   τὰ ἅρματα] pr και o**I**$^{-15}$ z$^{-18'}$ 120 669 Aeth Sa^3

11:21 om πολυημερεύσητε καί **b** z 407' ^{Lat}codd 91 92 94-96

11:23 om πάντα o**I**$^{-15}$-72 z Aeth^{-M} Arm^{te}

11:23 ἰσχυρότερα] + υμων 72 **b** 246 134 z^{-83}

12:7   χεῖρας A B o**I**$^{-15}$-58-707 129 121-392 z^{-83}] + υμων rell

13:9   om καί 1° B <u>b</u> <u>z</u>⁻⁸³ 407' ᴸᵃᵗcod 100 Cypr <u>Fortun</u> 5
       Firm <u>Mat</u> XXIX 1 Luc <u>Parc</u> 2 Tert <u>Scorp</u> 2 Aeth⁻ᶜᴳ
       Armᵗᵉ

13:11 ἔτι ποιῆσαι] tr 426 <u>n</u> 68'-83-120

14:4   om ἃ 72 <u>b</u> 75' <u>z</u>

*15:6 om συ ult B 72 71'-527 <u>z</u>⁻⁸³ ᴸᵃᵗcod 100 Bo Sa¹ 3 = Ⓜ

15:11 om καί 426 <u>C</u>" <u>z</u>⁻⁸³ 55 59 319 646

*18:2 αὐτῶν B 82 52 <u>b</u> 458 <u>z</u>⁻⁶⁸' ⁸³ 646 Cyr I 861 Aeth
       Bo] αυτου rell

18:6   ἡ ψυχή / αὐτοῦ] tr V <u>n</u> <u>z</u> ᴸᵃᵗcod 100

*18:20 λαλῆσαι / ῥῆμα ἐπὶ τῷ ὀνόματί μου] tr B V <u>n</u>⁻ᵂᴵ <u>z</u>
       Arm Bo

19:3   καταφυγὴ ἐκεῖ] tr <u>n</u> <u>z</u> 646 Aeth Arm

19:9   ὁδοῖς] εντολαις <u>f</u>⁻⁵⁶ 129 <u>z</u>-68' 83

20:18 om πάντα 72 <u>d</u>⁻¹⁰⁶ <u>z</u>-83 630

26:8   καί 2°⌒ 3° 72 <u>d</u>⁻¹⁰⁶ ᵂᴵ <u>z</u>⁻⁶⁸' 83 59

26:17 θεόν 1°] κυριον <u>0</u>⁻⁸² 246 767 120-122-630' Phil V
       324ᵃᵖ Syh = Ⓜ

*27:26 om ἐν 426-<u>oI</u> 528 <u>z</u>⁻⁶⁸' ¹²⁰ Chr IX 188 X 335 XIII
       96 Cyr VI 649 X 965 Epiph I 331 Bo

*28:20 om ἕως ἄν 2° <u>d</u>⁻¹²⁵ <u>z</u>⁻⁶⁸' 83 646 Bo Sa³

28:67 om τό 2° C-761 18'-630' 407

29:7   πολέμῳ] pr τω A M <u>oI</u> 46ˢ 18'-120-630*-669

30:3   om σε 3° 618 77 <u>d</u> 68'-83-120

31:10 ἀφέσεως] pr της <u>oI</u> 246 <u>z</u>⁻⁶⁸'

31:21 καί 1°⌒ 3° M V <u>oI</u>-58 56 54-75 <u>z</u>⁻¹⁸ 55 ᴸᵃᵗcodd 100
       103 104 Aeth Arm Sa³ vid

33:16 τῷ] pr εν 376-o͟I͟ z$^{-68'}$ 55

33:28 γñ͟ç͟] pr τηç b͟ z͟ 407

Six of these 36 readings (6:6, 15:6, 18:2, 18:20,
27:26, 28:20) have Bo support. They have all been discussed earlier and shown to be of no serious consequence.
Bohairic was slightly influenced by the z͟ group.

M. The relationship of Bohairic to the textual
families and recension has been explored at length in
the previous pages. It is accurate to say that in
general Bohairic shows no substantial ties to any of the
textual groups. The b͟-n͟ group comes closest to Bo and
the C͟-s͟ group seems farthest away. The relationship of
the individual families to Bo is summarized in the
following table.

Section A of the table more accurately indicates
the relationship between Bo and any textual family. The
B section is included in the table (and was included in
the lists above) only to confirm any relationship
established in section A.

The table presents only a quantitative statement
of agreement between Bo and the families. The actual
number of agreements is indeed small in each case; an
analysis of the agreements has also shown that qualitatively the kinds of agreements are only seldom
significant and only rarely show a necessary relationship.

Table 1

Number of Agreements

Groups	Section A			Section B		
	Unique Readings of One Group			Readings Supported by Two Groups		
	Total Rdgs.	Bo Support	%	Total Rdgs.	Bo Support	%
Asterisked Plusses	134	16	12%	-	-	-
Non-Ast. Plusses	113	35	22%	-	-	-
Non-Hex. o (incl. oI oII)	87	8	9%	48	8	16.5%
c (incl. cI cII)	158	4	2.5%	115	19	16.5%
b	350	38	11%	75	14	19%
d	466	26	5.5%	175	13	7.5%
f	56	9	16%	18	3	16.5%
n	128	17	13%	53	6	11%
s	18	2	11%	98	17	17%
t	38	7	18%	155	9	6%
y	85	11	12%	23	6	26%
z	108	11	14%	36	6	16.5%

N. The previous discussions have shown that Bo is not
recensional in its character. The textual families and
the hexaplaric recension have been examined in places
where their readings deviate from original Greek, and
Bohairic has been shown to exhibit no substantial ties
to any of them.

If it is assumed that a source to which Bohairic
shows close affiliation is extant, the only possible witnesses that remain to be examined are those whose texts,
in general, are pre-recensional. These witnesses are the
uncials A, B, F, M, and V, the papyri 963 and 848, and
the unclassified mss 55, 59, 407, and 509. The versions
other than Sahidic are excluded from further discussion
since the likelihood of influence on Bo is remote. Patristic and N. T.materials are also disregarded.

The possible relationship of Bo to the 11 presumed pre-recensional witnesses will now be examined by
means of a list of their readings which deviate from
original Greek. Only such readings which can be shown in
Bo are included. Any relationship(s) of Bo to these
mss should become clear. Bo is always recorded first in
the list of evidence and is shown whether it supports the
lemma or the variant. Secondary Bo readings are not
recorded. If Bo supports neither the lemma nor any variant, its reading is recorded in Coptic as a variant.

The rest of the evidence is presented in this order:
Uncials in alphabetical order, papyri in numerical order, codices mixti in numerical order, an indication of
the extent of support by the textual families, Sahidic,
and the Massoretic text.

The papyri are recorded as both lemma and variant
because of their importance and of their fragmentary
nature. No e silentio conclusions are, of course, valid
where the papyri are not recorded. The general extent of
support by Greek families is indicated thus: A plus sign
(+) immediately after any witness indicates support by
not more than four mss. Support by five to 15 mss is
indicated by "pl" (plures), and wide support--16 or more
mss--is indicated by "mult" (multi). The siglum "al"
(alii) is used only after the variant and refers to all
the other presumed pre-recensional witnesses not specifically mentioned. Since it can be assumed that where
"al" appears there is also wide support from the families,
no indication of this support will be given, it being
irrelevant to the present investigation. Sahidic and
the Massoretic text are included for interest, the former
being the other major Egyptian dialect and possibly ex-
erting an influence on Bo--this will be investigated
subsequently--the latter for obvious reasons.

List 23

Deviant Readings of the

Presumed Pre-recensional Witnesses

†1:1   init Bo] pr και A

†1:1   Τόφολ] τοφελ Bo; τοφοα 509

†1:1   Αὐλῶν Bo] αυλον 59 509 pl

†1:1   Καταχρύσεα] катакрусеа Bo; καταχρυσαι V

1:3   ἐνδέκατῳ Bo] δεκατω B pl

†1:3   υἱούς] pr τους Bo F pl

1:3   κύριος Bo] + τω μωυση 509

†1:4   πατάξαι Bo A B V 509 mult] + αυτον al

†1:4   Σηών Bo B 59 509 pl] pr τον al; σιων 55 59 pl
        et semper

†1:4   Ἀμορραίων Bo] pr των A F 55 59 mult;
        55 et semper

1:4   Εσεβών] σεβων Bo 55+

†1:4   Ὢγ Bo] pr τον A 55 pl

†1:4   Ἀσταρώθ Bo] ασθαρωθ M V+

†1:4   Ἑδράϊν] αδραι Bo; εσδραειν V; εδραι 59;
        εδραειν al

†1:7   ὄρος] pr το Bo F 509 mult

1:7   Εὐφράτου Bo] pr ποταμου F M 407' mult

1:8   παραδέδωκα Bo] παραδεδωκεν B+

†1:8   εἰσελθόντες Bo] pr ην 509

†1:8   Ἰσαάκ Bo B* mult] pr τω al

†1:8 Ἰακώβ Bo B* mult] pr τω al

†1:10 ὑμῶν Bo] ημων A mult;om 59 pl

†1:10 ὑμᾶς Bo] ημας V pl

†1:10 τῷ Bo] om 509

†1:11 ὑμῶν Bo] ημων 59 mult

1:12 μόνος φέρειν Bo] tr A M pl

†1:12 ὑμῶν 2° Bo] om V+

1:12 καὶ 2° Bo] η V

1:13 φυλάς Bo] φυλακας 509+

†1:13 καὶ καταστήσω αὐτούς / ἐφ' ὑμῶν Bo] tr M

†1:13 αὐτούς Bo] om B V 407' pl

1:13 ἐφ ὑμῶν Bo] om 55 pl

1:15 καὶ 5° Bo]⌒ 7° 509

1:15 ὑμῶν ult Bo]⌒(16) 1° 407 mult

†1:16 ἀδελφοῦ] pr του Bo A F M pl

†1:16 ἀδελφοῦ B V 509 mult] + αυτου Bo al

1:17 ἐπιγνώσῃBo] επιγνωσεσθε A M mult

1:17 κατά 1° Bo] και 509

1:17 αὐτό 2° Bo] υμων B

1:19 ἐκ] εν Bo 509 pl

1:19 Χωρήβ Bo] σοχωθ A; χωριβ 55+

1:19 ἥν Bo] om 407+

1:19 Ἀμορραίου Bo]⌒(20) V

†1:19 ἡμῶν Bo] υμων 59 pl

1:20 εἶπα Bo 963] ειπατε 509

†1:20 ὄρους 963] pr του Bo B M mult; οδου 55

1:20 ὁ θεός Bo 963] om 509+

†1:20 ἡμῶν Bo 963] υμων 59 407'

†1:20 ὑμῖν Bo 963] ημιν A pl = Ⓜ

1:21 ὑμῖν 1° 963] om Bo A F M V 55 59 407 mult

†1:21 ὑμῶν 1° Bo A F M 963 407' mult Sa² ¹⁶ ¹⁷] ημων al

†1:21 ὑμῶν 2° Bo 963] ημων V+

1:21 κληρονομήσατε] + την γην 55

†1:21 ὑμῶν 3° Bo A F M 55 mult] ημων 963 al

†1:21 ὑμῖν 2° Bo 963] ημιν 407 mult

†1:22 ἐν αὐτῇ 963] επ αυτης Bo 509

†1:24 εἰς] επι Bo 59 Pl

†1:25 ἡμᾶς Bo 963] υμας 59 pl

†1:25 ἡμῶν Bo 963] υμων 59+; om 509 pl

†1:25 ἡμῖν Bo 963] υμιν 59 pl

1:26 καί 2° 963] αλλα Bo A F M 55 59 mult

1:26 κυρίου Bo 963] om 509 pl

†1:26 ὑμῶν Bo A F M 55 59 mult Sa¹ ⁷ ¹⁷ = Ⓜ] η;μων 963 al

1:27 κύριον Bo 963] om V+

1:27 ἡμᾶς 2° Bo 963] + κυριος V+

†1:27 χεῖρας 963] pr τας Bo A F M 55 mult

1:28 ἀδελφοί] pr δε Bo A F M V 963 55' 407 mult Sa¹ ²
(sed hab 7)

1:28 καὶ πολύ Bo] om V+ = Ⓜ

†1:28 ἡμῶν 3° Bo] υμων B* 55' pl

†1:28 καί 4°] om Bo 59+

1:29 πτήξητε μηδέ Bo 963] om 59

†1:30   ὑμῶν 1° Bo] ημων F M 963 407' mult

†1:30   ὑμῖν Bo 963] ημιν B 407' mult

1:30   γῆ Bo 963] om 55 pl = Ⓜ

1:31   εἴδετε Bo 963] + οδον ορους του αμορραιου B pl

†1:31   ἥν 2° Bo 963] pr εις B* pl; om M

†1:32   ὑμῶν Bo] ημων B V 963 59 509 mult Sa¹ ² (sed hab 17)

†1:33   δεικνύων Bo] pr και 407+

1:33   καθ'] om Bo 509 = Ⓜ

†1:33   ἐν αὐτῆς] επ αυτης Bo B 407 mult

†1:34   καί 1° Bo] + ως A

†1:34   καί 2° Bo] om A

†1:35   τήν 1° Bo] om B pl

1:35   γῆν Bo] post ταύτην tr B pl

1:35   ταύτην 963(vid)] om Bo V 407 mult Sa¹⁷ = Ⓜ

†1:35   ὑμῶν 963 mult = Ⓜ] ημων 509; αυτων Bo al

†1:36   ’Ιεφοννή] ιεφωνη Bo 55*(vid) pl; ιεφονη M 59ᶜ

1:36   τὴν γῆν Bo] ταυτην 407+

1:36   τά 963] om Bo 407+

†1:38   υἱός 963] pr ο Bo 509 pl

†1:38   κατακληρονομήσει 963] κατακληροδοτησει Bo A F Mᵗˣᵗ
       V 55 59 mult

1:39   init B 963(vid) 55 407' mult Sa²] pr και παιδια
       υμων α ειπατε εν διαρπαγη εσεσθε Bo al

1:40   ὁδόν Bo] om 509

1:41   καὶ εἴπατε / μοί Bo] tr B V pl

1:42   μή 1° Bo 963] om 407' mult

† 1:42 οὐ 1° Bo] ουδε V

1:43 τὸ ῥῆμα Bo] τα ρηματα 963

† 1:44 Ἀμορραῖος Bo] αμωρραιος 59

† 1:44 ὑμῖν Bo 963] ημιν 407 pl

1:44 κατεδίωξαν 963] κατεδιωξεν Bo A V 59 mult

† 1:44 ὑμᾶς 1° Bo 963] ημας 407 pl

† 1:44 καί 3° Bo] om B*

† 1:44 ὑμᾶς 2° Bo] ημας 407 pl

† 1:44 Σηίρ Bo pl] σιηρ 59 pl; οιειρ 407 pl; σηειρ 963 al; et semper

1:44 Ἑρμά 963]ερⲆⲙⲀ Bo; ερμαν 407 pl

1:45 κυρίου Bo 963] + του θεου ημων B 407' mult

1:46 ἐνεκάθησθε 2° Bo 963] pr ουκ 59

1:46 fin 963] + εκει Bo B* pl

2:1 ἔρημον Bo 963] om B*

† 2:1 τό 2°] om Bo F 55 407

2:4 Ἠσαύ Bo 963] σαυ 407+

† 2:4 εὐλαβήσονται Bo] + υμας B 55 407'

2:4 σφόδρα Bo 963] om 55

† 2:5 οὐ Bo 963] + δε 55

2:5 δῶ 963] δωσω Bo A+

2:5 κλήρῳ δέδωκα τῷ Bo 963] om B*

2:5 Ἠσαύ Bo 963] + δεδωκα B; + οι κατοικουσιν εις 509

† 2:5 τό 2° 963] om Bo V 407 mult

2:6 ἀργυρίου 1° Bo] om M 963 55 mult

2:6 καὶ ὕδωρ μέτρῳ λήμψεσθεBo 963] om 59+

†2:7 ἡμῶν 963] υμων Bo A mult; σου 55 mult = Ⓜ

2:7 μεγάλην Bo] πολλην 963

†2:7 τήν 2° Bo 963] om 59 pl

2:7 ταύτην A F M 963 = Ⓜmult] εκεινην Bo al

2:8 παρήλθομεν Bo] pr ου 407+

2:8 τους κατοικοῦντας Bo] του κατοικουντος 509

2:8 παρά] Ϩℇℕ Bo;κατα 407'+

2:8 Αἰλών] ελωμ Bo+; αιλωμ V 509+; αιδ 59

2:8 Γαβέρ Bo] βαγερ 55*

†2:8 παρήλθομεν] ανεβημεν Bo F 59 pl

†2:9 Ἀροήρ Bo] σηειρ B 963 509; ασηρ 55 pl; αρωηρ 59 pl; σιειρ 407 pl; et saepe

†2:10 Ομμίν 55ᶜ Bo pl] οομμειν A; ομμειμ M; οομμιν 55*; ομμειν al

†2:10 πρότεροι Bo 963] pr το A F M V 55 59 mult

†2:10 πρότεροι Bo B 963 509 pl] προτερον al

†2:10 ἰσχυρόν Bo 963] ισχυοντες B V 407' pl

†2:10 Ἐνακίμ Bo(vid) pl] ενακειν F(vid) Fˢ; ενακειμ 963 al

†2:11 Ῥαφαΐν pl] ραϥαιм Bo; ραφαειμ A M; ραφαην 59; ραφαειν al

†2:11 Ἐνακίμ Bo pl] ενακειμ al

†2:11 Ὀμμίν Bo] ομμιειν A mult; ομμειν al

†2:12 πρότερον Bo B* 963(vid) pl] pr το al

†2:12 οἱ Bo] om B V 509* pl

2:13 οὖν Bo] om 55 = Ⓜ

2:13 καὶ ἀπάρατε Bo] om A

†2:13 ὑμεῖς Bo] om 963(vid) 509 pl

†2:13 Ζάρεδ 1°] ϳαρεθ Bo; ζαρετ A B 509 pl

2:13 καὶ παρήλθομεν τὴν φάραγγα Ζάρεδ] om Bo A* F V
55 59 407' mult; tr post (14) Ζάρεδ 963

†2:13 Ζάρεδ 2°] ϳαρεθ Bo; ζαρετ B pl; ζαρε A

2:14 ἀπο Καδὴς Βαρνὴ ἕως οὖ παρήλθομεν Bo] om 407

†2:14 Ζάρεδ] ζαρεθ Bo F M pl; ζαρετ A B 509 pl

†2:14 γενεά B F 963 407 mult] pr η Bo al

2:14 πολεμιστῶν Bo F M V 963 55 59 Sa² ³ = Ⓜ mult] +
αποθνησκοντες al

2:14 κύριος Bo A F 963(vid)] + ο θεος (c var) al

2:15 θεοῦ Bo] κ̄ῡ A+ = Ⓜ

2:15 ἐκ Bo A F M V 963(vid) 55 59 407 mult Sa² ³] +
μεσου al

2:16 ἐπεί] επιδη Bo 407' mult

2:17 μέ] μωυσην Bo F pl

†2:18 Ἀροήρ] αρωηρ Bo 55 59; σηειρ B 963 509; σιειρ 407+

†2:19 καί 2°] ογλε Bo; om 963 407' mult

†2:19 μή 2° Bo] + δε 963 407' mult

2:19 Ἀμμάν 2° 963] ϵμμαν Bo; αμμων 59 mult

2:19 σοί Bo] υμιν 407+

2:19 ἐν κλήρῳ Bo] om 509+

†2:20 Ῥαφαΐν   Bo pl] ραφαειμ A M pl; ραφαραειν F*;
ραφαην 59+; ραφασιν 509+; ραφαειν 963 al; et saepe

†2:20 καί 2° Bo] om 963 407' mult

†2:20 Ἀμμανῖται Bo M 55 407 mult] αμανιται 59+;
αμμανειται 963 al

2:20 αὐτούς Bo] αυτην 407+

†2:20 ζομζομμίν pl] ζοζομμιν Bo 55

ζοχομειν B (-μμειν^c); ζοζομεν 963; ζομζομμην 59;

νοζομμιν V; ζομμειν F* pl; ζομζομμην 59; ζομζομμειν al

2:21 δυνατώτερον Bo 963] + ημων 407+; + υμων B 509 mult

†2:21 οἱ Bo A B* 963 mult =Ⓜ] pr και al

2:21 αὐτῶν 1° Bo] υμων 407+

2:21 καί ult Bo] om 963*

2:21 αὐτῶν 2° A* F V 963 55 pl Sa^2 = Ⓜ] + εως της

ημερας ταυτης Bo al

†2:22 τοῖς υἱοῖς Bo] οι υιοι V mult

2:22 ἐξέτριψαν] εξετριψεν Bo 55 mult

⌐ 2:22 καί 1° Bo] ⌒ 2° B^{txt}

†2:22 κατεκληρονόμησαν Bo B 963 407' mult] + αυτους al

2:22 ἡμέρας Bo] pr σημερον 509+

2:23 Ἀσηρώθ Bo 963] ασηδωθ B 407+

2:24 ἐξελθόντες Bo] κατοικουντες 509

2:24 Καππαδοκίας Bo 963] καπαδοκιας F 407+

2:24 οὖν Bo 963] om A mult

2:24 καὶ παρέλθετε Bo 963] om B*

2:24 Ἐσεβὼν τὸν Ἀμορραῖον Bo 963] των αμμορραιων 55

2:25 τρόμον 963] et φόβον tr Bo V 55 407 mult

†2:25 σου 2° Bo] om V 963

2:26 ἀπέστειλα Bo] απεστειλαν 55+

2:26 Κεδμώθ Bo] κεδαμωθ B

2:27 οὐδέ Bo 963] ουτε A V mult

2:28 τοῖς ποσίν Bo] δια της γης σου 55

†2:28 fin B 963 407' mult] + μου Bo al

†2:29 ἐν 1° Bo] om 59

†2:29 Μωαβῖται Bo] μωαβειται A B* F* V pl

†2:29 ἡμῶν Bo 963] om 59 pl

†2:29 ἡμῖν Bo] om 509+; υμιν 59 pl

†2:30 ἡμῶν Bo] υμων 59+

2:30 ὡς] om Bo   963 407' mult

2:31 πρὸ προσώπου Bo] εις τας χειρας 55 509

2:31 πρὸ προσώπου σου] σοι A

2:31 τὴν γῆν αὐτοῦ Bo] om 509+

2:32 Σηών Bo 963 mult Sa² ¹⁷ = Ⓜ] + βασιλευς εσεβων al

†2:32 εἰς 3° Bo] om B+

2:32 Ἰάσα 963 pl] σιασσα 59; ιασσα Bo al

2:33 ἡμῶν 1°] + εις τας χειρας ημων Bo M 963 mult Sa

2:33 πρὸ προσώπου ἡμῶν Bo] om 963 pl (homoiot.); + και
       παρεδωκεν αυτον κ̅ς̅ 59

2:33 καί ult Bo] ⌒ (34) 1° 55

†2:35 πλήν Bo 963] + και V

2:35 ἐπρονομεύσαμεν Bo 963] + εαυτοις A F M 55 59

2:36 χεῖλος Bo] τειχος F 59 509+

†2:36 τῇ Bo] om 59

†2:36 πάσας Bo] + ας V

†2:36 ἡμῶν 1°Bo] υμων 59+

†2:36 ἡμῶν 2° Bo] υμων V 59+

†2:37 γῆν] pr την Bo 59 pl

2:37 εἰς γῆν υἱῶν Bo] εγγυς B; om V

2:37 Ἀμμάν 963] αμμων Bo B* 407 mult = Ⓜ

2:37 προσήλθομεν Bo] προσηλθον 407+

2:37 χειμάρρῳ Bo 963] om 407+

†2:37 Ἰαβόκ Bo 963] pr ΔΕΡΝωΝ Bo; αρνων V; ιαβωκ 55 pl

†2:37 ἡμῖν Bo 963] υμιν 59+

3:1 Βασάν 1° Bo 963] θαλασσαν 59*

3:1 Ὢγ Bo] γωγ B*; νωγ 509+

3:1 αὐτοῦ Bo] + μετ αυτου A F M V 55 59 mult

†3:1 Ἐδράϊν Bo pl] εδραειμ B pl; εδραει M pl; εδραην 59; σαραειμ 509; εδραειν 963 al

3:2 λαὸν αὐτοῦ Bo 963] ⌒ (3) 509

3:3 ἡμῶν 1° Bo 963] ⌒ 2° 59+

3:3 ἡμῶν 2° Bo 963] + αυτον A V+

3:3 Βασάν Bo 963] Βασσαν 59 pl

†3:3 καί 4° 963] om Bo 59

3:4 καιρῷ Bo] om V

†3:4 πάντα Bo] pr και V+

3:4 περίχωρα Bo] pr συνκυρουντα B*

†3:4 Ἀργόβ] Δρκωβ Bo; αργωβ 59 407; αρβοκ 55

†3:4 βασιλείας Bo] pr και 55

3:5 πόλεις Bo] pr αυται V 59 mult

†3:5 Φερεζαίων] ΝΙΦΕΡΕϹΕΟϹ Bo; φερεζεων V pl; φαρεζεων 509

3:5 πολλῶν Bo] + εκεινων 407+

†3:6 αὐτούς Bo] om 407' pl

†3:6   γυναῖκας B V 963 407' mult = Ⓜ] + αυτων Bo al

†3:6   παιδία] + αυτων Bo V pl

3:8   χειρῶν Bo 963] χειρος M mult = Ⓜ

†3:8   ἕως A F M 963 55 59 mult = Ⓜ] pr και Bo al

3:8   Ἀερμών] pr ορος Bo F 59 mult

†3:9   Ἀερμών 963] ερωογ Bo; αυτο B; αρμων B*+; ερμων 59 pl

†3:9   Σανιώρ Bo 963] ανιωρ 59; σανειωρ 509+

†3:9   Σανίρ] ⲤⲀⲚⲒⲰⲢ Bo; σανειρ A B M 963 pl; σανιειρ V;
       σανιηρ 59 407+

†3:10   πόλεις 1°] pr αι Bo V 963 509 mult

†3:10   Μισώρ] ⲚⲒⲤⲰⲢ Bo; μεισωρ A B 963 509 pl; μιωρ 59

3:10   Γαλαάδ Bo] βαλααν 509

†3:10   Σελχά+ = Ⓜ] ελκα 59 pl; σελχαν 407+; ελχα Bo al

†3:10   Ἐδράϊν Bo mult] εδρειμ A B; εδραει M+; εδραειν al

†3:10   βασιλείας Bo] βασιλειαι B 407'+

3:10   Ὢγ Bo] γωγ 509

3:10   τῇ Bo] γη 407+

3:11   ὅτι πλήν] tr Bo 407 mult

3:11   Ὢγ Bo] νωγ 509

3:11   Ἀμμάν] αμμων Bo B* 59 407 = Ⓜ

†3:11   αὐτῆς 2° 963] om Bo B*

3:11   ἐν πήχει ἀνδρός Bo] om 509+

†3:12   Ἀροήρ Bo 963] αρωηρ 59 pl

†3:12   Ῥουβήν Bo 963] ρουβιμ 59 mult

3:13   Γαλαάδ Bo] γααδ 59+

3:13   Ὢγ Bo] γωγ B*

†3:13   Μανασσή Bo 963] μαννασση A et semper

†3:13   περίχωρον B 963 pl] pr την Bo al

†3:13   Ἀργόβ] οργοβ Bo; αργωβ 59 407 mult

†3:13   πάσαν 3° Bo] pr και V 59 mult

†3:13   Ῥαφαΐν mult] ραφαιμ Bo; ραφαειμ M; ρα[φα]εν 963; ραφαην 59; ραφαειν al

†3:14   Ἀργόβ Bo] αρβοκ B*; αρβοη 963; αργωβ 59 407 mult

†3:14   Γαργασί Bo mult] γαρτασει B*; γαργασειν963; γαργασιν 55; γαργαση 59 pl; γαργασσει 509; γαργασει al

†3:14   Ὀμαχαθί pl] ΗΟΓΑΘΙ Bo; ο ιαειρ (c var) A F M V 55 59 407; ομαχατει 963; ομαχαθηκ 509; ομαχαθει al

  3:14   αὐτάς Bo B pl] αυτος V; αυτην 55; om 407; αυτον 509+; αυτο al

†3:14   Βασάν Bo] βασα V

†3:14   Αὐώθ 963] ΔΥΒωΔ Bo; υιωθ V

†3:15   Μαχίρ Bo mult] μαχειρ 963 al

  3:16   Γάδ Bo 963] γαδδ B*; γααλδει 509

  3:16   μέσον — ὅριον 1° Bo 963] om B*+

  3:16   ὅριον 1° Bo 963] οριων 59+

  3:16   ὅριον 1° Bo 963] ∩ 2° 509+

†3:16   Ἰαβόκ 963] ΔΒΟΚ Bo; ιαβωκ 55 59 pl

†3:16   Ἀμμάν 963] αμμων Bo pl = Ⓜ; αμαν 59

  3:17   Ἀραβά Bo 963] αραβια V mult; ραβα 59+

†3:17   Μαχανάραθ Bo B 963 407'] pr απο al

†3:17   Μαχανάραθ 963 pl Sa¹ ²] μαχαναρεθ Bo B 509; μαχενερεθ A F M 55+; χενερεθ V pl; μαχανερεθ 407 pl; μαχενερεθ al

3:17 Ἀραβὰ θαλάσσης Bo 963] om V+; ραβα θαλασσης 59+

†3:17 ὑπό Bo] απο M V 963 mult

†3:17 φασγά] ⲧⲁⲥϧⲁ Bo; φαραγγα 963 407; φαραγγαν 59

†3:18 ὑμῶν 1° Bo] ημων B V 963 407' mult

†3:18 ὑμῖν 2° Bo 963] ημιν 407' pl

†3:18 ὑμῶν 2° Bo 963] om 59

3:19 ὑμῶν 2° Bo 963] ⌒ 3° M pl

†3:20 ὑμῶν 1° Bo] om A pl; ημων 963 407' mult

†3:20 ὑμᾶς Bo 963] ημας 509+

3:20 θεός 2° Bo 963] + των πατερων 407+

†3:20 ὑμῶν 3° F M V 59 mult = Ⓜ] ημων Bo 963 al

3:21 Ἰησοῦ Bo 963] ιησοι B+

†3:21 ὑμῶν 1° Bo] αυτων 963; ημων 55 pl

†3:21 ὑμῶν 2° A pl = Ⓜ] om Bo; ημων 963 al

3:21 κύριος 2° Bo mult = Ⓜ] + ο θεος ημων 963 al

3:22 init — ὑμῶν 1° Bo] om 509

3:22 ἀπ' αὐτῶν] om Bo B 407 pl

†3:22 ὑμῶν 1° Bo mult = Ⓜ] ημων al

3:22 αὐτός Bo] ουτος 407 mult

†3:22 ὑμῶν 2° Bo] ημων 407 mult

3:23 ἐδεήθην Bo] + εναντιον B*

3:23 κυρίου] + του θεου Bo 407' mult

3:23 λέγων Bo] om 509

3:24 κύριε κύριε Bo 963] κ̅ε̅ ο θ̅ς̅ B*+

†3:24 χεῖρα 963] + σου Bo F pl = Ⓜ

†3:24 τῷ 2° Bo 963] om A F M V 55 59 407' mult

†3:24 τῆς Bo] om V 963(vid) 407' pl

3:24   ἐποίησας Bo 963] + κατα τα εργα σου M 55 mult = Ⓜ

†3:24   καί ult Bo 963] om 55 pl

3:25   τοῦτο Bo] om B* F 963(vid) 59 pl

†3:27   ὀφθαλμοῖς 1° A B M 963 509 pl] + σου Bo al

3:28   Ἰησοῦ Bo 963] ιησοι A B

†3:28   καί 2° Bo] om 963 pl

3:28   κατίσχυσον Bo] et παρακάλεσον tr 55 407 mult

3:28   αὐτόν 1° Bo] ⌒ 2° 59 509+

3:28   αὐτός Bo] ουτος 55 407 mult

3:28   τήν γῆν Bo] pr πασαν 55 407' mult

†3:29   Φογώρ Bo] φο]ρογ 963*; φωγωρ 59+

4:1   κριμάτων Bo] ρηματων A+

4:1   ζῆτε] + και πολυπλασιασθητε Bo B 963 407' mult Sa

†4:1   ὑμῶν Bo] om 407+; ημων 963 55 509 mult

†4:1   ὑμῖν Bo] om V+

4:2   πρὸς τό Bo] om 963

4:2   ὑμῖν 1° Bo A B* F M V 963 59 mult Sa = Ⓜ] + σημερον
       al

4:2   τὰς ἐντολάς Bo] pr πασας 407 mult

†4:2   ὑμῶν Bo] ημων B V 963 509 mult Sa¹ ² (sed hab 17)

4:2   ὑμῖν 2° Bo] σοι B*

†4:3   ἡμῶν Bo 963] υμων A 59 pl

†4:3   ὑμῶν 2° B* 55 59 pl = Ⓜ] ημων Bo 963 al

†4:3   ὑμῶν 3° 963] om Bo; ημων B* 407' mult

4:4   κυρίῳ Bo] om 963

†4:4   ὑμῶν A B* F V 55 59 mult Sa¹ = Ⓜ] ημων Bo 963 al

4:5 δέδειχα Bo 963] δεδωκα 55+

4:5 κύριος B 963 55 407' mult Sa] + ο θεος μου (om Bo)
Bo al

4:5 οὕτως B 963 407' mult Sa² ¹⁷ = Ⓜ] + υμας Bo al

4:6 τῶν ἐθνῶν Bo] om των B* 59; + των υποκατω του
ουρανου V

†4:7 αὐτῷ Bo 963] om 509 pl

†4:8 αὐτῷ Bo] om 963 509

4:8 κατὰ πάντα Bo 963] om 407

4:8 ἐνώπιον ὑμῶν Bo 963] υμιν B*+

†4:9 σου 1° Bo] om 963

†4:9 λόγους Bo 963] + σου 509

4:9 τῶν υἱῶν Bo 963] om 55*+

†4:10 ὑμῶν Bo A M V 407 mult Sa] σου F 59 pl = Ⓜ; om 55+
ημων 963 al

†4:10 τὸν λαόν Bo] pr παντα 55; + μου V

†4:11 ὑπό Bo] επι 407 pl

4:11 ὄρος 1° Bo] ⌒ 2° 59*

4:11 θύελλα 963] + φωνη μεγαλη Bo (pr οχος) 59 407'
mult

4:12 κύριος Bo A B* F M V 963 55 59 mult Sa = Ⓜ] + ο
θεος al

4:12 ὑμᾶς B^txt 963 mult Sa¹ ² = Ⓜ] + εν τω ορει Bo al

4:12 fin Bo] + ρηματων 509

4:14 διδάξαι ὑμᾶς Bo] om 509

4:14 ὑμας 1° Bo] ⌒ 2° 59

4:15   κύριος Bo] bis scr 59

4:15   Χωρήβ Bo] χωριβ M+

4:16   ποιήσητε Bo] pr μη 55 pl

4:16   ἤ Bo] και A+

4:16   ἡ θηλυκοῦ Bo] om 59+

4:18   ὁμοίωμα 1° Bo] ομοιωματι V

4:18   ὑποκάτω Bo] + και υποκατω 509

4:19   αὐτοῖς 1° ⌒ 2° Bo 963*+

† 4:19   σου 963] πεν- Bo; om V pl

4:19   αὐτά Bo] om 407' mult

4:20   ἔλαβεν Bo B 963 407' mult Sa¹] + κυριος al

† 4:20   ὑμᾶς Bo 963] ημας B pl; + εκ γης αιγυπτου B

4:20   ὡς Bo 963] om 59 pl

4:21   κύριος 1° 963] + ο θεος Bo 407' mult

† 4:21   ὑμῶν Bo 963] ημων A pl

† 4:21   θεός 963] + σου Bo B M pl = Ⓜ

4:22   τοῦτον 963] om Bo B^txt Sa¹ (sed hab2) = Ⓜ

† 4:23   μή Bo 963] pr και 509+

† 4:23   ὑμῶν] ημων Bo V 963 mult Sa²

4:23   διέθετο] + κ̅ς̅ ο θ̅ς̅ υμων ποιησαι 509

4:23   ὑμᾶς 963] + και ανομησετε Bo 407' mult

4:23   συνέταξεν Bo] pr ου V pl

4:23   σοί Bo 963] om B* 509 mult

4:24   ὅτι Bo 963] ο γαρ 55

4:25   υἱούς 2° Bo 963] θυγατερας 509

4:25   χρονίσητε Bo 963] χρονιση 509

4:25   πάντος Bo 963] om 407

4:25   τὸ πονηρόν Bo 963] τα πονηρα B* V pl

†4:25   ὑμῶν Bo 963] ημων V 59 509 mult

4:26   αὐτήν Bo] om B 963 pl

†4:27   καί 1° Bo] om 963

4:27   τοῖς 2°] pr πασιν Bo A 509 mult

†4:27   ὀλίγοι Bo] ολιγω A mult; εν 509

4:28   ὄψονται Bo] + ουδε μη λαλησωσιν 509+

†4:28   οὐδέ 2° 963] deest Bo; ουτε B 407 pl

4:28   οὐδέ 3° Bo 963] ουτε B 407' pl

†4:29   ὑμῶν Bo 963] ημων A B M 59 509 mult

†4:29   εὑρήσετεB 963 407' pl = Ⓜ] + αυτον Bo al

4:29   ὅταν Bo] + εκει 509

4:29   σου 1° 963] υμων Bo 407 mult

4:31   θεός 1° Bo] pr κυριος ο F V 59 mult; + σου F

4:31   κύριος ὁ θεός σου Bo] om V+; om ο θεος F

4:31   ὤμοσεν Bo 963] + κ̅ς̅ ο θ̅ς̅ 509

4:31   fin Bo 963] + κυριος 407 mult

4:32   προτέρας 1° Bo] om 509 mult; ⌒ 2° 59+

4:32   ὁ θεός Bo] pr κ̅ς̅ V

†4:32   ἄνθρωπον Bo] pr τον A+

†4:32   τό 1° Bo] om 963+

†4:32   ἄκρου] pr του Bo 407 pl

4:32   οὐρανοῦ 1° Bo] ⌒ 2° 963 59 pl

4:32   εἰ ult Bo] ⌒ (33) A+; om 59

4:33   θεοῦ Bo] κ̅υ̅ 59

4:34 χειρὶ κραταιᾷ Bo] et βραχίονα ὑψηλῷ tr V

4:34 καὶ ἐν ὁράμασι μεγάλοιςBo] om B^{txt}

† 4:34 ἐποίησεν Bo 963] + υμιν F M V 59 mult = Ⓜ

4:34 κύριος Bo] om B*+

† 4:34 ὑμῶν V 59 mult = Ⓜ] ημων Bo 963 al

4:35 οὗτος] αυτος Bo A F M 407 mult

† 4:35 θεός 2° Bo] om V 407+; + σου 509+; pr o 509 = Ⓜ

4:35 ἔτι] αλλος Bo A

† 4:36 init Bo] pr και 407

† 4:36 τῆς Bo] om 407+

4:37 ἀγαπῆσαι Bo 963] ακουσαι 509

† 4:38 init Bo 963] pr και B

4:38 αὐτῶν Bo 963] ταυτην F 59 509 pl

† 4:38 κληρονομεῖν Bo 963] κληρονομιαν 407 pl

4:39 γνώσῃ Bo] γνωσεσθε M+

4:39 ἐπιστραφήσῃ Bo] + σημερον 509; επιστραφησεσθε M+

4:39 τῇ διανοίᾳ Bo] om 509

4:39 οὗτος] αυτος Bo 407+; + εστιν Bo 407

4:39 θεός 2° Bo] om 55

4:40 φυλάξῃ Bo] φυλαξασθε B

4:40 αὐτοῦ 1° Bo] ⌒ 2° 509

† 4:40 μακροήμεροι Bo] μακροχρονιοι A

4:42 φονευτήν 963] + ος αν φυγη εκει και ζησεται Bo (pr ο̣ρ̣ο̣ς̣)
407' mult

† 4:42 πλησίον 963] + αυτου Bo 407 pl Sa^{17} = Ⓜ

4:42 αὐτὸν πρὸ τῆς Bo 963] τον πλησιον η V

4:42 καί 2° Bo 963] ουδε B*

4:42 τρίτης Bo 963] pr προ της B* V pl

4:43 ἐρήμῳ Bo 963] πεδιω F

† 4:43 ʿΡαμώθ Bo 963] ραμμωθ A+; ραβωθ 55+; ραμααθ 59+

† 4:43 ἐν 3° Bo 963] om 59+

† 4:43 Γαλαάδ Bo 963] pr τη V pl

† 4:43 Γαδδί] ⌐αλλιΝ Bo; γαδ 59 pl; γαδδει B V 963 407 pl

    Sa² (sed hab 17); γααδδι M; γαδαει 509

† 4:43 Γαυλών Bo] γαυρων 963; γαυλον 59+

4:45 μαρτύρια Bo] et δικαιώματα tr 963* 407

4:45 καὶ τὰ κρίματα Bo] om B^txt 407 mult

4:45 ἐλάλησεν Bo] ενετειλατο F 59 mult

4:45 ᾽Ισραήλ B 407' mult = Ⓜ] + εν τη ερημω Bo 963(vid)

    al

4:46 ἐν τῷ] om Bo 407

4:46 οὺς Bo B* 963 pl] ον al

† 4:46 αὐτῶν Bo] om V+

4:47 γῆν 2° Bo] om 509

4:47 ᾽Ωγ Bo] γωγ B*

† 4:47 πέραν Bo] pr εν τω M

† 4:48 Ἀροήρ Bo] αρωηρ 59; αρηρ 509

† 4:48 ἐπί 1° Bo] παρα B* pl

† 4:48 Σηών] cΔΝιωρ Bo; σιων 55 509 mult

† 4:48 Ἀερμών Bo] αερμου 59

4:49 πέραν Bo] pr ο εστιν A

† 4:49 ὑπό Bo] απο A B* V 59 407

† 4:49 Ἀσηδώθ Bo 963] σηδωθ V; ασειδωθ 59

5:1   ’Ισραήλ 2° Bo A B F M V 55 59 mult Sa = Ⓜ] +

παντα al

†5:1   ἐγώ Bo] om 59+

†5:2   ὑμῶν Bo] ημων 55 59 mult = Ⓜ

†5:2   ὑμᾶς Bo] ημας 59 509*+ = Ⓜ

5:3   κύριος Bo] om A+

†5:3   ὧδε Bo 963] δε 407 mult

5:3   ζῶντες Bo] om 59+

†5:4   πρόσωπον Bo] προς ους 407

5:4   κύριος Bo] + ο θ̄ς̄ V

5:4   ἐν τῷ ὄρει Bo] om A

5:5   ὑμῶν Bo A B Mᵗˣᵗ V 963 55 407' mult] pr ανα μεσον al

5:5   καιρῷ Bo] ορει 509+

5:5   τὰ ῥήματα Bo] ενωπιον A

5:6   σου 963] υμων Bo 55

5:6   σε Bo] υμων 55 pl

5:6   γῆς Bo 963] της 407+

5:7   πρὸ προσώπου μου B Mᵗˣᵗ 963 pl Sa] πλην εμου Bo al

5:7   μου Bo] σού V 509

5:8   γλυπτόν Bo 963] ειδωλον B 407' pl

5:8   ἄνω Bo] om 963+

5:8   τοῖς ὕδασιν Bo 963] τω υδατι A M mult

5:9   οὐδέ Bo 963] και A Mᵗˣᵗ pl

†5:9   ὅτι ἐγώ Bo] εγω γαρ B* 407

5:9   σου Bo 963] υμων 55 pl

5:9   γενεάν Bo] om 963+

5:9 μέ Bo] om 963+

†5:10 τοῖς 2° Bo] om 55 pl

5:11 κύριος Bo] + ο θεος σου (om σου 407+) V 407 mult

†5:12 σου Bo] om 407 mult

5:14 σάββατα Bo 963] + αγια 55

5:14 ὁ υἱός Bo 963] οι υιοι B* 59 509 pl

†5:14 σου 7° Bo 963] om 509+

†5:14 καί 6° Bo 963] om B*

5:14 ἐντος τῶν πυλῶν σου (c var) M^{txt} V 963 55 407'
mult Sa = Ⓜ] παροικων εν σοι Bo al

5:14 ἵνα ἀναπαύσηται ὁ παῖς σου Bo 963] om 55

5:14 παιδίσκη σου 2° Bo A B^{txt} F M V 963 59 Bo mult
Sa^{1 16 17} = Ⓜ] + και το υποζυγιον σου al

†5:15 γῆ Bo] pr τη 509

5:15 κύριος 1° Bo] om V+

†5:15 ἐν 3° Bo] om 59+

5:15 φυλάσσεσθαι Bo B* 59 pl] + σε 963 al

†5:16 σοί 1ᶜ Bo] om B*+

5:16 ἵνα 2°] om Bo 55 pl

5:17 comma Bo B V 963(vid) 407' mult Sa] et 18 comma tr
al

5:21 σου 1° Bo] ⌒ 2° 407' mult

5:21 οὔτέ 1° B V 407' mult Sa³] ουδε Bo al

5:21 οὔτέ 2°] ουδε Bo A pl

5:21 οὔτέ 3°] ουδε Bo A 55 pl

5:21 οὔτε 4°] ουδε Bo 55

5:21 οὔτέ 5°] ουδε Bo 963 pl

5:21 ὅσα Β* 963 mult] pr παντα Bo al

5:22 λιθίνας Bo] om Β*

5:22 fin A Β* F M V 55 59 mult Sa^{1 2} = Ⓜ] + κυριος
Bo al

5:23 προσήλθετε] προσηλθον Bo 407' mult

†5:24 ἡμῖν Bo] om Β*+ 963(vid)

†5:24 ἡμῶν Bo 963] om 509 pl; υμων 59+

5:24 δόξαν Bo] δεξιαν V

5:24 ὁ θεός 2° Bo] pr κ̅ς̅ V

5:27 συ1° Bo] ουν V 59

5:27 καί 1° Bo] ⌒ 2° 963*

5:27 ὅσα 1° A Β^{txt} F V 963^c 59 mult] pr παντα Bo al

5:27 ἡμῶν 1° Bo 963^c] σου 509 Sa¹ (sed hab 2 3 17)

5:27 ἡμῶν 1° B 407' mult = Ⓜ] + προς σε Bo 963^c al

5:27 καί 2° Bo] ⌒ 3° Β^{txt}+

5:28 τῶν λόγων 2° Bo 963] om 509 pl

5:28 ἐλάλησαν 1° Bo 963] ελαλησεν F V 55 509 pl

5:28 σε 963] με Bo 509 pl

5:28 ἐλάλησαν 2° Bo 963] ελαλησεν 59 509*+

5:29 εἶναι Bo 963] om 59

5:29 τὴν καρδίαν αὐτῶν ἐν αὐτοῖς Bo 963] om 509

†5:30 εἶπον Bo 963] pr και 407' mult

5:31 ποιείτωσαν A Β* F M 963 mult Sa^{1 2 3} = Ⓜ] + ουτως
Bo al

†5:32 σου Bo] om 509

5:32 ἐκκλινεῖς Bo 963] εκκλινειτε B V 55 pl

5:32 δεξιά 963] pr εις Bo A B F M 55 59 pl

5:32 ἀριστερά Bo] pr εις A B F M 55 59 pl; ευωνυμα V
963 mult

5:33 σου Bo] ημων 963 pl = Ⓜ; + συ 59

5:33 πορεύεσθαι A F M 963 59 mult = Ⓜ] + εν αυτη Bo al

†6:1 ἐνετείλατο Bo 963] + μοι V

†6:1 ὑμῶν Bo V 55 59 mult = Ⓜ] ημων 963 al

†6:1 ποιεῖν Bo 963] pr και V

†6:1 fin 963] + αυτην Bὐ B* mult = Ⓜ

†6:2 ὑμῶν Bo B M* 55 59 407 mult] ημων 963 al

†6:2 οἱ 2° Bo 963] om 59 pl

6:3 ὅπως] ινα Bo 509 pl

6:4 δικαιώματα Bo] + ταυτα V

6:4 κύριος 1°] μωυσης Bo F V 407 mult Sa

6:4 ἐν τῇ ἐρήμῳ Boj om B^txt

†6:4 ἡμῶν] πεκ- Bo; υμων 59+

6:5 διανοίας B 963 509 mult] καρδιας Bo al

6:5 ψυχῆς σου Bo 963] + και εξ ολης της ισχυος σου 55+

6:5 δυνάμεως Bo] διανοιας 55 pl

6:6 ταῦτα Bo] om 55+

6:7 αὐτά Bo 963] om B* +

6:7 ἐν 2° Bo] ⌒ 3° 509

†6:7 ἐν οἴκω] + σου Bo 963 pl Sa¹ 2 3 = Ⓜ

6:8 ἔσται Bo] om 407+

6:8 ἀσάλευτα Bo] ασαλευτον A B 55 509

6:9 γράψετε Bo 963(vid)] γραψεις A M pl = Ⓜ

6:9 ὑμῶν 1° Bo] ⌒ 2° 963* pl

†6:10 σου 1° Bo] om 509+

6:10 ὤμοσεν Bo] + κ̅ς̅ B 963+

†6:10 τῷ] om Bo 963(vid) mult

†6:10 Ἰσαάκ Bo] pr τω F 59 509 mult

†6:10 Ἰακώβ Bo 963] pr τω F 59 509 mult

†6:11 ἀγαθῶν Bo 963] pr των V+

6:12 μή Bo 963] + πλατυνθη η καρδια σου και A F M V 55
59 407 mult

6:13 κύριον Bo] και 407

6:13 φοβηθήσῃ Bo] προσκυνησεις A+

6:13 αὐτῷ B F^{txt} M 55 59 407' = Ⓜ] + μονω Bo A V 963
Sa^{1 2 3} al

†6:13 τῷ Bo B* 963 pl] pr επι al

6:14 θεῶν 2° Bo] αλλοτριων V

6:15 θεός 1° Bo 963] om V

6:15 ἐν 1°Bo] om 963

6:15 σοί 1° Bo] ⌒ 2° 963* 509 pl

6:15 θυμῷ Bo 963^c] om V+

6:15 ἐν σοί 2° Bo 963] om 55 pl

†6:15 ἐξολοθρεύσῃ Bo B V 963 407' mult] pr και al

†6:17 θεοῦ 963+] + σου Bo al

†6:17 τὰ μαρτύρια B V 963 407' pl = Ⓜ] pr και Bo al

†6:17 μαρτύρια Bo B V 963 407' pl] + αυτου al

†6:17 δικαιώματα Bo 963] + αυτου F mult Sa

6:18 ἀρεστόν Bo B 963 509 mult Sa = Ⓜ] et καλόν tr al

6:18 σου 1° Bo 963] υμων B*+

6:18 κύριος Bo] om 963 Sa² ³; + δουναι A+

6:18 σου 2°] υμων Bo A B* M V 963(vid) 55 mult

6:19 fin A F M 59 pl Sa² ³] + κυριος Bo al

✝6:20 ἡμῶν Bo 963] υμων 59 407+

✝6:20 ἡμῖν Bo 963] υμιν 407 pl

6:21 τῷ υἱῷ Bo 963] τοις υιοις 55 407'+

6:21 κύριος Bo] + ο θ͞ς 55; om 509

6:22 κύριος Bo] om 59 pl

6:22 πονηρά] φοβερα Bo 59

6:22 τῷ Bo] pr πασιν 509

6:22 αὐτοῦ Bo 963] + και εν τη δυναμει αυτου F M mult

6:23 ἐξήγαγεν Bo 963] + κυριος ο θεος υμων A F M V 59 mult

6:23 ἵνα εἰσαγάγῃ ἡμᾶς Bo] om B^txt

6:23 δοῦναι 1° Bo] om 509*

6:23 ὤμοσεν] + κυριος Bo A F M 55 59 mult

6:23 δοῦναι 2° B V 963 509 mult Sa² ³] om Bo 407 mult = Ⓜ; post fin tr al

6:23 fin Bo] + ημιν A F M 55 pl; + υμιν 59

6:24 κύριος Bo] + ο θεος 55 pl

6:24 πάντα τὰ δικαιώματα ταῦτα Bo 963] πασας τας εντολας και τα κριματα A F M 55 59 mult

6:24 εὖ ἡμῖν ᾖ Bo] πολυημεροιωμεν A 55 pl

6:25 ταύτας Bo 963(vid)] om F pl

6:25 ταύτας Bo 963(vid)] + του νομου τουτου F V 59 pl

6:25 fin A F M V 55 59 mult = Ⓜ] + κυριος Bo 963 al

7:1 ἐαν δὲ εἰσαγάγῃ σε κύριος ὁ θεός Bo B 963 407'
    mult Sa = Ⓜ] και εσται εν τω εισαγαγειν σε
    κυριον τον θεον al

†7:1 κληρονομῆσαι B 963(vid) 407' mult] + αυτην Bo al

7:1 καὶ πολλά] + και ισχυρα Bo 509+; + και ισχυροτερα
    407; om B^{txt}+

†7:1 Χετταῖον Bo] χετγαιον 55

†7:1 τόν 2° Bo 963] om B V

7:1 Γεργεσαῖον Bo] et Αμορραῖον tr B*; γεργεσεον 509

†7:1 τόν 3° Bo 963] om B V 509+

†7:1 τόν 4° Bo 963(vid)] om A B V 407' mult

†7:1 Χαναναῖον Bo] χανανεον 509

†7:1 τόν 5° Bo 963(vid)] om A B V 407' mult

†7:1 Φερεζαῖον] ⲫⲉⲣⲉⲥⲉⲟⲥ Bo; φερεζεον V

†7:1 τόν 6° Bo 963(vid)] om B V 407' mult

7:1 μεγάλα 2° Bo B V 963(vid) 407 mult] + και πολλα al

7:1 μεγάλα καί 2° Bo] om 509+ = Ⓜ

†7:1 ὑμῶν Bo] ημων V 59 509 pl

†7:2 σου 1°] ⲧⲉⲛ- Bo; om 59 pl

†7:2 ἀφανισμῷ Bo 963^c] pr και 407

7:2 οὐδέ Bo] ουτε V pl

7:2 ἐλεήσῃς] ελεησητε Bo B* V 509

7:3 οὐδέ Bo] ουτε V pl

†7:3 πρός Bo] om 55+

7:4 ἀφ' ἐμοῦ Bo] αφ ημων 509

7:4 θυμῷ Bo] om 55

7:5 τά 1° Bo] ⌒ 2° 59+

7:5 τῶν θεῶν Bo] om 407' pl = Ⓜ

7:6 τῆς γῆς Bo] pr πασης 509 mult

7:7 init — ἔθνη Bo] om 509

†7:7 προείλατο Bo 963] pr και 509

7:7 ἐξελέξατο] + κυριος Bo 963 pl

†7:7 ὑμᾶς 2° Bo] om 407; ημας 509

†7:7 τά Bo] om V

†7:8 καί 1° Bo] om A+

†7:8 ὑμῶν 1° Bo 963] ημων V+; om 509+

7:8 κύριος Bo 963] om 55

†7:8 ὑμᾶς 2° Bo 963] ημας V+; + εκειθεν A F V 59 407

7:8 καὶ ἐν βραχίονι ὑψηλῷ Bo] om B^{txt}+ = Ⓜ

†7:8 σε Bo 963] om B* 509 pl; + κυριος 509 mult

†7:9 ὁ 2° Bo] om B 963* pl

7:9 ὁ 3° Bo] και 963

†7:9 διαθήκην 963] + αυτου Bo 509 mult Sa$^{2\ 3}$

†7:9 τό Bo] om B* 963 pl; ποιων V

†7:9 ἔλεος 963] + αυτου Bo F M 59 407 mult Sa$^{2\ 3}$

7:10 καί 2° Bo] ⌒ (10) 1° 55 509

†7:11 ἐντολάς] + αυτου Bo B* pl

†7:11 δικαιώματα] + αυτου Bo B*

7:11 ταῦτα Bo] om F pl = Ⓜ

7:12 ἡνίκα Bo] om B*+

7:12 πάντα] om Bo B V 509 mult = Ⓜ

†7:12 αὐτά Bo] om 509 mult

7:12 διαθήκην Bo] + ταυτην 55

7:12 σου 2° Bo Sa+ = Ⓜ] ημων V pl; υμων 963 al

7:13 σε 1° Bo 963] + κ̅ς̅ B*

†7:13 καί 5° Bo 963] om A

†7:13 τὰ βουκόλια Bo] pr και V 963 mult Sa² ¹⁷

7:15 κύριος Bᵗˣᵗ 55 mult Sa² ³ = Ⓜ] + ο θεος σου
      (om σου Bo B M pl) Bo al

7:15 ἃς ἑώρακας Bo] και τας κακας V

7:15 πάντας Bo] om 407 pl

†7:15 τῶν Bo] om 59

†7:16 σου 1° Bo 963] om 55+

7:16 καί 2°] ΟΥΔΕ Bo; om 407' pl

7:17 ὅτι Bo] om 55 = Ⓜ

7:17 αυτους Bo] ∩ (18) B* 59

7:19 τὰ μεγάλα ἐκεῖνα Bo 963] om B* = Ⓜ; om ἐκεῖνα V

†7:19 ἡμῶν 963] πεκ- Bo Sa¹⁷ = Ⓜ; υμων 407' pl

7:19 πᾶσι τοῖς ἔθνεσιν Bo] om 407

7:20 init — (21) αὐτῶν Bo] om Bᵗˣᵗ

7:20 ὁ θεός σου Bo] om 59+

7:20 κεκρυμμένοι Bo] + προσωπου 509 pl = Ⓜ

7:21 τρωθήσῃ Bo] + εν σοι 407

7:21 θεός 2° Bo] om 55

7:22 γένηται Bo] + το ταχος 509

7:24 ὑμῶν Bo] σου 509 pl = Ⓜ

†7:25 οὐκ Βο] pr και Α Μ mult

7:25 καί Β*+ = Ⓜ] η 55 mult; ουδε Βο al

7:25 καὶ οὐ λήμψῃ (om και Β* 407 Βο) Βο Β V 407' mult
Sa$^{2\ 3}$ = Ⓜ] λαβειν al

†7:26 τοῦτο Βο] pr και 407 pl

†7:26 προσοχθιεῖς] + -ΟΥ Βο; + αυτω 55

8:1 ἐντολάς Βο Α Β^{txt} Μ^{txt} 55 59 mult Sa$^{2\ 17}$ = Ⓜ] +
ταυτας al

8:1 ὑμῖν Βο] σοι Β* V 55 pl = Ⓜ

8:1 γῆν Βο] + την αγαθην Α F Μ V 55 59 mult

8:1 κύριος Βο] + ο θ̄ς̄ υμων Β

†8:1 ὑμῶν Βο] ημων V pl

8:2 σε 1° Βο] om 59+

8:2 διαγνωσθῇ Βο] pr ινα 55+

†8:3 καί 1° Βο] om 59+

8:3 καί 2° Βο] ⌒ 3° 407+

8:3 μάννα] + εν τη ερημω Βο 407' mult

8:3 σου Βο] υμων V

†8:3 ὸ 1° Βο Α Β F Μ V 59 509 mult = Ⓜ] om al

†8:3 τῷ Βο] om Α 55 mult

8:4 οὐ κατετρίβη] ου κατετριβησαν Βο V 407 pl; ουκ
επαλαιωθη Β

8:4 οἱ πόδες Βο] pr τα υποδηματα σου κατετριβη απο
σου Β

8:4 τεσσαράκοντα ἔτη Βο] μαθηση V

8:5 ὸ θεός Βο] om V

† 8:5   σου 2° Bo] om 509 pl

† 8:6   σου Bo] om 59

† 8:7   γῆν Bo] pr την A 59 pl; + την A 59 pl

† 8:7   πηγαί B*+ = Ⓜ] pr και Bo al

  8:7   πεδίων Bo B V 407' mult Sa = Ⓜ] et ὀρέων tr al

† 8:8   συκαῖ] pr και Bo F V 407 mult Sa¹ 2 3 17 (sed hab 15)
        = Ⓜ

† 8:8   ῥόαι] pr και Bo V 407' mult = Ⓜ

  8:8   ἐλαίου Bo] ⌒ (9) οὐ 59

  8:9   ἐνδεήθησῃ Bo] + σοι 59

† 8:9   αὐτῆς 2° Bo] om B V 407' mult

  8:10 fin] + κυριος ο θεος σου Bo 407' mult

  8:11 κρίματα Bo] et δικαιώματα tr V pl; + αυτου Bo V
        pl Sa² ¹⁷ = Ⓜ

  8:12 καὶ κατοικήσας Bo] om 59

  8:13 βοῶν Bo] et προβάτων tr V 509 mult

† 8:13 σου 2° Bo] om F V pl

† 8:13 σοί 1° Bo] om B*+

  8:13 σοί 1° Bo] ⌒ 2° 55 509 pl

  8:13 πληθυνθέντος A B pl = Ⓜ] πληθυνθεντων Bo al

  8:13 σοί 4° Bo] om V 407' pl Sa¹ ² = Ⓜ

† 8:14 καρδία B 55 407' mult] + σου Bo al

† 8:15 σε Bo] om 59

† 8:15 διά] εκ Bo 59

† 8:15 καί 1° Bo] om 59+

  8:15 ἐκείνης Bo] om V+ = Ⓜ

† 8:15 οὗ 2° Bo] om 59 509 pl

8:15 fin Bo] + ζωντος 509+

8:16 τοῦ Bo] και V

8:16 ᾔδεισαν οἱ πατέρες σου] ηδεις συ και ουκ ηδεισαν
οι πατερες σου Bo 509 mult

8:16 ἐκπειράσῃ Bo] pr ινα A F M V 59 mult = Ⓜ

† 8:16 εὖ Bo] pr και B 509 pl; pr οπως V

8:16 σου 2°] των ημερων Bo B* 407'(om των) mult

† 8:17 init Bo B V 55 407' mult] pr και al

8:17 τῆς χειρός Bo] των χειρων 407+

8:18 αὐτός Bo] ουτος V pl

† 8:18 ἰσχύν Bo] pr την B*

† 8:18 καί 2°] om Bo A 55 mult = Ⓜ

† 8:18 αὐτοῦ] om Bo B^{txt}

8:18 ὤμοσεν] + κυριος Bo B 55 407' mult Sa[1] [2]

8:19 καὶ προσκυνήσῃς αὐτοῖς] om Bo B* mult

8:19 σήμερον B^{txt} pl = Ⓜ] + τον τε ουρανον και την
γην Bo al (c var)

8:20 κύριος] + ο θεος Bo 407 mult Sa[1] [2]

† 8:20 ὑμῶν 2° Bo] ημων M 59 mult

9:1 κληρονομῆσαι Bo B F M V 55 59 407 mult Sa = Ⓜ]
pr και al

9:1 μᾶλλον ἢ ὑμεῖς Bo] σου 407' mult

† 9:1 πόλεις] pr και Bo 55+

9:2 Ἐνάκ Bo] εννακ 509+

9:2 οὕς Bo] om 59

9:2 συ 2° Bo] ους 509

9:3 ὁ θεός Bo] om V

9:3 καί 3°] pr εξολεθρευσει αυτους Bo A F M 55 59 mult Sa[lte 2] = Ⓜ

9:3 καὶ ἀπολεῖς αὐτούς Bo] om 55 59

9:3 ἐν τάχει Bo] om B+

9:4 ἐξαναλῶσαι Bo] + αυτους 407' mult

9:4 τὰ ἔθνη ταῦτα Bo] om 407' mult

†9:4 σου 3° Bo] om B

9:4 τὴν δικαιοσύνην B] τας δικαιοσυνας Bo al

9:4 ἀλλά — fin Bo] om B+

9:5 οὐδέ Bo] και A+

†9:5 συ Bo] om 59 407 pl

†9:5 αὐτῶν Bo] om 407+

9:5 ἀσέβειαν Bo B 407' pl] ανομιαν al

9:5 κύριος 2° Bo] om B 59 509 pl Sa[13]

†9:5 διαθήκην B 407 mult Sa[lte 2]] + αυτου Bo al

†9:5 ὑμῶν Bo] σου 407 pl Sa[1ap 13] = Ⓜ; ημων V pl

†9:5 τῷ B V 55 407' mult] om Bo al

†9:5 Ἰσαάκ Bo] pr τω B V 509+

†9:5 Ἰακώβ Bo] pr τω B V 407'

9:6 σήμερον Bo] om A

9:6 τὴν δικαιοσύνην Bo 59 mult Sa[1ap 13]] τας δικαιοσυνας al

†9:6 σου 2°] deest Bo; om A 59 pl

9:6 ταύτην Bo] om F

9:7   ἐξήλθετε Bo] εξηλθες· 407 = Ⓜ

9:7   Αἰγύπτου A B 55 407' pl Sa^{1ap}] pr γης Bo al

9:7   ἕως Bo] και B+

9:8   κύριος Bo] om B+

†9:9   διαθήκης Bo] om 509; pr της Bo V+

†9:10 ἐν 1° Bo] om 55 pl

9:10 λόγοι Bo] + κυ του θυ V

9:10 ὑμᾶς Bo] μωυσην V

9:10 ὄρει Bo A* B 55 407' Sa pl] + εκ μεσου του πυρος al

†9:11 τεσσαράκοντα 2° Bo] pr δια F V 509 mult

†9:11 διαθήκης] pr της Bo A+

9:12 κύριος Bo] + ο θεος 55 pl

†9:12 κατάβηθι Bo B M 59 mult = Ⓜ] pr και al

†9:12 παρέβησαν Bo] pr και 407 mult

†9:12 ἐποίησαν Bo] pr και B+

9:13 μέ Bo] + λεγων 407' mult

†9:13 λέγων Bo] ελεγον 59

9:14 init Bo] pr και νυν B+

9:14 τοῦτο Bo] τουτους 407

9:15 πυρί Bo] + εως του ουρανου B

9:15 πλάκες Bo B 407'] + των μαρτυριων (c var) al

†9:16 ὑμῶν] om Bo; ημων V 55 59 mult

9:16 χωνευτόν B 407' mult] pr μοσχου Bo al

9:16 παρέβητε Bo B V 509 Sa pl] + ταχυ al

9:16 fin Bo] + ποιειν F M V 55 59 pl

9:17 τῶν δύο χειρῶν Bo] της χειρος 55

9:17　δύο 2° Bo] om A F M V 59 407 mult Sa^{1 2 3}

9:17　αὐτάς 2° Bo] om B 407' pl

†9:18　τό 2° Bo] om 509

†9:18　ὑμῶν 2°] deest Bo; om B; ημων 59 pl

9:19　ὀργήν A B F M 59 pl] et θυμόν tr Bo al

†9:19　ἐν Bo] om 509+

†9:19　καί 4°] om Bo M V 59 407' mult Sa^{1 2 3 13}

9:19　ἐκείνω Bo] τουτο B F V 55 59 mult Sa

9:20　κύριος σφόδρα Bo] om B

†9:20　καί 3°] om Bo 59 509 pl

†9:21　αὐτόν 2° Bo] om 509

†9:21　καί 3° Bo] om 509

†9:21　καταλέσας Bo B 407' (c var) mult] pr και al

9:22　fin B+ = Ⓜ] + τον θεον υμων Bo al (ημων 59 pl)

†9:23　καί 1° Bo] om A F M 55 59 mult

†9:23　δίδωμι] pr εγω Bo A M 55 407' mult

†9:23　ὑμῶν Bo] ημων V 59 509 pl

9:23　αὐτῷ και ούκ εἰσακούσατε Bo] om V

9:24　init Bo] pr αλλα M mult

†9:24　ἀπο τῆς ἡμέρας ἧς Bo B 407' mult Sa] αφ ης ημερας al

†9:25　ἐδεήθην 1° Bo] + εγω 407' mult

9:25　ὅσας ἐδεήθην Bo] om 509+

9:25　κύριος Bo] om 55+

9:26　τον θεόν Bo] pr κυριον V 509

9:26　κύριε 2° Bo] om B 509+

9:26　θεῶν] εθνων Bo 407' pl

9:26　κληρονομίαν Bo] μεριδα B V 55 pl Sa^{2 12}

9:26 ἐν τῇ ἰσχύι σου τῇ μεγάλῃ Bo] om B Sa

9:26 μεγάλη 1° Bo] ⌒ 2° 55 407 pl

†9:26 ἐν 2° Bo] pr καί 59

9:26 τῇ μεγάλῃ 2° Bo] om 963(vid) pl Sa² ³ ¹² (sed hab 17)

†9:27 μή Bo] pr καί 59+

†9:27 ἐπί 2° Bo] om B V

9:27 ἀσεβήματα Bo] αμαρτηματα A F M 55 59 pl; + αυτων Bo A F M 59 pl Sa

†9:27 ἐπί 3°] om Bo B V pl

9:27 ἁμαρτήματα Bo] ασεβηματα A F M 55 59 pl

9:28 εἴπωσιν Bo B 407' mult] pr ποτε al

9:28 μισῆσαι Bo B 407' mult] + κυριον àl

†9:28 ἀποκτεῖναι] + αυτους Bo B+ = Ⓜ

9:29 οὗτοι] ουτος Bo 407' pl Sa² ³

9:29 κλῆρος] κληρονομια Bo 59 pl Sa

9:29 μεγάλῃ] + και εν τη χειρι σου τη κραταιαν Bo B

†9:29 ἐν 2° Bo] om 55 509+

10:1 ποιήσεις] ποιησον Bo 55

10:2 γράψω Bo] γραψεις B; γραψον 59 pl

10:2 πλάκας Bo] pr δυο 55 pl

10:3 δύο 1° Bo] om B

†10:3 ἐπί] εν Bo 407' pl = Ⓜ

10:3 χειρσίν Bo] pr δυσιν F V 59 mult

10:4 πλάκας Bo] pr δυο 59 pl

10:4 πυρός Bo] + εν τη ημερα της εκκλησιας M pl = Ⓜ

†10:6 Ἰακίμ 509 pl] ⌂ΚΙΜ Bo; ιακειμ 963 al

†10:6 Μισαδαί F M V 59 407 mult] ⲘⲓⲤⲀⲀⲀⲒⲎ Bo; μεσσαδαι
     55; μεισαδαι 963 al

†10:6 ἐκεῖ Bo] pr και A

  10:7 Γαδγάδ 1° Bo] γαλγαλ F 55+

  10:7 Γαδγάδ 2° Bo] γαλγαλ 55

†10:7 εἰς 2° Bo] pr και 55

†10:7 Ἰετεβάθα M V 59+] ⲓⲈⲐⲈⲂⲈⲐⲀ Bo; ετεβαθα 509 pl;
     ιτεβαθα F+; ταιβαθα B; τεβαθα 407 Sa[3]; ιεταβαθα al

  10:7 χειμάρρου] χειμαρροι Bo B 509 pl

†10:8 init Bo] pr και 59+

  10:8 ἐπεύχεσθαι] ευλογειν Bo 407+

†10:8 ἐπί Bo] om 55

  10:8 ἕως τῆς Bo] πασας τας 509

†10:9 init Bo] pr και 59

  10:9 καί] ουδε Bo 407' mult

  10:9 κύριος Bo] + ο θεος M 55 mult

  10:9 αὐτοῦ] αυτων Bo M 407' mult

  10:9 αὐτῷ] αυτοις Bo M 407' mult

  10:11 fin 963] + αυτην Bo A+

  10:12 αἰτεῖται] ζητει Bo 55 407 mult

†10:12 πορεύεσθαι Bo] pr και B

  10:13 σου Bo] + και τα κριματα αυτου M

†10:15 ὑμῶν Bo] ημων 59 mult

  10:15 κύριος Bo] om 509+

  10:16 ὑμῶν 1° Bo] ⌢ 2° 509

  10:16 ἔτι] om Bo B+

†10:17 τῶν 1° Bo] om 55

†10:17 ὁ ἰσχυρός Bo A pl = Ⓜ] καὶ ισχυρος al

†10:17 ὁ φοβερός Bo A B F M V 59 pl = Ⓜ] om ὁ al

10:18 προσήλυτον Bo] πλησιον A

10:20 αὐτῷ Bo] + μονω A mult Sa

10:20 κολληθήσῃ Bo] + και αυτω λατρευσεις 59

†10:20 τῷ Bo 963] pr επι A F M 55 59 mult

10:21 init Bo] pr οτι 509

10:21 αὐτός 1° 963] ουτος Bo B 407' mult

10:21 αὐτός 2° Bo] ουτος B 55 407' pl

†10:21 ἐν Bo B V 407' pl] om al

10:22 ἑβδομήκοντα B M 509 mult Sa³ = Ⓜ] + πεντε Bo al

†10:22 σε Bo] om 59*+

†10:22 σου 2° Bo] om V 55

11:1 αὐτοῦ 1° Bo] ⌒ 2° V+

11:1 ἐντολάς Bo] et κρίσεις tr 407+ = Ⓜ

11:1 καί 4° Bo] ⌒ 5° B+

11:2 παιδείαν Bo] φωνην 55 pl

11:2 μεγαλεῖα αὐτοῦ Bo] εργα αυτου τα μεγαλα 55

11:3 τέρατα Bo] εργα 509 pl = Ⓜ

11:3 Αἰγύπτου 1° Bo] ⌒ 2° 59+

11:4 αὐτῶν 2° Bo] + και την δυναμιν αυτων B

11:4 κύριος Bo] + ο θεος A F M V 55 407 mult

†11:6 Ἀβιρών Bo M 509 pl Sa³] αβηρων 59 407 pl; αβειρων al

11:6 Ἀβιρών Bo A B 509 mult] pr τω al

11:7 ὅτι] om Bo 407' mult

11:7 ἑώρων] εωρακαν Bo B+

11:7 τὰ μεγάλα Bo] om B

11:8 σοί Bo B V 407' mult = Ⓜ] υμιν al

†11:8 καί 4°] om Bo B pl

11:10 ὑμεῖς εἰσπορεύεσθε Bo (om υμεις)] εισπορευη B pl

11:10 ἐκεῖ Bo] om 407+

†11:10 ἐστιν 2°] om Bo A V

†11:10 ποσίν] + αυτων Bo B

†11:11 εἰς Bo] om 509+

†11:11 εἰσπορεύῃ Bo B 59 pl] pr συ al

†11:11 ὀρεινή Bo] την ορινην V

†11:13 αὐτοῦ Bo] om B

11:13 ἐξ 1° Bo] ⌢ 2° V+

11:13 ὅλης 1° Bo] ⌢ 2° 407^txt+

†11:13 σου 3° Bo] om A+

11:14 καθ' ὥραν] εν τω καιρω αυτου Bo 407' pl Sa = Ⓜ

11:14 εἰσοίσεις] συναξεις Bo 407 pl

11:14 σῖτον Bo] σπορον 407

11:15 δώσει Bo B V 509 mult Sa] δωσεις al

11:16 πλατυνθῇ] πλανηθη Bo 407'

11:16 σου Bo] υμων 407 mult = Ⓜ

†11:17 ὀργισθῇ] οργη Bo B F 407 pl

11:17 κύριος 2° Bo 963] θεος A+

†11:19 διδάξετε 509 pl] + αυτα Bo al

†11:19 αὐτά Bo] εν αυτοις B

†11:19 καθημένους Bo] καθημενου σου B pl

†11:19 πορευομένους Bo] πορευομενου σου B pl

†11:19 διανισταμένους Bo] διανισταμενου σου B pl

11:20 ὑμῶν 2° Bo] σου 407

11:21 πολυημερεύσητε Bo] πληθυνθωσιν 407' pl; + και
πληθυνθωσιν αι ημεραι υμων M 407' mult

11:21 ὑμῶν 2° Bo] σου 407' pl

11:21 αὐτοῖς Bo] σοι 407' pl Sa³

11:22 init — (32)fin Bo] om 55

11:22 ἀκοῇ Bo] om 59+

11:22 ὑμῖν] σοι Bo B 407'

†11:22 ὑμῶν M 407 mult = Ⓜ] ⲡⲉⲕ Bo; ημων al

†11:22 πορεύεσθαι Bo B 407' mult] pr και al

11:23 κύριος Bo] + εφ υμας 59

†11:23 ἰσχυρότερα Bo] ισχυρα B pl

11:24 τοῦ ποδός] των ποδων Bo F+

11:24 ποταμοῦ 1° Bo] ⌒ 2° 59 pl

11:24 ποταμοῦ 2° Bo] om V 509 pl

11:24 ὑμῶν 2° Bo] σου B pl

11:25 τρόμον B pl] et φόβον tr Bo al

11:25 ἐλάλησεν B+ = Ⓜ] + κυριος Bo al

11:25 προς ὑμᾶς Bo] επ αυτης F

11:26 εὐλογίαν Bo] et κατάραν tr 407 (c var)

11:27 την εὐλογίαν Bo] τας ευλογιας F V 59 407 mult

11:27 σήμερον Bo] ⌒ (28) 59 509

11:28 ἑτέροις Bo] om 407+

11:28 οἷς οὐκ οἴδατε Bo] om V

†11:29 τήν 2° Bo] om B

† 11:29 Γαριζίν Bo] γαριζειν B F M V 509 mult Sa³;

γαζιρειν A

† 11:29 Γαιβάλ Bo] γεβαλ 59 mult

11:30 ἐν — δυσμῶν 2° Bo] om 509

11:30 δυσμῶν 2° Bo] + ηλιου 407

11:30 Γολγόλ Bo] γολγωδ 407; γοδγοδ V

† 11:31 ὑμῶν 1°] om Bo; σου 407'+; ημων A M V 59 pl

11:31 ὑμῖν Bo 963] σοι 407

† 11:31 καί 1°] om Bo 407' mult; ⌒ 2° B 963 Sa¹

11:31 καί 2° Bo] ⌒ (32)1° F+

† 11:31 ἐν αὐτῇ 963] επ αυτης Bo 407 Sa¹ ²

11:32 ταῦτα 963 Sa¹ ³+] μου A+; αυτου Bo al

11:32 ταύτας Bo] αυτου A F M V 59 mult

† 12:1 ἐπί 1°] εν Bo B+ = Ⓜ

12:2 πάντας τοὺς τόπους Bo] παντα τα εθνη A

12:2 τὰ ἔθνη Bo] om A B+

† 12:4 ὑμῶν Bo] ημων 59 509 pl

12:5 ὑμῶν 1° Bo] σου B

12:5 φυλῶν Bo] πολεων B

12:6 ἐκεῖ Bo] om B* V+

12:6 καὶ τὰ θυσιάσματα ὑμῶν] om Bo V 407 pl

12:6 ὑμῶν 3° Bo] om V+

12:6 ὑμῶν 3° Bo] ⌒ 4° A pl

12:6 ὑμῶν 5°] + και τας ομολογιας υμων Bo B 55 407' mult

12:6 καί 6° Bo] om B F M 55 59 407' mult

12:6 ὑμῶν ult Bo] om V+

†12:7 ἐπί] εν Βο Μ+

12:7 ἐπιβάλητε τὰς χεῖρας Βο] επιβαλεις την χειρα 407; επιβαλητε την χειρα Β 509

†12:7 χεῖρας Α Β pl] + σου 407; + υμων Βο al

†12:7 ὑμεῖς Βο] om M 55

12:8 πάντα] pr κατα Βο 407' mult = Ⓜ

12:8 ἡμεῖς ποιοῦμεν Α Β 55 407' mult = Ⓜ] υμεις ποιειτε Βο al

12:8 σήμερον Βο] om 407 mult

†12:9 ὑμῶν Βο V 407 Sa¹ ³ mult] om 509 pl; ημων al

12:10 πάντων] om Βο 509

12:11 ἐκεῖ 2° Βο] om Β 59 pl

†12:11 ἐγώ] om Βο 407' mult Sa¹ ³

12:11 θυσιάσματα Βο] θυσιαστηρια 407

12:11 ὑμῶν 3° Βο] ⌒ 4° 59 509 pl

12:11 καί 5° Βο] ⌒ 6° Β+ Sa = Ⓜ

†12:11 ὑμῶν ult Βο] om Β

12:12 ὑμῶν 4° Βο] σου 407

12:12 μερίς Βο] et κλῆρος tr 509+

12:12 οὐδέ Βο] η 509+

12:14 φυλῶν Β pl = Ⓜ] πολεων Βο al

†12:14 σου 3° Βο] υμων Β; om 59+

12:15 ἐπιθυμίᾳ Βο] + της ψυχης 55

12:15 κατά] + την επιθυμιαν της ψυχης σου Βο 407' mult Sa¹ ³

12:16 ἐπί Βο] pr αλλα 963 pl Sa

12:17 καί 1° Bo] + το επιδεκατον 407

†12:17 τά Bo] pr και V+

12:17 σου 5°] ⌒ 6° B

†12:17 εὐχάς Bo A B M 55] + σου 509 mult = Ⓜ ; pr τας al

†12:17 ὑμῶν ult Bo] om B+ = Ⓜ

12:18 σου 1° Bo] υμων 407

12:18 σου 2° Bo] υμων 407

12:18 παιδίσκη σου Bo] + και ο λευιτης A F M V(om και)
       55 59 mult = Ⓜ

12:18 πόλεσιν σου Bo] πολεσιν υμων B pl

12:20 ὥστε Bo] om 407+

12:20 ψυχῆς Bo] καρδιας A

†12:21 μακρότερον] μακραν Bo B pl

†12:21 σου 2° Bo] om 509+

12:21 ἐκεῖ Bo] post σου 2° tr B

⸰12:21 δῷ B V 59 pl] + σοι κυριος Bo 407' mult; + κυριος
       F pl; + σοι A F M 55 pl

†12:21 ὁ θεός σου 2° Bo] θεος σοι B pl

12:21 ἐνετειλάμην] ενετειλατο Bo V 407' pl Sa¹ (sed hab 3)

12:22 ἀυτό Bo] αυτα 407 Sa¹ ³

12:23 ὅτι τό Bo(om το) 407' mult] το γαρ al

12:23 ψυχή 1° Bo] ⌒ 2° 509

†12:23 ἡ Bo] om A M 55 pl

12:25 σέ Bo B 407' mult Sa¹ ³ = Ⓜ] εις τον αιωνα al

†12:26 ἃ Bo] om B pl

12:26 αὐτῷ] om Bo B* 55 pl

†12:27 κρέα 1° Bo] pr δε B 509+

12:27 κρέα 1° Bo] ⌒ 2° B

12:27 κυρίου τοῦ θεοῦ σου 2° Bo] om 55+

12:28 σοί 1°] + σημερον Bo M 55 407' mult Sa[1] [3]

†12:29 συ] om Bo B pl

12:29 αὐτούς Bo] αυτην B

†12:29 ἐν Bo] om 407+

12:30 μή — αὐτῶν 1° Bo] om B

12:31 κυρίῳ Bo] om B

12:31 τούς Bo] pr και F M V 59 mult = Ⓜ

†12:32 ὁ Bo] om 59+

12:32 σοί Bo] υμιν B = Ⓜ

12:32 τοῦτο] om Bo V 55

†13:1 ἡ Bo] om V pl Sa

†13:2 καί 2°] om Bo 407

†13:3 θεός 55 407 mult] + σου B 509; + υμων Bo al

13:3 εἰδέναι] ιδειν Bo 407+

13:3 κύριον Bo] om B

13:3 ὑμῶν 2° Bo] σου B

†13:4 ὑμῶν Bo] ημων V pl

13:4 αὐτόν Bo] τουτον B pl

13:4 καί 2° Bo] ⌒ 3° B+

13:4 ακουσεσθε Bo B 407' pl Sa[1] [3]] και αυτω δουλευσετε al

13:5 ἐκεῖνος 2° Bo] om 509 mult Sa[1] [3]

†13:5 τῆς 1° Bo] om 59+; γης 509

13:5 ἀφανιεῖς Bo B 509 pl = Ⓜ] αφανιειτε al

† 13:6   γυνή B 407 pl = Ⓜ] + σου Bo al

† 13:6   φίλος] + σου Bo mult Sa^2 = Ⓜ

13:7   τῶν θεῶν Bo] om 407 pl

† 13:8   καί 2° Bo] om 55 pl

13:8   αὐτῷ 2° Bo] ⌢ 3° M V+

† 13:8   ἐπ´ Bo] om 509+

† 13:8   οὐδέ] om Bo; και ου 55 407

† 13:9   καί 1° Bo] om B 407' pl = Ⓜ

13:9   αἱ χεῖρες 1° Bo] η χειρ A F M V 55 59 mult Sa^1 (sed hab 3) = Ⓜ

13:9   ἔσονται Bo] εσται A F M V 55 59 mult = Ⓜ

13:9   αἱ χεῖρες 2° Bo A B F M V 55 59 407] η χειρ al

† 13:10   σε 2° Bo] om 59+

13:11   φοβηθησεται] φοβηθησονται Bo M 55 407' pl = Ⓜ

† 13:12   πόλεως Bo F M V 59 509 mult] + σου al

† 13:12   σε B 407' mult Sa^{1} ^{3}] om Bo al

† 13:13   ὑμῶν Bo B 55 509 mult] ημων al

13:13   πάντας Bo] om 407 = Ⓜ

13:13   πόλιν Bo] γην B

13:13   καί 2°] om Bo 407

13:14   καὶ ἐτάσεις] om Bo B 407'+

† 13:14   καί 2° Bo] + στας 407'

13:15   πόλει Bo] γη B

13:15   καί Bo] ⌢ (16)1° V 407+

13:15   τά] οσα εστιν Bo 509 mult

13:16   αὐτῆς 1° Bo] της γης 55

†13:17 init Bo] pr και B

13:17 ἐλεήσει Bo] et πληθύνει tr A

13:17 σε 2° Bo] + καθ ως ελαλησε σοι A F M V 55 mult

13:17 κύριος] om Bo B+ = Ⓜ

13:18 ἐάν Bo] + δε F 59 407 mult

13:18 ἀκούσῃς B] ακουσητε 59 pl; ακουση V+; εισακουσητε
Bo al

13:18 σου 1°] υμων Bo 509 pl

13:18 πάσας 1° Bo] om B 407+

13:18 καλόν Bo] et ἀρεστόν tr B pl

†14:1 ὑμῶν 1° Bo] ημων V 59 pl

14:1 οὐ φοιβήσετε Bo] om B^{txt}+

†14:1 ὑμῶν 2° Bo] om V+

†14:2 σε 1°] deest Bo; om F M+

14:2 σε 2° Bo] om A mult = Ⓜ

†14:4 ἐκ 2° Bo] om 509

14:5 ἔλαφον Bo] om 407

14:5 καί 2° Bo] ⌒ 3° B

†14:5 ὄρυγα Bo B 407' pl] pr και al

14:6 φάγεσθε Bo] ⌒ (7) 59 pl

14:7 ἀναγόντων Bo] pr μη 59+

†14:7 δασύποδα] pr τον Bo 55 pl = Ⓜ

14:7 ταῦτα 1° Bo] om B 407' pl

14:7 ταῦτα 2° Bo] om A F V mult

14:8 ὀπλήν Bo] om A pl

14:8 τοῦτο 3°] + εστιν Bo 407' pl (tr post υμιν 509)

†14:8　καί 4°] om Bo B

14:9　φάγεσθε 2° Bo] pr ταυτα A pl

14:10　καί 2° Bo B 407 pl] ουδε al

14:10　ταῦτα] om Bo B 407

†14:12　τόν 2° Bo] om 59

14:12　ἀετόν Bo] + και τον γυπα 407

14:13　καὶ τὸν γύπα] om Bo V

†14:13　τόν 1° Bo] om 59

14:13　αὐτῷ Bo] αυτων 407 pl

14:14　καί 1° Bo] ⌒ 3° A^{txt} B 55 Sa^1 mult

14:14　αὐτῷ 1° Bo] αυτων 407 pl

14:14　αὐτῷ 2°] om Bo; αυτων 407 pl

14:16　ἔποπα Bo] + και πορφυριωνα A F M 59 mult = Ⓜ

14:16　καὶ ἔποπα Bo] post (17) αὐτῷ tr M V pl = Ⓜ

14:17　καὶ πελικᾶνα Bo] om V

14:17　αὐτῷ] om Bo; αυτων 407 pl

14:17　καὶ πορφυρίωνα Bo B 55 407' mult Sa] om al

14:18　ταῦτα A M V 59 mult = Ⓜ] om Bo al

14:19　comma Bo] om 509

†14:20　καί init] om Bo B pl = Ⓜ

14:20　fin Bo] + ος γαρ ποιει τουτο ωσει θυσει ασπαλακα
　　　　μηνιμα εστι τω θεω Ιακωβ 55 407 pl

14:21　τὸ γένημα Bo] τα γενηματα 407

†14:21　σου 2° Bo] om 55 = Ⓜ

†14:22　καί 1°] om Bo F 407+

†14:22　τῷ Bo] om A mult

14:22 ἐκεῖ] bis scr Bo 407' mult

14:22 οἴσεις] οισετε Bo B 407 mult Sa

†14:22 τά 2° B 55 pl] pr και Bo al

14:23 init — (15:4)fin Bo] om 55

14:23 ἡ ὁδός] ο τοπος Bo 407'

†14:24 σου 2° Bo] om A+

14:24 αὐτόν] om Bo 407 pl; + επικληθηναι το ονομα αυτου
   εκει 407' mult

†14:25 τό Bo] om B

14:25 σου 1° Bo] ⌒ 2° B 509

†14:25 ἥ 2° Bo] om 59+

14:25 ἐπι οἴνω A F M V 59 pl] pr η Bo al

14:25 καὶ εὐφρανθήσῃ Bo] om A

14:27 αὐτό] αυτα Bo 407+

†14:28 ἔργοις B pl] + σου Bo al

15:3 τοῦ ἀδελφοῦ] τω δε αδελφω Bo A F M V 59 mult
   Sa¹ ³ (om δε V 59 pl)

15:4 ὅτι 2° Bo] + δια το ρημα τουτο 407' mult Sa¹ ³

15:4 σου 1° Bo] ⌒ 2° 59+

†15:5 δέ Bo] om 55

15:5 εἰσακούσητε] εισακουσης Bo A; εισακουση 55 407 = Ⓜ

15:5 ὑμῶν Bo] σου 55 407 = Ⓜ

15:5 καὶ ποιεῖν Bo] om A

15:5 ταύτας Bo] αυτου 407+ Sa¹ ³

15:5 σοί Bo] υμιν 407+

†15:6 σου Bo] om 59 407 mult

15:7   ἐν σοί Bo] om 509+

15:7   τῶν 1° B 509+] pr εκ Bo al

15:7   σοί 2° Bo] + εν κληρω A

15:7   ἀποστέρξεις B pl = Ⓜ] αποστρεψεις Bo al

15:8   τὰς χεῖρας Bo] την χειρα 55 59 pl = Ⓜ

† 15:8   δάνειον Bo] pr και M 407' mult = Ⓜ

† 15:8   καθ᾿ Bo] pr και A F M 55 59 mult

15:8   καθ᾿ — fin Bo] om 509 pl

15:9   ἔτος 2°] om Bo V pl

15:10   ἐπιδέηται Bo] + σου A F M V 55 59 mult; + καθοτι ενδεειται B pl

† 15:10   σου 4° Bo] om B

† 15:11   γῆς Bo B 407' = Ⓜ] + σου al

15:11   τοῦτο 1° Bo] ⌒ 2° V

15:11   ποιεῖν Bo] om A 55 Sa³ (sed hab 1) mult

15:11   τας χεῖρας Bo] την χειρα 59 pl = Ⓜ

† 15:11   καί Bo] om 55 59 mult

† 15:12   ἡ Bo] om V 59 mult

15:12   σου 2° Bo] ⌒ (13) B^txt 407^txt mult

15:14   κύριος Bo] om 407'

15:14   σου 4° Bo] ⌒ (15) 59+

† 15:17   καί 1° M 407' mult = Ⓜ] om Bo al

15:17   θύραν] + επι τον σταθμον Bo 407' mult

† 15:17   σοί Bo] om V

15:19   init — (17:1)fin Bo] om 55

15:19   τα ἀρσενικά Bo] om 509

15:19 τὸ πρωτότοκον Bo] τα πρωτοτοκα B

15:20 τοῦ θεοῦ σου Bo] om B pl

15:20 ἐξ ἐνιαυτοῦ Bo] om 59

†15:21 ἐαν δέ Bo] και εαν B

15:21 χωλόν] pr η Bo 59 407 Sa³ (sed hab 1)

15:21 ἡ καὶ πᾶς Bo] om B

†15:23 αἷμα Bo A B 407' mult Sa¹ ³] + αυτου al

15:23 φάγῃ] φαγεσθε Bo B pl

†16:1 τῷ 2° Bo] om F V 407 mult

16:2 ἐν τῷ τόπῳ Bo] om 509

16:3 ἄζυμα Bo] om 509

16:3 Αἰγύπτου 1° Bo] + νυκτος A M 407' mult

16:3 ἵνα Bo] om A

†16:4 init Bo] pr και 407' mult = Ⓜ

†16:4 σοί] om 59+ Bo; υμιν 407+

16:4 θύσῃς] θυσητε Bo A F V 59 mult

16:5 ὁ θεός Bo] om 509

†16:6 τόν Bo] om V+

16:6 θύσεις] pr εκει Bo 407' mult Sa¹ ³

16:6 ἐξ] εκ γης Bo A F M V mult Sa

16:7 καὶ φάγῃ Bo] om 509

†16:7 τὸ πρωί Bo] pr εις V+

16:8 ψυχῇ Bo] pr παση M pl

16:9 ὁλοκλήρους Bo] om B+

16:10 σοὶ καθότι εὐλόγησεν σε Bo] om B

†16:11 συ Bo] om B 59+

16:11 ὁ υἱός Bo] οι υιοι 59+

16:11 ὁ ἐν ταῖς πόλεσίν σου Bo] om B

†16:11 ὁ ὀρφανός Bo] om ο 59+

†16:11 τῷ Bo] om 509

16:11 αὐτόν Bo] om B pl = Ⓜ

16:12 ταύτας Bo] αυτου 407+

16:14 ἐν τῇ ἑορτῇ σου Bo] om A F M^txt 59 407 mult

16:14 σύ Bo] pr εναντι κυροου του θεου σου A F M V 59
407 mult; om 59

†16:15 τῷ 2° Bo] om 59

16:15 αὐτόν Bo B 509(αυτω) pl Sa³] + επικληθηναι το
ονομα αυτου εκει al

†16:16 σου 1° Bo] om F V pl

16:16 αὐτόν Bo] om A M^txt 407 mult = Ⓜ

16:16 κύριος A F M^txt V 59 pl] + ο θεος σου Bo al

16:18 πάσαις Bo] om B+

16:19 οὐκ 1° Bo] ⌒ 2° B+

16:19 οὐκ 2°] ουδε Bo 407' mult

16:19 δῶρα 1°] δωρον Bo B 407 pl

16:21 ὁ ποιήσεις σεαυτῷ] om Bo 407 mult

†17:1 σου 2° Bo] om 59 509 pl

17:2 ἐν σοί Bo] om B+ Sa³ 11

17:2 ὧν Bo] om V

17:2 πονηρόν Bo] ρημα τουτο 407

17:3 ἤ 1°] και Bo 407+; om 59

17:3 οὐ Bo] om 59+

17:3 fin Bo] + σοι F M V 55 59 mult

17:4 ᾽Ισραήλ Βο] υμιν 55

17:5 ἐκείνην Βο Β 407'+ Sa³ ¹¹] + οιτινες εποιησαν

το πραγμα το πονηρον τουτο επι την πυλην (c var) al

17:5 λιθοβολήσετε Βο] λιθοβολησουσιν Α V 55 407+

17:6 ἐπί 2°] om Βο F pl = Ⓜ

17:6 μάρτυσιν 2°] om Βο V mult

17:7 πάντος Βο] om Β+

17:7 ἐξαρεῖς Βο Β pl Sa³ ¹⁴ = Ⓜ] εξαρειτε al

17:8 init — (19:15)fin Βο] om 55

17:8 αἷμα αἵματος Βο] om αἷμα 59 pl; et κρίσις κρίσεως
tr 407

17:8 καὶ ἀνὰ μέσον ἀφή ἀφῆς Βο] om 407

17:8 σου 2°] υμων Βο Β 407' mult

17:8 ἐπικληθῆναι — fin Βο] om Β

17:10 ῥῆμα] προσταγμα Βο+; πραγμα Β 407' pl Sa³ ¹⁴

†17:10 σου Βο] om 59+

17:10 ἐπικληθῆναι τὸ ὄνομα αὐτοῦΒο] om Β

17:10 φυλάξῃ Βο Α Β V pl = Ⓜ] + σφοδρα al

17:10 κατά Βο] om Β

†17:10 σοίΒο] om 59+

†17:11 ῥήματος Βο] + σου 59 509+

17:11 οὐδέ Βο] η 407 pl

17:12 ἐξαρεῖς Βο] εξαρειτε F pl

17:13 ἔτι Βο] om 59

17:14 ἐάν Βο] om 59+

17:14 εἰσέλθῃς] εισελθετε Βο 848

† 17:14 θεός 848+] + σου Bo al

† 17:14 σοί Bo 848] om 509

17:14 σοί B 848+ = Ⓜ] + εν κληρω Bo al

17:14 ἄρχοντα Bo 848] αρχοντας A V+

† 17:15 αὐτόν Bo] om V+

17:15 ἐπί Bo] om 59+

17:16 διότι Bo] πλην A F M 59 mult = Ⓜ

17:16 ὅπως] ϨΙΝΑ Bo; οτι 407'

17:16 ὑμῖν] om Bo B 407' mult Sa³

17:17 οὐδέ μεταστήσεται Bo B 407' mult Sa³ = Ⓜ] ινα
μη μεταστη al

† 17:18 ἔσται Bo] om B pl Sa³

17:18 τοῦ δίφρου] om Bo B V 407' pl Sa³

† 17:19 αὐτοῦ 3°] ΠΕΝ Bo; σου B 407' pl Sa³; om 848(vid)

† 17:19 φυλάσσεσθαι Bo] pr και B pl

17:19 ταῦτα Bo] αυτου 407 mult

17:19 ταύτας Bo] αυτου F pl

17:19 αὐτά Bo] om B 407' mult

† 17:20 ἐντολῶν Bo] + αυτου V+

17:20 αὐτοῦ 4° A* B F 59 mult = Ⓜ] + μεθ αυτου Bo al

† 18:1 τοῖς 2° Bo] pr και V

18:1 καρπώματα Bo] καρπωμα A 407 pl

18:1 αὐτῶν Bo] αυτου V+

18:2 αὐτῷ 1°] αυτοις Bo B 407' mult

18:2 αὐτοῦ 1°] αυτων Bo B pl; om 407 mult

† 18:2 αὐτοῦ 2°] −οι Bo; om 407^{txt}

18:4 τῶν προβάτων Bo] om V

†18:5 αὐτόν Bo] εν αυτω 407'

18:5 κύριος B 848] + ο θεος σου Bo al

†18:5 σου 2° Bo 848] om B+

18:5 αὐτοῦ 1° Bo B V 848 407' mult Sa] κυριος al

18:5 ἐν τοῖς υἱοῖς Ισραήλ Bo B M V mult Sa³] om 848 al

18:5 πάσας τας ἡμέρας Bo] om B

†18:6 ὑμῶν Bo 848] om B

†18:6 τόν Bo] om 59+

18:6 κύριος A B F M mult = Ⓜ] + ο θεος Bo al; om B

†18:7 init Bo 407' mult] pr και al

18:7 ἐκεῖ / ἔναντι κυρίου] tr Bo 509; εκει 407

18:7 fin Bo] + του θῡ σου B V

†18:8 πράσεως Bo] + αυτου V mult = Ⓜ

†18:8 κατά Bo] παρα 407+

18:9 εἰσέλθῃς Bo] εισελθητε V+

†18:9 σου Bo] om A mult

18:10 ἤ Bo] και B = Ⓜ

18:10 αυτου 2° Bo] + μετ αυτου 509

18:10 ἐν πυρί Bo] om V 59+

†18:10 κληδονιζόμενος Bo B 407' mult = Ⓜ] pr και al

18:10 φαρμακός Bo] φαρμακοις B 59 407'

†18:11 καί 2°] ΟΥΔΕ Bo; om B 407' mult

18:12 ὁ θεός σου] om Bo B 407' pl

†18:12 σου 2°] deest Bo; om V pl

18:12 προσώπου Bo] om B V+

18:14 οὗτοι] om Bo = Ⓜ; ουτε 59

18:15 σου 1° Bo 848] υμων 407+

18:15 σοί Bo 848] om 407 mult

18:17 fin Bo] + προς σε B

18:18 ἐκ Bo B V 407' mult] + μεσου al

18:18 το ῥῆμα Bo] τα ρηματα B = Ⓜ

† 18:19 ὁ 1° Bo] om 407' mult

18:19 ἄνθρωπος Bo] + εκεινος A F M V 59 mult

18:19 τῶν λόγων αὐτοῦ] om Bo V 407' pl

18:19 προφήτης Bo] + εκεινος B+

18:20 ῥῆμα / ἔτι τῷ ὀνόματί μου] tr Bo B V pl

† 18:20 προσέταξα B 407' mult] + αυτω Bo al

18:22 προφήτης 1° Bo] + εκεινος B+

† 18:22 καί 1° Bo] om 509

18:22 το ῥῆμα 1° Bo] om B+

18:22 τοῦτο Bo] om V pl

† 18:22 ὁ 2° Bo] om F pl

18:22 οὐκ Bo] om 59 pl

18:22 κύριος Bo] + ο θεος 407' mult

18:22 ἐκεῖνος Bo] om A* F M V 59 mult = Ⓜ

19:1 κύριος ὁ θεός σου Bo] om V

19:1 αὐτῶν 1° Bo] om B+

† 19:1 καί 1° Bo] om V+

19:1 κατακληρονομήσητε Bo B 963 407' mult] -μησης al

19:1 κατοικήσητε B 407' mult] κατοικησης (c var) Bo al

† 19:2 θεός 848 59+] + σου Bo al

19:4 δέ] om Bo V

† 19:4 πλησίον 848 407' mult] + αυτου Bo al

19:4   καί 3° Bo] ουδε 963 pl

✝19:5   πλησίον 1° B 848 407' mult] + αυτου Bo al

✝19:6   καρδία B 848 407' mult] + αυτου Bo al

19:6   καὶ ἀποθάνῃ 963] om και Bo; om B 407' mult = Ⓜ

✝19:8   θεός 848(vid) pl] + σου Bo al

19:8   ὤμοσεν] + κυριος ο θεος Bo 407' mult Sa³

19:8   σοί 848 pl] + κυριος Bo al

19:8   πᾶσαν Bo] pr ο θ̅ς̅ V

✝19:9   καί 1° 848 mult = Ⓜ] om Bo al

✝19:9   ἐν Bo] om 509

19:9   τὰς τρεῖς Bo] om V+; + πολεις A+ Sa³

19:10   αἷμα — σοί 2° Bo] om 59

✝19:10   σου 1° Bo 848] om B pl

✝19:10   σου 2° Bo 848] om A+

19:10   σοί 1° Bo] om 848(vid)

19:10   οὐκ Bo 963(vid)] om 848 = Ⓜ

19:11   γένηται Bo 848] + εν σοι B pl

✝19:11   πλησίον B 848 407' mult] + αυτου Bo al

19:11   καί 3° Bo 848] ⌒ 4° 59

19:11   ψυχήν Bo] om 59+

19:12   τῷ ἀγχιστεύοντι Bo] των αγχιστευοντων B pl

19:14   πατερες Bo] προτεροι A M V 407' pl Sa³

19:14   κληρονομῆσαι 848 = Ⓜ] + εν κληρω κληρονομησαι
        αυτην Bo M 407 mult; εν κληρω al

19:15   εἷς 848(vid)+ = Ⓜ] + μαρτυρησαι Bo al

19:15   καί 1° Bo] ⌒ 2° 848(vid) pl Sa³

19:15 ἥν ἄν ἁμάρτῃ Bo] om 59

19:17 αὐτοῖς Bo] om 407+

† 19:17 ἡ Bo] om 55+

19:19 τῷ ἀδελφῷBo 848 407' mult] κατα του αδελφου al

19:19 ἐξαρεῖς B pl = Ⓜ] εξαρειτε Bo al

19:21 fin B^txt F V Sa³ pl = Ⓜ] + καθοτι αν δω μωμον
τω πλησιον ουτως δωσετε αυτω Bo al

20:1 ἐχθρούς Bo] ⌒ (3) 55

† 20:3 πόλεμον Bo] pr τον B M pl

20:3 ὑμῶν 1° Bo] ⌒ 2° 59

† 20:4 διασῶσαι B 848(vid) 407' pl = Ⓜ] pr και Bo al

20:5 αὐτήν 1° Bo] om 848(vid)

† 20:5 καί 3°] om Bo 509

20:5 εἰς την οἰκίαν αὐτοῦ Bo] om 407

20:8 καρδίαν Bo] + αυτου και A

20:8 ἡ αὐτοῦ Bo] om 59

20:10 αὐτήν Bo] αυτους B

20:11 init Bo] pr και εσται 407' mult = Ⓜ

20:11 αὐτῇ Bo B F V 59 mult = Ⓜ] τη πολει al

20:11 σοί 3° Bo] om A pl

20:12 init — (21:4)fin Bo] om 55

† 20:12 περικαθιεῖς Bo 848] pr και 407' mult = Ⓜ

20:13 καί 1° Bo] εως αν B

20:13 παραδώσει Bo] παραδω σοι B 848 pl

20:16 init — τούτων] om Bo B pl

† 20:16 τῶν ἐθνῶν] deest Bo; om A M V pl

20:17 ἀπ᾿ αὐτῶν Bo] om B pl = Ⓜ

20:17 ἀναθέματι Bo] om F M 59 pl

†20:17 τόν 2° Bo] om B pl

†20:17 τόν 3° Bo] om B pl

†20:17 τόν 4° Bo] om A B M 509 pl

†20:17 τόν 5° Bo V 59 mult = Ⓜ] om al

20:17 Ἰεβουσαῖον] et Γεργεσαῖον tr Bo B V 407' pl

20:17 καὶ Γεργεσαῖον Bo] om B^{txt}+ = Ⓜ

†20:18 ὑμῶν Bo] ημων V pl

20:19 ἀγρῷ Bo B 848 407' mult] δρυμω al

†20:20 ξύλον B 848(vid) 407' pl] pr το Bo al

20:20 ὅτι Bo] + ξυλο[ν] 848 cf Ⓜ

20:20 ποιεῖ] ποιησει Bo 407' mult

†21:1 γῇ Bo] + σου 407 mult

21:2 ἐξελεύσονται Bo 848+] εξελευσεται al

†21:2 γερουσία F 848(vid) pl] + σου Bo al

†21:2 κριταί 848(vid) 407+] + σου Bo al

†21:2 ἐπί Bo] om A+

21:3 λήμψονται 848] λημψεται Bo al

†21:4 τήν Bo] om B+

†21:5 θεός B 848(vid) pl] + σου Bo al

†21:5 αὐτοῦ Bo 848] om 59+

21:5 ἀντιλογία] et ἀφή tr Bo 55 407' mult

21:6 νίψονται Bo] pr και 848+

21:8 κύριε B 848(vid)+ = Ⓜ] + εκ γης αιγυπτου Bo al

21:9 αὐτῶν] + και ευ σοι εσται Bo V 55 407 mult

21:9 ποιήσῃς Bo B 407' mult Sa = Ⓜ] ποιησητε al

21:9   ἀρεστόν V 848 pl Sa] et καλόν tr Bo al

21:10   init — (21)fin Bo] om 55

21:10   πόλεμον Bo] πολιν V

†21:10   σου 1° Bo] om 59

21:10   σοί B 848 509 mult = Ⓜ] om Bo al

21:10   σοί B 848(vid) 407' pl] + αυτους Bo al

21:10   σου 2° Bo] ⌒ 3° V+

†21:12   αὐτήν 2° Bo] om 407' mult

†21:13   πατέρα] + αυτης Bo A V 407 mult Sa^8 = Ⓜ

†21:13   μητέρα] + αυτης Bo V mult Sa^8 = Ⓜ

21:15   ὁ 1° 848+ = Ⓜ] om Bo al

21:15   ὁ 2° 848+ = Ⓜ] om Bo al

†21:16   υἱοῖς 848(vid)] + αυτου Bo al

†21:18   πατρός B 407' mult] + αυτου Bo al

†21:18   μητρός B 407' mult] + αυτου Bo al

†21:19   καί 1°] om Bo 509 pl

21:19   τοῦ τόπου Bo] της πολεως A+

†21:19   καί 3° B+] om Bo al

21:19   αὐτοῦ 3° A B F M^{txt} V 59 mult = Ⓜ] αυτων Bo al

21:19   αὐτοῦ 4° A M^{txt} V mult = Ⓜ] αυτων Bo al

21:20   τῆς πόλεως Bo] του τοπου 59 mult

21:20   αὐτοῦ A V 407 mult = Ⓜ] αυτων Bo al; + λεγοντες
       Bo 407' mult

†21:20   οὐχ Bo] pr και 509 mult

21:21   ἐν λίθοις Bo] om 407+

21:21   ἐξαρεῖς Bo] εξαρειτε 407 mult

21:21 οἱ ἐπίλοιποι] πας ισραηλ Bo 407' pl = Ⓜ

† 21:22 δέ Bo] om V

22:1 ἀδελφῷ σου 2°] + και αποδωσεις αυτω (c var) Bo B
F V 59 407' Sa

22:2 αὐτα ἔνδον Bo] om 848(vid)

† 22:2 ἀποδώσεις B 848(vid) 509 pl] + αυτα Bo al

† 22:3 εὕρῃς B V 407' mult] + αυτα Bo al

† 22:3 ὑπεριδεῖν A* B F 59 407 mult = Ⓜ] + αυτα Bo al

† 22:4 ἀναστήσεις] + −οϒ Bo; + αυτα A 59 pl; + αυτους 407
mult

22:4 μετ᾽ αὐτοῦ Bo] om 407+

22:5 ὅτι Bo] om A

† 22:6 σου Bo] om 59+

† 22:8 δέ Bo 848] om B pl

† 22:8 καί 1° B 407 mult = Ⓜ] om Bo 848 al

22:8 ἀπ᾽ αὐτοῦ Bo 848] om 407

22:9 καὶ τὸ σπέρμα Bo] om 55

22:9 μετα τοῦ] και το Bo 848 = Ⓜ

† 22:9 σου 2° Bo 848(vid)] om V = Ⓜ

22:11 κίβδηλον Bo] κιβδηλα 407 pl

22:11 ἔρια 848] εριον Bo 55 pl

22:12 τεσσάρων Bo] om 509

† 22:14 αὐτῆς 2° Bo] om 59

22:14 καὶ λέγῃ] λεγων Bo 509

22:16 γυναῖκα Bo] om 509

22:17 νῦν αὐτός] tr Bo A F M 55 59 mult

22:17 πόλεως] + εκεινης Bo 407' mult

22:18 ἐκείνης] om Bo 55 pl

22:21 θύρας Bo B 848(vid) 407' pl] + οικου al

22:21 αὐτήν Bo] om 848(vid)+

22:21 ἐν λίθοις] om Bo 848 55+

22:21 Ἰσραήλ 848(vid)+ = Ⓜ] pr υιοις Bo al

22:21 ἐξαρεῖς Bo] εξαρειτε 848 407' pl

22:22 κοιμώμενος Bo] om F mult

22:22 καὶ τὴν γυναῖκα Bo] om 848(vid)+

22:22 ἐξαρεῖς] εξαρειτε Bo V 407'

22:22 Ἰσραήλ 848] υμων Bo F 59 mult Sa³

†22:23 πόλει] pr τη Bo 407+

22:24 αὐτῶν Bo] εκεινης V pl = Ⓜ

†22:24 ἐν 2° Bo] om M 59

†22:24 πλησίον B 407' mult] + αυτου Bo al

22:24 ἐξαρεῖς Bo] εξαρειτε 509 mult

22:25 τὸν ἄνθρωπον Bo] om B 407' pl

22:26 τῇ δέ Bo] και τη B 407' mult Sa³

†22:26 πλησίον B 848(vid) 407' mult] + αυτου Bo al

22:26 αὐτοῦ Bo] om 848(vid) pl

†22:27 ἐβόησεν Bo] pr και 509 pl Sa³

†22:27 αὐτῇ Bo] om 407

†22:28 βιασάμενος B 407' mult] + αυτην Bo al

†23:1 καί] ιε Bo; ουδε B

23:2 οὐκ Bo]∩(3) A* Bᵗˣᵗ F+

23:3 καί 1°] ουδε Bo B

23:3 καί 2° Bo] ∩ 3° 407

†23:4 Βεώρ Bo] βαιωρ 55 pl

†23:6 σου Bo] om F 55 pl

23:7 αὐτοῦ A B M V 848 mult Sa³ = Ⓜ] αυτων Bo al

23:9 παρεμβαλεῖν Bo] + εις πολεμον 55 509 mult Sa³

23:9 σου Bo] υμων 848 pl

†23:9 καί] om Bo 848(vid) pl

23:9 ῥήματος Bo] πραγματος A V 55*+

23:10 ἐάν] + δε Bo V+

23:10 ῥύσεως Bo] + σωματος 55

†23:10 καί 1°] om Bo V 848(vid) 509 mult

†23:10 καί 2° Bo] om V = Ⓜ

23:10 οὐκ 2° Bo] om 59+

23:10 καί 2° Bo]∩(11) 1° B+

23:13 πάσσαλος Bo] πας ο λαος 407+

23:13 ἐν αὐτῷ 2° Bo] om B+ = Ⓜ

†23:14 σου 2° Bo 848(vid)] om A pl

23:14 παραδοῦναι Bo 848] + σοι A M 55 pl

†23:14 σου 3° Bo 848] om 59

23:14 πρὸ προσώπου σου B 848 407' mult = Ⓜ] εις τας
          χειρας σου Bo al

†23:15 κυρίῳ B 848(vid)] + αυτου Bo al

23:16 κατοικήσει 1° Bo 848]∩2° F 55 pl

†23:16 κατοικήσει 2° Bo 848] pr και 407

23:16 ἐν παντι τόπῳ Bo 848] om B

23:17 θυγατέρων 2°] υιων Bo V 407'+

23:17 τελισκόμενος Bo] + προς πασαν ευχην A M 407' mult

23:19 τόκον 2° Bo]∩3° V

23:19 fin] + τω αδελφω σου Bo M pl Sa³

23:20 ἐκτοκιεῖς 1°]∩2° Bo 509+

†23:20 δέ] deest Bo; om V 59 mult

†23:20 εἰσπορεύῃ Bo] pr συ 55 pl = Ⓜ

23:21 τῷ θεῷ Bo] om 407' mult

23:22 μή Bo] om 509

23:23 κυρίῳ Bo] om B pl

†23:23 σου 2° Bo] om B 59

†23:24 ἀμητόν 1° Bo] pr τον V 407' mult

†23:25 τόν Bo] om M pl

†23:25 φάγῃ Bo] pr και 407' mult = Ⓜ

24:1 init — (26:15) ἐποίησα Bo] om 55

†24:1 δώσει] + αυτο Bo 509

24:2 ἀπελθοῦσα Bo] + η γυνη 509

†24:3 ἀνήρ 2° Bo A B pl Sa³ = Ⓜ] + αυτης al

†24:4 αὐτήν 2° Bo] om 59+

24:4 σου 2° Bo B 407' pl = Ⓜ] ημων M pl; υμων al

24:4 σοί B 407'+ = Ⓜ] υμιν Bo al

†24:7 τῶν 1° B 407' mult] pr εκ Bo al

24:7 ἐξαρεῖς Bo B mult Sa³ = Ⓜ] εξαρειτε al

24:8 σφόδρα Bo] om 407

†24:9 θεός 848(vid) 407 mult] + σου Bo al

24:9 ἐξ Bo 848] εκ γης 509 pl; εκ της 407

24:10 δέ Bo 848] om A B 407' mult

24:10 ὀφείλημα 2°] om Bo 407 pl Sa³

† 24:10 ἐνέχυρον] + αυτου Bo B pl = Ⓜ

† 24:11 σου] om Bo 407 pl

24:12 ἐνεχύρῳ] ιματιω Bo F V 59 mult

† 24:13 ἀποδώσεις] + αυτω Bo F M V 59 mult Sa³ = Ⓜ

24:13 ἐνέχυρον B 407' mult = Ⓜ] ιματιον Bo al; ιματιον
το ενεχυρον αυτω V

† 24:15 ἐν 2° Bo] om M 407' mult

† 24:16 υἱοί Bo] pr οι 59 407* pl

† 24:17 καί 3° Bo] om 59 pl; ⌒ (18)1° 509+

24:18 τοῦτο 1° Bo] ⌒ 2° 59

24:19 ἐάν Bo A F M V 59 mult] + δε al

† 24:19 ἀμητόν Bo] + σου A F M V 59 mult = Ⓜ

24:19 σου 1° Bo] ⌒ 2° B* 407ᵗˣᵗ 509 pl

24:19 αὐτό B 848(vid) 407'+] + τω πτωχω και Bo al

24:20 comma Bo] post (22)fin tr F 59 407

† 24:21 δέ Bo 848] om F 59+

24:21 αὐτόν 848(vid)] om Bo A F M V 59 407 mult = Ⓜ

† 25:2 καί 2° 848(vid)] om Bo B mult

25:2 ἐναντίον αὐτῶν Bo] om 407+

25:3 προσθῶσιν Bo] προσθης B 509; προσθη 407 pl

25:5 ἀδελφοί Bo] pr δυο 407

25:5 ἀποθάνῃ Bo] + ο αδελφος ο 848

25:5 εἷς B 848(vid)+] + εξ Bo al

25:5 ἔξω Bo 848] om V 407

† 25:6 κατασταθήσεται Bo] pr και V+; + το πεδιον V

† 25:7   ὁ 1° Bo] om A

25:7   τοῦ ἀδελφοῦ Bo] om A 407 pl

25:7   οὐκ — fin Bo 848] om 509 pl

25:8   αὐτοῦ B 848 V+ = Ⓜ] εκεινης Bo al

25:9   αὐτοῦ 1° B 848 407' mult] + προς αυτον Bo al

† 25:9   καί 2° 848] om Bo 407' mult

25:9   αὐτοῦ 2° Bo] ⌒ 3° 59

† 25:9   εἰς τό Bo] κατα B+

25:9   ἀποκριθεῖσα Bo 848] om F 59 407 Sa³

† 25:10   καί] om Bo 59

25:11   ἄνθρωποι B^txt F V 59 mult = Ⓜ] pr δυο Bo al

† 25:11   ἢ Bo] om B F M V 59 pl

† 25:11   χεῖρα] + αυτης Bo 407' mult = Ⓜ

25:13   στάθμιον 1° Bo] ⌒ 2° 407 pl

25:13   ἤ] και Bo 407 mult = Ⓜ

25:14   ἤ] και Bo 407' mult

† 25:15   σοί 1° Bo 848] om 407 mult

25:15   σοί 1° Bo] ⌒ 2° B^txt F pl

† 25:15   σου Bo 848] om 59+

25:16   κυρίῳ 848] + τω θεω σου Bo al

† 25:16   πᾶς 2° Bo] pr και 509 pl

25:16   ἄδικον] αδικα Bo 848 407 mult Sa³

25:17   σου] υμων Bo 848 407' mult; om 59

25:17   ἐκ γῆς B 848] εξ Bo al

25:18   ἐφοβήθη] εφοβηθης Bo V 59 407' mult

† 25:19   σου 3° Bo] om F M V 59 mult = Ⓜ

25:19 ἐν κλήρῳ κατά] om Bo B

†25:19 κληρονομῆσαι A B F M V 59 mult] + αυτην Bo al

26:1 ἐν κλήρῳ Bo] om B+

26:1 καὶ κατακληρονομήσῃς] om και Bo; κατακληρονομησαι B Sa³

26:2 κύριος ὁ θεός σου 1° Bo] om V

26:2 σοί] + εν κληρω Bo A F M V 59 mult

26:2 ἂν ἐκλέξηται κύριος ὁ Bo] om V

26:3 μου Bo] σου M pl = Ⓜ

26:3 δοῦναι ἡμῖν Bo] om 407 pl

26:4 ὁ ἱερεύς Bo] οι ιερεις 848

26:7 κύριον Bo] om 509

26:7 τῶν πατέρων Bo 848] om B+

26:8 ἐξ Αἰγύπτου Bo] om 509

26:8 ἰσχύι Bo] + αυτου τη B

26:8 καί 2° Bo] ⌒ 3° 59 pl

†26:8 βραχίονι Bo V mult Sa³ = Ⓜ] + αυτου τω al

26:8 ἐν ult Bo] om V mult

26:9 ἡμᾶς Bo] + εις την γην ταυτην A

26:9 τοῦτον Bo] om 59+

26:9 γην 2° Bo] om V

26:10 ἔδωκάς μοι κύριε] εδωκε μοι κυριος Bo F 59

26:10 αὐτά] αυτο Bo F M V mult; αυτον 59

†26:10 σου Bo] om M+

26:10 προσκυνήσεις B+ = Ⓜ] + εκει Bo al

26:11   εὐφρανθήσῃ] + εκει Bo 407' mult

26:12   γενημάτων B 848+ = Ⓜ] + της γης Bo al

† 26:12   φάγονται] + αυτα Bo 407' mult

26:13   καί 3° Bo] ⌒ 4° V

26:13   κατά Bo] και 407+

† 26:13   ἐντολάς Bo A B V 407'] + σου al

† 26:14   καί 1° Bo] om V pl

26:14   αὐτῶν 1° Bo] ⌒ 2° B^txt+

26:14   αὐτῶν 2° Bo] ⌒ 3° V+

26:14   οὐκ 3° Bo] ουδε 407' mult = Ⓜ

26:14   μου 2° Bo] ημων B

26:15   σου 2° Bo] pr εκ του υψους 509

26:15   ἡμῖν Bo 848] αυτοις 407 Sa^16

26:16   ταῦτα Bo 848] om B pl Sa^16

† 26:16   καί 2° Bo] om 509

26:16   και ποιήσετε Bo 848] om 55

26:16   ὑμῶν 1° Bo] σου V 848 407' pl = Ⓜ

26:16   ὑμῶν 2° Bo] σου V 407+ = Ⓜ

26:17   ταῖς Bo] pr πασαις B+

26:17   δικαιώματα Bo A B F M V 55 Sa^16] + και τας εντολας
        αυτου al (om αυτου 407'); + αυτου Bo V pl Sa^16 = Ⓜ

26:18   εἶπεν B pl Sa^16] + σοι Bo al

26:18   πάσας Bo] om B+

26:19   σε 1° Bo] + αυτω 509

27:1   πάσας Bo] om 407 mult

27:1   ταύτας 848] om Bo F 407 mult = Ⓜ

27:3 λίθων Bo 848] + τουτων B

27:3 εἰσέλθητε Bo] εισελθης A M 55 59 mult

27:4 τούτους Bo] om 509+

27:4 ὑμῖν Bo 509 mult = Ⓜ] σοι al

† 27:4 Γαιβάλ Bo A B F M V 55 407 mult] γεβαλ al

27:5 θυσιαστήριον 1° Bo] ⌒ 2° 407+

27:5 αὐτούς] αυτο Bo B 407' pl

27:6 τό] om Bo B V+

27:6 ὁλοκαυτώματα Bo] pr τα B pl

27:7 θύσεις A F Mᵗˣᵗ V 848 55 59 mult = Ⓜ] + εκειBo al

27:7 σωτηρίου B M 848 mult = Ⓜ] + κυριω τω θεω σου Bo al; om 407+

27:7 ἐκεῖ] om Bo B+

27:7 καὶ εὐφρανθήσῃ Bo] om 509

27:8 λίθων Bo 848 963] + τουτων 55 407 pl

27:8 πάντα Bo] om 55+

27:9 Μωυσῆς Bo] μωσης 848 pl

† 27:9 οἱ 2° Bo] pr και M pl

27:11 τῷ] pr παντι Bo 407 mult

27:12 εὐλογεῖν τον λαόν Bo] om 509

27:12 Γαριζίν Bo 59 mult] γαριζειν al

27:12 Ἰουδάς Bo] ιουδα B+

† 27:12 Ἰσσαχαρ] ᴴⅭᴀᕽᴀᑭ Bo; ισαχαρ F pl

† 27:12 Βενιαμίν Bo] βενιαμειν A B F M V 407' mult

† 27:13 Γαιβάλ A B F V 55 mult] Γᴀᗸᗅλ Bo; γαιβακ 509; γεβαλ al

27:13 Ἀσήρ] ασσηρ Bo 509

†27:13 Νεφθαλί pl] νεφθαλιμ Bo V pl; νεφθαλει A B F 407; νεφθαλειμ 963 al

† 27:15 ὁ 1° Bo 963] om B 848 mult

27:15 καί 1° 848 963] η Bo 407+

27:15 χειρῶν Bo] om 407+

27:15 θήσει 848+ = Ⓜ] + αυτο Bo al

27:15 πᾶς Bo] om B Sa

27:16 ἐπικατάρατος Bo] + ο α̅ν̅ο̅ς 59

† 27:16 αὐτοῦ 1° Bo] om 59 407 pl

27:17 ἐροῦσιν Bo] ερει 407' mult = Ⓜ

27:18 comma Bo] post (24)fin 848(vid)

27:18 ἐροῦσιν Bo] ερει 59 407' mult = Ⓜ

27:19 ἐροῦσιν Bo] ερει V 59 407 = Ⓜ et saepe

27:20 ὁ 1° Bo] pr πας V pl

† 27:20 αὐτοῦ 1° Bo] om M

27:21 comma] post (22)fin tr Bo(vid) 407'

27:22 ὁ 1° Bo] pr πας V+

† 27:22 ἐκ 1° Bo] om B+

† 27:22 ἐκ 2° Bo] om B pl

27:23 fin Bo 848] + επικαταρατος ο κοιμωμενος μετα αδελφης γυναικος αυτου και ερουσιν πας ο λαος γενοιτο B pl

† 27:24 πλησίον 848] + αυτου Bo B V mult

27:24 δόλῳ Bo] om 848(vid)

27:25 ὃς Bo] pr πας V+

27:25 δῶρα] δωρον Bo 59+

27:25 αἵματος Bo] om 848(vid) 509

28:1 ἔσται B 848 pl = Ⓜ] + ως αν διαβητε τον ιορδανην
εις την γην ην κυριος ο θεος υμων διδωσιν υμιν Bo
al

28:1 ἀκούσῃς B = Ⓜ] εισακουσητε Bo al

28:1 σου 1° B = Ⓜ] υμων Bo al

✝28:1 αὐτοῦ Bo] om A+; ταυτας B

✝28:1 σου 2° Bo 848(vid)] om A+

28:1 τῆς γῆς Bo] om 407'+

28:2 εὑρήσουσιν Bo] ευλογησουσιν 509

28:2 ἀκούσῃς 848(vid) 963 pl Sa³(vid) = Ⓜ] pr ακοη
Bo al

28:6 συ 1° Bo] om 848

28:6 σε 1° Bo] om 848

28:6 συ 2° Bo] om 848

28:6 σε 2° Bo] om 848

✝28:7 παραδῴη Bo] + σοι M pl Sa¹⁶

28:7 προσώπου Bo] om 509+

✝28:8 καί] om Bo 407' Sa¹⁶

28:9 κύριος B 848(vid) 963 pl Sa¹⁶ = Ⓜ] + ο θεος σου
Bo al

28:9 τῆς φωνῆς Bo] om 963+

✝28:9 ἐν Bo] om 848(vid) 407' mult

28:9 ταῖς Bo] pr πασαις B

✝28:10 τό Bo] om V+

28:11 ἐκγόνοις τῶν κτηνῶν] et γενημασιν της γης tr Bo
B V 407' mult Sa³ ¹⁶

28:12 σοί] om Bo 407+

† 28:12 αὐτοῦ 2° Bo] om B 407' mult

† 28:12 συ 2°] om Bo B V+

28:13 κύριος ὁ θεός σου Bo] om 848

28:13 ἀκούσῃς Bo] ακουσητε 963 pl; pr ακοη Bo V;
εισακουσητε της φωνης κυ του θεου υμων και
μνησθηση V

28:13 τῶν ἐντολῶν Bo 963] της φωνης B

28:13 σου 2° Bo] υμων 963 pl

28:13 σοί Bo 848] υμιν 963 pl

28:13 καὶ ποιεῖν Bo 848] om B

28:14 πάντων Bo] om 509+

28:14 οὐδέ Bo B F V 407' pl] η al

28:15 εἰσακούσῃς Bo] pr ακοη 407 pl

28:15 σου] υμων Bo 407 mult

28:15 καὶ ποιεῖν] om Bo B+

28:15 σοί Bo] υμιν V

† 28:17 init Bo] pr και V+

28:18 σου 1°∩ 2° Bo 509

28:19 εἰσπορεύεσθαι Bo] et ἐκπορεύεσθαι tr B 55

† 28:21 συ] om Bo B pl

28:22 και φόνῳ] om Bo B

28:23 σοί Bo 963] om A F M 59 Sa³

28:24 κύριος Bo 963] + ο θεος σου B

28:24 ἐπι σε Bo 963] om B

28:24 fin Bo] + εν ταχει B

28:25 ἐναντίον 963] om Bo 407

†28:25 σου Bo] om B+

†28:25 ἐν 4° Bo] om F 59 pl

†28:28 καί 1° Bo] om B 963 509

†28:28 καί 2° Bo] om 963(vid) 407'

†28:29 ὁ 1°] om Bo B+

28:29 σοί Bo 963] om B pl = Ⓜ

†28:29 ὁ 2° Bo 963] om V 407

28:31 ἐναντίον σου Bo] om 59+

28:31 ἐξ Bo] om V

28:31 σοί 1° Bo] om˙ V+

28:31 καί ult Bo] ⌒ (32)2° B^txt

†28:32 θυγατέρες 848(vid)] + σου Bo al

28:32 εἰς Bo] om 848(vid)+

†28:32 καί 3° Bo 848 963] om B+

28:32 ἡ χείρ σου Bo 963] om 509; om σου 59+

28:36 οἱ πατέρες Bo] ο πατηρ 59+

28:38 αὐτά Bo] αυτο 407 = Ⓜ

28:40 σοί Bo] om F 59 pl

28:43 ἐπι σε] om Bo B pl

†28:45 αὐτοῦ 2° Bo] om B

†28:46 καί 3° Bo] om B pl

28:47 ἐν 2° 963] om Bo A^txt B 407' mult

28:47 διά Bo 963] om 59

28:48 λατρεύσεις] + εκει Bo 963 407' mult Sa^3

28:48 κύριος Bo A B 963 mult Sa^3 = Ⓜ] + ο θεος σου al

28:48 ἐν 2° 963] om Bo A 509 mult

† 28:51 τά 3° Bo] om A F M 59 407' mult

† 28:51 τά 4° Bo] om 59 407 mult

28:52 καί 1° Bo] + εως αν 407' mult

28:52 πάσαις 1° Bo] om B+ Sa³

28:52 σου 1° Bo] + αις εδωκε σοι κυριος ο θεος 55 pl

† 28:52 σου 2° Bo] om B

28:52 πάσαις 2° Bo] om B

28:52 κύριος ὁ θεός σου Bo 963(vid)] om B+

† 28:53 σου 2° Bo 963] om F+

† 28:53 σου 3° Bo] om 963 55+

† 28:53 σοί Bo] om 509 mult

28:53 κύριος B 963 pl Sa³] + ο θεος σου Bo al; om B

28:53 fin] + εν ταις πολεσι σου Bo 407' mult

† 28:54 ἀφθαλμῷ B 963 mult Sa³] + αυτου Bo al

† 28:54 ἀδελφόν B 963 pl] + αυτου Bo al

† 28:54 γυναῖκα 963] + αυτου Bo A Sa³

† 28:54 κόλπῳ Bo B 963 59 pl] pr τω al

28:54 καταλειφθῇ Bo] καταλειφθωσιν F 407

† 28:54 fin B 848(vid) 407 pl Sa = Ⓜ] + σοι 509 pl;
        + αυτω Bo al

28:55 δοῦναι Bo] + σε 407

28:55 ἐνὶ αὐτῶν Bo] αυτω 55+

† 28:55 στενοχωρία] ⲡⲓⲕⲁϩⲓ Bo; + σου B pl

† 28:55 σου 1° A B F M 55 mult Sa³] om Bo al

28:55 οἱ ἐχθροί Bo] ο εχθρος A+

28:56 τρυφερά B 963 pl Sa³ = Ⓜ] + σφοδρα Bo al

28:56 τρυφερότητα Bo] et ἁπαλότητα tr 963 407 mult

28:56 τῷ ὀφθαλμῷ αὐτῆς Bo] om 55

† 28:57 αὐτῆς 1° 963] om Bo 55 pl

† 28:57 τό 2° Bo 963] pr και 407+

† 28:57 τέκνον B 963 407' mult Sa³] + αυτης Bo al

† 28:57 γάρ] om Bo; παρ 963 55 mult Sa³

28:57 κρυφῇ Bo] τρυφη 59+

† 28:57 στενωχωρίᾳ] + σου Bo B+ Sa³

† 28:57 θλίψει 1°] + σου Bo B pl Sa³

28:57 ταῖς Bo B 848(vid) 963(vid) mult Sa = Ⓜ] pr πασαις
al

28:58 εἰσακούσῃς B+ = Ⓜ] εισακουσητε Bo al

28:58 ἔντιμον Bo] + τουτο F+

† 28:58 καί Bo 848] om B

28:59 σου και τας πληγάς Bo 963] om F

† 28:60 καί 1°] om Bo 963

28:60 ἐπὶ σε Bo 963] om B

28:61 πᾶσαν 2° Bo] om A+

28:61 μή Bo] om 407

28:61 γεγραμμένην B^txt M^txt 848 963 55 59 mult Sa³ ¹⁶ =
Ⓜ] + και πασαν την γεγραμμενην Bo al (tr post
τουτο Bo B^mg)

28:61 βιβλίῳ Bo 963] + τουτο 55 pl

28:61 τοῦ νόμου τούτο Bo 963] του 509; om 55 pl

28:62 ὑμῶν Bo] σου B = Ⓜ

28:63 ἐφ᾽ ὑμῖν 2° Bo] om 55+

†28:63 εἰσπορεύεσθε Bo B F 963 55 pl Sa³ ¹⁶] pr υμεις al

†28:64 γῆς 1° Bo] + σου 407

†28:64 γῆς 2° Bo] + σου 407

28:65 ἔθνεσιν Bo] om 59

28:65 ἐκεῖ Bo 963] om 848(vid)+

28:65 ἀθυμοῖσαν Bo 963] ετεραν απειθουσαν B+

†28:67 τό 2°] om Bo 407 pl

†28:68 ἐν 2° B = Ⓜ] pr και Bo al

†28:68 ᾗ Bo] om B+

29:2 κύριος A B 963 pl Sa³ ¹⁶ = Ⓜ] + ο θεος υμων (ημων
   Bo F) Bo al

29:2 πάντα Bo 963] om 55

29:2 γῆ 1° Bo] om 407'

†29:2 ἐνώπιον ὑμῶν] om υμων Bo; om 55

29:2 τοῖς Bo B F 848 963 pl Sa³ ¹⁶] pr πασι al

29:3 ἐκεῖνα Bᵗˣᵗ 848 963 pl Sa³ ¹⁶ = Ⓜ] + την χειρα
   την κραταιαν και τον βραχιονα τον υψηλον Bo al

29:4 ὁ θεός Bo] om 55+ pl = Ⓜ

29:5 ἐπαλαιώθη] επαλαιωθησαν Bo A pl

29:5 κατετρίβη Bo] επαλαιωθη 407' Sa³ ¹⁶

29:6 οἶνον 963] pr και Bo 407 mult Sa³ ¹⁶ = Ⓜ

29:6 καὶ σίκερα Bo 963] om 407+

29:6 οὗτος Bo 963] om B F 59 509+

29:6 fin Bo 963] + εγω B

29:7 init — (17)fin Bo] om 55

29:7   fin Bo] + εν τω πολεμω M pl

29:8   Γαδδί] γαδ Bo F 407 mult Sa³ ¹⁶

29:9   πάντας Bo] om 407+ = M

29:9   ταύτης Bo] + ποιειν αυτους A F M 59 mult = Ⓜ

29:10 ἐστήκατε 963] + ωδε Bo 407' mult

29:10 πάντες] om Bo 963 407 pl

29:10 πᾶς ἀνὴρ 'Ισραήλ Bo 963(vid)] om 509

† 29:11 init 963] pr και Bo A M 59 mult

29:11 ἔκγονα B 963 407' mult] τεκνα Bo al

† 29:11 ὑμῶν 3° Bo 963] om 59

† 29:11 καί 3° Bo B 963 407' mult] om al

29:12 σε 1° Bo F 963 407' mult = Ⓜ] om al

29:12 σου 1° Bo 963] υμων B

29:12 ὁ θεός Bo] om 509

†29:13 καί ult Bo] om 509

†29:15 ἡμῶν 1°] υμων Bo A 963 59 407 mult Sa³

†29:15 ἡμῶν 2° mult = Ⓜ] υμων Bo al

29:15 ὧδε 2° Bo] om 963+

29:15 ἡμῶν 3° A F M mult = Ⓜ] υμων Bo al

29:15 fin] + εναντι κυριου του θεου υμων Bo 407+

† 29:16 καί] om Bo B 963

29:16 οὕς] ως Bo B 407' mult

29:17 ἃ Bo] om 963 407+

29:18 ἐν ὑμῖν 1° Bo 848 963] om 407 mult

† 29:18 ἤ 2° Bo 963] om 59+

† 29:18 λατρεύειν Bo 963] pr και 509 pl

29:18 ἐκείνων Bo 963] om 407 Sa³

29:18 ῥίζα Bo] + πικριας A F

29:19 ὅτι Bo] om 509

† 29:20 ὀργή Bo] pr η 407' mult

29:20 τοῦ νόμου τούτου Bo 963(vid)] om B+ = Ⓜ

29:21 αὐτόν Bo 963] αυτους 407+

29:21 τὰς γεγραμμένας Bo] της γεγραμμενης A F M 59 mult
       = Ⓜ

29:21 τοῦ νόμου Bo] om 509

† 29:22 οἱ 2° Bo 848] om 407+

29:23 ἀναβῇ Bo] om 55

†29:23 Σεβωίμ Bo] σεβωειμ B M 963 mult; σεβωειν A F Sa³+;
        σεβοειμ 55 407 pl; σεβμας 509; σεβοην 59;

29:23 κύριος 963] + ο θεος Bo 407 pl

† 29:23 fin Bo] + αυτου A F M 59 mult = Ⓜ

29:24 ἔθνη] + της γης Bo 963 pl Sa³

29:24 κύριος Bo] + ο θεος 407

29:24 οὕτως] post ταυτη tr Bo 407

29:26 καὶ προσεκύνησαν αὐτοῖς Bo 848(vid)] om B+

29:26 οὐδέ — fin Bo 848(vid) 963(vid)] om 55

† 29:27 τάς 1° Bo] om 509

29:27 κατάρας B 848 407' mult Sa³ = Ⓜ] + της διαθηκης
        Bo (+ ΝΑΙ-) al

29:27 τούτῳ 848+ = Ⓜ] του νομου τουτου Bo al

29:28 ἐξῆρεν Bo] εξηγαγεν 407+

29:28 αὐτούς 2° Bo] + κυριος 509

† 29:29 ἡμῶν 1° Bo] υμων B 55 509 mult

† 29:29 ἡμῖν] υμιν Bo B 848 509 mult

† 29:29 ἡμῶν 2°] υμων Bo B 55 59 509 mult

30:1 κύριος Bo B 848(vid) pl Sa] + ο θεος al

30:3 κύριος 2° B 848 407' mult Sa³] om 55 pl; + ο θεος σου Bo al

30:4 σου 2° Bo] ⌒ (5)1° 55 pl

30:4 fin A F M 59 pl = Ⓜ] + κυριος ο θεος σου Bo 963 al

30:5 κύριος ὁ θεός σου Bo 963] om 509 pl Sa¹⁷; om κύριος B

30:5 ποιήσει 1° Bo] 2° 55 509 pl

30:6 fin A*(vid) B F M 848(vid) 59 mult = Ⓜ] + και το σπερμα σου Bo al

30:7 ὁ θεός σου Bo] om A 407

† 30:9 ἐν 2°] pr και Bo 407' Sa³ mult

30:9 γενήμασιν τῆς γῆς B 848 407' mult Sa³] et ἐκγόνοις τῶν κτηνῶν tr Bo al

30:9 ἐν τοῖς ἐκγόνοις Bo] om 55 pl

30:10 τάς 1° B 848+ = Ⓜ] pr και ποιειν πασας Bo al

30:10 ἐάν 2°] + δε Bo 407; και 55+

† 30:11 ἔστιν 2°] om Bo B pl

30:12 οὐρανῷ] + ανω Bo B 407 mult

30:12 ἡμῖν 1°] om Bo 55

30:13 comma Bo] om B^txt+

30:13 αὐτήν 1° Bo] ταυτην 407

30:13 ἀκουστὴν ἡμῖν ποιήσει] ακουσαντες Bo A F M 55 59 mult Sa³

† 30:15 τό 2° Bo] om 59+

30:16 σου 1° B pl Sa³] υμων Bo al

30:16 σοί Bo 963] υμιν F 59 407 mult

30:16 ταῖς 848(vid)+ = Ⓜ] pr πασαις Bo al

† 30:16 φυλάσσεσθαι Bo B 848(vid) 407' mult] pr και al;
＋ τας εντολας αυτου και Bo A pl = Ⓜ

30:16 καὶ τὰς ἐντολάς αὐτοῦ Bo] om B 848(vid) pl Sa³

30:16 αὐτήν Bo] om 963(vid) 509

30:17 καὶ ἐάν] εαν δε Bo 407' mult

30:18 καί — γένεσθε Bo] om 407

30:18 γῆς B pl = Ⓜ] + ης κυριος ο θεος σου διδωσι σοι
Bo al

30:18 εἰς — ἐκεῖ Bo] om 55

† 30:19 καί 4° 848(vid) 963] om Bo B pl

30:19 ζωήν 2° 963] ευλογιαν Bo 55 407' mult

31:1 πάντας 1° Bo] om 407+ = Ⓜ

† 31:1 υἱούς] pr τους Bo V 407 mult

31:2 προς αὐτούς Bo] om 509

31:3 σου 3° Bo] ⌒ 4° 55+

31:4 κύριος Bo] + ο θ̅ς̅ σου B pl

† 31:4 Σηών 963] σιων Bo 55 mult

† 31:4 τοῖς Bo] om A F M 59 mult

† 31:5 ἐνώπιον ὑμῶν] ⲈⲚⲈⲦⲈⲚⲊⲓⲊ Bo; υμιν B 407' mult

31:5 ἐνετειλάμην] ενετειλατο Bo 407+

31:6 οὗτος A F M V 848 59 mult] om Bo al

31:6 ἐν ὑμῖν Bo B 848(vid) 407' mult] om al

† 31:7 ἡμῶν Bo] υμων F M 59 407 mult; αυτων A pl = Ⓜ

† 31:7 αὐτήν Bo] om B 509 mult

31:8 συμπορευόμενος Bo 963 55 59 407' Sa³(vid)] + σοι al

31:8 σε 1° Bo 963] om 407+

31:8 μη φοβοῦ μηδε δειλία Bo] om 509

31:9 τά 963] pr παντα Bo A F M V 509 mult

† 31:9 ἔδωκεν A B Mᵗˣᵗ 55 59 407' mult] + αυτω Bo al

† 31:11 τῷ 2° Bo] om 407 pl

31:11 κύριος A* B F M mult] + ο θεος σου Bo al

31:12 σου 963] υμων Bo B 407' mult

31:12 ἵνα 2°] om Bo 963 pl

31:12 κύριον Bo] om 59

† 31:12 ὑμῶν Bo 963] ημων V 59 pl

† 31:13 ὑμῶν Bo] ημων V pl; om 55

31:13 ἐκεῖ 963] om Bo 55 509 pl

31:14 κάλεσον Bo] + ουν 407 mult

31:14 καί ult Bo] ⌒ (14)1° V 509 pl

31:15 νεφέλη B 848 407' pl Sa] στυλω νεφελης Bo al

31:15 καί 2° Bo] ⌒ 3° V+ = Ⓜ

31:15 καί 3°] ⌒ (16)1° Bo 55 mult

31:15 fin] + του μαρτυριου Bo 963 59 407 mult

31:16 οὗτος 2°] om Bo 407 mult

31:16 εἰσπορεύεται] εισπορευονται Bo 55 pl; -ρευεσθε 407

31:16 ἐκεῖ] om Bo 407' mult

31:17 ἔσται] εσονται Bo V pl

31:17 πολλά Bo] μεγαλα F

31:17 ἐρεῖ Bo] ερουσιν V+

31:17 ἐμοί Bo] ημιν F M V mult Sa³; υμιν A pl

31:17 τά Bo] pr παντα V

31:18 ἐποίησαν Bo] εποιησεν V+ = Ⓜ

31:19 γράψατε Bo] + ωδε 59

31:19 αὐτήν 1° Bo] om A+ Sa³

31:19 εἰς 2°] om Bo 407' pl

31:20 αὐτῶν Bo] + δουναι αυτοις B pl

31:20 fin pl = Ⓜ] deest B 59 407' pl; + ην διεθημην
      αυτοις Bo al

31:21 init B M V 55 59 407 509 mult Sa³(vid)] pr και
      εσται οταν ευρωσιν αυτον κακα πολλα και θλιψεις
      Bo al

†31:21 πρόσωπον B 848 59 pl] + αυτων Bo al

31:21 στόματος B 848 963 pl Sa³ = Ⓜ] pr στοματος αυτων
      και απο Bo al

31:21 ποιοῦσιν Bo 848 963] pr αυτοι 407; + μοι A pl

31:21 ὧδε Bo] om 848

31:21 αὐτούς Bo] αυτον 848

31:22 Μωυσῆς Bo] μωσης 848 pl

31:22 ταύτην Bo 963] om F+

31:23 ἐνετείλατο B 963 pl Sa³ = Ⓜ] + μωυσης Bo al

31:23 ᾿Ιησοῦ B V 963+] + υιω ναυη Bo al

31:23 εἶπεν B V 59 pl Sa³] + αυτω Bo al

31:24 Μωυσῆς Bo] μωσης 848 pl

31:24 γράφων Bo 848] om 55+

31:24   τούτου Βο 848] + και εγραψεν αυτους 55

31:24   ἕως εἰς τέλος Βο 848(vid)] om 55 407

31:25   τοῖς 2° Βο] om 848(vid)

31:26   τῆς κιβωτοῦ Βο 963] om 848(vid) 55+

† 31:26   ὑμῶν Βο 963] ημων V 59 mult

31:27   σου 1° Βο] ⌒ 2° 59

31:28   ὑμῶν 1° Βο] om 848(vid)

31:28   ὑμῶν 1° Βο] ⌒ 2° Β+

† 31:28   ὑμῶν 4° Βο] om 509+

31:29   καὶ ἐκκλινεῖτε Βο 848] om 59

31:29   καὶ συναντήσεται ὑμῖν Βο 848] om Β+

31:29   κυρίου 848] + του θεου υμων Βο 407' mult

31:30   Μωυσῆς Βο] μωσης 848(vid) pl

31:30   πάσης Βο] om 407

31:30   Ἰσραήλ Βο] om Β Sa³

† 32:3   ὄνομα] pr το Βο Β+

32:3   τῷ] pr κυριω Βο 59 509

32:4   ἀδικία Α Β Fᵗˣᵗ V 848 963 55 pl = Ⓜ] + εν αυτω
        Βο al

32:6   σε 2° Βο] ⌒ 3° Β 848(vid)+

32:7   τὸν πατέρα Βο] τους πατερας 59+

32:8   υἱῶν V 848 pl] αγγελων Βο al

† 32:10   ἀνύδρῳ] pr Μᾳ- Βο; pr γη Β

† 32:17   πρόσφατοι Βο Β F pl] pr και al

32:17   οὓς οὐκ ᾔδεισαν 2° Βο] om 55

32:19   αὐτοῦ Βο Α Β F Μ V 55 59 509 pl Sa] αυτων al

32:20 ἐσχάτων Bo] + ημερων B; + των ημερων 59+

†32:24 γῆς] pr της Bo A mult

†32:25 ταμιείων Bo] + αυτων 59 pl

†32:26 δή] δε Bo B F M 848 55 509 pl

†32:27 ὑψηλή A M V 55 509 Sa³] pr η Bo al

32:27 πάντα Bo] om 963 55

32:28 ὅτι Bo 963] om B

†32:28 καί Bo 963] om V

32:28 αὐτοῖς Bo 963] αυτω 59

32:31 ἡμῶν 2° Bo] υμων 407+

32:34 ταῦτα Bo A B F M V 55 Sa³ = Ⓜ] +
       παντα al

†32:41 ἐχθροῖς]+ μου Bo 59 407 pl Sa³ ⁶ = Ⓜ

32:42 ἐχθρῶν Bo B F M 55 pl Sa³ ⁵ ⁶ = Ⓜ] εθνων al

32:43 αὐτῷ 1° Bo] αυτοις 407

32:43 υἱοί A B Mᵗˣᵗ 509 pl Sa³] αγγελοι Bo al

32:43 αὐτῷ 3°] αυτων Bo A* F 59 pl Sa⁵ ¹⁶

32:43 ἄγγελοι Bo] υιοι 55 407 mult

†32:43 ἐχθροῖς Bo] + αυτου A F M V pl Sa⁴ (sed hab 3 6 16)
       = Ⓜ

32:43 μισοῦσιν] + αυτον Bo 59 407 mult Sa³ ⁶ ¹⁶

32:44 Μωυσῆς 2°] + προς τον λαον Bo A F M V mult

32:44 τοῦ νόμου τούτου Bo] τουτους 407

32:45 λαλῶν B 848 59 407' mult Sa³ ¹⁶] + τους λογους
       τουτους Bo al

†32:46 καρδίᾳ B 848(vid) pl] + υμων Bo al

32:47 ὅτι Bo] om 55

32:47 ἐκεῖ Bo] om 55+ Sa³ ¹⁶

† 32:47 κληρονομῆσαι B 848(vid)+] + αυτην Bo al

† 32:49 Ἀβαρίμ Bo pl] αβαρει 407'; αβαρειν B pl; αβαρικ V
αβαρειμ al

† 32:49 ὅρος 2°] pr το Bo 59 509 mult ˅

† 32:49 Ἰεριχώ Bo] ιερειχω B* F M 55 pl

32:50 ἐν Ωρ τῷ ὅρει Bo] om 407

32:51 Σίν] σινα Bo V 509 mult Sa³ ¹⁶

32:51 ἐπί — fin Bo] bis scr 509

† 32:51 ἀντιλογίας A B V 55 407'] pr της Bo al

32:52 ὅτι] om Bo B 59 407' mult Sa³ ¹⁶

† 33:1 καί] om Bo F 407' pl

33:2 κατέσπευσεν] κατεπαυσεν Bo 55 407' pl

33:3 ἐφείσατο Bo] + κ̅ς̅ 59 pl Sa³ ¹⁶

33:3 σου] αυτου Bo 59 pl

† 33:4 ἡμῖν Bo] υμιν 59 mult

33:5 ἄρχων Bo] om A pl

33:5 ἀρχόντων Bo] om 59+

33:5 λαῶν Bo] λαον 55

33:5 φυλαῖς Bo] φυλης 59 pl

33:6 καί 2° Bo] + συμεων A M V pl; om V

33:7 Ἰούδα 1° Bo] + και ειπεν 59 mult = Ⓜ

† 33:7 φωνῆς] pr της Bo A 59 pl

† 33:7 αί] pr και Bo B V 407'+

† 33:7 αὐτοῦ 2° Bo] om B

†33:8 Λευί 1° Bo] λευει B 407+ Sa³ ¹⁶

†33:8 Λευί 2° Bo] λευει B 407+ Sa³ ¹⁶

†33:9 πατρί B pl] + αυτου Bo al

†33:9 μητρί B+] + αυτου Bo al

 33:9 καὶ τοὺς υἱούς αὐτοῦ οὐκ ἐπέγνω Bo] om 55 pl

 33:9 οὐκ ἐπέγνω(c var) Bo F M 59 407 mult] απεγνω al

†33:12 Βενιαμίν Bo] βενιαμειν A B Fᵗˣᵗ M V Sa³ (sed hab 16)

†33:13 ἀπό 2° Bo] om 59

†33:14 καί 1° Bo] om 407 pl

†33:15 καί 1°] om Bo B 407' mult

 33:15 κορυφῆς 1° Bo] ⌒ 2° 59 pl

 33:16 γῆς πληρώσεως] tr Bo 55

†33:16 πληρώσεως Bo] + αυτου 59 pl = Ⓜ

†33:17 ἐπ᾽] om Bo 59 pl

†33:17 γῆς] pr της Bo A F 55 mult

†33:17 μυριάδες] pr αι Bo V+

 33:18 Ἰσσαχάρ] ισαχαρ Bo 59 pl

†33:18 αὐτοῦ Bo] om 407; σου V pl = Ⓜ

 33:19 ἐπικαλέσεσθε Bo] επικαλεσονται 59 pl

 33:19 θύσετε Bo] θυσουσι 59 pl

†33:21 γῆ] pr η Bo V mult

 33:22 Δάν 2° Bo] om 407 mult

 33:22 Βασάν Bo] κασαν 509

†33:23 Νεφθαλί 1° M pl = Ⓜ] νεφθαλιμ Bo 407 pl;
        νεφθαλει A Fᵗˣᵗ 55* pl Sa⁵; νεφθαλειμ al; et saepe

 33:25 ἔσται Bo] om 407 pl

†33:25 καί 2°] om Bo B 407' pl

33:27 σκέπασις] σκεπασει σε Bo M 407 mult

†33:27 σου Bo] om 59 mult

33:28 πεποιθως μόνος] tr Bo A F M V 407 mult Sa

†33:28 γῆς] pr της Bo 407 pl

33:28 ἐπί 2° Bo] + γης 59 mult Sa³ 16 = Ⓜ

33:28 αὐτῷ Bo] σοι B 59 mult Sa³ 5 16

33:29 τὸν τράχηλον] των τραχηλων Bo 59

34:1 Ἀραβώθ Bo] αραμωθ V Sa³ (sed hab 16)

†34:1 ἸεριχώBo] ιερειχω B* F M 55 mult et saepe

34:1 γῆν Bo] om 509 pl

†34:2 τῆς 1° Bo] om 59 pl

†34:4 ἔδειξα Bo A F* M V mult = Ⓜ] pr και al

†34:4 ἔδειξα   B 407' mult = Ⓜ] + αυτην Bo al

34:5 ἐκεῖ] om Bo B 59 407' mult

34:6 ἐν γῇ Μωάβ] om Bo B 59 407' mult Sa³ 16

34:6 ταφήν Bo] τελευτην A mult

34:7 ἐφθάρησαν Bo B 55 509 pl Sa³ 5] + τα χελυνια αυτου (c var) al

34:8 ἐπί Bo] εν τω περαν 59 pl

34:10 ἔτι Bo] om V pl Sa⁵ (sed hab 3)

34:11 αὐτόν Bo A B F M V 407 mult = Ⓜ] om al

34:11 Φαραω] pr εν Bo 407+

34:11 τοῖς 2°] pr πασιν Bo 55 mult Sa³ 5 = Ⓜ

34:11 πάσῃ] om Bo A M mult

34:11 αὐτοῦ 2° Bo 963] αιγυπτου 59 pl

†34:12 $\kappa\alpha\iota$ 1° 963] om Bo B 59 407' pl
34:12 $\kappa\alpha\iota$ 2° Bo B 963 55 59 407' Sa^{3} ^{5} mult] + $\pi\alpha\sigma\alpha\nu$ al

The above list of 2098 readings consists of all
the deviant readings of the 11 presumed pre-recensional
witnesses which could have been shown by the translator
of Bo. The following analysis of the list does not include secondary readings of the papyri since their texts
are fragmentary; they will be discussed separately. An
analysis of the remaining 2060 readings reveals the following number of deviations from original Greek by each
of the 10 complete pre-recensional witnesses.

Table 2

Deviations from Original Greek

Pre-recen. Witness	No of Deviations
M	424
F	443
A	483
B	529
55	532
V	576
Bo	633
59	647
509	677
407	702

These figures include many unique readings of
each ms and thus may only indicate how carefully or care-
lessly each ms was written. It may be observed even in
this full list that the mss 407 and 509 exhibit a high
deviance from original Greek, and mss A F and M show a
high correlation with it. Bo and the remaining witnesses are relatively similar in their percentage of
deviation.

In order to perceive the textual affiliations of
Bo more clearly it is necessary to exclude from further
consideration a number of textually insignificant readings in the list. Exclusion is made in keeping with the
guidelines outlined in Chapter V and readings thus elim-
inated are marked in the list by a † before the chapter
number. When a lemma has more than one variant, the
† appears if at least one of the variant readings is considered textually insignificant. Instances of this kind
are few and the insignificant reading(s) can be easily
identified in each case. Greek itacistic variant spellings of proper names are not included. Since the goal
of this investigation is to determine the nearest extant
Greek neighbour to Bo, the unique readings of Bo are not
included.

The number of significant variants which remain
is 1304. The total number of deviations of each of the
ten witnesses is set out in table 3.

348

Table 3

Significant Deviations from Original Greek

Pre-recen. Witness	No of Deviations	Percentage
M	231	17.6%
F	252	19.3%
A	271	20.8%
B	311	24 %
V	323	25 %
59	325	25 %
55	326	25 %
Bo	355	27.2%
509	411	31.5%
407	467	36 %

The picture changes slightly when the larger list
is pruned. The mss A F and M are again least deviant
and 407' most deviant from original Greek. The mss B
V 55 and 59 are closer to each other in their percentage
of deviation than they were in Table 2. Bo is again
relatively normal in its percentage of deviation.

The 355 deviant readings of Bo are of primary interest. A clearer picture of the relationship of Bo
to the other witnesses should emerge from an analysis
of these readings. The following table lists the joint
support of Bo and each of the other pre-recensional
witnesses for a variant reading.

349

Table 4

Deviant Readings Jointly Supported by Bo and

Each Pre-recensional Witness

Manuscript	No of Joint Deviations	Percentage
407	223	63 %
509	190	53.5%
55	150	42.2%
V	134	37.7%
59	130	36.6%
M	128	36.1%
F	126	35.5%
A	119	33.5%
B	90	25.3%

It would appear from this quantitative analysis
that Bo deviates most often in the direction of 407 and
509 and least often with B. It may be observed that Bo
seems to follow the A-type text more often than the B-type
when the uncials divide. Bo supports the reading of B
only 90 times whereas it supports the A F M reading about
120 times. The text of V seems closer to the text of
A F M than to the text of B. The nearest neighbour to
Bo after 407' is 55.

The 355 joint deviations of Bo and the other
witnesses break down into 93 specific combinations. These
are listed in Table 5 below in descending order of
frequency.

Table 5

Specific Mss and Combinations Joining Bo in

Support of a Deviant Reading

Manuscripts	Deviations
407'	43
A F M V 55 59 407'	33
407	29
B	17
B 407'	17
A F M V 55 59	17
A B F M V 55 59 407'	14
509	13
55	12
V	8
B 407	6
59	6
A	5
B 55 407'	5
A F M 55 59	5
F 59	4
A F M V 55 59 407	4
A F M V 59	4
55 407	4
B V 407'	4
B V	3
F	3

Table 5 (Continued)

Manuscripts	Deviations
M 55 407'	3
V 55 407'	3
V 407'	3
B V 55 407'	3
B 59 407'	3
A F V 55 59 407'	3
M	2
A F M V	2
V 59	2
59 407	2
A 509	2
A 55	2
F 59	2
M 407'	2
F M V 55 59 407'	2
F M V 59	2
B F M 55 59 509	2
A B F M 55 59 407'	2
V 55 407	2
A F M 55 59 407'	2
V 55 59 407'	2
A M	1
A F	1
A V	1

Table 5 (Continued)

Manuscripts	Deviations
A F V 59	1
A M 55 59 407'	1
A V 59	1
A F M 407	1
A F M V 59 407	1
A B F M 509	1
A B F M V 55	1
A 55 407	1
A F V 55 59 407	1
A B 407'	1
A F M V 407	1
A F M V 59 407'	1
A F 59	1
A F V 407'	1
A F M 55 407'	1
A B F 59	1
A B M V 55	1
A 59 407	1
A M 55 407'	1
A F M V 509	1
A F M V 55	1
B 509	1
B 55	1
B 59 407	1

Table 5 (Continued)

Manuscripts	Deviations
B F V 59 407'	1
B 55 407'	1
B V 509	1
B F 55 59 407'	1
B V 59 407'	1
B M 59 407'	1
F M V 59 509	1
F V 55 59 407	1
F V 407'	1
F V 59	1
F V 407	1
F 55 59 407'	1
F 407'	1
M 407	1
M 59 407'	1
M V 55 407'	1
V 55	1
V 509	1
V 59 407	1
55 407	1
55 509	1
59 509	1
59 407'	1

Analysis of the above list confirms the close
relationship of Bo to 407 and 509. The combination 407'
alone supports a deviant Bo reading 43 times--10 more
times than any other combination or single ms in the list.
Further, Bo and 407' deviate from LXX, both alone and in
combinations with other mss, a total of 165 times. Table
4 shows the joint deviations of Bo with each pre-recensional witness. Were 407' to be included as a unit in
that table, it would be third highest in the number of
joint deviations from LXX, being exceeded only by its
individual members 509 (190 times) and 407 (223 times).
This shows the affinity of 407 to 509 and of 407' to Bo.

The above comparison of the number of joint deviations of Bo and two mss (407') with those of Bo and
single mss is not a fair one. The meaning of the 165
joint deviations of Bo and 407' is more fairly shown
when these deviations are compared not with single mss
but with combinations of two mss. Bo deviates 58 times
with B and 407, 44 times with A and 407, 24 times with
B and V, 99 times with A and M, 85 times with M and V,
89 times with A and V, 91 times with 55 and 59, etc.
Clearly Bo deviates with the combination 407' more
often than with any other combination of two mss. All
but 30 of the 93 combinations in Table 5 include 407
and/or 509, and one or both of these mss support 249
of Bo's 355 deviant readings (70%).

Textual conclusions based only on a quantitative analysis can be, of course, misleading. Investigation of the readings jointly supported by Bo and 407 and/or 509 reveals that qualitatively the relationship is also significant. A clear indication of such a relationship would be a plus uniquely attested by the two related sources. Such plusses are indeed widely attested by Bo and 407'. For example, additions of the divine name appear in 3:23, 4:21, 8:10, 8:20, 19:8, 29:23, and 31:29. Such additions alone would not be significant, but in view of the quantitative picture, they indicate more than a coincidental relationship.

A more meaningful kind of plus is found in 4:23 where και ανομησετε is added. The addition of ος αν φυγη εκει και ζησεται in 4:42 is ex par (cf. the C group p. 206), but the probable source of the reading of Bo is now more clearly obvious. The phrase εν τω ερημω is added in 8:3, την επιθυμιαν της ψυχης σου in 12:15, and εν ταις πολεσιν σου in 28:53. The addition of εναντι κυριου του θεου σου in 29:15 is attested by Bo and 407. (The margin of A also contains the reading.) This indicates that only Bo and 407 now preserve this early variant reading known to the corrector of A.

Bo and 407' also attest change in lexemes. For example, only these three pre-recensional witnesses read εθνων for θεων in 9:26, ευλογειν for ἐπεύχεσθαι in 10:8, and πλανηθη for πλατυνθῇ in 11:16. The lexemes in the second instance are quite different in form from each other, i.e., palaeographic similarity did not give rise to the variant text. Bo and 407' are the only two witnesses to ο τοπος as a variant of ἡ ὁδός in 14:23, for ιδειν as a variant on εἰδέναι in 13:3, and for πας ισραηλ as a variant on οἱ ἐπίλοιποι in 21:21. Bo 55 and 407' support ευλογιαν as a variant of ζωήν in 30:19, and in 33:2 the same sources support κατεπαυσεν for κατέσπευσεν.

The transposition of verses 21 and 22 of Chapter 27 is particularly interesting as a comment on the relationship of Bo to 407'. The extant Bo text has the contents of verse 22 (with slight variations) both before and after verse 21. The only Greek sources which attest any kind of alteration to the sequence of these verses are 407', which transpose vs. 21 post 22 fin. The content of this chapter is repetitive, and it is fully possible that this transposition by Bo and 407' is independent in origin; but in the light of all the foregoing, it is significant that these sources should alone support such a variant reading.

This quality of evidence makes it fully clear that Bo is closer to 407 and its congener 509 than to any other extant Greek mss.

0. Only two questions remain to be investigated, the relationship of Bo to the papyri where they are extant

and the possible relationship of Bo to Sahidic. The first
of these questions will now be considered.

The papyri are so fragmentary that extensive comparison with Bo is impossible, but some attempt to test
the possible relationship of Bo to the papyri (especially
to 963) can be made.

Papyrus 963 is recorded in List 23 above a total
of 470 times. In 347 of these instances (74%) it is
support for the lemma, and in 244 of these instances Bo
also supports the lemma. Twenty-eight of its 123 variant
readings (22.7%) are shared by Bo, 10 of which are textually significant. These are 2:33, 4:1, 4:45, 6:13,
6:25, 7:7, 29:24, 30:4, 31:12 and 31:15. Such a quantitative statement says nothing of the possible relationship of Bo to 963. The papyrus is so important, however,
that some further analysis must be attempted. The first
six chapters are virtually complete, so a careful comparison of the deviant readings of Bo and 963 in this
section could give some clearer indication, however
tentative, of the nature of any relationship between
these two sources.

Eighty-three of the 123 deviant readings of 963
obtain between Chapters 1-6. Among these 83 readings are
38 which are useless for showing any textual relationship to Bo. These include 16 changes of pronouns as a
result of itacism (ημων/υμων, etc.), five additions/

omissions of καί, two additions/omissions of the definite
article, and 15 itacistic variant spellings of proper
names. Five other variants are unique to 963 and most
probably are mistakes.

Forty meaningful deviations remain and 19 of these
(49%) are shared by Bo. These are found in 1:28, 2:30,
*2:33, 3:10, 3:20, *4:1, 4:3, 4:4, 4:19, 4:23, 4:34,
*4:45, 5:21, 5:27, 6:7, 6:10, *6:13, 6:18 and *6:25.
Five of these 19 readings are of textual interest and
are starred. These all consist of additions, i.e., of
εις τας χειρας ημων in 2:33, of και πολυπλασιασθητε
in 4:1, of εν τη ερημω in 4:45, of μονω in 6:13 and of
κυριος in 6:25. Such plusses indicate that there is
some connection, though slight, between the text of 963
and the parent text of Bo.

The sampling available for comparison of Bo and
963 is small but the following seems clear. Bo and 963
are early witnesses to LXX as their low percentage of
deviations shows. They jointly support a deviant reading in only a few significant instances, and thus their
texts appear to be related but not intimately.

The valuable papyrus 848 appears only 181 times
in List 23 and as variant in 50 of these instances. The
text is extremely fragmentary so no more than a quantitative statement of comparison with Bo is possible. Ten
of the 50 deviant readings are jointly attested by Bo

but only two of these are textually significant--22:21
and 25:16. The text is early and in such places where
it exists it has often been used alone to reconstruct
LXX. As a result of this, only 53 of its 131 readings
supporting the lemma are also shared by Bo.

P. The final question to be investigated is the
possible relationship of Sahidic to Bohairic. Since Bo
and Sa are the main dialects of the Egyptian version of
the LXX, one has tended to assume some mutual influence
of these dialects on each other, but the validity of
the assumption has never been tested. This task will
now be attempted.

The extant witnesses to the Sa of Deut are quite
numerous though some are only fragmentary.[5] Only one
ms, Sa^{17}, contains the entire book but the text is not
always clear. For this reason Sa^{17} can be used as
evidence only where it is cited. The next most complete
ms is Sa^{3} which contains only a few lacunae. Sa^{2} is
virtually complete for the first nine chapters, and Sa^{1}
obtains (with lacunae) from Chapters 1-16. The rest of
the evidence consists of small fragments of different
sections of the book. This means that several of the
extant Sa mss may all support some verse(s), whereas
the support for a whole verse or chapter may consist
only of a single ms, or may be entirely lacking. In
these circumstances, all variant readings of Sa mss
are recorded in List 23. When Sa mss support both lemma

and variant they are so recorded and so counted. These
instances are few and the statistical picture changes
only slightly on account of this procedure.

The possible relationship of Bo to Sa may be
tested by an analysis, first of all, of the variant
readings jointly attested by both dialects. A word-by-
word comparison of the two dialects would probably re-
veal a high percentage of similarity in phraseology and
translation technique, but dependence would not necessarily be indicated. Sa and Bo are, after all, dialects
of the same language so the contents of Chapter V, for
example, might well apply in large part to Sa also.
Agreement of Sa and Bo on the translation of a Greek
word or phrase may thus indicate only Coptic translation
technique. No word-by-word comparison is attempted for
these reasons. However, List 23 which shows meaningful
deviations of all pre-recensional witnesses from LXX
may conveniently serve as a basis for testing any
Greek-based relationship of Bo to Sa.

It has been shown (see Table 2) that Bo diverges
a total of 633 times in that list. Bo and Sa jointly
support 180 (28%) of these deviant readings. Both
textually insignificant and significant agreements are
included in this figure so the real correlations are
even less. All but 67 of these variant readings are
also attested by the majority of extant Greek mss.
Actually, the joint reading of Bo and Sa is unique in

361

only one instance (7:19) and this is the addition of
ΠEK- = Ⓜ , and most likely mere coincidence. It
appears from the foregoing statements that there is no
mutual influence between Bo and Sa; these translations
were certainly independent in origin.

Independence of Bo and Sa is confirmed by the
140 deviant readings of Sa in the list. This figure
does not include unique secondary readings of Sa; such
were not recorded and, in any event, their existence
makes the case for influence on Bo even less strong. Only
a few examples of these deviant Sa readings need be shown.
In each of the following instances Bo supports the lemma.

Sa supports the omission of αυτου from δικαιώματα
in 6:17, of δύο in 9:17, and in 9:19 Sa supports τουτο
against ἐκείνω. In 10:20 Sa adds the equivalent of μονω
to αυτῷ, and in 11:31 Sa supports the omission of καὶ
κληρονομήσετε αὐτήν in keeping with B and 963. This
omission could have occurred through parablepsis on
καί in each case so that its existence in these witnesses
would be mere coincidence. Sa omits ἐκεῖνος 2° in 13:5,
and καὶ πάντα κόρακα καὶ τὰ ὅμοια αὐτῷ in 14:14; Sa
adds δια το ρημα τουτο in 15:4, omits ἐν σοί in 17:2,
and in 19:9 adds πολεις to τὰς τρεῖς. Sa supports
και τη against τῇ δέ in 22:26, the addition of
εις πολεμον in 23:9, and προτεροι as a variant to

πατέρες in 19:14. Sa omits καὶ τὰς ἐντολὰς αὐτοῦ in
30:16, and supports the addition of κυριος to ἐφείσατο
in 33:3, and of γης to ἐπί in 33:28. Most of these
deviant Sa readings are omissions and thus not as con-
clusive indicators of Vorlage as additions or substitutions. The list contains several kinds of variants,
however, which taken together further show that the
translations of Bo and Sa were independent in origin.

A third indicator of independence of Bo and Sa is
the list of 252 deviant Bo readings when Sa support for
the lemma is certain. A few striking examples from that
list follow.

Bo supports the variant πλην εμου in 5:7 and in
5:14 παροικων εν σοι contra ἐντος τῶν πυλῶν σου. At
6:19 fin Bo supports the addition of κυριος, and in
10:22 the addition of πεντε to ἐβδομήκοντα, and in 19:2
of καθοτι αν δω μωμον τω πλησιον ουτως δωσετε αυτω.
The transposition of ἀρεστόν and καλόν in 21:9, and the
addition of σφοδρα to τρυφερά in 28:56 are supported by
Bo. Bo supports the addition of και πασαν την
γεγραμμενην in 28:61, and in 29:3 of την χειρα την
κραταιαν και τον βραχιονα τον υψηλον. Bo supports the
variant στυλω νεφελης in 31:15, and in two instances in
31:21 it supports the addition of significant plusses,
i.e., και εσται οταν ευρησωσιν αυτον κακα πολλα και
θλιψεις at the beginning of the verse, and στοματος
αυτων και απο before στόματος.

These readings are mostly Bo plusses, quite long in some cases and all unattested by Sa. Were Bo and Sa mutually dependent, a high degree of agreement on deviant plusses could be expected, but this is clearly not the case. In view of this kind of evidence, it is now conclusively clear that although Sahidic and Bohairic are good early witnesses to original Greek, there is no trace of influence of one upon the other.

References

[1] See Sigla and Abbreviations.

[2] J. W. Wevers (ed.)., _Septuaginta, Vetus Testamentum Graecum_, Bd I. _Genesis_. Cf also THGG.

[3] Cf. _THGG_ p. 136f.

[4] _Ibid_ p. 62f.

[5] See Sigla and Abbreviations.

Chapter VII

SUMMARY STATEMENT

There are eight extant mss dating from the ninth
to the eighteenth centuries which contain the Bohairic
of Deuteronomy. These fall into two groups, one consisting of six mss and the other of two. The better
text is found, in general, in the smaller group and in
the absence of a critical edition one of these two mss
may be used.

The two printed editions of the Bo of Deut are
untrustworthy primarily because the older of them,
edited by David Wilkins, contains several readings which
are unsupported by Coptic mss. These readings have in
turn been copied by Paul de Lagarde, the editor of the
more recent edition. Many of the unique readings of the
Bo editions, i.e., readings not found in above mss, are
based on the Sixtine edition of the Greek.

The inherent differences in the Greek and Coptic
language systems make it impossible to show certain Greek
variants in Bo and, because of the nature of the Bo translation of Deut it is difficult to precisely determine its
Greek Vorlage in certain instances. Such instances often
involve the presence or absence of Greek και, addition or

omission of the possessive pronouns, and the presence
or absence of a resumptive pronoun/particle. Despite
such features it is possible to make valid comparisons
of Bo with Greek.

Bohairic is not hexaplaric in character. A comparison of Bo with hex asterisked plusses and with
plusses from which the hex asterisk is presumably lost
shows a low percentage of agreement in either case. Even
where there appears to be agreement, it is often on the
addition of the possessive pronouns or of the co-ordinating conjunctions and because of Bo translation
technique, the agreement is probably due to coincidence.
The relationship of Bo to the textual families is similar
to its relationship to the hex recension. The deviant
readings of all the families are recorded and Bo ex-
hibits no strong connection quantitatively or qualitatively to any of them. It thus becomes apparent that
Bo is probably pre-recensional in character. Analysis
reveals that Bo is indeed a good witness to the pre-
recensional text, rarely deviating from LXX. Of the
Greek mss whose texts are also presumably pre-recensional,
Bo is most similar to 407 and 509. When the uncials
divide Bo is closer to the A F M V group than to B.

The papyri are too fragmentary to warrant extensive comparison with Bo. In the six chapters of
continuous text of 963, Bo shows a slight textual
connection to it.

The Sahidic of Deut is contained in several mss. Some of these are only fragmentary, but together they provide an adequate basis for comparison with Bo. An analysis of readings of Bo and Sa which deviate from original Greek reveals that while Bo and Sa are both good early witnesses to the text of the Septuagint, their translations were independent of each other.

APPENDIX

Damaged Verses in Br. Mus. Or. 422 = Bo^D

```
 1:   3 4 9 10 17 18 19 24 25 31 33 39 40 41 46
 2:   1 2 3 8 14 15 22 23 29
 3:   5 6 19 25 26
 4:   3 4 9 14 15 20 21 26 27 32 33 38 39 43 44
 5:   2 3 4 5 11 12 13 19 20 21 24 25 26 31 32
 6:   3 4 11 13 19 20 21
 7:   1 2 7 8 13 19 26
 8:   4 5 13 14 19 20
 9:   4 5 9 10 18 23 24 25
10:   1 2 7 8 14 15
11:   1 2 8 9 13 14 21 26 27 28
12:   1 2 6 7 12 13 14 18 19 24 25 30 31
13:   5 6 11 12 13
14:   1 2 8 9 23 24
15:   2 3 11 12 21 22
16:   6 7 8 15 16
17:   2 3 10 11 18 19
18:   6 7 16
19:   1 2 6 7 8 13 14 20 21
20:   5 6 13 14 19 20
21:   7 8 14 15 16 21 22 23
22:   5 6 15 16 17 22 23 24 29 30
```

368

Appendix (Cont'd)

```
23:   1  10  11  12  19  20
24:   2  3  4  10  11  12  19  20
25:   4  5  11  12  19
26:   1  7  8  13  14  19
27:   1  2  9  10  17  18  25  26
28:   7  8  13  14  22  23  45  46  47  52  53
29:   11  12  13  18  24  25
30:   2  3  15  16  20
31:   1  2  6  7  11  12  16  20  21  24  25  26
```

BIBLIOGRAPHY

Botte, B. "Versions Coptes", Orientales de la Bible
    (Versions) III: Dictionaire de la Bible Supplement
    dir. H Cazelles 6. (Paris, 1960)

Brooke, A. E. "Sahidic fragments of the Old Testament."
    The Journal of Theological Studies, VIII, 1906,
    pp. 67-74

_____ "The Bohairic Version of the Pentateuch."
    The Journal of Theological Studies, III, 1902,
    pp. 258-259

_____ and N. McLean (Eds.). The Old Testament in
    Greek according to the Text of Codex Vaticanus,
    Vol. I., pt. 3 Cambridge, 1911

Budge, E. A. Wallis. Coptic Biblical Texts in the Dialect
    of Upper Egypt. London: 1912

Ciasca, A. Sacrorum Bibliorum Fragmenta copto-sahidica
    Musei Borgiani iussu et sumptibus S. Congregations
    de Propaganda Fide edita. Tom I, Rom 1885

Clear, John. "The Ethiopic of II Chronicles." Unpublished
    Ph.D. dissertation, University of Toronto, 1971

Crum, W. E. Catalogue of the Coptic Manuscripts in the
    British Museum. London: Longmans, 1905.

_____ A Coptic Dictionary. Oxford, 1939

Delaporte, L. "Catalogue sommaire de Manuscripts Coptes
    de la Bibliothèque Nationale." Revue de l'Orient
    Chrétien, Paris: 1909-1913

Erman, A. Bruchstücke der oberagyptischen Uebersetzung
    des alten Testaments (Nachrichten von der königl.
    Gesellschaft der Wissenschaften und der G. A.
    Universität zu Göttingen. Göttingen 1880, n° 12)
    Göttingue, 1880.

Goodwin, William Watson. Greek Grammar. revised by Charles
    B. Gulick. Waltham Mass: Blaisdell Publishing Co.
    1958

Grabe, Johannes Ernestus S. T. P (Ed.). Septuaginta
Interpretum Tomus I. continens Octateuchum quem ex
Antiquissimo Codice Alexandrino Accurate Descriptum
. . . Oxford: 1707

Hallock, Frank H. "The Coptic Old Testament." American
Journal of Semitic Languages 49, 1932-33, 325-33.

Hatch, Edwin and Henry H. Redpath. A Concordance to the
Septuagint and Other Greek Versions of the Old
Testament. (Including the Apocryphal Books). 2 vols
and supplement. Oxford, 1897-1907.

Hebbelynck, Adolphe. "Le versiones coptes de la Bible."
Muséon 16, 1897, 91-93.

_____. "L'unité et l'âge du papyrus copte biblique
Or 7594 du British Museum. Muséon 34, 1921, 71-80.

_____. "Les κεφάλαια et les τίτλοι des Evangiles."
Le Muséon, Louvain, 1928, p.118.

_____. and A. Van Lantschoot. Codices Coptici Vaticani;
Barberiniani Borgiani Rossiani. Tomus I.
Codices Coptici Vaticani. Bibliotheca Vaticana 1937.

Holmes, R. (Ed.). Vetus Testamentum Graecum cum variis
lectionibus. Tom I. Oxford, 1798.

Hyvernat, Henry. Bybliothecae Pierpont Morgan Codices
Coptici: photographice expressi. Rome 1922.

_____. A Checklist of Coptic Mss in the Pierpont Morgan
Library. New York. 1919.

_____. Album de Paléographie copte, Rome, 1888.

_____. "Etude sur les Versions Coptes de la Bible."
Revue Biblique Internationale, VI. Paris, 1897.

Jellicoe, Sidney. The Septuagint and Modern Study. Oxford:
Clarendon Press, 1968

Kahle, P. E., Bala'izah: Coptic Texts from Deir al-Bala'izah in Upper Egypt. Vol.I, Oxford 1954.

Kammerer, W., A Coptic Bibliography. Ann Arbor 1950.

Kasser, R., Papyrus Bodmer: Deuteronome I-X en sahidique.
Geneve 1962.

372

_____. "Les dialectes coptes en les versions coptes bibliques." _Biblica_ 46 (Roma 1965) 287-310.

Kittel, R. (Ed.)., _Biblica Hebraica_, third ed., Stuttgart: Württembergische Bibelanstalt, 1937.

Lagarde, Paul de, (Ed.)., _Der Pentateuch Koptisch_. Neudruck der Ausgabe 1867. Osnabrück: Otto Zeller, 1967.

Lefort, L. Th. Les manuscrits coptes de l'universite de Louvain. I. Texts litteraires (Louvain 1940). (cf. "Coptica Louvaniensia" _Le Muséon_ 50, 51, 53.)

Liddell, Henry., and Scott, Robert., _A Greek-English Lexicon_, 9th edition, revised by H. S. Jones, Oxford: Clarendon Press 1940, reprinted 1961.

Mallon, Alexis., _Grammaire Copte_. 4th ed. Beruit, 1956.

Maspéro, G., Fragments de la version thébaine de l'Ancien Testament (Mémoires publies par les membres de la mission archaeologique francaise au Caire, VI, fascicule 1), Paris 1892.

Peterson, Theodore., "The Biblical Scholar's Concern with Coptic Studies." _Catholic Biblical Quarterly_ 23 (1961) 241-249.

Pietersma, Albert., "A Text Critical Study of Genesis Papyri 961 and 962"(Chester Beatty Papyri IV and V) Ph.D. dissertation, University of Toronto, 1970, (in Press).

Pleyte, W. and Boeser, P. A. A., Manuscripts coptes du Musée des Antiquités des Pays-Bas à Leide, Leiden 1897.

Rahlfs, A, (Ed.)., _Septuaginta_, Stuttgart, 1935.

Rhode, J. F., The Arabic Versions of the Pentateuch in the Church of Egypt. Leipzig 1921.

Schleifer, J., Sahidische Bibel-Fragmente aus dem British Museum zu London. _Sitzungberichte der Kaiserl. A. d. W. in Wien, philos-hist. Kl._ 162, 6, Wien 1909; 164, 6, Wien 1911.

_____. Bruchstücke der sahidischen Bibelübersetzung. _id._ 170, 1, Wien 1912.

Swete, H. B., _An Introduction to the Old Testament in Greek._ Cambridge: University Press 1914.

_____. _The Old Testament in Greek according to the Septuagint._ Cambridge: University Press 1897

Till, Walter C., "Coptic Biblical texts Published after Vaschalde's Lists." _Bulletin of the John Rylands Library_, 42 1959.

_____. _Koptische Grammatik._ Leipzig, Veb Verlag Enzyklopadie, 1970

_____. **"Saidische Fragmente des Alten Testamentes."** _Le Muséon_ 50 (Louvain 1937) 175-237.

_____. and Sanz, P., Eine griechisch-koptische Odenhandschrift, Monumenta biblica et ecclesiastica 5. Rome 1939.

Van Ess, Leandri. (Ed)., _Vetus Testamentum Graecum_ iuxta Septuaginta Interpretes ex autoritate Sixti Quinti Pontificis Maximi editum iuxta Exemplar Originale Vaticanum. Romae 1835.

Vaschalde, A., "Ce qui a été publié des Versions coptes de la Bible." _Revue Biblique_ 1919-1922; Muséon, 43, (1930), 45, (1932).

Von Lemm, O., Sahidische Bibelfragmente III. _Bulletin de l'Académie Impériale des Sciences de St.-Pétersbourg._ Ve Série, XXV, 4. St Pétersbourg 1906.

Weigandt, Peter., "Zur Geschichte der koptischen Bibelübersetzungen." _Biblica_ 50 (1969) 80-95

Wessely, Carl., Griechische und Koptische Texte theologischen Inhalts II, III, IV. _Studien zur Paleographie und Papyruskunde_ IX, XII, XIV. Leipzig 1909-1914.

Wevers, John William., (Ed.) _Septuaginta, Vetus Testamentum Graecum,_ Bd I _Genesis._ Göttingen, Vandenhoeck and Ruprecht, 1974.

_____. _Text History of the Greek Genesis._ Mitteilungen des Septuaginta-Unternehmens (MSU) XI. Göttingen, Vandenhoeck and Ruprecht, 1974.

_____. "A Note on Scribal Error" _Canadian Journal of Linguistics_ XVII (1972), 185-190

_____. "The Textual Affinities of the Arabic Genesis of Bib. Nat. Arab 9." Studies of the Ancient Palestinian World, ed, by J. W. Wevers and D. B. Redford (Toronto Semitic Texts and Studies II). Toronto 1971.

Wilkins, David., Quinque Libri Moysis Prophetae in Lingua Aegyptia. London 1731.

BS
1274
C66
P47

Peters, Melvin K. H
    An analysis of the textual character of the
Bohairic of Deuteronomy / Melvin K. H. Peters.
-- Chico, CA : Scholars Press, c1979.

    xv, 374 p. ; 22 cm. (Septuagint and
cognate studies ; no. 9)
    Bibliography: p. 370-374.

19979

    1. Bible. O.T. Deuteronomy. Coptic--versions.
2. Bible. O.T. Deuteronomy--manuscripts, Coptic.
3. Bible. O.T. Deuteronomy--criticism, textual
I. Society of Biblical literature.   II. Title.
III. Series.